Alessandro Manzoni

The Manzoni Family

ALSO BY NATALIA GINZBURG

All Our Yesterdays
Family Sayings
The Little Virtues
The City and the House

NATALIA GINZBURG

The Manzoni Family

*Translated from the Italian
by Marie Evans*

SEAVER BOOKS
New York

First published in the United States in 1987 by
Seaver Books, 521 Fifth Avenue, New York,
New York 10175.
Distributed by Henry Holt and Company, Inc.,
521 Fifth Avenue, New York, New York 10175.
Originally published in Italy under the title
La famiglia Manzoni.

Library of Congress Cataloging in Publication Data
Ginzburg, Natalia.
The Manzoni family.
Translation of: La famiglia Manzoni.
1. Manzoni, Alessandro, 1785–1873—Biography—
Family.   2. Manzoni family.   3. Authors, Italian—
19th century—Biography—Family.   I. Title.
PQ4715.G4713   1987   853'.7   87–9892
ISBN 0-8050-0613-3

First American Edition
Printed in the United States of America

1 3 5 7 9 10 8 6 4 2

ISBN 0-8050-0613-3

Contents

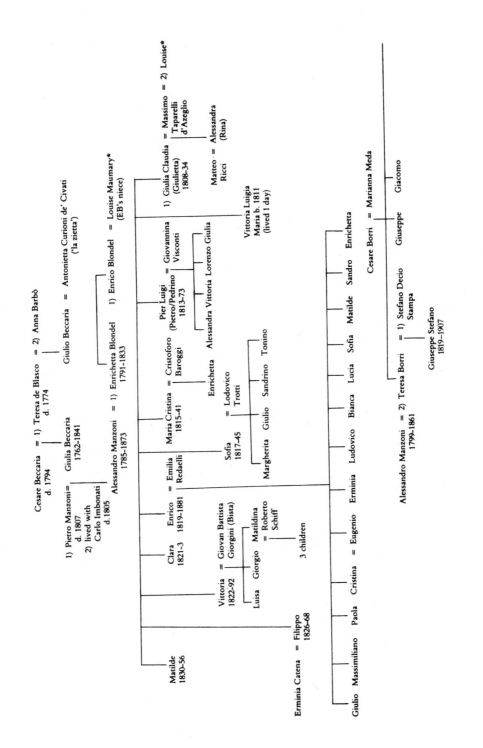

Foreword

The book is intended as an attempt at a detailed reconstruction and a reshaping of the story of the Manzoni family, through their letters and the things we know about them. It is a story that is scattered in various books, most of them unobtainable in bookshops. It is full of gaps, absences, obscurities, like any family history one might try to piece together. These gaps and absences cannot be filled.

I had never written a book like this, requiring other books and documents. I had written novels born of invention or of my memories, dependent on nothing and no one outside myself.

Therefore I must thank some people who have helped me.

I must thank Donata Chiomenti Vassalli. The first thing I read was her book, *Giulia Beccaria*, published some years ago by Ceschina and never republished, goodness knows why. I must thank her for her very fine book. And I must thank her for listening to me, lending me books, making suggestions.

I must thank Cesare Garboli for listening to me, making suggestions, and for his usual great, irascible, generous patience.

I also thank Signora Letizia Pecorella and Signorina Maria de Luca of the Braidense Library; Signora Jone Caterina Riva of the Centre for Manzoni Studies, in Milan; and in Rome, Signora Annamaria Giorgietti Vichi, Director of the Biblioteca Nazionale, and Alessandro Florio. They have helped me in many different ways, making books and letters available to me.

Finally I thank Enrica Melossi and Augusta Tosone, who provided the illustrations [not included in this edition].

I dedicate this book to my friend Dinda Gallo. She knew all about the Manzoni family, and I nothing. I just felt a simple curiosity about this family's destiny. The desire to know it more intimately and thoroughly grew out of my conversations with

7

her. And so, as I wrote, I would take the pages to her to read. She shared my perplexities and uncertainties. She shared my frustration at the gaps and absences. She was a generous guide and companion along the way. Without her I would not have written this book, which is why I dedicate it to her.

Some letters were in French in the original, and were translated into Italian by Natalia Ginzburg, though she 'would have preferred to leave them in French'. All the letters between Manzoni and Fauriel were in French, except the first in Italian from Manzoni. All the letters addressed to Fauriel, from Giulia, Giulietta etc., were in French. Enrichetta's letters were all in French, as were those following: Giulietta to Cristina (from Andeer), Giulietta to her father (from Castello d'Azeglio), Giulia to her friend Euphrosine Planta, and Teresa to Aunt Notburga.

Part One
1762–1836

Giulia Beccaria I

Giulia Beccaria had red hair and green eyes. She was born in Milan in 1762. Her father was Cesare Beccaria and her mother Teresa de Blasco; he belonged to the nobility, she was the daughter of a colonel. The marriage had met with bitter opposition. The couple had financial difficulties, but they always lived extravagantly. When he was very young Cesare Beccaria wrote a book which brought him a certain fame, *Of Crimes and Punishments*. Teresa was a graceful woman with black hair. She became the mistress of a rich man called Calderara. A frequent visitor to their house was Pietro Verri, economist, philosopher, lover of one of Cesare's sisters. Relations between Verri and the two Beccarias were always somewhat stormy, they would quarrel and make it up again.

Giulia was four when her sister Marietta was born. The same year her mother contracted venereal disease, but she continued to travel and lead a worldly life. Then she gave birth to a boy who died immediately. The father longed for a son. Giulia and her sister were brought up by servants, because their mother, although ill, was always travelling. In 1774 she died of her illness in appalling suffering. The father was in despair. The day she died he demanded an inventory of her many clothes and jewels. He called the two little girls to him and said 'It's all yours'. He clasped them in his arms, weeping. But the girls never saw the clothes and jewels again. He went off to weep in the opulent house of his wife's lover, Calderara. The girls stayed home with the servants. A few days later Calderara was astonished to see him having his hair curled by the barber. He told Calderara: 'I want to keep up appearances.' Forty days after his wife's funeral he became engaged to a beautiful rich woman, one Anna Barbò. Three months later he married her. In the end he had by her the son he wanted. Meanwhile Giulia had been put into a convent. Marietta stayed at home because she was frail, rickety and hunch-backed. She was put in an iron corset and consigned to a life of domestic slavery. In the convent Giulia was utterly forgotten. Her paternal grandparents were dead, and a maternal uncle who was fond of her was abroad at the time living in Brazil. The only person who remembered Giulia was Pietro Verri. He used to come and see her occasionally in the convent parlour. When she was eighteen, he persuaded her father to take her back into his house.

Giulia was a very beautiful, healthy, intelligent girl with a strong character. From the first she had violent quarrels with her father. Then she fell in love with Giovanni Verri, a younger brother of Pietro, Knight of the Cross of Malta, an idle, elegant man with girlish features. But there could be no question of marriage. Neither the Verris nor her father would consider it. Giulia was not rich. So Pietro Verri and Cesare Beccaria looked round and hit on a certain country nobleman called Don Pietro Manzoni, a childless widower of forty-six, not rich but with a modest affluence. He had a property near Lecco called Il Caleotto where he used to spend the summer. In the winter he lived in Milan in a house on the Navigli in via San Damiano. He proved reasonable about the dowry. Thus the marriage was swiftly arranged. Giulia simply wanted to get out of her father's house.

Don Pietro Manzoni lived with seven unmarried sisters, one an ex-nun, and had a brother, a Monsignore, who was a canon at the Cathedral. Giulia was very unhappy from the start. She quarrelled with her husband and her sisters-in-law were hostile. The house on the Navigli was ugly, small, damp and dark. Her husband seemed to her a wretched creature, without intelligence, without great wealth and without prestige. He was conservative and clerical, while she had breathed in new liberal ideas, both in her father's house and in the Verri family. She was desperately bored. She continued to see Giovanni Verri and to frequent the fine Verri house, always full of guests and gaiety. She led a brilliant life and aroused in her in-laws increasingly manifest hostility, and in her husband the urge to spy on her.

Three years after her marriage, on 7 March 1785, she gave birth to her first and only son, Alessandro. He was named after the father of the Manzonis, and baptised at the church of San Babila. His birth pleased nobody. Quarrels between Giulia and her husband became more bitter. People were talking.

The baby was immediately put out to nurse at Malgrate, near Lecco. Giulia took up her old life again. But she was tired of Giovanni Verri and he of her. She had a relationship with a certain Taglioretti. Meanwhile Alessandro was growing up with the nurse in a peasant home, loved by the nurse and her many relatives. His mother rarely came to see him. Then he was taken back to Milan, but always returned to the nurse for long periods. Andrea Appiani painted a portrait of Giulia with the little boy, in which she is dressed in a riding habit. Her face is hard, bony and weary. She is gazing into space, and shows no sign of maternal affection for the little four-year-old boy leaning against her knee. Giulia gave the portrait to Giovanni Verri.

It was at that time that she got to know Carlo Imbonati. She met him in the salon of his sister, who had been a schoolfriend of hers at the convent. There is a second portrait of Giulia painted by a woman called Cosway not many years after the Appiani with the child. It was painted in Paris where Giulia was living with Imbonati and where she was happy. In this one she is wearing a little white cap and veil. Her nose is delicate and there is a certain humorous shrewdness in the faint smile on her lips. She looks very young. The years and the bitterness have fallen from her face.

Carlo Imbonati came from a rich, aristocratic family. As a boy, Parini had been his tutor. As an adult he lived abroad for a long time. He had only just returned to Italy when he and Giulia met. They became lovers. Giulia promptly decided to leave her husband. Love gave her strength and she resolved to bring things to a head. During her relationship with Giovanni Verri she had not thought of asking for a separation, feeling she lacked moral and material support, and also feeling infected by his idleness. Now it was all different. She wrote to Pietro Verri. He was the only person who had come to see her in the convent; and he had given her some support, even if it had proved to be very dubious since he had combined with her father to lead her into that unhappy marriage. She wrote to him:

'It is absolutely impossible for me to live with a family who are all hostile to me. My husband, fired by sacred zeal, wishes

13

at all costs to procure me a place in Paradise through suffering here below; Monsignore [the canon of the Cathedral] sits in his villa refining ideas to impose upon his brother, who comes home, scours all the rooms and even searches behind the pictures, I suspect. The ex-nun takes it upon herself to keep creeping downstairs to hear what is being said, and then goes to report it all to the worthy Prelate, who, poor fellow, is troubled by a fairly obvious beam in his own eye. This is the picture of my family life. I have opened my heart to you by word and by letter, for I felt I must invoke your humanity on my behalf. Unfortunately I fear I may be deceiving myself, since I see you still maintain that friendship to which I was once innocently sacrificed. But at the time my father alone was responsible for my unhappiness; he knew me and the man he intended me to marry. You knew none of the circumstances, so your concern for my establishment arose from your affection for me and my father. Now things are quite different. Now that you are aware of my desperate circumstances, can you wish for a reconciliation which would make me a wretched, unhappy slave, simply because you are reluctant to oppose the effects of my father's despotism? He does not feel the horror of my situation, but is merely annoyed to see me shake off a yoke he imposed upon me. Forgive, Count Verri, the liberty I take in writing like this, but I am using the one thing no one can give or take from me, that is a strength of character that makes me speak the truth in the same voice whoever I am speaking to. A separation is essential; I can bear my present situation no longer.'

Don Pietro Manzoni then made a bid to keep his wife. She despised him because he did not belong to the high nobility, so he persuaded his brothers to put forward a petition for them to be admitted to the golden book of patricians. The petition was rejected. In any case, the rejection reached him when Giulia had already left.

The separation was legally granted in February 1792; Don Pietro Manzoni pledged himself to make a quarterly allowance of 2,000 lire to his wife; Giulia was supposed to move to the house of her maternal uncle, Michele de Blasco, who had meanwhile returned from South America; nothing was said about the boy, and it was therefore understood that he was to remain in the care of his legitimate father, Don Pietro Manzoni. Giulia took the boy to Merate, to the College of the Somaschi Fathers, and left him there. Before setting off for Merate, she took him to see his grandfather, Cesare Beccaria, who with the years had become enormously fat; Alessandro, who was seeing him for the first time and would never see him again, later recalled him rising heavily from an armchair to get him a chocolate from a drawer. He did not seem too pleased at their visit. Alessandro was then seven.

In 1788 Marietta, Giulia's sister, had died at twenty-two without ever having left her father's house, leading the obscure life of an invalid in the servants' quarters. At her death Giulia had brought an action against her father to obtain the right of inheritance to a portion of her mother's goods; separated from her husband, she devoted herself more passionately to this legal procedure. She presented a long memorandum of accusations against her father in which she recalled how he had forced her into a marriage which filled her with 'agitation and repugnance' and had cheated her of all her maternal inheritance, allotting her a wretched dowry, although after the death of his own father, the Marquis Saverio, he found himself in quite a flourishing situation financially, with lands and houses. But in November 1794, Cesare Beccaria died suddenly, in his room, of an apoplectic fit; Anna Barbò, his widow, decided to come to terms with her step-daughter, and Giulia received much of what she was demanding. She left for Paris with Carlo Imbonati in the autumn of 1796. In May of that year, the French under Napoleon had entered Milan.

Sad and solitary, Don Pietro Manzoni contemplated both the end of his marriage and the end of an era; disorder and confusion reigned in his city; it was thronged with soldiers he hated; he belonged to the past, and all around him he saw the civil and religious stability in which he had lived swept away by a hurricane; he left his home on the Navigli which held too many memories, and moved to a house in Santa Prassede Street; but he spent much of his time in the quiet of Il Caleotto; he rarely sent for the boy. One day he received a complaint from the Head of the College of the Somaschi Fathers. Alessandro had cut off his pigtail in an attempt to express his sympathy for the new ideas which were blowing throughout Europe.

In 1797 Pietro Verri too died of an apoplectic fit. As for his brother, Giovanni Verri, he had gone to live at Belvedere on Lake Como with his mistress, one Signora Curoni, and her husband.

Giulia was happy in Paris. At last she had everything she had lacked hitherto. She was free. She lived with a man she loved who loved her, in a great city where the fact that they were not married created no problems, a man with a noble mind and generous nature, a handsome man, who was rich, admired and esteemed by all. They had a fine house in a fine district, in Place Vendôme. They had lots of friends. Suddenly she was pleased with her maiden name of Beccaria, which was known to everyone in cultured and worldly circles. She met with a cordial and lavish reception whereever she went. Everyone remembered her father and his famous book *Of Crimes and Punishments*. Her long legal battle and bitter, humiliating clashes with her father, and the rancour and resentment that had built up inside her against him, poisoning her life so long, now seemed quite remote and in any case soothed and almost effaced by his death. She rarely thought of her little boy at Merate at the College of the Somaschi Fathers. He was part of a dark former life she despised, and over the boy's head hung shadows and a sense of guilt that she did not wish to recall. She never wrote to him.

The dearest friends she and Imbonati had in France were a couple who like them lived together unmarried, Claude Fauriel and Sophie de Condorcet. They lived at Meulan near Paris in a house called *La Maisonnette* that had once been a monastery. Giulia too dreamed of having a house in the country, that she would call *La Chaumière*.

Sophie de Condorcet was then about thirty. She was dark-haired and olive-skinned. She had led a very eventful life. Her husband, the Marquis de Condorcet, philosopher and mathematician, was a Girondin; when the Girondins fell in 1792, he was pursued and threatened with arrest; he hid in a peasant house; his wife would come to see him dressed as a peasant, and meanwhile she had sued for divorce in order to save their confiscated goods. Then Condorcet tried to escape, was captured, and poisoned himself with stramonium, which he got

16

from a doctor friend, Pierre Cabanis. To support her daughter, her sister and an old governess, the widowed Sophie went to the prisons every day to paint portraits of people condemned to the guillotine. She retrieved part of the confiscated property. One day she met Claude Fauriel walking in the Jardin des Plantes; they shared a love of botany. She took him from Madame de Staël, with whom he had a relationship at that time. But Madame de Staël and Fauriel remained friends.

Fauriel was a philologist. He was born in modest circumstances in a village in the Cévennes, Saint-Etienne. He studied at Tournon. In 1793 he was made lieutenant in an infantry battalion. During the Directorate he retired to Saint-Etienne and studied Greek, Latin and Turkish. He was a friend of Fouché and on his return to Paris he became his secretary and inspector of police. As a police official he was extremely attentive to the needs of those about him, sympathetic to their misfortunes and swift to help. He resigned when he was about to make a successful career, for he had no ambition and no wish to attain too high a rank. Sainte-Beuve called him a perpetual resigner. He loved botany, nature and especially the countryside on the banks of the Loire, and the places around his village. He loved to wander through the country in the early morning gathering plant specimens. Again in the words of Sainte-Beuve, he always loved to return to the origins of things: he liked 'the sources of rivers, the birth of civilizations', art and poetry in their primitive forms and, when he was botanizing, he concentrated on mosses in particular. He was very handsome and popular with the ladies: Stendhal said he was the handsomest man in Paris. He was tall and dark, with very full lips, strongly marked features, and sad, pensive eyes. He had a strong sense of friendship. He would become passionately interested in the topics his friends were studying and take them up in his turn. He was a good listener and everyone confided in him. He had many friends; Cabanis, Madame de Staël, Benjamin Constant, and later, Manzoni. He was an extraordinary translator. A vain man, he loved to hear his works praised, especially the translations. Sophie de Condorcet lived with him for twenty years, but she would not marry him, because he was not noble and belonged to a class inferior to her. It would have been a *mésalliance*. The Revolution had taken place, and Sophie de Condorcet was in many ways a

17

person without prejudices, but the idea was deeply rooted in her mind that it would be humiliating to marry a man of humble origins. Many years later when Sophie died, Fauriel was rejected and scorned by her relatives, with whom he had lived for so long on the most intimate terms. They broke off all connection with him.

Sophie de Condorcet's manners were polite and easy, and yet controlled and proud. Giulia admired her but went in awe of her, for the other woman's manner was distant and protective. Giulia displayed her affection for Sophie impulsively, and received courteous but cold responses. She was hurt and confided in Fauriel: 'It is a cruel thing for love to be unrequited, but it is no less a torment to feel loved against your wishes: this is precisely the situation between me and that unique and gracious lady for whom I have and always will have the liveliest affection, and friendship between us must be reciprocal, or I can not and will not sue for it.'

It has been thought that Sophie de Condorcet might have been very jealous of Giulia, and for this reason sometimes cold with her.

Nevertheless, at a moment of great distress Giulia received very real and strong support from Sophie de Condorcet. Carlo Imbonati died suddenly of bilious colic. He had suffered from liver trouble for some time, but nobody had realised the gravity of his illness. Sophie de Condorcet, Cabanis and Fauriel were the first to hasten to the house in Place Vendôme. Giulia was sobbing upon the corpse which she refused to leave. Sophie suggested that Giulia should have the body embalmed and taken to Meulan to the garden of *La Maisonnette*. No priest was asked to bless the body. In the course of an afternoon Sophie found an embalmer. There was a chapel in the garden of *La Maisonnette*, but it had long remained unconsecrated. The embalmed body of Carlo Imbonati was placed there, violating all the ecclesiastical laws which forbade burial in unconsecrated ground. Giulia felt bound to Sophie by eternal gratitude.

Carlo Imbonati had made a will years before in Milan, when he and Giulia were about to leave for France. On his death the will was opened before a lawyer in Milan and communicated to Giulia who had remained in Paris. She already knew its contents, because Imbonati had told her, but she did not know how they were expressed. There were fourteen legacies to relatives and domestic servants; the rest was left to Giulia. 'Of all my other goods, chattels and estates, investments, accounts and shares, and anything of which I die possessed, I have pronounced and do pronounce my sole heiress Giulia Beccaria Manzoni. . . and this my free and incontrovertible decision stands as a solemn public testimony to the pure and just feelings I owe to and feel for my aforesaid heiress for the constant and virtuous friendship I have professed for her, from which I gain not only complete satisfaction in the years I have spent with her, but an intimate conviction that I owe to her virtue and disinterested attachment that peace of mind and happiness which will go with me to the grave; for which, since I can never find words to express all that I feel in my heart for my aforesaid heiress, I pray Almighty God, Father and Creator of us all, to receive the humble prayers I offer in the fullness of my heart for the greatest good of my aforesaid heiress, and that He will grant that we may bless and adore Him together in all eternity.'

Carlo Imbonati had died on 15 March 1805; he was fifty-two and Giulia forty-three. The closing words of the will turned her thoughts to God. She had never thought of Him much. The ambience in which she lived was devoid of any religious thinking. She went to see a Protestant minister, Federico Menestraz, whom she had met at the house of an elderly Genevan lady, Carlotta Blondel. She asked him for consolation and advice. He exhorted her to dedicate her life to the sufferings of her fellows. At that time she conceived the idea of becoming a hospital nun. She gave away furniture and household objects, and wrote to Carlo Imbonati's sisters offering them part of the inheritance left to her in the will. She did not want to go back to the house in Place Vendôme, so she took an apartment in rue Saint-Honoré. In the summer her son arrived. Then they moved to a bigger house in rue Neuve du Luxembourg.

Giulia Beccaria II

When he was twelve Alessandro left the College of the Somaschi Fathers which he hated. ('Filthy sheepfold' he was to call it later.) He was transferred to the Longone College in Milan, which he hated just as much. But he made friends, there; Arese, Pagani, Confalonieri, Visconti. He stayed there until he was sixteen. Then he went to live in the house in Santa Prassede Street, where he was received by the dark melancholy of Don Pietro, the gloom of the maiden aunts, Uncle Monsignore with the beam in his eye, and everything that had bored and depressed Giulia when she lived among these people. As for Don Pietro, he felt neither affection nor hostility for the boy. His presence in the house disturbed him, as it reminded him of Giulia and his unfortunate marriage. However, he felt it his duty to behave with decorum. The law had consigned this boy to him, and he placed law in the highest sphere of the human condition. But he could offer him only a severe and weary gaze and inhibited, speechless protection. Moreover, the boy himself was uncertain how to behave towards this melancholy man. He was ill at ease. He had a group of friends and imitated their behaviour. He talked with them about women, and in the evenings went to gamble at the Ridotto della Scala. It was at that time that he got to know the poet Vincenzo Monti, and saw in him an authoritative presence, a model to be emulated. He wrote verses which Vincenzo Monti read. One evening in the theatre, sitting in a box beside a certain Contessa Cicognara, he saw Napoleon Bonaparte; like a flash of lightning, the General's gaze alighted for a moment on the Contessa who he knew loathed him, and then moved scornfully away; those penetrating, scornful eyes remained in the boy's memory for ever.

Vincenzo Monti was the guest of Giulia and Carlo Imbonati

during a visit to Paris not long before Imbonati died, and he spoke of Alessandro. Then Imbonati wrote to Alessandro inviting him to visit them. He was curious to make his acquaintance and felt guilty since he and Giulia had never given a serious thought to the boy growing up far away. In fact, he had taken his mother away from him. Perhaps he also had a subconscious premonition of his death and wanted Giulia to have her son beside her. Alessandro was then nineteen. When he received Imbonati's letter, he asked Don Pietro for the money for the journey. Don Pietro gave it to him and thought of his departure with a sense of liberation. In the spring the news of Imbonati's death reached them. Alessandro left for Paris in June.

In Paris, in rue Saint-Honoré, mother and son found themselves face to face like two people who had never met before. They were not mother and son but a woman and a man. She was suffering a recent bereavement and bore the traces of grief in her face. He felt suddenly called upon to sustain her. They were not mother and son because the maternal and filial bonds between them had been severed over the years in which they had been living far from each other, each wanting to forget the other. In his memory was buried the image of the mother who had abandoned him and vanished, and it bred anguish and a confused rancour. . . In her was buried the image of an infant to whom she had given no motherly affection and from whom she had fled, and it bred anguish and remorse. All these buried emotions suddenly flared up briefly between them before sinking back again into obscurity, but not without emitting flashes and clamour which dazzled and bemused them. A new life was beginning for both.

Alessandro fell in love with Giulia, and not only with her but suddenly with everything around her, with the memory of Carlo Imbonati, with Paris, Sophie de Condorcet and Fauriel. Later a very real and profound friendship would develop between Manzoni and Fauriel, but at this early stage he was only someone dear to Giulia and illuminated by her radiance.

He sent his verses to Fauriel who gave his opinion of them. Alessandro replied: 'Knowing you were so well informed about Italian literature, I was afraid to show you my verses: and the same reason makes your reception of them all the more flattering. . . I close, assuring you of my real distress that I can not

21

express my feelings to you in person. Shall I never clasp that hand which placed my dear, unhappy mother's in the cold hand of her and my Carlo? But our hands can only be joined by my mother's.'

He wrote a long hymn, *On the Death of Carlo Imbonati*, dedicated to his mother. Later he came to dislike it, and rejected it.

To his friend Pagani in Milan he wrote that he wished from now on to be called Alessandro Manzoni Beccaria. 'Yesterday I had the honour of dining with a great man, a supreme poet and superb lyricist, Le Brun. Having honoured me with the gift of one of his printed works, he insisted on writing on the copy, which I shall keep for ever: to Monsieur Beccaria – *C'est un nom – he said – trop honorable pour ne pas saisir l'occasion de le porter. Je veux que le nom de Le Brun choque avec celui de Beccaria.* I had the honour of placing two kisses on his wan, emaciated cheeks, sweeter to me than if I had plucked them from the lips of Venus.'

Alessandro and Giulia wrote a joint letter to Vincenzo Monti in Milan, telling him of their meeting and their happiness. In him it was the happiness of one who had left grey, empty days behind him. In her it was mingled with the torment of her recent misfortune. Together they were seeing the world with new eyes. Manzoni wrote: 'I have felt a real need to write about my happiness to you who predicted it; to tell you I have found it in a mother's arms; to say this to you who have so often spoken to me of her and know her so well. Oh Monti, I do not seek to dry her tears: I weep with her: I share her profound, but sacred and tranquil grief. . . I do not know when I may see you. I live only for my Giulia, and with her to adore and emulate that man you used to tell me was virtue itself. . . Love me and write to me. Now I willingly pass the pen to my Giulia, who is almost snatching it from me to write a few lines to her Monti.' And Giulia: 'Dear Monti, I should like to add a line or two to what my Alessandro has written. Oh, you who love him, you who *really* know him since you could propose my beloved Carlo as a model to him, you can measure the immense love I bear him by the immense love and sacred, incurable grief I feel for Carlo. Oh! do not tell me yet to seek distraction or consolation, you cannot imagine how I aspire to set these tears in the eternity which has already begun for me since it has closed upon him.

Oh Monti, do write to me, so that I may write to you.'

Giving up the plan of going to Geneva to become a hospital nun – which, in any case, she had never seriously intended to do – Giulia devoted herself to her son. She was a practical person with her feet on the ground. She had learned to organize her own life with great good sense. She thought her son's exalted love for her could be a heavy encumbrance on their daily life, wearing and painful for both of them, and that in the long run they would tire of being alone together. Her son must marry as soon as possible, and have a family and children, so that she would have a firm, clearly defined role and, surveying this new landscape, peopled and cheerful, she would grow old in wisdom and happiness. But it was essential to choose the right person, one who would intuitively know her place between the two of them. So she must look around, either in France or in Italy. Imbonati had left her, among all the other things, a large property at Brusuglio, near Milan. It would be a good thing to go and see it. Mother and son set out. Here is a letter to Fauriel from Genoa: 'I was lying in bed this morning, thinking how long we had been waiting to hear from you, when I heard my mother shout: Alessandro, a letter from Fauriel; I jumped out of bed, ran into her room, and we savoured your dear letter together. I cannot tell you the pleasure I get from the growing hope that I will be your friend, and this hope is also the joy of my mother, who keeps saying: Oh, if only you could become necessary to that divine Fauriel! Don't be angry, the epithet slipped from my pen.' Immediately after that, still in Genoa, he received a letter from Milan saying that Don Pietro Manzoni was very ill; 'I set off at once,' he wrote to Fauriel, 'my good mother accompanied me; but on my arrival they told me I was not to have the consolation of seeing my father, for the very day on which I heard of his illness was his last.' He did not go to see his dead father; he did not stop in Milan; 'Peace and honour to his ashes,' he wrote to Fauriel. He and Giulia spent a few days at Brusuglio, then went to Turin for a month. Don Pietro Manzoni had made a will: he left his possessions to Alessandro, and begged him 'not to forget the maxims and principles' in which he had sought to bring him up. 'To my lady wife I leave two diamond pendants as a token of my esteem and remembrance of her.'

23

Enrichetta Blondel I

There are several portraits of the young Alessandro Manzoni which vary greatly although they were painted within quite a short space of years. In one his hair is arranged in tight little symmetrical waves, his nose is pointed, and he has a judicious look. In another he has a thick, dishevelled mane and cloudy eyes and looks like Ugo Foscolo. In another he has a big nose and sulky mouth. In yet another he has hollow cheeks, a penetrating gaze, and crisply curling whiskers.

There is one portrait of the young Enrichetta Blondel in her bridal veil. She has a round, childlike face with gentle, unformed features. She was born in 1791 at Casirate d'Adda in the province of Bergamo. Her father was called Francesco Blondel, her mother Maria Mariton; he was Swiss, she came from Languedoc. They were Calvinists. They had eight children, four boys and four girls, and Enrichetta was the third. All the children had been baptised Catholics, because the father wanted them to be the same as everyone else. The mother had made no objection, although she hated the Catholic religion and brought her children up in the Protestant faith. The father was of a gentle disposition, the mother severe and authoritarian. He had made money out of a silk-farm. He traded in silk and had many mills. Early in the century they bought the Imbonati house in Marino Street in Milan. They were related to the Carlotta Blondel who in Paris, after the death of Carlo Imbonati, had sent Giulia to Pastor Menestraz.

Enrichetta was small, fair and graceful, with fair eyelashes. She had modest, submissive ways and said little. To Giulia she seemed the ideal daughter-in-law she had long imagined. She seemed quite perfect, created to slip gently and harmoniously into their little world. She was considered during a second trip

24

to Italy, after two or three other matrimonial plans had come to nothing. One was with a certain 'angelica Luigina', whom they had known to be already promised, and another with a French girl, daughter of friends of Fauriel called De Tracy, who had thought they were not sufficiently aristocratic.

In October 1807, shortly after meeting Enrichetta, Manzoni wrote to Fauriel from a friend's house at Belvedere sul Lago: 'I have something to tell you in confidence; I have seen in Milan the girl I told you about; I thought she was very charming; my mother who has also spoken to her and at greater length, thinks she has an excellent heart; she thinks only of her home and the happiness of her parents who adore her; in short, she is full of family feelings (and I'll say in your ear that she's the only one here with such feelings). For me there is another advantage, and a very real one in this country, at least for me: she is not an aristocrat, and you know Parini's poem. Moreover, she is a Protestant; in fact, she's a treasure, and it seems to me before long there will be three of us wanting your company; as yet, however, nothing is settled, and she herself knows nothing of it. I think, when it happens, it will be my duty to inform the worthy man whose alliance I was hoping to obtain, so please tell me what you think about it. For the moment it must be kept completely secret. . . My mother has just interrupted to tell me to say that the little girl I speak of speaks French all the time, is sixteen, and is simple and unpretentious. So now you know it all.'

And in another letter when the marriage was about to take place:
'So I can tell you that my bride is sixteen, has a sweet nature, upright feelings, the greatest affection for her parents and apparently some little for me. . . She shows such love mingled with respect for my mother you would think she was her own daughter; and indeed she always calls her 'Mama'. No doubt you will think I have been rather hasty, but as soon as I really got to know her, it seemed pointless to delay. Her family commands respect for the harmony that prevails among them, and for their modesty, goodness and every estimable sentiment. In short, I am certain that this will bring happiness for me, and for my mother, without which there could be none for me.'

Enrichetta and Alessandro were married in Milan in February

1808 in a Calvinist church. He would have needed a dispensation for a Catholic wedding, since she was of a different faith despite her baptism. But he was in a hurry and neglected to ask for the dispensation. He wrote to Fauriel that the priests had refused to celebrate his marriage because of the difference of religion. This delighted all the Blondel family. Giulia did not attend the ceremony because she was indisposed. There was no wedding breakfast. A Swiss pastor blessed the couple in the house in Marino Street which had once belonged to the Imbonatis. Immediately after Manzoni hurried to his mother's bedside. The marriage was bitterly criticized in the town, for it was generally thought scandalous that a nobleman, related to 'monsignores', should marry a Protestant.

'I have spent two months between pain and pleasure,' Manzoni wrote to Fauriel in the spring. 'My mother has had a terrible sore throat, which has recurred three times; however, she now seems free of it. Meanwhile, I have got married, which speeded my mother's recovery, as it has filled, indeed *flooded* her heart with happiness. We are all three as happy as can be; this angel was created just for us; she shares all my tastes, and I don't think there is one important matter on which her opinions differ from mine.'

But Giulia, albeit happy, was in a black mood; she was excessively irritated that the town should speak ill of them. In a corner of her estate at Brusuglio she had already had a *tempietto* built the year before and had arranged for Carlo Imbonati's body to be brought there from France, and this too had been considered scandalous. She could not wait to leave *ce vilain Italie*; she longed for Paris and her friends who understood her. She often went to Brusuglio to linger at the little tomb; also to supervise the work begun a year before; on the estate there was a farm which was to be transformed into a spacious, comfortable house in which they would enjoy living. But all this failed to soothe her.

So it was decided to return to Paris. The three of them set off in the summer, and took a house on the boulevard des Italiens.

Enrichetta was taken to *La Maisonnette*, and presented to Madame de Condorcet and Fauriel. But she was bored at *La Maisonnette*; Alessandro and Fauriel went off to talk literature and philosophy; Giulia and Sophie de Condorcet chatted

26

together about people in Paris whom she did not know. She did not like Sophie de Condorcet; she dared not converse with Fauriel as she feared she was too ignorant; she felt awkward, out of her element, lost. She was homesick for Italy and her family. Giulia, on the other hand, was cheerful again in Paris.

In December 1808, in the house on the boulevard des Italiens, Enrichetta and Alessandro's first daughter was born. She was officially registered by Fauriel and a friend. She was called Giulia Claudia. Her grandmother expressed a wish that she should be baptised, and Enrichetta made no objection. It was decided to baptise her at Meulan, where a priest friend of Fauriel would make no difficulties about the non-Catholic marriage of the parents. In her first month the baby girl became seriously ill. Manzoni wrote to Fauriel: 'Poor Giulietta has had German measles and thrush at the same time – two deadly illnesses at the age of twenty days; it's all over now, but what a harsh entrance into the best of all possible worlds.' Meanwhile he was finishing a short poem called 'Urania', and thinking of another to be called 'La vaccina'.

Giulietta was not baptised until the summer, at Meulan as had been decided; and Enrichetta was sad because she felt they were separating her from her daughter, since she herself had grown up in another faith. The christening was organized by Madame de Condorcet whom she knew to be an unbeliever; and Fauriel was an unbeliever and he had been chosen to act as godfather to the baby girl; and he, an unbeliever, recited the *Credo* and *Abrenuntio*. For Enrichetta any religious event was a very serious matter.

In Paris the Manzonis frequented a group of people Enrichetta liked, some Piedmontese patriots who had been friends of Imbonati. They led a strict life and seemed imbued with great moral severity. Enrichetta felt happy in their company, much more than at *La Maisonnette*. One evening there was a discussion of the Catholic faith. Count Somis de Chavrie was there, a Turinese, Councillor at the Court of Appeal. 'I believe in it,' he said simply. Enrichetta was struck by these forceful words. She went up to him and asked him to suggest an expert in the Catholic faith who might talk to her and offer her some illumination. Somis recommended Abbé Degola.

Abbé Degola was a Jansenist priest from Genoa, then about fifty. In 1801 in Paris he had taken part in the Second Council, and there he had become a friend of Bishop Grégoire, whom he helped to compile the *Annals of Religion*. Between 1804 and 1805 he travelled with Grégoire, visiting England, Holland, Germany and Prussia; at Hamburg he heard that Liguria had been annexed to the Empire by Napoleon, and he sent a protest against this action. At Genoa, with his friend Father Assarotti he founded an institute for deaf-mutes. Degola, according to his friend Achille Mauri who wrote his biography, was 'well-proportioned with a gentle, benevolent countenance, and clear, bright eyes'. Nevertheless, in his portraits his face does not convey great gentleness or benevolence. Achille Mauri also says of him: 'All things combined to adorn him with rare gifts: philosophy, letters and religion inclined him to virtue. A heart ever open to indulgence, sincerely amiable manners, a pleasing discourse remote from any rusticity won the love and respect of people of every order. . . He set religion above all other thoughts, and it made him humble, mild and patient. . . When he became a priest, all his actions revealed his conviction that the priesthood is an honourable bondage, imposing on all who undertake it a constant and diligent concern for the needs, passions and sufferings of all.' It was said that he was without ambition. But he was ambitious to convert souls to the Catholic faith. From his travels with Bishop Grégoire there remain five notebooks in which he wrote down his impressions: he made dry judgements on the people he met, collected together thoughts and utterances he heard, listed facts and details, keeping a keen eye on everything around him.

> Erfurt. There are regular and Benedictine canonesses. At the Fort there were four canonesses, one a Benedictine who seemed to me something of a coquette; she allowed the Commandant Dall' Alba to stroke her hand. I spoke Latin to an old Augustinian. . . In Leipzig there is a great loosening of moral standards. Divorce is common. But still more so in Halle; you have only to pay for it. . . Among the Lutherans it is said that Luther was a horse and Melanchthon the bridle to restrain him. . . In Wittenberg 31st July: we were at the

28

Temple of the Court and University, where they never observe communion or baptism. We saw, among other things, two hollows in which the bodies of Luther and Melanchthon had rotted, and behind them their portraits. Luther in a sort of cassock and yellow boots, Melanchthon (to whom I said *Anathema Melanctoni*) a black robe with fur at the edge like a Professor of Greek. There is a table with two inscriptions in bronze; the first which I traced contemptuously with my foot was as follows [the inscription followed]. I went up into the pulpit and from there I said: *Anathema Lutero*, and repeated it in the hollow, where I had already said: *Maledictus qui posuit carnem. . .* Berlin. Conversation with Ancillon, Calvinist minister; he agreed that religion there is declining rapidly as regards worship and faith. Tolerance, he said, was the *fin mot* to neutralize religious opinions and lead to universal indifference. – He agreed that the demands of the reformers *en voulant emporter la broderie, ils ont déchiré la robe*. As for literature, he said they were accustoming the young to *légèreté*, and making them *voltiger*.

At Strasbourg Degola parted from Grégoire and prepared to turn homeward. The next day, still at Strasbourg, he met a boy, one Teofilo Geymüller, whose mother had been converted to Catholicism. She wanted her two young sons to be converted too.

I spoke of conversion to Teofilo, who said at once, speaking of Calvinism: *J'y tiens, oui, et je ne changerai pas*. I exhorted him to seek instruction, I spoke to him openly and affectionately: I talked about his mother's conversion and excellent conduct, I gave him the note which I had copied. The next day, at seven in the evening, he began to tell me he felt moved to do as his mother had done. I encouraged him.

The day after that, at Buchten (Switzerland), he and Teofilo attended a Catholic wedding.

The parish priest, to whom I spoke, but who did not say much to me, held by the breviary; he told me there were five thousand inhabitants there, all Catholics, he said the prayers in Latin: I did not hear the act of consent; I thought he asked it very quietly. I blessed the couple, the priest sprinkled holy

29

water on the congregation. On the way out Teofilo said to me: *A présent il faut que je conserve cette bénédiction pour toujours.*

When he got back to Genoa in 1805, Abbé Degola stayed there. He had the two sons of Signora Geymüller with him. Teofilo was converted in 1806; Luca, the younger son, two years later. Their mother was living in Paris. Enrichetta met her, and from her too heard of Abbé Degola; she asked to meet him if he should come to France.

Alessandro and Enrichetta had come to a joint decision to regularize their marriage in the eyes of the Church. After the baby's christening, this seemed right and proper to both of them. The Catholic wedding ceremony took place in the private chapel of a friend of theirs, Count Marescalchi, on 15 February 1810.

Enrichetta had seen Abbé Degola for the first time in the autumn of 1809; he had come to Paris because he had been invited to Port-Royal. In the spring of 1810 her discussions with the Abbé began. Manzoni chose to be present, though remaining silent.

When she got home after every discussion, Enrichetta, at Degola's request, was to write a brief summary of the chief points discussed; this is what Signora Geymüller had been required to do; then Degola read and corrected the summaries. Signora Geymüller's summaries, with Degola's corrections, have been preserved, but Enrichetta's have been lost. At Manzoni's death his son Enrico found among his papers a few summaries in Manzoni's own hand; so he too wrote summaries, without being required to do so, when he attended these discussions. We have Enrico's word for this, but the summaries later disappeared, and nobody knows what happened to them.

On 2 April 1810 the wedding of Napoleon and Marie-Louise of Austria was celebrated in Paris. There were great crowds in the streets, among them Alessandro and Enrichetta. Suddenly mortars were fired. People panicked and began to run to and fro in confusion, and in this panic there were dead and wounded. Alessandro lost sight of Enrichetta. He seems then to have experienced a malaise, a giddiness, and he feared he was going to faint; he went into the church of San Rocco. He found Enrichetta shortly after. They say that there, in the church, he prayed a real prayer to God for the first time in his life, asking Him to let him find his wife again safe and sound. 'Entering the church of San Rocco one day, he prayed feverishly and rose from his knees a believer,' says Abbé Zanella, who was a friend of his. 'It was the grace of God, my son, the grace of God,' Manzoni replied much later to his stepson Stefano, who asked him when he had found faith, and where, and how. He would never add to these words. A tablet has been placed in the Church of San Rocco which states that Manzoni's conversion happened at that place and that moment.

The malaise and vertigo which led him to seek refuge in the church were a real *crise de nerfs*, the first in his life. From then he realised he was liable to convulsions, or afraid of experiencing attacks. And this fear caused him palpitations and vertigo. In fact, his grandfather, Cesare Beccaria, had been convulsionary, and his uncle Giulio Beccaria, son of Cesare. Abbé Degola was also subject to convulsions, and this probably created mutual understanding between Manzoni and Degola.

'He rose from his knees a believer.' He was in a frantic state when he knelt to pray: he had felt he was fainting or dying; his prayer had been 'feverish'; feverishly he had begged God to restore Enrichetta to him, and also to restore to him a less hateful image of himself, for in the confusion of his malaise he had looked at himself with disgust; his faults had seemed very great: he had been cynical, fatuous, indifferent to his neighbour, and cruel; this is how he saw himself at that moment, and he had never believed in God. From then, he suffered frequent crises of acute anguish; he kept remembering that moment; he was oppressed by remorse, and felt that his faith was never sufficiently strong, limpid or sure.

The three of them became Catholics: Enrichetta, Alessandro, Giulia. They were strongly united but profoundly different, and each arrived at the Catholic faith in a different way. Enrichetta had to break the bonds that bound her to her family and childhood, as it were with blood and toil. Alessandro bore within him that burden of secret remorse, doubts and travail. Giulia rushed forward, stumbling and breathless, like someone afraid of missing an appointment; but she moved forward with a light tread, for she was always ready for any change or turn and faced the future eagerly, whatever new form it might take; she too bore a sense of remorse and guilt, but it never completely darkened her path. They were at one in deciding to go back and settle in Italy; all three wanted to change their life and breathe new air. Giulia remembered *Ce vilain Italie* with affection; Enrichetta had never liked Paris, and now Alessandro hated it.

On 22 May, in the Church of Saint-Séverin in Paris, Abbé Degola received Enrichetta's abjuration and her profession of faith in the Catholic Church. It was a solemn ceremony, attended by Somis, the President of the Court of Appeal Agier, Signora Geymüller with her two sons, lofty prelates and magistrates, and many ladies. One of Enrichetta's uncles who lived in Paris got to know of it, and immediately informed the Blondel family in Milan, who knew nothing of it.

'I, Enrichetta Luisa Manzoni, née Blondel, called by the grace of Almighty God to return to the bosom of the Church, recognize the errors of the Calvinist sect in which I had the misfortune to be brought up, sincerely abominate them, and henceforth wish, with the help of divine mercy, to live in the bosom of the Catholic Church, which is the pillar of truth. I firmly believe all the teachings of the Catholic Church, and wish to abjure the Calvinist heresy; of my own free will resolved upon this act for no other reason than to work for the glory of God and to provide for my eternal salvation, I pray the Church to accept for her ministry my abjuration, and to welcome me into her bosom in the name of Jesus Christ and of His charity.'

For some time Enrichetta's parents had been inviting Enrichetta, Alessandro and Giulia to be their guests on their arrival in Milan, and they were eager to meet the baby girl they had never seen. The news of the abjuration took them by surprise and roused them to a tremendous anger, especially the mother. Until then relations had been perfect between the two families, but they were spoiled at that moment and never fully recovered. Mariton, the mother, thought Giulia was to blame for Enrichetta's abjuration and cordially detested her.

The Manzonis left Paris at the beginning of June. When they got to Lyons, Giulia fell ill, and the baby too. Enrichetta was pregnant, or thought she was; she was suffering from stomach upsets that seemed to her to indicate pregnancy. Manzoni had to have a tooth out. They spent several days at Lyons, where the echoes of the Blondel anger reached them. They were sad days. As they were leaving Paris a letter had come from Fauriel, who was going back to Meulan without calling to say goodbye. 'Today I am leaving this Paris where soon you will be seen no more, my dear friends, – he wrote – I could not come to see you last night, and I feel I was right to spare myself such a sad moment. . . We will meet again one day. I need this hope, and flatter myself it will be realized. . . Farewell, I press you all to my heart. Kiss little Giulietta for me a thousand times.' He had the greatest respect for other people's ideas; this triple conversion and Enrichetta's abjuration disturbed him, but he never mentioned it. From Lyons Manzoni answered: 'Dear friend, after knowing and esteeming you, why can I not remain with you longer? . . . Indeed, you are the only link binding me to Paris for which otherwise I feel no affection. . . We all send our love, including Giulia, who will certainly have learned to call you *caro padrino* (dear godfather) when you come to Italy. . . Remember that I am never completely happy away from you.'

In Turin, at the Albergo della Moneta, Enrichetta met her brother Carlo who spoke harshly to her. She wrote to her father. 'It is with a heart full of pain and fear that I venture to send you this letter, dear Father! . . . Oh, if only I could hope you do not judge your daughter too severely! I need this hope if I am not to give way completely to the bitter pain I feel at the threats and the suffering of the mother I have always adored. . . Dear God! I can not bear the idea of being banished from the presence of parents who have always been precious to me; and what I have done does not seem to me to merit such severity! . . . Why is my dear mother so angry with me? What I have done, I did for my salvation; can she harbour resentment against a daughter who has acted for her eternal happiness? . . . My dear parents, dearest Father and Mother, may God bless you, this is my constant prayer. And I beg Him to grant me courage and resignation, for I see I shall have great need of both, oh God!'

Somis wrote to Abbé Degola: 'Yesterday at one in the afternoon I had the consolation of seeing that beloved family of whom I can not speak, especially to you, without strong emotion. Poor creatures! they had to stay two weeks at Lyons, all more or less ill, and you can imagine in what discomfort. But God reserves His greatest tests for his elect. Yesterday Signora Enrichetta received two letters from Milan which caused consternation in her tender, affectionate heart. The news of her abjuration has aroused tumult, fire and frenzy in her mother. Our virtuous Catholic suffers unspeakable torment at this clash between her holy and irrevocable resolution and her natural filial sentiments. Help her with your fervent prayers and wise counsel. . .'

Enrichetta was bled twice on that unhappy journey, at Lyons and Turin; they hoped this would improve her health and cure the malaise she was suffering, but from then on she was never really well again. From Turin they went on to Brusuglio, where Enrichetta received a letter from her mother agreeing to see her; she went on her own. 'Neither my mother nor I could go,' Manzoni wrote to Degola, 'as my mother was excluded quite rudely, and I was invited in a way that was more like a dismissal.' At Brusuglio Enrichetta was bled for the third time. However, the air was healthy there, and in a few days the baby was rosy and blooming, Manzoni enjoyed the house and park, and wrote to Fauriel: 'It seems centuries since I heard from you; write soon, tell me what you are working on at *La Maisonnette*, and when you are thinking of coming to Italy. Really the climate is much better here, the sun is inspiriting, and I have become a real farmer. I've seen the cotton grown from the seed I sent from Paris which Monsieur Dupont was good enough to give me; some plants are already a foot high. . . I asked what had become of the ones I sowed myself two years ago, and they showed me a basket full of bolls, some quite mature. . . I have planted medicinal herbs; clover grows naturally here among the ears of corn and between the hedges. . . You must come; we will grow things, you can botanize; oh, how happy I'd be!'

When they left Paris, Abbé Degola gave them a letter for a Canon Luigi Tosi, parish priest of Sant' Ambrogio, in which he commended the Manzoni family to him, and asked him to continue their religious instruction which he had begun.

Canon Luigi Tosi was born at Busto Arsizio in 1763. Like Degola, he was a Jansenist. He was no genius, but a limited, modest man, with a high sense of the proper duties of a priest, and with great human warmth.

34

It was Giulia who took the letter to him. She and the priest met in the street as he was going home from church. He read the letter and was profoundly disturbed by it. So the lady before him was Giulia Beccaria, who had been talked of so much in the town, friend of Imbonati, and mother of the Manzoni who had caused a scandal by marrying a Protestant. He felt unprepared and inadequate for the charge Degola was entrusting to him. But he could only accept it. He came to Brusuglio to meet Enrichetta, who was ill and feverish after a second visit to her family, during which her father had hardly spoken to her and her mother had renewed her bitter complaints.

Tosi wrote to Degola: 'My friend, at the beginning of July, when Madame Beccaria gave me your letter in the street as I was walking home, I was so stunned I could hardly find words to answer her. It was the greatest surprise to me, after such little as I had heard of this family; I was so afraid the matter was beyond my strength that I felt discouraged. Since I have been a priest, and especially in the last ten years, I have been so oppressed with every sort of care, that I can tell you truly I have not read a single book. . . Moreover, this anxious life, beset with constant worries, has greatly undermined my health, quite blunted the power of my spirit, destroyed my memory, and so confounded my mind that I must constantly blush for myself. . . In such a state, how could I not feel dismayed and discouraged before a task which demanded an enlightened mind, consummate wisdom, alert attention, as well as a certain practice in matters of which I have no experience? It was well for me, and for you who had erred so gravely in your choice, that the Lord has wrought all things in this family. He gave all three such simple docility as I have never seen in twenty years of ministry, not even in people of the lowest orders. Oh, what a miracle is this Divine Mercy! Not only Enrichetta, who is an angel of innocence and simplicity, but Madam, and even the proud Alessandro are lambs, who receive with the utmost eagerness the simplest instruction, foresee people's wishes before they are spoken, by their encouragement help their interlocutor to speak freely, and turn all things to their sanctification. They live together in the wisest way; their hearts are wonderfully united, and they conspire to encourage and strengthen each other and to scorn all worldly considerations. Our town is highly edified by this miracle of God's right hand.'

Giulia received the eucharist at Brusuglio on 15 August. Two days before she was writing to tell Father Tosi that her engagements prevented her leaving Milan: 'I commend myself to your prayers in the most important act of my life, which I cannot contemplate without the greatest anxiety; I cannot yet conceive how I dare approach the Sacred Table. . . In God's love tell me if I really can approach the altar. In my heart of hearts I feel I am the lowest and most unworthy of creatures, I am truly convinced of this yet in saying it I feel a sense of pride is mingled in my confession, I am lost in this terrible contradiction and I realize that even good things become bad when they are in me or issue from me. I could not help this outburst; perhaps I have done wrong, and ought to act with greater simplicity? I wait for you to tell me, in charity, what I must do. I have done and am doing what you told me for my preparation, and after dinner I read some chapters of the fourth book of the *Imitation of Christ*, especially the second and ninth chapters in which I find the most sublime prayers.' Enrichetta was unwell on the morning of the 15th and could not leave her room; she wrote to Tosi: 'This morning as I stayed behind in bed while the others were at Mass, I did my best to follow the service; but the singing of the band of faithful caused me to burst into tears: at the same time I thanked God for the small trial He set me and asked Him for strength and resignation to bear it, and my heart cried louder still. . . Oh God, I see you find me unworthy to be among those faithful, since you keep me here: you find me too great a sinner and I have not yet sufficiently lamented my faults!' She received the eucharist a month later. Manzoni went up to the altar the same day as his mother, with Rosa, the daughter of Somis, who was their guest at the time. Her father wrote to Rosa: 'My beloved Rosa, Donna Giulia has written to tell me that after the confirmation you joined those God-fearing people, your hosts, in their devotions.' The Somis family were not well-to-do and lived modestly, and the father was pleased that his daughter could enjoy a different way of life in those summer months: 'I hear that, donna Enrichetta's health permitting, they are thinking of moving on to Milan, and from there to Lecco. I feel these little journeys, and the chance to see new and beautiful places, should afford you delightful distraction; enjoy it in all innocence. . . I consider you should not deprive yourself of the innocent novelty of seeing the celebrated neighbourhood of Lake Como. Who knows when you might go again?' There was indeed a plan to move on for a while from Brusuglio to Il Caleotto, the property near Lecco which Manzoni had inherited from Don Pietro, but they had to give up the idea, because Enrichetta was unwell; they could not make out if she was pregnant or not; they called a surgeon; in the end she had a miscarriage.

From Abbé Degola, Enrichetta had received a copy of the *Regolamenti*, indicating how to lead a truly religious life, written by Signora Geymüller. Enrichetta and Giulia read them again and again with dismay; perhaps they suited Signora Geymüller, who enjoyed better health and a less demanding domestic life, but to them they seemed severe and difficult to carry out. They seemed intended to impose an iron discipline upon existence, and Giulia was by temperament capricious and intolerant of discipline. Enrichetta suffered indifferent health, and one was supposed to get up in the cold night to pray. Nevertheless they submitted to it. As for Manzoni, he was causing the two ladies grave anxiety with his bouts of anguish and *crises de nerfs*; at times he felt as if a chasm was opening at his feet, and they had to run up with a chair to fill the void he felt before him. He was terrified of going out alone, and someone always had to accompany him on the walks he so much enjoyed in the park; one day when he was alone, feeling he was about to faint, he dashed a bottle of sparkling water called 'acqua di Lecco' into his face, and it caused an inflammation of the eyes which kept him in bed in a darkened room for several days.

Father Tosi saw fit to make 'a few small modifications' to the *Regolamenti*, but they still remained severe. '1. God shall be your first thought on waking. . . 2. As soon as you are dressed, prostrate yourself at the feet of Christ. . . 3. After a moment's silence which is a confession of your nullity, a profound lamentation upon your wretchedness, and a filial yielding to Divine Mercy, you will recite the *Morning Prayers*. . . 4. After the prayer follows the reading of the Holy Gospel. . . 5. In the course of the day do not forget to offer to God your every action, working, eating and sleeping. . . 6. You will occupy yourself with your domestic tasks, for this too is a duty imposed on you by Providence. . . 7. Work must be considered part of the general penitence imposed by God upon the sons of Adam. Add to this consideration the duties of your estate, the providence required by a wise and well-regulated domestic economy, the dangers present in a single moment of idleness, the need to give a good example of a useful life. . . If time remains after you have accomplished the duties of your house, you will work for the poor. . . 8. But the work I particularly recommend in this respect is the religious, moral and civil instruction of the local children. Well-directed, their education will extend the Church, regenerate manners, and make for good family life. . . 9. In the course of your work, manual or educational, lifting your heart to God, seek to animate your thoughts by the divine presence. You may be helped to this end by some pious reading. . . 10. You will set aside a little quarter of an hour before meals for a moment of meditation, a brief examination of conscience. . . some reading of the Psalms in Monsieur De Sacy's interpretation, or of some other pious and sound writings. . . 11. After meals, do not turn at once to work. Profit when you can from conversation, but in such a way as it may always be of some utility. . . 12. Towards evening rest a little so that you may more easily resume your evening occupations. About ten, devote a little time to meditation and reading, as before dinner. In general, seek to sanctify every meal by some self-denial. Evening prayers and examination of conscience about eleven o'clock. Then choose some pious thought to fill your heart before sleep and in the wakeful hours of the night. Your rest may last from that time until five or six in the morning. . . 13. On Sundays and feast-days you will follow the offices of the Church. Each month set aside a day of retreat to examine your conduct, thank God for the good actions He has permitted you to perform, lament your faults, and seek effective means to correct them. . . 14. I exhort you each year to make a pilgrimage to Port-Royal and a visit to the cemetery of Saint-Lambert, to thank God for all his gifts in which you have enjoyed the first fruits of His spirit, to ask for grace to persevere in good by the intercession of the Saints, who in solitude, by their piety, their penitence and their works have spread throughout the Church the good odour of Jesus Christ.'

This is only a very brief and superficial outline of the

Regolamenti, but perhaps it gives some idea of the attitudes they imposed, and which might seem at first sight not too difficult to adopt; but it was arduous to maintain them constantly, day in, day out. The *Regolamenti* demanded absolute dedication; they barred the way to idleness, fantasy, free and various choices, they ruled out any possibility of shaping life hour by hour, according to one's own inclinations and whims, or the thousand unpredictable chances that might arise. Observing them by the letter, one would hardly have time to breathe.

Giulia sent Father Tosi a 'questionnaire on how to pass the hours of the day', which reveals how she was seeking to soften the impact of the *Regolamenti*. 'I am almost always wakened by Fanni [her French maid] more or less late, but I hardly ever get up at her first call so that as soon as I am dressed I go out to church with her in order not to waste her time. If I were to get up the first time she comes into my room, I would have time to say my prayers before going out. . . I pray for my spiritual benefactors who have helped me and do help me to serve the Lord, for all those converted by the particular intercession of the Blessed Virgin, and finally for the unbelieving Hebrew heretics and for those I have had the misfortune to lead into trespass in some way. If Fanni is taking Holy Communion, I stay in church as long as she is there.' The priest replied: 'I have not much to add to the system you describe: *promptness* and *fidelity* are the essentials; so when it is time to rise, rise at once and expiate by this promptness all you have lost by such idleness especially in remaining so long in bed. If your state of health requires you to stay there a little longer, never let this be a time of idleness, but even in bed employ it at once in thanks, sad lamentations and offerings. . . Never neglect those prayers you mention for sinners etc. These are your special brothers.' Giulia: 'When I return home I go to the room of my son and daughter-in-law for breakfast and usually waste a great deal of time there. I must remark that except on the day when I also take coffee with them because it would seem odd if I did not do so, I could easily stay in my own room to take my chocolate on the other days.' The priest: 'Time spent with your family for breakfast should not be too long. It would be well if you were told when it is almost ready to be served, and then stayed no more than an hour. . . Neglect no opportunity to say some good word, or

39

make some timely suggestion. Be on your guard at these and all times, against excessive love for little Giulietta.' Giulia: 'Most Reverend Sir, you suggested as a practice of Christian penitence that I should rise from my bed at night to pray at least for a few minutes; I have only ever found courage to do so a few times. . . May God illumine my heart, and inspire you in all charity to impose upon me a way of life that will lift me out of my lethargy and perhaps out of perdition. – I have put myself under the particular protection of the holy penitent Maria Egiziaca.' The priest: 'This practice of rising at night, if not essential, is none the less most opportune. Start doing it one or two nights a week, not getting out of your bed in the winter, but sitting up well covered, or at least adopting a position which allows you to take your crucifix in your hands. . . as for the table, I have nothing to suggest but simplicity, and not too much anxious regard for health. . . In conversation return constantly to the Lord with some secret prayer, and take the greatest care not to become too involved and heated in discourse. Always remember that silence becomes a sinner.'

Meanwhile Manzoni was writing to Fauriel: 'As for me, I shall continue in the sweet habit of speaking to you of what is nearest my heart, at the risk of being tedious. And so I will tell you that above all I have been occupied with the most important thing in life according to the religious notions that God sent to me in Paris, and the more I advance, the more my heart finds contentment and my mind delight. Dear Fauriel, allow me to hope that you will do the same. It is true that I fear for you those terrible words: *Abscondisti haec a sapientibus et prudentibus et revelasti ea parvulis* [Thou hidest these things from the wise and prudent, and hast revealed them unto babes]; but no, I do not fear them, for the goodness and humility of your heart is as great as your intellect and understanding. Forgive the sermon this *parvulus* takes the liberty of addressing to you. Apart from this, I am up to my eyes in agricultural plans. . . the cottons have been sent off for this year, apart from the nankin, from which I shall collect a little seed. . . And now the errands with which I mean to trouble you. I should like some trefoil, for myself and for a friend. . . Make haste then, and buy me nine pounds of trefoil and give it to Fayolle [a Parisian publisher], to whom I have written to send them on to us by a coachman. . .'

40

In the winter Enrichetta was pregnant again. Her father had a paralytic attack. Relations with her mother and relatives were still rather cold. She wrote to Abbé Degola that winter: 'Your prayers go straight to God: pray that, by His grace, I may by my behaviour and my words edify my parents and contribute in some way to their sanctification.' And she wrote to Canon Tosi: 'God bless you, my dear Father, and please give me your holy blessing in your turn, which I receive as coming from God Himself who has made you so good and so necessary to the souls He has entrusted to you.' She signed the letter: 'Enrichetta Manzoni, Catholic by Divine Mercy.'

Enrichetta Blondel II

Enrichetta's existence revolved around four main preoccupations: marriage, motherhood, illness, religion. She never had many distractions or friendships; she sometimes wrote to Rosa Somis in Turin, or to Carlotta de Blasco, a cousin of Giulia's maternal uncle; she recounted the small minutiae of domestic life, the illnesses of local ladies, her ailments in pregnancy, blood-letting, and the progress of her babies. When she wanted to confide in someone, she wrote to Abbé Degola. Canon Tosi was dear to her, but Degola always remained her real spiritual guide. But all three led an austere life without much in the way of amusements at Brusuglio, in the big house buried among the trees.

'We await your arrival with eager confidence,' Manzoni wrote to Fauriel. He had promised to come to Italy. But he did not come, and they heard nothing from him for many months. At last a letter arrived. 'A letter from you, who are ever more dear to me,' Manzoni wrote, 'would always cause me great excitement, but it so happened that the excitement was increased in an extraordinary way; I was in my room and I heard shouts in the hall of "Fauriel, Fauriel"; I rushed out like a madman, and saw only my mother and my wife, whose faces showed me at once that I had made a ridiculous mistake; only then did I have time to reflect upon the absurdity of thinking I might see you here in this season, without hearing a word about your coming, etc. But if anything could console me in my *disappointment*, it was your letter. How it made up for your silence! Every line is precious to me. . . and what about your marvellous project on Dante?' Fauriel was thinking of writing a book on Dante, and wanted to dedicate it to Manzoni (the book appeared posthumously many years later).

In the winter of 1810 the Manzonis took a rented house in Milan, in via San Vito del Carrobbio. But they still spent a great part of the year at Brusuglio. In September 1811 a second baby girl was born at Brusuglio, called Vittoria Luigia Maria; she was born prematurely and lived for only one day. Manzoni wrote to Degola: 'I am writing to tell you of the happy issue of Enrichetta's troubles which happened yesterday when a millstone was removed from her. In the end her pains yesterday were quite atrocious but brief, and led happily to her delivery, with no need of intervention.' These words sound strange and brutal in speaking of a baby girl who received a name and lived a day. Manzoni wrote an epitaph to be inscribed on her tomb: *immature nata illico praecepta – coelum assecuta* [Untimely born, summoned at once, she sped to heaven]. It was the first of the many funeral epitaphs he would be called upon to write in his life. Sophie de Condorcet wrote to Giulia: 'Dear friend, I feel the warmest sympathy for all that you have gone through with Enrichetta. Her good health at the birth is a great consolation for the loss of that poor little creature that was not aware of its existence. Delicate as Enrichetta is, it is a great thing if her confinements do not cause you too much anxiety. As she grows older and stronger, and with a little rest, it should be possible for her to give a brother to the delightful Giulia.' This letter is melancholy, and full of affection for her distant friends; and she seems to have lost her proud, haughty ways; she had been very ill with *une goutte à la tête*, and Fauriel had been ill too with *une fièvre pernicieuse*; the friends in Italy heard about it only when it was all over. 'I have difficulty in writing. I have suffered so much for five months! Goodbye, dear friends, I hug and love you all, each in a different way, but each with a true love which hates this absence. . . I assure you that, as I lay in my bed twenty days out of every month, it broke my heart to receive no news of you, and I would say to myself, I love them more than ever. . . and will always do so.'

In the winter of 1812 Enrichetta's father died of an apoplectic fit. He had resumed relations with his daughter, but they would not see Manzoni. 'I haven't seen him once since my return to Italy,' Manzoni wrote to Fauriel, 'and though it's true neither he nor I was to blame, it continues to distress me. He died mourned by all, especially the poor; he died after making a for-

43

tune, always deservedly maintaining his general reputation not only for total probity, but for great delicacy and generosity; all of which should give you some idea of the quality of his mind and at the same time of his moral qualities.' They used the money Enrichetta inherited from her father to buy a house in via del Morone, 'a town house with garden' as it was called in the deed of purchase; it cost a hundred and six thousand lire.

A brother for the 'delightful Giulia', that is little Giulietta, was born in July 1813 at Palazzo Beccaria, where the Manzonis were the guests of Giulio Beccaria, the half-brother of grandmother Giulia, whom she had sought out on her return to Italy and whom she loved dearly. They had moved out of the house in via San Vito and the new house was not ready. Grandmother Giulia wrote to her uncle Michele de Blasco on 24 July: 'On the 21st, at seven in the morning, our dear, beloved Enrichetta presented me with a fine little boy right on my birthday and in the very house where I was born; her pains did not last many hours, she is very well and is breast-feeding this handsome, bonny, splendid boy. You can imagine our joy.' She does not say the new baby had been named Pier Luigi, but was to be called Pietro: this was Alessandro's choice, in memory of the gloomy, elderly man whom he remembered with remorse and whom he had not seen on his death-bed; Grandmother Giulia did not call this first grandson Pietro, but almost always Pedrino, or 'el Pedrin'.

Imbonati's corpse was no longer in the park at Brusuglio; Canon Tosi had told Giulia it would be well to dispose of it elsewhere, so it was taken to the neighbouring cemetery, and as there was no room there it was buried along the perimeter wall by the roadside.

In the winter Manzoni wrote to Fauriel after a long silence: 'Madame de Condorcet has been informed by Mother of the birth of a baby boy who, after causing my Enrichetta a lot of trouble in pregnancy, now rewards her and consoles us almost every moment of the day by his good health, placid cheerfulness and *goodness*. Enrichetta is feeding him herself and is very well. He was born weak and sickly by a mother in the same state, but little by little both have gained strength, so that Enrichetta (apart from a few little problems she is never free from) is an excellent nurse and my little Pietro is one of the bonniest babies you could wish to see. Giulietta is well and profits by the education we try to give her, of which dear Enrichetta has special charge. As for me, I am here with my family, the trees and my verses. [He was writing the *Sacred Hymns*.] We have bought a house with a big garden of about a tenth of an acre, in which I immediately planted some *liquidambar*, sophoras, thujas and firs which, if I live long enough, will come up through the window one day looking for me. I have written another two Hymns, and mean to write a lot more. . . When things are quieter, I will send them to you for your opinion, which is always the most authoritative for me. . . Does it not seem strange that I talk about such things in the midst of all this tumult? But you know that it is one of the advantages of poets, *among so many showered on them by Heaven*, always to find a moment to talk of their own verses.'

A great deal of work was required in the new house, and there were expenses for the property at Brusuglio; the Imbonati inheritance had diminished, and they had financial worries. Besides, they had to pay very heavy taxes; money was demanded from the citizens to pay for the defeats Napoleon had suffered in battle. Many had died in Russia and in the fighting on the Elbe. For some time disorder had reigned in Milan and throughout Lombardy; there was violence in the streets, theft and looting. On 19 April in that year, 1814, a petition was signed for the convocation of the Electoral Colleges, to be presented to the Senate; among the hundred and twenty-seven signatories was Manzoni, Alessandro, landowner. On 20 April occurred the murder of Giuseppe Prina, the finance minister hated by the people for his subservience to the French; he had imposed tremendous taxes in response to the demands of Napoleon. Manzoni wrote to Fauriel, in a letter addressed to Paris to be delivered by his cousin Giacomo Beccaria: 'My cousin will tell you about the revolution that has taken place here. It was unanimous, and I must say wise and pure, although it was unhappily stained by an assassination which those involved in the rebellion (that is, the major and better part of the population) had no share in; nothing could be further from their nature. It was the work of people who took advantage of the popular movement and turned it against a man who was the object of public hate, the finance minister, who was slain in spite of the efforts of many to snatch him from their hands. You will know in any case that the people are always a better jury than judge; but decent people were saddened by this deed. As it happens, our house is very close to the one where he was living, so that for hours we could hear the shouts of the people searching for him, which kept my mother and wife in a state of cruel anxiety, as they feared the people might not stop at that. And indeed, some men of baser motives tried to take advantage of the momentary anarchy and prolong it, but the civil guard were able to check it with courage, wisdom and diligence worthy of the highest praise.'

Among the many who had fought to snatch Prina from the fury of the crowd was Ugo Foscolo, and Manzoni must have known it. In his heart he must have compared the physical courage of Foscolo (who fought with great bravery) with his own fear at any shouting or violence and bloodshed. He must have shared the 'cruel anxiety' experienced by his mother and wife, to an even greater degree. Those moments were deeply distressing to him, either because a man was murdered only a few steps from his house, or because he had not the strength to go and defend him.

Foscolo and Manzoni respected but did not like each other. They were too different. In 1806, when he was in Paris, Foscolo had called on Manzoni whom he already knew. He had read the verses 'On the Death of Carlo Imbonati' and he admired him. He expected an enthusiastic welcome, but was received coldly either by Alessandro or by Giulia, for no obvious reason; perhaps Giulia's nerves were bad that day. On his return to Italy, Foscolo expressed his admiration for Manzoni's poem in a note to the *Sepolcri*. But he had been upset by that cold reception and many years later he still remembered it with displeasure.

'We are all longing to leave for the country,' Giulia wrote to her uncle Michele de Blasco in the summer, '. . . But all our houses have been chock-full of soldiers. . . at Brusuglio we had forty soldiers; I got them to move out, because we need to go there for the sake of our health, especially Enrichetta who had been ordered to take baths; in fact, all things being equal, we are going tomorrow. It is so hot here; Milan is full, because it's swarming with soldiers. They are about to create a square, demolishing the house of the former finance minister; I mention it because it's so close to us. . . Giulietta sends you a hug, as Pedrino will do one day, I'm sure. On his birthday and mine, the 21st July, I surprised his mother by giving us a portrait of this lovely baby boy.' They spent some months in the winter at Lecco, at Il Caleotto: 'Our poor house had been full of soldiers for a year,' Giulia wrote again to her uncle de Blasco in Milan, 'so we've had to remove all the mattresses in the house, and replace everything, including the kitchen utensils. . . We were happy there, but we had to come back here very soon, because they wanted to billet men in our own rooms, and we really haven't one that you could call a spare room.' Meanwhile Abbé Zinammi had died, an old friend of the family, administrator and friend of Imbonati while he lived; he had been 'stricken by the universal fate', wrote Giulia, giving details of his death; he fell into a lethargy, 'consulted a doctor, was bled in the neck, and finally died on the fifth day. . . Oh, you can see that such happenings are not cheering, but deeply thought-provoking; God grant our thoughts be profitable, that we may trust in the mercy of the Lord, and not indulge in vain melancholy. Apart from this, Giulietta is well; Pedrino is well and walking on his own like a footman; Alessandro is a bit tired by business matters; I have a cold, and am confined to the house because the streets are so bad; Enrichetta, who is ever more dear to me, and who was so well at Lecco, is now suffering her old troubles all the time. . .' 'I must tell you, dear friend, that I have been leading a very sedentary life for more than two months, and have even been obliged to stay in bed for some time; in the last two or three days I have felt some relief from my pains, but I am still living more or less in enforced idleness because any occupation upsets me,' Enrichetta wrote to her cousin Carlotta. She was pregnant again; in July Maria Cristina was born.

'Enrichetta is nursing a little Cristina,' Manzoni wrote to Fauriel. It was difficult to get the letter to France, as the postal services were not functioning properly; they had to seize opportunities which did not occur often. 'Not one letter, nor two, nor a whole volume would suffice for all I have to tell you, and all I would like to ask you; I have to keep alive the hope of

47

seeing you, of spending a little time with you, so that the memory of your friendship may not be as sad and painful as it is dear.'

In June, when the news of the defeat at Waterloo reached Milan, Manzoni was leafing through books in a bookshop, and he fainted with shock; he had placed his hope in Napoleon once again during the Hundred Days, and all hope crumbled with this defeat; from then on his nervous troubles grew worse. He was deeply embittered; an Austrian governor had returned to Milan, imposing iron repression; for a moment he had thought the Allies would establish an independent regime, but he had soon realized this was an illusion. He described his condition to Fauriel: 'It's a case of worries and anguish causing a strange state of depression. . . Travel might do me good, but where can I go? Society rarely proves a distraction; so many people urge you to forget your ailments and remind you of them just as you were thinking of something quite other; it's a strange sort of consolation to hear people say ten times a day: "Cheer up", that's all you need to feel wretched. Of course, the remedy is excellent, but suggesting it is not the same as administering it. They don't realize that "Cheer up" means "You are being miserable", and that nothing could be less cheering than such a suggestion.' He was writing a tragedy, *Il Conte di Carmagnola*. But Canon Tosi insisted he should finish a religious work instead, one that he was working on in weary fits and starts: *Osservazioni sulla morale cattolica*. He felt impatient of Canon Tosi and everyone about him: his schoolfriend Ermes Visconti, Vincenzo Monti, the Greek Mustoxidi. He found them all tiresome. In fact he had a great urge to return to France. He wrote to Fauriel: 'I have never felt so keenly the value of your friendship or so longed for your company. That little room in *La Maisonnette* that overlooks the garden, the little hill of Saint-Avoie, the ridge from which you can look down on the course of the Seine, that island covered with willows and poplars, the fresh, peaceful valley – these are places where I am always wandering in imagination.'

At that time the marchese Parravicini di Persia and his wife were frequent callers, and were the only people he was pleased to see. They were preparing to leave for France and he had a sudden idea of going with them. He would send for the family if he felt he could find comfortable accommodation for them in Paris; if not he would return, having at least had the pleasure of spending a few days with Fauriel. He was held back by the fear of being a nuisance to the Parravicinis on the journey with his health problems; and then there was the difficulty of obtaining a passport at once, and suddenly having to drop so many things, so much family business; 'all this,' he wrote to Fauriel, 'made me step hurriedly down from the stage-coach in which, in my imagination, I had already taken my seat.' The Parravicinis left without him.

But the desire to go to Paris haunted him. He was thinking about it all the time and formulated a concrete plan. But he did not want to go alone, so he applied for passports for all the family. Giulia was happy, but Enrichetta was dismayed and anxious. She remembered Paris with dislike; she feared the upheaval and toil both of the long journey with three little children, and of settling such a big family in a foreign city. But most of all she feared the ambience awaiting them. It was a world which might distract her husband from the religious life, a world of unbelievers. And he was going through a strange period; he had been neglecting his religious practices for some time and his relations with Canon Tosi had become cold. It would be dangerous for him to be surrounded by those people at such a time. He might lose his faith for ever. On the other hand, he was not well, and the journey seemed the only thing that might soothe him. 'Pray for us,' she wrote to Abbé Degola, 'that this plan may not be contrary to God's will.'

What happened between Enrichetta and Alessandro at that period? They were probably dark days for both of them. Alessandro was in a gloomy mood; the life he had led till then had suddenly become hateful to him. He did not want simply to travel to Paris, he wanted to shake off the dust of many years, and take on a new persona. And she was deeply worried and judged him severely, feeling intuitively that in his dark mood, his intolerance, and eagerness to get away there was something 'contrary to God's will'.

But the plan came to nothing. The passports were refused. They had presented medical certificates, saying the journey was essential to their health, but just then a police decree was issued banning journeys undertaken on health grounds. Manzoni was regarded with distrust by the Austrian authorities. He had refused to collaborate on a pro-government newspaper, and he had friends among the opposition. So they had to give up the idea of travelling.

Canon Tosi was delighted. He had told Manzoni this journey was 'a great mistake'. Some even suspected Canon Tosi had approached the authorities to get them to refuse the passports. Certainly like Enrichetta he was profoundly alarmed by Manzoni's behaviour at that time; he seemed to think of nothing but France and his friends there; and he felt his faith had diminished, perhaps was already spent. At last he heard they were not going after all. He wrote to Degola:

'Enrichetta has already written to tell you the outcome of the projected journey, and how well Alessandro has taken the rejection. I must add that, after the grace received in Paris, of which you were the chief instrument, this is the greatest favour the Lord could grant. This fine young man is changed almost entirely. . . he has placed himself in God's hands; he has already received the holy sacraments twice; he has returned to his original confidence in me, which had been chilled by the perhaps excessive freedom with which I had expressed myself; he hardly ever talks of politics now, or does so with moderation. . . he is serene with the family, self-denying at table, moderate in his planned expenditure; in short he has been greatly blessed by the Lord. . . even Donna Giulia, who with a touch of proud vexation was the last to mend in this matter, is now quiet and content; and I hope that she too will turn her heart to do what I am always telling her, to attend seriously to the prime object of life.'

And Enrichetta to Degola: 'God grant this peace may continue between us; I hope you will understnd what peace I mean, for, thanks be to God, we do not wish for any that is merely an outward show.' Outward peace had perhaps never been lacking in the house, but it had concealed serious personal differences and disharmony; these gradually disappeared and things returned to their original state. But Enrichetta had to resign herself; the idea of the journey to Paris was never abandoned, and they applied again to the police.

That year, 1817, Uncle Michele de Blasco died; in November another baby girl was born and called Sofia; the last but one, Cristina, was dark, *ma petite noiraude*, her mother called her, the

50

only dark one among the siblings who were all blond. Sofia again was blonde and fair-skinned. Enrichetta nursed her. Then she became pregnant for the fifth time. As always, she had kidney trouble, and at this time she began to suffer with her eyes: they were always inflamed, and her sight deteriorated.

In 1818 they sold Il Caleotto, which cost a great deal to maintain and gave no return. In the garden there was a little temple containing the tomb of Don Pietro, which passed, with all the rest, into the hands of Signor Scola for the sum of a hundred and fifty thousand lire.

'Oh my friend, "caro padrino" of our Giulietta, friend of Alessandro and of us all, perhaps all these appellations are nothing but an empty sound to you? Why this stubborn and cruel silence?' Giulia wrote to Fauriel, who had not written for some time. She was thinking of 'the prime object of her life', that is the salvation of her soul and expiation of her sins; but this did not dispel the fond memories of happy years, loyalty to those she loved, and nostalgia. 'My son wanted to write to you, but you would not believe or imagine how dearly he has to pay for any strong emotion; joyful sensations may produce a salutary excitement, but thoughts of sadness, of absent friends, friendship or searing memories – oh, these give him such pain. . . Oh, dear friend, if you were to see him! And why do you not see him? . . . He said to me a few days ago: this morning a particular group of trees at Meulan so filled my heart that I felt I was suffocating.'

In 1819, changes took place among the government authorities which proved favourable to them, and this time their passports were granted; they began to prepare for their departure; Enrichetta had to supervise it all as serenely as possible, although now the big family was even bigger: in July 1819 Enrico was born. She was feeding him.

'We propose to set out at the beginning of September, see something of Switzerland, and go on to Paris via Basle and Alsace,' Manzoni wrote to Fauriel. 'We are bringing you a Giulietta, in whom you will see all the seriousness that was in her portrait [they had sent a portrait of her to Madame de Condorcet], a Pietro who is an indomitable imp, a Cristina who does her best to imitate him, a Sofia who is beginning to look round to see if the world offers her some similar occupation,

51

and an Enrico at the bosom of my Enrichetta. We'll get by as best we can, but after seeing the English travelling with a veritable Noah's Ark, one is not so frightened of journeys *en grande famille*. As you can imagine, we hope to be staying in rue de la Seine, or as close as possible, so we are relying on your kind friendship to find lodgings for us. . . Addio. Do you know what it means to me to be able to end a letter to you with "Arrivederci"? Addio, addio.' Giulia: 'Mio caro padrino, fondest love to my dear Sophie. I am relying utterly on you for all my caravan. Oh, God willing, we shall be reunited, dear friends, and I do so hope my poor son will regain his health; addio, addio, we will write again.'

They planned to pause on the way to rest at Chambéry, where Somis was now living. 'My fancy feeds upon this promised delight,' wrote Somis, 'but also on the pain it will cost me to see you go. But I shall console myself with the thought that your stay will have been useful to you, and it will afford me further proof of the truth that we must not count on lasting pleasures in this life. I have found a coachman here who has three carriages; one will take six people inside and two outside; the two others are the usual size. I have good reports of the coachman.' There were ten in their party as they set off: eight of them and two servants, Fanny and her husband Jean.

They gave up the trip through Switzerland and arrived in Paris at the end of September. They put up at an hotel where they found a letter from Fauriel. He was ill, wretched, feverish. *La Maisonnette* was full of guests at that moment, but Madame de Condorcet was adding a few lines to invite them to come. '*La Maisonnette* is yours, as ever.' The words were affectionate, but the signature abrupt: Condorcet. Giulia wrote a letter of acceptance and thanks; they would come in two days, they had sent their linen to be washed and were waiting for it to be returned. She explained they would need three rooms at *La Maisonnette*, one for Enrichetta and Alessandro, one for herself and Giulietta, and those must be connected; one for Fanny and the other children, and this one must have a fire so she could change the little baby; the man-servant could sleep anywhere. 'Taking the liberty of a sister,' she warned that she would need soup without meat on days of abstinence, and the same for Giulietta and the servants; then simply eggs and potatoes, 'and, if possible, fish for me.' She said they intended to pay for their daily keep; they could come to some agreement about this. 'We are sisters, you are my dearest, my only friend, and we must act accordingly. After nine years I breathe again because I shall breathe with you.' Finally she asked whether, if they could not leave all the luggage in safe-keeping at the hotel, it would be possible to fit it into some corner in the villa. 'I look forward to a word in answer. . . Addio addio.'

They stayed at *La Maisonnette* for more than a month. Then they found an apartment in Paris, in Faubourg Saint-Germain. They bought furniture and fitted it up, and moved in in November. They were thinking of selling Brusuglio and the Milan house, and settling in France for good. Enrichetta did not want to and actually feared the idea. In any case, it was a confused notion. They gave Uncle Giulio Beccaria, Giulia's half-brother, the job of going to Brusuglio to find out if it would be possible to sell the estate advantageously. Giulio Beccaria went, walked about examining the estate carefully, and was left 'somewhat mortified' to find it poor, 'lacking in mulberries, vines and timber'. He asked for precise instructions. If the properties were not to be sold, they should make new plantations of mulberries. He contacted a certain Signor Poldi, who was a possible purchaser. But later he wrote: 'Signor Poldi has decided against and no other purchaser has come forward.' And he observed sagely: 'The worst position of all is to hang fire between selling and not selling. . . The thought of selling postpones the question of repairs. . . The same applies to the house in Milan.'

Canon Tosi was still vexed that Manzoni had left Italy without finishing *La morale cattolica*, and that latterly he had thought of nothing but his tragedy, *Il conte di Carmagnola*. Since Abbé Lamennais was living in Paris, he hoped Manzoni would seek his acquaintance, and also that of Bishop Grégoire. Years ago, Manzoni had translated part of one of Lamennais' works, 'Essay on indifference in the matter of faith'. Canon Tosi wrote to Lamennais about Manzoni. He sent him the first volume of *La morale cattolica* which had appeared in print. Abbé Lamennais, in a reply to the Canon, spoke flatteringly of *La morale cattolica*. 'I am delighted that you found the work of my friend Manzoni well-written and interesting,' the Canon wrote back, 'I have frequently urged him to work on the second volume which is promised. . . he has recently written to say he is working on it seriously. . . My persuasion carried less weight than those friends who urged him to finish a tragedy which he had begun a long time ago; he finished it on the very last day before he left here, and it is being printed with a few corrections he has sent from Paris, after which I believe he promptly devoted himself to the more important and profitable work of the 2nd volume. . . What pleasure it would give me if you were to correspond with this author, whose gifts of heart are even more rare and precious than his gifts of mind! But I dare not yet give you his address, as, because of his vertigo which I think is rather worse than better after this journey to Paris with his family which I so deplored, because of the shyness which makes him shrink from new contacts, and also because of family circumstances, I must wait for him to resolve to seek you out. . .'

Manzoni and Enrichetta called on Bishop Grégoire with a letter from Degola, shortly after they arrived in Paris, and received a kindly welcome; they returned a few times but did not find him at home, 'and for the time being,' Manzoni wrote to Canon Tosi, 'we do not think it right to disturb him.' Bishop Grégoire had been elected a député and was extraordinarily busy. He was an extreme anti-monarchist: in the past he had thundered against the monarchy: 'The tree of liberty can prosper only if it is watered by the blood of kings', and 'kings are in the moral order what monsters are in the natural order', and again 'the destruction of a fierce beast, the end of a plague, the death of a king, are sources of rejoicing to humanity'; and his nomination as a député had a precise political significance, it was a slap in the face to the monarchy. It was strange to think of the gentle Enrichetta sitting in amiable conversation with a man who had written such bloody words, and just as strange for Manzoni who had a horror of blood, of political hatred and of violent, inflated language; moreover, how could Christian piety and such furious hate be reconciled in the person of the Bishop? Enrichetta and Alessandro must both have been baffled and disturbed by all this, but they must have said to themselves that these were strange, torn and bitter times in which they were living.

As for Abbé Lamennais, Manzoni took care not to seek him out, and the two men never met, then or at any other time.

Although he had admired the 'Essay on Indifference', Manzoni distrusted Lamennais, who seemed to him a sectarian, factious priest, and after reading a new book of his in Paris, his distrust turned to real aversion. This aversion was, moreover, shared by Abbé Degola, who wrote to Tosi describing Lamennais as 'a fanatic' and 'a Sulpician madman'. The parish of Saint-Sulpice was worldly and Jesuit, and was opposed to the Jansenist parish of Saint-Séverin. Bishop Grégoire had been full of praise for the parish of Saint-Séverin, when Enrichetta and Alessandro called on him.

Manzoni's health did not improve in Paris. The apartment in Faubourg Saint-Germain was noisy because the windows over-looked the market. The children were often ill, Enrichetta tired. Little Enrico was growing up delicate, late in cutting his teeth and generally slow. Manzoni led a rather solitary life in Paris. There had been an imperceptible cooling-off in relations between his mother and Sophie de Condorcet; Sophie could not recognize her former friend, idle, witty, light-hearted, in the Giulia who now appeared before her, an elderly lady completely absorbed in her grandchildren and her devotions. The friendship with Fauriel remained unbroken, but they did not often go to *La Maisonnette*, and when they did, they returned home before evening. Manzoni went for long walks about the city with his friend Ignazio Calderari; he always maintained that it suited him to take a lot of exercise, but felt unequal to going out alone; in the winter Calderari left. Now he was homesick for the garden at Brusuglio and the surrounding countryside, and the people he used to see in Italy: Ermes Visconti, Tommaso Grossi, friends with whom he had a different relationship from Fauriel, less passionate, more easy-going, familiar and joking. He wrote to Tommaso Grossi: 'I can't wait to be sitting in my study with Grossi at my side reading his new novella. . . how we will chat and improvise as we walk to the little bridge! It's impossible to work here, I can't put together a single verse.' He sent cuttings to Uncle Giulio Beccaria, to give to the agent at Brusuglio for grafting; they had given up all idea of selling Brusuglio and the house in via del Morone; there had been no buyers, and any intention of staying in France for good had evaporated. 'I am sorry your health is no better; but I hope preparations for your return will take you out of yourself, and your native air will prove beneficial,' Giulio Beccaria wrote to Manzoni. 'One does not know how to treat nervous disorders; I still suffer from them, and don't know what to do about it. Distraction and motion are the only things that seem to help. You apply too little of the first of these remedies, and at times a bit too much of the second, for I have found by experience that it may help momentarily to tire oneself when one has an attack of convulsions, but afterwards it is harmful, like taking strong drinks when one has indigestion: it seems to give relief, but in fact it aggravates the trouble and the difficulty of overcoming it. I consider that the effect of the convulsions is to make the nerves oscillate in an irregular way, and that excessive activity increases this uncomfortable oscillation which must be dangerous for such a weakness.' Uncle Giulio thought of everything, went to Brusuglio to talk to the agent, sent off parcels with copies of *Il conte di Carmagnola*, and busied himself in an unpleasant law-suit which some relatives of Don Pietro, 'le consorti Manzoni', had brought against Alessandro concerning the inheritance.

Il conte di Carmagnola was dedicated to Fauriel, 'as a testimony to my cordial and reverent friendship'. It was printed by Ferrario of Milan, at the author's expense. It met with approval and criticism in the papers, but did not have much success with the public. Fauriel wrote a French prose translation of it.

They planned to return to Italy in May. 'It is as if I were not in Paris at all,' Giulia wrote to Canon Tosi. There was some truth in it, but she liked to emphasize to the canon what a strict life she was leading. 'In the morning I leave for church with Alessandro, or on my own when he cannot come. . . otherwise, because of the winter weather, I am cooped up in these little rooms, but now Calderari has gone it will be better for me to go out a bit with Alessandro. Giulietta wants me to send you her love, she is still not well at all, she is a bit homesick for Milan and asks you to pray for her.' Giulietta suffered from such severe headaches that they had to call a doctor and apply leeches to her legs. 'Every day I see more clearly that my strength, my head, my *knowledge*, as well as the continual bustle around me make it quite impossible for me to establish a plan of education,' Enrichetta wrote, also to the Canon. As the children were so often ill, the idea of sending the bigger children to school was put aside, and a governess was taken on, a certain Mademoiselle de Rancé, adopted daughter of an old friend of Giulia's; she was always dressed in black although very young, she had a gentle but firm manner, and was extremely religious: for a week she had prayed to God that they would appoint her, although she had an excellent situation with a rich aristocratic family, but when she saw the Manzoni children she thought them so charming that she wanted to be called to educate them. Enrichetta thought she had been sent to them from Heaven, but she soon realised she was something of a fanatic: she belonged to the parish of Saint-Sulpice; she had enflamed political ideas of a 'sulpician' character, that is to say, monarchical and reactionary, which she communicated to the children, and Enrichetta did not like this at all. 'Besides,' she wrote to Canon Tosi, 'everyone in France is obsessed with politics, or so it seems to me, since even women are involved in politics in an extraordinary way; but I think this is bound to create difficulties in educating children.' 'I feel that a cool, balanced temperament is required with children'. She was preparing to dismiss Mademoiselle de Rancé. I am quite sick at heart when I think I may find myself once again in the old difficulties with the education of my children. . . My weak head and poor sight rule out any hope that I could take on the task myself.'

From Abbé Billiet, whom they had met at Chambéry the previous year, they had bad news of Councillor Somis: he had an eye disease, and was apparently going blind. He spent his days sitting in an armchair in his study, far from the fire and the light which hurt him; 'plunged into a darkness,' wrote Abbé Billiet, 'which must inevitably turn the whole year for him into a long, weary night'; he had been forced into debt for treatment, and he was living in sadly straitened circumstances; he had a large family, five daughters to provide for, of whom the youngest was consumptive. Enrichetta was distressed by these painful details, the misfortunes of their friend caused her great anxiety; and the words 'a long, weary night' seemed directed at her, since she had eye trouble and was afraid of losing her sight in her turn. Shortly after they heard, again from Abbé Billiet, that Somis had moved from Chambéry to Turin, where he had received good treatment, and his condition was improving. But they felt they were surrounded by misfortunes; in those last months of their stay in France they met a young poet called Charles

Loyson, and Alessandro, who was reluctant to see anyone at that time, became friendly with him, but Loyson was consumptive, with no hope of a cure. The friendship between him and Manzoni was brief; Loyson died in June, and for a few days the news of his death was kept from Manzoni who had been seriously ill for a month.

On 10 May Manzoni fainted, then developed a high temperature. Enrichetta wrote about it either to Canon Tosi or to her friend Signora Parravicini, who often saw the Canon, and from the letters she received from them both in reply she felt they had understood neither her fears nor the gravity of his fever: the Canon continued to lament the delay in their departure. Enrichetta wrote again in a state of agitation: 'Opening a letter in which I saw the handwriting of two people, each of whom has so much claim on my affection, respect and gratitude, I hoped, since my poor heart is in such great need at the moment. . . I hoped, I say, to find in it some words of consolation. . . I was disconcerted by this complete silence about a matter which could only be a great sadness to us.' She was then moved to convey to the Canon thoughts which must surely have been weighing on her heart for some time. 'The joy Alessandro anticipates in seeing his friends again knows no bounds, except in the idea which irritates him a little at times, that those friends feel they must call him to account, not for his actions, but actually for his intentions; he is often tempted to respond in the same way; I should certainly like to see him more humble and I try to persuade him. . . but he always answers: *that if a man has nothing with which to reproach himself in his relations with other men, he can at least expect from them interest free from continual censure.*' These words clearly refer to the Canon; he was the friend who had badgered Manzoni in the past, calling him to account and censuring him, and especially tormenting and oppressing him with demands to write on religious matters. 'Please have a little pity on me,' she wrote again to the Canon some time later, to excuse her own veiled but bitter resentment. 'I've always had a poor head, but after my own troubles, and all the tribulations, great and small, which make up our lives here below, I have become. . . I dare not say a complete imbecile, in deference to the good Lord, but often I really don't know where I am.'

As for Giulia, her letters to the Canon were full of piety as usual, but they too expressed resentment. The Canon kept writing that they must leave, but the return journey seemed to them fraught with risk. 'Indeed the Lord knows how disappointed I am at this unexpected delay,' Giulia wrote to the Canon. But after that fainting turn Alessandro had not recovered his health, and besides there was little Enrico 'in travail with 4 teeth, with continual diarrhoea and feverishness' and 'our beloved Pietro not at all well after his father's accident, which he witnessed.' A letter from the Canon to Alessandro with various complaints and entreaties that they should set out had put him in a bad mood. 'I must confess to you, and I beg you for the love of God not to take amiss what I am about to say, which is that your letter to Alessandro has upset him,' Giulia replied to the Canon. 'Anything that serves to remind him of objections made to his decisions or his point of view puts him in rather a bad mood, and I have not the right, and still less the power to influence in any way his view of things. This is right and proper because he is a man not a boy, and you know how sensitive he is about such things.' Giulia had given the Canon the job of contacting a certain Giuseppino, who had been in service in their house in the past, and persuading him to come back; she was hoping to find him at Brusuglio on their return. On her side Giulia was to obtain some books and take them to the Canon. 'I have already obtained the books you commissioned me to find, now I will look for the others.' About Abbé Lamennais whom the Canon so much hoped Alessandro would approach, Giulia revealed her own perplexity. 'They say that the Abbé de Lamennais will soon bring out the second volume of his work, but I must confess that I am not looking forward to it, this author is at present involved in so many of those blessed political writings, that really do not seem suited to his ministry and it is a pity that with his talent for writing on religion he should waste it criticizing governments and people. I am simply telling you my opinions, because we hardly ever talk about him.'

Meanwhile Manzoni was getting worse all the time. After that fainting turn on 10 May, his temperature had remained high, he could not get out of bed and he was not eating. The doctors diagnosed a bilious fever and inflammation of the brain and chest. Enrichetta and Giulia did not trust the Parisian doctors and wrote to their family doctor in Italy, Doctor Cozzi, who sent advice. Their letters to the Canon were more and more anxious. They asked him to pray for them. 'I am sorry to hear that so many people we care about are not well, and especially our dear, good Signora Parravicini. I do not ask you to pray for us,' wrote Giulia, 'I know you will all do so. Oh, for the love of charity, do not stop!' Slowly the invalid recovered. He could sip a little *eau de poulet* and a little *eau de violette*. Slowly he got back on his feet. Giulia to the Canon: 'These last few days he has had a touch of diarrhoea which seems more or less to have gone today, he is taking a *decoction blanche de Siduham* and that is all, the doctor says not to take any medicine but to leave it to Nature, he eats a little and often and takes his chocolate every day, but he's so thin and wasted you would hardly know him; I've been reading aloud to him and still do so almost all day to distract him, but today he wanted to read himself, which worries me, but I can't say a word. Only the good God can guide him!' They had to tell him his young friend Loyson was dead, and he recited the De profundis, with tears in his eyes.

On 6 July the departure began to seem possible. Giulia to the Canon: 'Oh God! please, please pray for us and welcome us with true love and charity. I am so exhausted that all I want is to creep into a corner to recover. . . Alessandro is better, but he has so little strength! and his nerves! and his imagination! Oh, please pray for us and *keep all these things in your heart.*' That is to say, the Canon was to say nothing, to anyone, about the sometimes indignant letters he had received from them. 'It is a relief to know we will definitely have Giuseppino.' The servant they wanted was ready to welcome them. 'Please be so kind as to see that Giuseppino gets a jar of barley water and Sant Agostino lemon juice so that it is waiting for us when we arrive at Brussú. . . I shall seize the first possible opportunity to set off because we know to our cost that he who hesitates is lost, and I have been hurrying to pack the *valises.*'

They finally left Paris on 26 July. In spite of the heat, the journey went well. They stayed with the Somis family in Turin for a day. Manzoni went to call on Abbé Lodovico di Breme, whom he had met years before, when they passed through Turin in that distant summer of 1810 when Giulietta was a tiny baby. Lodovico di Breme had had an adventurous and unhappy life. It was said he had had a mistress among the aristocracy – a sister of the marchesa Trivulzi – and that 'he unintentionally caused her death with a potion, to free himself rather than her of the scandalous consequences of their love', according to Niccolò Tommaseo. He had been one of the group collaborating on the newspaper *Il Conciliatore*, which had gone out of production in 1819. Di Breme was now suffering from an incurable disease, and felt his faith in God fading with his life. It seemed that death appeared to Manzoni at every turn at that time. Many years later Tommaseo recounted that last meeting between Manzoni and di Breme: 'When "il Nostro" [Manzoni] was passing through Turin on his return from Paris, di Breme, already close to his end, sent for him to discuss his doubts on matters of faith, and his squalid appearance with his hair standing on end was fearful to behold.' Manzoni was deeply distressed. The abbé died in August.

And there they were at last at Brusuglio, at Brusú or Brussú as they usually called it, with the welcome cool of the spacious rooms and the shady trees in the garden. And to think they had intended, not many months ago, to sell this house! It was such a welcoming, restful, hospitable place. Manzoni found all his old friends. Canon Tosi had become more cautious and considerate, and stopped badgering him about the *Morale cattolica*. Immediately after their arrival the philosopher Victor Cousin, a friend of Fauriel, stayed with them; he was going through a difficult spell; chiefly because he too was in poor health, but also because he was being attacked in France for political reasons, and they wanted to deprive him of his teaching post; he too felt better in the peace of the countryside. When Cousin left them, Manzoni gave him a parcel of books he wanted Fauriel to read, among them *Ildegonda*, a novella in verse by Tommaso Grossi. In the letter he enclosed with the parcel, he told Fauriel about the friends he had met again in Italy, Berchet, Visconti, Grossi, and about a new tragedy he was thinking of beginning, about the end of the reign of the Longobardi. Fauriel was slow to reply and they still had not heard from him in the winter, that is, several months after leaving Paris, and all the news they had of him was in a few brief lines from Madame de Condorcet.

That winter Enrichetta realized she was pregnant again. 'It is my ninth pregnancy,' she wrote to Cousin Carlotta de Blasco.

She had not written to her for a long time; the cousin meantime had married a certain Signor Fontana. Enrichetta told her everything; how they had gone to Paris, their eight months there, Alessandro's illness, their return. She described her five children one by one. Now she had to prepare herself for the arrival of the sixth. 'I assure you this new task is a great distress to me. . . but we must submit to the will of God.'

They spent the winter months in Milan, in the house in via del Morone; this too they had wanted to sell, but now it seemed very dear to them as well. They went back to Brusuglio in the spring. The governess they had brought back from France with them, successor to Mademoiselle de Rancé, was called Perrier. But the air, either in Milan or at Brusuglio, did not suit her, and she left after less than a year.

'Dear Fauriel, I prefer to send a very short, sad letter than to let slip another opportunity of writing to you. We've been in the country for a few days and mean to stay all summer,' Manzoni wrote to Fauriel. It was Spring 1821, the dark days of the proceedings against the Carbonaria. 'Mother, as usual, is *not-ill* rather than well. Enrichetta is in the seventh month of a difficult pregnancy, which gives hope of a happy outcome, to be achieved by a lot of patience and rest. As for me, it would be better to say nothing. I can get by when I can work: this gets me through four or five hours in the morning, and then I am too tired to think for the rest of the day; but for some time I've all too often had days of enforced idleness, because I simply cannot get my head working, and these are often rather gloomy days. I must bow my head and let the storm pass over; it's true it could happen that we must pass on, before the storm. In these *black* days, I pick up a book, read a couple of pages, put it down and take another, which meets with the same fate. . . When will we meet again, dear Fauriel? Addio. If you write to me, it will indeed be a charitable office.' The word 'black' is underlined, and evidently refers to the political situation.

In April that year Manzoni began to write a novel. The title was *Fermo e Lucia*. Then he abandoned it to finish the tragedy about the end of the Longobardi: *Adelchi*. Meanwhile he was reading historical novels: he got his antiquarian friend Gaetano Cattaneo to look for them: '*The Abbot,* or *The Monastery,* or *The Astrologer (sic)*: something for pity's sake.' These were three novels by Walter Scott. He gave Cattaneo no peace with his constant requests for books. 'Here I am as usual, pestering you like a baker for bread. I would like the Dictionary of the French Academy. . . Here I am again. I would like the *Crusades* of Michaud, in the original or in translation, it doesn't matter.' He apologized for never going to see him: 'Remember a poor convulsive can't go and see his friends when he'd like to, and please continue to love your grateful friend.'

In July of that same year 1821, in the *Gazzetta di Milano* appeared the news of the death of Napoleon. He had died two months before, on 5 May. Manzoni spent three days writing the ode which was to become famous. 'Ei fu. Siccome immobile, / dato il mortal sospiro. . .' These verses were written while Enrichetta sat at the piano and played non-stop any piece of music that came into her head, at his request.

In August a baby girl was born, and was called Clara. Enrichetta became seriously ill with puerperal fever. She nearly died but they managed to save her.

'I told you my tragedy *Adelchi* was finished, apart from some revising I still have to do, so I must add that I'm not at all pleased with it, and if in this brief life some tragedies had to be sacrificed, then this one of mine ought certainly to be suppressed,' Manzoni wrote to Fauriel, who had written at last. Fauriel's letter was brief, and was brief 'particularly on those matters I should like to hear you discuss more fully', that is, the work on which the lazy and never-satisfied Fauriel was engaged. Manzoni, by contrast, wrote pages and pages to him. 'How often have I, even more than usual, cursed the distance that separates us. . .' 'How I reproach myself with not having made you talk more when I was lucky enough to be near you, with not having had the impudence of the customs officer to search in your portfolio.' 'I can't finish without saying something of a matter which has sadly preoccupied us and caused us to spend days I would rather forget. You know from Madame de Condorcet that my Enrichetta has been so ill as to cause us anxiety. Slowly but surely she is now recovering. Never have I felt so keenly the uncertainty, danger, and even terror which underlies even the most peaceful happiness. As for me, I am better than when I last wrote to you: I work, and my nerves leave me more or less in peace the rest of the time.'

The next year Enrichetta was pregnant again. A young Scot turned up at Brusuglio, recommended by Fauriel, and was taken on as a tutor. In the summer there was a tremendous hailstorm at Brusuglio that devastated fields, vines and mulberries. 'This disaster came straight from Heaven,' Giulia wrote to Sophie de Condorcet, 'so that we cannot and must not complain about it; by the same token we should be resigned to all the rest; but the problem is that your friendship is strong and generous, and mine tearful, which make it almost a duty for you to sustain and console me.' Sophie de Condorcet was gravely ill, but they did not know; and consolation and support would never again come to Giulia from that quarter. The children had scarlet fever, Giulia a very painful whitlow, and 'my Enrichetta,' wrote Manzoni to Fauriel, 'without staying in bed, is always indisposed, and her sight is pitifully weak, which grieves us very much; but we are led to hope, indeed we are assured, that this new weakness is the result of her pregnancy and the birth will cure it.' Regarding his novel, he wrote, he was half-way through the second volume; regarding the *Adelchi*, he had delivered it to the printer. Fauriel was translating the *Adelchi* into French, and they had decided, he and Manzoni, that the French edition should appear at the same time as the Italian; so the Italian publisher had to delay the appearance of the book until the French edition was also ready. 'Believe me, it will be a happy moment for both of us when we can write to each other without always having the tedious *Adelchi* as a burdensome third party between us.'

The news reached them that Sophie de Condorcet was poorly, yet she seemed to be already on the road to recovery. On 12 September Manzoni wrote congratulating Fauriel on her recovery. But she had died four days before.

On 17 September another baby girl was born, and was called Vittoria. Enrichetta's sight did not improve after the birth; the hope had proved illusory. The doctors advised a change of air. They planned to go to Tuscany. Meanwhile they had heard of the death of Sophie de Condorcet: they thought they might persuade Fauriel to join them in Tuscany. But Alessandro could not interrupt his work on his novel and the project was abandoned. They did not write to Fauriel immediately. Instead Visconti wrote to him in October: 'Grossi and the Manzoni family ask me to send you their love. Manzoni wanted to write to you, but after the loss of Madame de Condorcet didn't know how to touch upon a matter too painful to you, as to him and to all his family. In sending you my sincere condolences, I think I should tell you that, after this sad news, Manzoni cannot regard as definitive the final date fixed by you for the publication of the *Adelchi* for the twentieth of this month. But he is waiting for you to fix a later date.'

The *Adelchi* was published in Italy in November. It was dedicated to Enrichetta with these words, in which there is a strange commemorative and funereal note:

'To his beloved and revered wife Enrichetta Luigia Blondel / who together with conjugal love and maternal wisdom / was able to preserve a virginal soul / the author dedicates this *Adelchi* / regretting that he has no more splendid and lasting monument / to which to commit her dear name and the memory of such virtues.'

Fauriel

'Giulietta is drawing a little head for you,' wrote Grandmother Giulia to Madame de Condorcet. It was summer 1822; Sophie de Condorcet would be dead a few weeks later. 'Pietro is studying French. They are all well and drink tea from the little Easter tea-cups [perhaps a gift from Sophie de Condorcet]. At last I've had a letter from you, my dear friend . . .' This was Giulia's last letter to Sophie, and the drawing was sent with it. It was found by Jules Mohl and Cabanis' daughter among Fauriel's papers when he died many years later. There was also a portrait in miniature of a little girl which Cabanis' daughter thought must be Giulietta. Portrait and drawing were sent back to the Manzonis.

In 1822 Giulietta was fourteen, almost the age at which her mother had married, and her awareness of this made her grown-up, sensible and motherly towards her brothers and sisters. She led a sober, disciplined life, without much in the way of amusements and without many friends of her own age; she did not go to school but was taught at home by a governess; after Mademoiselle Perrier, who went back to France because the climate did not suit her, a governess called Mademoiselle Burdet was sent by Abbé Billiet. Long summers at Brusuglio, long foggy winters in Milan. At home, whether at Brusuglio or Milan, there were always plenty of visitors, friends of her father. It would have been a monotonous existence without the comings and goings of visitors, her noisy brothers and sisters and the bustle of the servants. It would have been a peaceful life without her mother's poor health, her father's nerves, and the illnesses of the many little siblings.

That summer of 1822, Tommaso Grossi was writing a poem, 'The Lombardians at the First Crusade'. Manzoni was writing

66

the second volume of his novel. Ermes Visconti had finished a very lengthy essay *On Beauty*; he sent it to Fauriel: 'I am just writing a few lines, my dear Sir, to tell you I have at last sent off the manuscript of *On Beauty* by the mail-coach, addressed to you. . .' When *la petite caisse* containing the manuscript arrived, Fauriel had other things to think of: Sophie de Condorcet had died. Knowing the essay was on its way, he had planned to have it translated into French by *cette angélique créature que nous n'avons plus*, that is by Sophie; some time later he glanced at the great bundle of paper, spoke to Cousin about it, and they both set about trying to find another translator. Fauriel was a generous, patient man, always ready to listen even when most absorbed in his own affairs; always ready to collaborate with others, and place his time and intelligence at their service.

'I put off writing to you after the misfortune that overwhelmed me,' said a letter from Fauriel. Almost three months had gone by. He was answering a letter Manzoni had finally written to him. 'I don't think I have been weak in my misfortune; at least I have tried not to be; I have tried not to exaggerate my loss; but the riches I have lost are not such as can be named on earth, such as can be sought and found: and this knowledge makes my tears flow more freely perhaps than if my grief were more vulgar and easily expressed. I weep for something heavenly and pure. . . My heart is not dead to life's interests or to human affections; but alas! even if I should still find some happiness or remnant of happiness along the road that lies before me, I shall never forget that Heaven has taken from me a greater treasure than I deserved, and which I am no longer allowed even to desire. Forgive me, dear friend – dear friends, since I am writing to you all; I weep with all of you; forgive me this slight and fleeting effusion of a grief that words cannot express, and which you will understand better than I am able to describe it; it is a grief that deserves your grieving, it has nothing at all to do with those feelings that humanity condemns, and this I dare to testify by that supreme power before which man is as nothing. . . There is much I could tell you about my present situation, but so little can be said in a letter, especially things of this nature. I will just say that all the family of this angel who has gone from me have proffered every comfort and attention I could wish; and if I have suffered at the hands of *one person*, at least there was no personal motive involved. My friends, too, have done everything that could be done for a fellow human being in such circumstances, in particular Thierry [the historian Augustin Thierry, then twenty-seven, and very close to Fauriel], and Cousin, who chose to spend the first week of my distress with me in the country. So I lack neither friendship, nor comfort, nor attention; neither do I lack the means to lead a peaceful and independent little life. But the fact is that, by some unhappy concatenation of chance circumstances and events, my life becomes more bitter and disturbed every day. . . . There are very bitter particulars in my general misery: at present I feel quite incapable of finding distraction in any serious work, and disinclined to seek distraction outside my usual habits; which all combines to leave such scope for memories, laments, comparisons between what remains and what I have lost that I would fall into a state of discouragement and despair, if I did not create for myself a perspective which gives me strength to bear my present situation for a time, on condition that I may change it soon, or as soon as possible. I feel a pressing need, both moral and physical, to temper my shattered being in a new atmosphere, among old friends and new objects. Do you know where I have found this perspective? You will have guessed, I hope, dear friends: in your midst. To come to you, spend some time with you, find you all unchanged, and love you even more than I have done till now, work with my dear Alessandro, and at his side try to create something worthy of him, this has been for three months my fondest dream, the only one which satisfies every present need of my heart. This project, then, is the refuge and dwelling-place of my hopes. Do you approve of my plan, dear friends? you have no objections? does it appeal to you at all? The sooner you reply, the better, for in my present state my sick heart and mind need some secure resting-place. Once I have received your reply, I can discuss in more detail this delightful dream which today I can only mention in passing.'

The phrase 'if I have suffered at the hands of one person' refers perhaps to Sophie de Condorcet's daughter, Eliza, or to her husband, General O'Connor; perhaps they showed some coldness to Fauriel, or hurt his feelings in some way. Eliza had always found it hard to accept that her mother lived with Fauriel, and now that her mother was dead, perhaps a long-standing resent-

ment erupted. Fauriel's relations with Sophie's family deteriorated thereafter, the 'comfort' and 'attentions' did not last long.
Certainly when Sophie died Fauriel found himself in a difficult
and delicate situation, made more difficult by the fact that he
had no money. In all this his susceptibilities suffered. He left *La
Maisonnette* at once and moved to a small apartment in Paris, in
rue des Vieilles Tuileries, and it was from there that he was
writing.

Manzoni wrote back telling him to set off at once. Everybody
was waiting for him. The house in via del Morone was in a state
of confusion as they had had to bring in workmen to do repairs,
but Fauriel could share the confusion with them. Besides, they
were thinking of a trip to Tuscany in the spring, recommended
by the doctors for Enrichetta, because the air was better there,
and Fauriel could go with them. However, a year passed and
Fauriel had still not stirred from Paris. In any case, the Manzonis
too had put off the trip to Tuscany, either because they wanted
to go with Fauriel, or because, as Manzoni wrote to Fauriel,
'*mon ennuyeux fatras*', my tedious scribbling, in other words the
novel, was occupying him a great deal, and he felt he could
neither abandon it at that point, nor take it with him.

In summer 1823, Fanny, the Manzonis' French maid, went to
Paris to the help of her sick mother. She took a letter to Fauriel.
'My dear, and ever dearer friend, here is an unexpected
messenger, but misfortunes make travellers almost as much as
boredom', Manzoni wrote to Fauriel. The *Adelchi* had meanwhile appeared in France, in Fauriel's translation and with an
introduction by him. 'Oh, my friend! what have you done?
what have you said?' wrote Manzoni. 'I am quite confused; I do
not speak of the pleasure it has given me to see my sketchy
thought so well rendered, or rather developed and perfected by
your style: I anticipated this pleasure. But once again, what have
you said of your poor author! You make me blush, and I hardly
dare raise my head. Let's speak of something else, and above all
of this journey conceived so joyfully but constantly delayed. My
dear friend, we cannot possibly leave here before the winter.
The inconveniences arising from the work on our house in
Milan have taken up the time which should have been spent on
preparations essential for a large family. . . At the same time we
have had preoccupations in which inconveniences were certainly

69

the least painful of our problems.' Clara, the last but one of the children, had died. 'Pietro, Cristina and Sofia have had measles which proved to be quite a long, painful illness for them, but from which they have happily recovered. I cannot say the same of our poor dear little Clara, who was just two years old; after seeing her suffer for a long time, we lost her. And so we found ourselves close to the time when we had hoped to begin that blessed journey. We have been obliged to put the plan off again until next spring, and even then with some doubts arising from a host of possible and predictable obstacles, and also, when all's said and done, from our tendency to give in to them too easily.' Then he talks of the *fatras*, the novel: All I can say is that I have tried to achieve a precise knowledge of the time and place in which I have set my story, and to depict it faithfully. There is no shortage of material: everything that shows men in a wretched light is there in abundance: confident ignorance, pretentious folly, bare-faced corruption, were, alas, among others of the same kind perhaps the most striking characteristics of the period. Fortunately there were also men and traits which did honour to the human race, characters endowed with strong virtue, outstanding in proportion to the obstacles and opposition they encountered, and by their resistance, or sometimes their submission to conventional ideas. I've put in peasants, nobles, monks, nuns, priests, magistrates, scholars, war, famine. . . [here the page is torn and the phrase is illegible], which means it's quite a book!'

In 1823 Canon Tosi was appointed bishop at Pavia, so he left them. 'I need hardly repeat how warmly you are remembered in our family,' Manzoni wrote to him, '. . . I would not have presumed to ask you to write to me sometimes in the little spare time that will remain to you; but since you have deigned to promise to do so, I remember your promise with the sincerest gratitude. Meanwhile, the hope of seeing you again, after a long interval, is one of the thoughts I turn to in those moments when physical and mental labours make me feel the need of some living, tranquil consolation.' Canon, now Bishop, Tosi displayed some anxiety about the work on which Manzoni was engaged. He wrote: 'I cannot refrain from an urgent personal plea that you curb this tendency to throw yourself so whole-heartedly into all the writing schemes you dream up. I observe that your health suffers from occupations that involve you in too intense meditation. Moreover, I see that the fruit of such labour must be very slight, for the interest of the world will be short, and the dissension, malignity and envy of the literati may cause you grave anxiety. My son, if you must consume yourself, let it be for things that bear real fruit. And what is this real fruit, other than the reward you can expect from the Lord?' Canon, now Bishop, Tosi was still hoping Manzoni would resume his *Morale cattolica*. Manzoni replied: 'Since you have deigned to show some anxiety for the ill effects which the work on which I am at present engaged may produce on my health and my peace of mind, I will admit, as for the first, that the research I am absorbed in is indeed somewhat fatiguing, but I try to combine work and rest so that the former shall cause me no serious indisposition, and indeed for some time, apart from the occasional grey day, I have been keeping quite well. As for literary hostility, I think I can rest assured that the publication of my scribblings will provoke none. Since I trace ideas as carefully as possible and commit them faithfully to paper as I find them, it is true I find myself in opposition to many people, but not in league with any party. . . My lone, dispassionate opinions may seem exravagant or foolish, but not provocative; and the poor author may perhaps inspire scornful pity, but, I hope and think, no anger.'

'I still don't know how I'll set out,' Fauriel wrote in October. 'They want to embark me with a great Russian gentleman whom I don't know, and who, they say, would be very pleased to take me to Italy, where he is going. I will see him, but I don't think I'll accept this mode of travel, however convenient it may seem. On the other hand, I have promised two English ladies, who are at present in Switzerland preparing to go on to Italy, to pick them up if I should happen to travel at the same time as them; I don't quite know what detour or delay this promise might involve; in short, it's not certain whether I will descend, like Hannibal, from Mont Cenis, or, like so many others, from the Simplon. If we discount the Russian, it seems likely that I'll set out with Fanny.'

Fauriel arrived in Milan, at via del Morone, a month later.

71

The two English ladies were with him, so he had stopped in Switzerland, and probably always intended to do so. The two English ladies took lodgings at the *Pension Suisse*. They were a mother and daughter called Clarke; with the daughter, Mary Clarke, Fauriel was having an amorous relationship which had begun a few months before Sophie died.

Mary Clarke was then twenty-nine. She was born in London, her mother in Scotland; the mother, a captain's widow, had settled in France with her two daughters when her husband died. Mary Clarke had brown curly hair, and was small and graceful though very slightly hunch-backed; she was attractive rather than beautiful. She painted; she loved paintings and music, and liked to travel and to meet artists.

This is how the relationship between Mary Clarke and Fauriel had begun; she had written to Fauriel asking him to pose for her; she intended to give the portrait to Augustin Thierry: 'You are more dear to him than anyone, and nothing could please him more.' She had had a relationship with Augustin Thierry which she wanted to bring to an end. Fauriel wrote agreeing to the proposal; he was not happy about this portrait, because he did not like the idea that his picture should be a farewell present for poor Thierry: 'But if I am to have only one opportunity in my life of obeying you, I shall obey you sadly, but with all my heart.'

Fauriel posed for Mary Clarke, and the portrait was completed; then she left for England and a steady exchange of letters began between them. *Mon ange*, she wrote to him; *ma chère douce amie*, he wrote to her. At first he said nothing of Sophie, as if she did not exist. He mentioned her later, in August; for weeks Mary had heard nothing from him and he begged her pardon: '*chère douce amie*,' he wrote, 'dear, sweet friend, the last time I wrote to you, I promised to write at least a few lines every day. . . I made this promise from the heart, or rather I felt such joy in promising it to myself that you would have loved me at that moment. And yet I have not written, dear friend; indeed I chose not to write to you: for if I had written then, either I would not have told you what I felt, which is inconceivable, or I would have upset and saddened you, which I did not want. The fact is, I have spent the saddest month I could ever have imagined. Madame de Condorcet has been extremely ill, in a way that has worried her family and friends, and me more than anyone. This anxiety was so overwhelming that for some days I suffered physically more than I could say or reveal. In this sad space of time every sort of anguish came thick and fast upon me: the memory of you and hope of a letter from you were my only consolation. I resume this letter, which was interrupted this morning, as I return from my evening walk, which I almost always take alone, and which I enjoy only if I am alone. Only then can I think of you at my ease, immerse myself in memories of the time when you were here, and in sweeter dreams of the day when I shall see you again. I think a great deal about that day, but the past and absence are strong, and I do not want to struggle too much against them; there is no bitterness in the sadness they can cause me and which may sometimes appear in my letters, as they do on my face and in my manner: for me one idea and one feeling dominate all others, the idea and the feeling that I am loved by you, only I tremble slightly at the thought that you may not be sufficiently convinced of all you mean to me: and when I hear you say that I don't love you enough, I feel a spasm of fear that this means I am incapable of making you happy: oh! how could I prove to you that my heart has never known such enchantment as you have created for me? I could not resume this letter after I broke off. I have not been feeling very well in the meantime, and have been acutely distressed, since my usual anxiety for the sick friend I spoke of has redoubled. . . But whether I write a lot or a little, briefly or at length, I implore you not to forget, my dearest, that I see you and speak to you every moment, and at every moment seek your voice and your image. . . Goodbye for today, *my sweet hope* [in English in original]; goodbye, be near me a while in spirit, and let me hear you say it to me.' Mary Clarke replied angrily: 'What on earth is this Madame de Condorcet? I didn't know the illness of any lady could be enough to make you ill: what on earth is a lady to you, that her illness should be more distressing to you than to her own family? to the extent of preventing your writing to me? . . . I wrote back the day your letter arrived, in all the bitterness of my first reaction, but thank Heaven I put aside that letter and after reading it the next day before posting it, I decided not to send it, but however I may control myself, I cannot pretend. . . Just imagine if I wrote to you like that and spoke to you of a man whose name you had never heard me pronounce before? . . . I have some sort of confused notion about this Madame de Condorcet that is painful to me, but I can't remember what it was, how I came by it or what it relates to; I've never heard you mention her, and I don't even remember who did, unless it was Amédée Thierry, brother of Augustin – . . . I thought I would not speak my mind, partly because I don't want to upset you, but I couldn't help it and a slight squall is better than perpetual clouds.' This letter was dated 3 September: Sophie de Condorcet died the next day.

A year passed in which Mary Clarke was again often away; she and Fauriel wrote many letters to each other; they planned the Italian trip, and here they were at last in Milan together.

Mary Clarke became very friendly with the Manzoni family. She and her mother spent the whole of that winter of 1824 in Milan, and they used to spend the evenings at the Manzoni house. Many years later Mary Clarke remembered those evenings clearly; she described them in a letter to someone who had asked her about them (it was Angelo de Gubernatis, who was writing a study of the relationship between Manzoni and Fauriel). They were happy evenings; the children played blind man's bluff and Enrichetta and Mary Clarke joined in, while Giulia and Mrs Clarke chatted by the fire, with Manzoni, Fauriel, and other friends who called every evening: Grossi, Visconti, Cattaneo, a poet called Giovanni Torti, and Luigi Rossari, who was an Italian teacher. In this letter Mary Clarke presented a different and unusually youthful image of Enrichetta: 'You would have thought she was the sister of her older children,' Mary Clarke observed. 'You've been enjoying yourself, little wife,' Manzoni said once to Enrichetta, who was rosy and excited after one of these games of blind man's bluff, putting his arm round her waist, and she agreed. But is was certainly a modest sort of entertainment, playing blind man's bluff with the children through the rooms of the house; the Manzonis did not frequent high society, they never went out in the evenings, and in Milan they had the reputation of being unsociable.

During this visit from Fauriel, the friendship between him and Manzoni changed, and became somehow more simple and natural. Fauriel would chat for a long time with Enrichetta and Giulia, and play with the children. A real affection grew up

74

between him and the children, in the light of which Enrichetta too became his friend, more than she had been in the past. The children called him Tola, a name invented by one of the little ones.

In the spring, the two Clarkes set off for Venice, and Fauriel followed them. From Venice he wrote to Manzoni: 'We were a bit chilled and weary arriving here, but otherwise fairly well. In spite of its ruined palaces, and pretty unbearable weather with rain and cold, I like this Thousand and One Nights town very much. . . Goodbye for now my dear friend, I hug you all, each and every one of you, again and again, my dear "god-mother", and your Enrichetta who is so close to my heart. Tell my dear little Giulia I have no one to play skittles with, which is very sad; and I have no one to ride on my shoulders or to call me Tola. Mrs and Miss Clarke talk of nothing but you, of all of you.' Fauriel was working on a collection of Greek folk songs, and there was a very large Greek colony in Venice: with a friend of his and of Manzoni, the Greek Mustoxidi, he went to Trieste, where there was also a Greek colony, parting from the two Clarkes who wanted to tour Italy. Fauriel to Mary Clarke, from Trieste: 'I am not sorry to have come here: Mustoxidi knows everyone here, and is liked by many people who have welcomed me for his sake. . . I spend all my evenings at the theatre, where they act tragedies and comedies quite well, or no worse than in Milan; I don't enjoy it very much, as you can imagine; but at least the evenings are less tedious to me there than elsewhere, and I can see more people without being obliged to talk. Three or four boxes are available to me, and I can choose to be alone or in company. . . I don't know yet whether I'll set off alone or whether Mustox is coming with me; he is still the best of men, but I do wish he could think of one thing for ten minutes on end, and that he was not so addicted to his pipe. Goodbye, dear life of my heart, I must go out and rush round, think about my departure, and I can't talk to you any longer. Goodbye, say you haven't forgotten me among all the grand things you are seeing; I assure you I love you more than ever.'

Fauriel to Mary Clarke from Venice, where he had paused before returning to Milan (Mary and her mother, meanwhile, were in Rome): 'I can't open my eyes or take a step without seeing something that reminds me that you were here with me, and I have to fight against tears; and I don't always succeed, especially when I am alone in my room. I really don't know why, but I came back to our hotel, though I did take care to find a nook as far as possible from the rooms we had then: but this precaution avails me little, for I keep returning instinctively to those rooms, and I have to turn back on my tracks, with a suffocating sense of the unspeakable pain of your absence. Yesterday, in an unguarded moment, I suddenly found myself standing in the middle of my old room, face to face with a man glued to the table at which he was writing, and looking at me in astonishment; I babbled a few laborious words of apology about my memory. . . . I haven't had the courage to go back to the Lido where we once saw the sea in its awful beauty. *Good-bye, my dearest life, I must end this letter, and I can end it only by telling you I love you, and that I love you as much as you can desire, and that I would do so even if you did not love me* [this in Italian, the rest of the letter in French]. Goodbye again, dear friend, my dear, sweet friend; this Italian language does not seem serious enough for a declaration of my love, so I repeat it in the language in which I said it for the first time and for ever.'

Mary Clarke to Fauriel, from Rome; he had now rejoined the Manzonis at Brusuglio (Bruzuglio, he and Mary called it) and was to spend the summer there: 'I am pleased to think you are at Bruzuglio and happier than in your letter, though you love me much more when you like the people about you less, and Manzoni and Cousin are a threat to me, while Musky [Mustoxidi] made you gloomy. . . . Goodbye then, my dear Dicky [she often called him this], I shall write to you sometimes poste restante, for they will think it strange that I write to you so often, and I prefer your friends to suspect nothing, because Signora Manzoni will think it wasn't very nice of me not to have told her about our relationship, and I don't want you to tell her about it, if I see her this autumn, *I* will tell her. Goodbye, my angel, write to me and be good and write masterpieces and judge them to be so, and be talkative, which is healthier; it hurt me more than I can say to go four months in Milan without really speaking; goodbye, my angel.' So she had been ill at ease in Milan among the Manzonis who did not know about her amorous relationship with Fauriel; and yet it seems impossible that they should not have guessed it.

From Brusuglio, Fauriel to Mary Clarke: 'You know the

friends I am with, so I need not tell you the welcome I got; I felt I was finding not just friends but something sweeter still: the children talked about me all the time, sometimes they dreamed of me, and whenever a carriage made a noise around midnight, they thought it was the stage-coach. They were delighted with the shells I brought them, and I hastened to explain that you had helped me gather them, so that I should not usurp your share in their gratitude. So much for the children. As for the grown-ups, they were no less delighted with the news they had had from you. . . Believe me, we have talked about you such a lot: and if I had no other reasons to love such excellent friends, I would have to love them for the affection they bear you. That is why I could not help being indiscreet with them about you: what they may have suspected about my feelings toward you, they now know completely and without a shadow of doubt. I told them I love you, that I love you with all my heart; I told them our plans for the future, without concealing the doubts I feel about my capacity to engender a happiness that I desire more than my own.' So perhaps Mary Clarke and Fauriel were thinking of getting married. but they never did.

Fauriel spent a peaceful summer at Brusuglio; he wrote the preface to the *Greek Songs*; he intended to join Mary and her mother in Florence in the autumn, and meanwhile he and Mary regularly exchanged long letters. The two Clarkes had been in Naples, and were now back in Rome; they were tremendously keen on Italy; Mary loved the Italians, but not the poor (*le bas peuple*) whom she thought fierce and brutal: They ill-treated horses. She had read Alfieri's *Memorie* with enthusiasm. She enjoyed being in Rome, but in the family boarding-house where they were staying the cooking was dreadful ('they cook like pigs') and she and her mother moved to Tivoli for the fresh air and better food: 'I need to cosset my stomach which is somewhat recalcitrant, although I'm a bit better after a week of complete rest during which I have amused myself painting, which has been like mother's milk to babes.' Talking of babies, she recalled freeing one from its swaddling-clothes on the outskirts of Naples: 'Poor creature! it was howling fit to burst and it was only two weeks old, and the weather was scorching; when we adults could hardly bear our loose clothing, the wretched little thing was all bundled up in swaddling clothes, tightly bound,

77

almost hidden from sight; as soon as we released it, it smiled and was quite happy. A young English painter I'm mad about told me he had freed at least a hundred in the three years he's been in Italy.' At one moment she and her mother were without money, and she wrote urgently to Fauriel asking him to send them some of his or ask Manzoni to lend some: but then their money arrived from England. 'Long live money!' she wrote. 'It's the key to everything: that's why I would like to be able to earn some and why I am so avaricious.' Her health improved at Tivoli, after the heat of the Roman summer: 'It isn't hot here, in fact it's almost cold in the evening, but there is no shade; fortunately Mama has found a painter's wife who is bored too and they keep each other company, otherwise I couldn't wait to set off again, and I've been cursing my life and especially the hateful box in which it pleased God to imprison me, because if I were a man, I ask you, would it be necessary for Mama and myself to be chained together? Ah, if I were asked: Would you rather be a woman or a galley-slave? I would say at once: Hurrah for the galley! . . . I am like a great eagle in a little cage, but enough, I must resign myself.' She often asked how Manzoni's novel was going, and she wanted to translate it into French; she knew that Fauriel had discussed it in Paris with another possible translator called Trognon, and she wanted to have the book as soon as it was printed to translate it at once, leaving Trognon empty-handed: 'If Signor Manzoni's first volume is printed, bring it with you, *possession is nine points in the law* [in English in original]: and if I had it before that beastly Frenchman, I would perhaps finish it first and then we'd see. You must realize, dear Dicky, I love money, and that's why I want to translate the book well or ill; *my own dear sweetie, do write to me, pray do*' [English in original]. However, in the end neither she nor Trognon translated the book.

In the autumn Fauriel went to Florence, where the two Clarkes were waiting for him; as he set off, he told the Manzonis to come and join him, or he would fly back to them; but the Manzonis went on postponing their trip to Tuscany; and Fauriel did not fly back to them, in fact after a short letter in December, they did not hear from him for several months. Pietro answered

that short letter: ' I am pleased to tell you we are all well; my
dear mother is taking walks which do her a lot of good. My
sisters Giulia, Cristina and Sofia and my brother Enrico send
you all their love; Vittorina calls *Tola* and then answers at once
"he don to Florence" – she gets sweeter every day, can recite the
verse about all the animals, sings and runs all round the house
like a big girl.' Enrichetta also added a few lines: 'We cannot get
used to your absence. . . We are always talking seriously of the
plan of joining you in the spring as long as we don't meet with
any obstacles. . .'

'Oh, our dear Tola, why did you leave us?' Enrichetta wrote
again two months later. 'My children often bewail your
absence, gratefully remembering your kindness and regretting
that they can no longer try your patience. . . I wanted to write
to Miss Clarke for news of you, and to ask her if you are so
absorbed in her as to forget, it seems, your friends in Milan; I
cannot altogether forgive her for taking you from us. . . she
was not wrong. . . but we are not wrong to lament your
absence. Giulia was supposed to write to you, but could never
find the courage; Pietro is a scatter-brain; even Alessandro does
not write, though he always means to do so, and it is, I imagine,
for the same reasons as you do not write; Mama is full of good
intentions. . . and I see I am the boldest, since I have dared to
write.' 'Enrichetta says I never carry out my intentions,' added
Giulia, the grandmother, 'the truth is that for more than
twenty-five years my intention has been to love you all my life,
and I carry it out every moment of my life, but you make me
pay dearly for it with all the anxiety you cause us! Here is the
whole family who love you dearly and who are consumed with
longing because of your silence. Oh, dear friend of us all, what
are you doing? where are you? you can't possibly have forgotten
us? it cannot be! then what is our *Tolla* doing, whom not even
Vittorina forgets? . . . I beseech you to write to us. . . Goodbye, dear friend – your room remains just as it was, but in vain,
it is empty.'

For Manzoni, the chief purpose of this famous trip to Tuscany, which kept being postponed, was to temper his style, for
he thought it was there that the true Italian language was
spoken; yet he never found the right time to go, perhaps fearing
that, if he went too soon before the novel had really taken shape,

79

the sudden encounter with a different idiom might be too much of a shock and strangle the novel at birth. But he certainly thought a great deal about the streets of Florence where that idiom was spoken, and where Fauriel was now walking. 'My son's book is very behind-hand, he still hasn't finished writing, revising and re-revising the 2nd volume,' Grandmother Giulia wrote again to Fauriel in the spring. 'So he will be occupied the whole summer, when I hope he will bring it all to a speedy close in the solitude of Brusú. Wherever he goes, the speech of the *Mercato Vecchio* is always on his mind, but that is really the only problem and I think he would find a few months in Tuscany in the autumn sufficient to resolve it. . . but we'll talk about it when it's convenient, meanwhile he afflicts our ears with all his "Tuscanisms".'

'Dear friend, oh! how happy Alessandro is, he has hit upon a good writing spell. . . We had vaguely hoped to see Mrs and Miss Clarke, thinking they would pass through Milan on their way back to France, but unfortunately this is not to be,' again Grandmother Giulia writing to Fauriel. He had finally announced he would be arriving soon. 'I think you will receive our letter, so I must tell you we cannot get to Florence this summer, so Brusú awaits you . . . We will remain in our Thebaid at Brusú; after all the plays, the balls and masquerades in Florence, I dare say you must be longing for your cell. Alessandro is overjoyed at the thought of having you with him, so you can have some good chats *over breakfast*; I need not mention Enrichetta and myself, for you know our feelings; your god-daughter loves you as dearly, but always imagines she is not loved. . . You will talk to Alessandro about the *Mercato Vecchio*, because it is for him the whole of Tuscany.'

'How can you be so good as to take an interest in the trifles that come from my pen?' Manzoni wrote to Abbé Degola, who had written again after a long silence. 'Do you know what sort of thing I am struggling with as if it were a matter of great importance? It is the sort of composition whose authors your Nicole – and mine – unhesitatingly called *empoisonneurs publics*. I have certainly done everything in my power not to deserve this title, but have I succeeded?' Pierre Nicole, a seventeenth century Jansenist, in his book *Les imaginaires et les visionnaires*, had launched a bitter attack against a satirical comedy by

80

Desmarets de Saint-Sorlin called *Les visionnaires*, which had offended Jansenist severity. Manzoni obviously thought his novel might offend Jansenist severity. 'When you have seen this work, I shall await your judgment with impatience and some little trepidation. I warn you, however, that, as a good author, I have prepared an apologia against any objections that could possibly occur to you, and I intend to justify my work not only against the reproach of perniciousness, but also on the score of utility. But these are jests: in all charity, pray to Him who is not deluded that He may condescend to keep me from wretched self-delusion. And since you want to know how far I have got, I will add that the 2nd volume is at the printer's, and I hope in three or four months to say the same of the 3rd and last.'

Fauriel spent the whole of the summer of 1825 at Brusuglio; in October he suddenly returned to Milan and left Italy. He left secretly, leaving a book as a present for Grandmother Giulia, a small sum of money for a doctor who had treated him, and a brief farewell note. He gave no reason for a departure so sudden and hasty as to seem a flight, and his friends never knew what it was; perhaps he had some money troubles; or perhaps he simply feared the commotion and tears of goodbyes. During the summer he had expressed the intention of leaving Italy for a short period, and then returning; but he never returned, and his friends never saw him again. In November he wrote from Marseilles: 'If anything could increase my unhappiness at leaving you, and my regrets for having left you, it would have been the inconveniences and delays I have suffered on the journey. I was obliged to spend three whole days in Turin, so I had time to digest the heavy beauty of the city, with the sole company, when I had it, of a Polish braggart and a mason from Milan, who was responsible for that wretched grave in which goodness knows how many people were buried last winter. Likewise I was held up at Nice where I was even more bored than in Turin, despite my walks by the sea, and my excursions into country-side which, like all the beautiful localities of Provence, looks rather like a garden set in a casket of rocks. . . As for Marseilles, I can't say whether I was amused or deafened by the noise, the bustle and activity of this mercantile population. . . Although

81

everything I've been seeing and hearing for some days convinces me I'm in France, I don't feel completely *repatriated*, and I grieve for something of Italy, especially you and everything about you. . . I can tell from here that in spite of so much that is dear to me there, I shall not like Paris at all. . . But since I have ceased to be one of you, I grow daily more impatient to get to Paris, and I am weary of highways and inns. – Adieu, I clasp you tightly, so tightly in my arms, all, grown-ups and little ones, those dear little ones whose beloved faces, voices, and even their merry noise, still seem to be with me, so that I look round expecting to see them. I would weep if I thought of them and of you all too often. . .'

From Toulouse, where he stopped for a few days to pursue his studies, he wrote to Mary Clarke: 'Since I left Narbonne, I have spent almost all my time in horrible places, with no company but my guides, exhausted by long walks on paths the like of which I have never seen in the wildest corners of the Alps. – Adieu, dear friend of my heart, we will meet soon. This is my fondest hope.' Although it was his fondest hope to see her again, and although she too expressed in every letter to him her desire to be near him, they made no attempt to be together always, and she wanted to keep their relationship hidden; perhaps he did too; this relationship of theirs was passionate but troubled and complicated, and they kept separating, and so it went on, with long separations and long exchanges of letters, for years, until he died.

Giulietta

'You've gone, dear, too dear friend to us all!' wrote Grandmother Giulia to Fauriel. ' You have left your family, ah, if you
knew how many tears you caused us to shed! the children are
inconsolable and Enrico threatens anyone who utters your
name. . . What can I say about Giulia or Pietro? in their sensitive
and reflective natures silence is eloquent, if I may put it like
that, while we could not appease Cristina's sobs. My Alessandro, ours and yours, feels your absence more than you can
imagine. Believe me, I am not exaggerating. Enrichetta regards
you as one of our family, and cannot be consoled for this sort of
laceration; it is as if you have scattered a bundle that was so
closely tied. And I who am writing this – I weep more bitterly
than all the rest.'

'Dear friend,' wrote Manzoni, 'the feelings your departure
left in our hearts cannot easily be expressed, and are not the sort
one likes to chat about. I can add nothing to what Mama has
said. You can imagine how impatient we are to hear from you.'

'My dearest godfather,' wrote Giulietta. It was the first of the
many letters she wrote to him. *Mon bien cher parrain; mon cher
parrain.* Writing to Fauriel became a fond habit and pleasure.
She wrote in place of her father, who was too busy. This first
letter is still timid. 'I am always being scolded because my
foolish timidity outweighs my desire to write to you. However
seeing that everyone keeps putting it off till tomorrow, and
Papa scolds us all, I am resolved to be the kindest, and to make
a virtue of something really very dear to me, of being able to
converse for a moment with you, as it's so long (long for me,
at least) since I bored you with my chatter, as I did when we had
the pleasure of having you here with us. After a month of waiting, and dare I say anxiety, we have had your dear letter. But

why keep us waiting and longing like that? And now who knows when we'll have another. You know how we love you, and (especially we women) how we tend to worry and imagine all sorts of misfortunes, so don't leave us to languish so long in fantastic suppositions, fortunately dissipated by your letters which always announce, somewhat belatedly, that you are in good health and that nothing unpleasant prevented you from telling us so before. Not a day goes by without our talking of you. . . Mother sends you her best regards, she is rather poorly these days, but as this is the result of her condition, nobody seems worried, which makes her say not only has she to suffer but also to hear everyone say it's quite natural and nothing at all, poor Mama! However, she feels the moment of her release can't come too soon.' Enrichetta was pregnant. She was so ill she thought she would die in childbirth, and towards the end of her pregnancy she made a will. She wrote a letter to her husband, which she kept hidden. 'To you, my beloved Alessandro, I venture to declare my intentions, in case God in His Divine Wisdom takes me from this world. . . Although I have very little to dispose of, I wish to leave at my death a little memento to those who were most dear to my heart.' There followed a detailed enumeration of her possessions, money, small jewels and shawls, which she wanted to go to her husband, her mother-in-law, her children, the servants and the poor.

In his letters Fauriel asked for news of 'Signor Blondel and the Signora', that is, Enrichetta's brother, Enrico Blondel, and his wife. After many years Enrico Blondel had renewed relations with Alessandro, which had been broken off at the time of the conversion; now the two brothers-in-law met often and exchanged books, ideas and affectionate letters. Manzoni had written to him once, when they had recently resumed relations: 'It happens all too often that differences of opinion, and especially of faith, freeze the good will between men. Such a difference existed between us but we never spoke of it; we both avoided any discussion that might expose it. Now we have broken the ice, I feel an even stronger need of reassurance that the friendship you have shown me, which is most precious to me, has not suffered thereby. Suffice to say that for me nothing has changed, and nothing can ever change, either the feelings of universal charity that bind me to you as to all men, or the particular feelings of esteem and friendship which I have vowed to you, or the happy relations created between us by the person who came from your family into mine, to be at once a consolation and an example to us.' Enrico Blondel had been seriously ill for years; his young wife looked after him; he had married Louise Maumary, who was his niece, daughter of a sister. Louise, *tante Louise*, would be very important in the life of the Manzoni family.

In January 1826 news came from Genoa that Abbé Degola had died. His nephew, Prospero Ignazio, wrote to Manzoni. 'Poor Don Eustachio had had bronchitic attacks two or three times over the last few years, and they became more frequent and led to vomiting. In order not to feed his illness he lived on a very strict diet, abstaining from any stimulants, and this caution enabled him to get through the summer and autumn reasonably well, but without succeeding in eradicating the germ of his illness, the symptoms of which reappeared at the beginning of December last. After two weeks of unavailing treatment, he was stricken by acute pains in the head, so persistent that they tormented him to the end. . . The patient went into a steady decline, and, losing his joviality, appeared indifferent to the company even of his best friends; finally he showed unmistakable signs of a failure of his mental faculties, often asking for the same thing, and talking quite at random. But it was not until Friday the 13th of this month that we began to fear for his life, as he lay in a deep lethargy. Then on Saturday he roused himself and was fully conscious to receive the last rites. Nothing could disturb his *tranquillity*. And therefore, setting aside all worldly thoughts, he turned only to thoughts of Heaven. . . What resignation between the spasms! What virtue! Four hours before his death he asked for some of his family, and summoning all his remaining strength to his cold lips, he took a tender farewell of us, and turning to me said *love me*, I promised it, whereupon he added *but if you love me, do what I have always told you*: words spoken with such effort and love that I shall never recall them without tears. . .'

In March 1826 Enrichetta had a baby boy who was called Filippo. She could not feed him herself, so a nurse was taken.

'My dear friend,' Fauriel wrote to Manzoni, 'It was double pleasure to receive your news from the amiable messenger who brought it, and who has so courteously passed on the news he has continued to receive from you.' The 'amiable messenger' was Giacomo Beccaria, Manzoni's cousin. 'I was most of all eager to have news of our very dear Enrichetta; so you can judge my delight to hear that she had safely given birth to a fine handsome little Filippo, who will, I hope, soon take over Enrico's place on my shoulders. . . I am still in rather low spirits, if less so than the last time I wrote: and perhaps this is why my health is not so good as when I left Brusuglio and the Pyrenees. Paris is not one whit more pleasing to me than when I first arrived, and I can't imagine I can stay cooped up here all summer. . . If I were free to consider only my own wishes, feelings and desires, I would fly back to you and find the well-being and calm that surrounded me, and I cannot bring myself to give up all hope of such a sweet prospect. But the fact is I have committed myself to some serious work with fixed dates for completion, which obliges me to use my time judiciously, and to remain in or near Paris. . . When I consider how much remains to be done to complete this task, it is quite frightening, so to avoid being frightened I try not to think too much about it, and to waste as little time as possible.' This letter was delivered by hand, with others for Giulietta and Ermes Visconti, by the Marchese Trotti and his wife, friends of the Manzonis, who often travelled between Paris and Italy. Giulietta replied: 'Papa says how sorry he is not to be able to write to you, but there is a storm brewing up and he feels so poorly that he really feels unequal to it (as you know, he always feels ill in stormy weather). He wanted to write something in reply to the letter you sent me by the Marchese Trotti; he was so touched that he keeps talking of it. . . . He also wanted to say how sad he is that you will not be at Brusú, which robs him of much of the pleasure he feels in going there. Papa longs to see fruit of your completed labours, which will be doubly pleasing because this liberation may lead to your coming here, so it is a sort of passport which he most eagerly desires. This is what he has told me over and over again to say to you, with such urgency and so little faith in my ability that he has made me more clumsy than usual. . . Filippino is doing very well with the new nurse; he is growing fast and laughs when you talk to him; if he is as cheerful as his nurse, he will be very cheerful indeed. . . I often talk about you to Cavalier Jacopetti who comes twice a week in the evening, and to Princess Pietrasante, and Jacopetti talks about you to please me, and he is not the only one. . .'

Manzoni to Fauriel from Brusuglio in the summer: 'I don't know (but I flatter myself it is so) if you can read into the first word of this letter everything I mean to convey by it: *Brusuglio!* this place you have made so difficult for us to live in now, where your absence is felt on all sides, where we all miss you every hour of the day!'

From Coprena that autumn, Giulietta to Fauriel (they had rented a house in Coprena, where they had all gone for a change of air. The Beccaria relations were also there): 'We are quite happy in this charming little house. . . We go for walks. We go to see all the fine country houses in the neighbourhood. . . I spend my time drawing, studying and reading: I am reading *Woodstock* in English. Have you read it? what do you think of it? It's Walter Scott, so we mustn't say a word. . . Vittorina is here beside me; I asked her what she wanted me to say to you, and she said: *Nuffing, 'cos he said Enrico was a bad boy, so he a naughty man.* You see how she bears malice. She's really very sweet, but as wilful as can be. Enrico hasn't got any further with his reading and writing since you left. . . Last Monday 9th October, Papa, Grossi, Cattaneo, young Capretti and Pietro set off from here for Como; Gallina went too with a pony carrying their baggage. . . I don't know yet when they'll be back. . . you can imagine how empty it is here without them! I don't know how we would bear it anywhere else! . . . Can we hope to hear from you at long last? Don't you know it really is too bad of you to behave like that? . . . As my letter had not been posted, I am opening it to tell you Papa is back. It rained a lot yesterday, and it wasn't very pleasant travelling on foot; when they got to Merate, they took a carriage and came back. . . To give you some idea of their high spirits, the gentlemen were talking about their adventures this morning, they said they had denied themselves nothing, only that at Bellagio they had eaten some excellent fish and had been foolish enough not to ask for more. What a shame!

87

Cattaneo said: It's worth going back to have some more. Quite right, said Grossi, such a foolish omission must be rectified. And Cattaneo: promise you'll keep me company if I go! So all four are setting off tomorrow at four, they will get to Como to cross the lake by steamer, they'll eat their fish at Bellagio, and return immediately. Sixty miles for a bit of fish! Pietro is delighted at this extension of the fun, but Papa won't go.'

Manzoni to Fauriel, from Milan in late autumn: 'For some time, more than two months I should think, I have been more than usually troubled by my real or imaginary ailments, but certainly real for me in either case; I confess that I am almost pleased to have the more obvious symptoms (especially the almost continual stomach aches), as they provide a reason for my low spirits and dejection which would be even more painful if I could not attribute them to some physical cause. My work proceeds pretty slowly, with long interruptions: I am enormously disillusioned, the only thing that keeps me going is the wish to be rid of it for once and for all, so you can imagine how cheerful that makes me. You must have had the first half of the 3rd volume from Signora di Belgioioso; since then I've only managed to put together about a third of the second half; and anyway, I hope to be rid of it before the winter is out.'

Gradually, as the novel progressed, Manzoni was sending it to Fauriel, sending groups of pages by people who were leaving for Paris; as soon as Fauriel received them, he passed them to his acquaintance, Auguste Trognon, who was to translate them into French. Trognon was a history teacher, and author of an historical novel in the style of Walter Scott, and he had translated, years ago in 1819, *Le ultime lettere di Jacopo Ortis*. He had long before expressed to Fauriel his wish to translate Manzoni's novel, and Manzoni had agreed. Mary Clarke had expressed the same wish, but perhaps Fauriel had thought Trognon more suited to the task.

Giulietta to Fauriel: 'We don't see Ermes so often in the evening since his brother got married, he says it's so nice by the fire in your own house when there's someone to talk to. That's just like Visconti, isn't it? They've just brought me some violets from Brusú, so I'll put one in for you. Think of us sometimes at poor Brusú! But think of us to some purpose! We talk of you so often and remember the past in order to imagine the

88

future. . . For three days Vittorina has been telling everyone she sees that Fauriel had written something about her, then she would run to me to get it right, but no sooner had I told her than she forgot it again. . . Enrico wants me to tell you he dreamt of you, I don't remember what the dream was. He has a master who teaches him various little things most patiently, and takes him out for walks. My sisters are making progress with their music; like Pietro, they have a teacher for French, History and Geography. Pietro has several others, and is progressing in every way, physically and morally. He still goes to the riding-school sometimes, and he skated while the ice lasted; he even hopes it will freeze again, but I'd be very surprised. We had a lot of snow which gave us a fortnight of slush and bad weather. Oh! I mustn't forget to mention Acerbi, he is still at Lake Como, and by now it is to be hoped he is quite out of danger. . .' (Enrico Acerbi was a friend of the family, a doctor, he had been very ill with an infection of the lungs; he used to give minute details of his health, especially to Grandmother Giulia, whom he called 'my second little mother', and who used to write to him and send him baskets of sweetmeats). . . 'Vittorina is in a corner of the room talking to herself; she says she's more sorry for Fauriel than Acerbi, because Fauriel is in Paris, poor man, and Acerbi isn't so far away. So far away all on his own! She wants me to tell you that if we send Giuseppe [the servant] all the way to Paris with letters for you, we just don't realize how tired he'll get!'

Giulietta to Fauriel, in the spring of 1827: 'Papa sends you his very best regards; he is working, and begs me to say he thinks he has at last almost reached the end of his endless work. But you know, a chapter often takes him weeks, because of his health which is always poor; so it's almost finished but when will it be really finished? . . . Thank you very much for enquiring about my health, I should say it is a bit better. . . even though I continue to lose weight. Pietro has my share of good health; the others are well except Filippino who has had teething troubles; he still takes only his nurse's milk although he is a year old. Mother has had a bit of toothache these last few days. she's also had spots on her face for two months which are very irritating. *Bonne maman* [their grandmother] is still the one with the best health, I assure you it's a joy for us to see her so well.

89

By the way, I want to enclose a violet again, which I picked myself this time at Brusú yesterday; I'm astonished you didn't find the two I put in my last letter. A week ago we had a Signor Orlandi here, who has flown with a winged balloon. He claimed he could adopt a precise direction but the fact is that he did fly very well indeed, but straight ahead, and he had to come down where he could and not where he chose; the weather was splendid and he came down very near the Arena from which he set out. . . Please don't go on like this without writing to us. Oh, if only we could see you soon! Will your journey last long? What are your plans afterwards? And you won't see Milan again for a long time, I hear? Oh, it would be really cruel of you, after raising our hopes! The whole family beg me to say so, and it's the endless refrain of all our friends! If Mrs and Miss Clarke are in Paris, please tell them we still have a happy memory of the little time we spent together.'

Ermes Visconti to Fauriel: 'I think I am right in assuming that the translation of that essay of mine on Beauty, – I sent you the manuscript approved by our censors years ago – has not come from the press yet? I think I am right, and I certainly hope so. I now wish with all my heart that the work should remain unpublished for ever, as I find it contains fundamental errors of the greatest importance. A great number of things are not considered from their more serious side, the only true side. Others present ideas which are incomplete and therefore false. Some other time I might perhaps recast the essay, remove the many, many faults I detect in it. . . Meanwhile, if we are still in time, I beg you, my excellent friend, to see that they give up all thought of a publication which has fortunately been so long delayed. . . I hope to hear from you soon to confirm all this. At your best convenience, and only at your convenience, I shall await Mr. Rémusat's clarification of the Chinese language. Alessandro is almost on the point of giving the last chapters of his Romance to the printers. I hope we shall have it in May. Excellent news of the Manzoni household, of Cattaneo and of Grossi. Addio.'

Giulietta to Fauriel, from Milan in June: 'Here I am again writing to you in place of Papa! . . . But once again he insists he means to write to you soon. At the first opportunity he will send you the remaining pages – I think there will be about four;

he is sending you eight this time, that's all that have been printed so far. . . Marchese Ermes is in the drawing-room and asks me to send you his best regards and to ask for a word in reply to his last letter. . . As for Papa, you will see that we can at last hope that everlasting novel will soon be published, it really is high time, for more reasons than one: because he's tired of working at it, and the others are tired of waiting for it. . . Papa has just come in to tell me to say he will have another opportunity on Monday, that he will certainly write to you and send you the rest, but you won't get it till the end of the month because it seems this person has to travel slowly. . . Mama's eye trouble has never been cured, in fact it has got worse in the last five months, it's a very long time, and though she is taking fresh-water baths, she has only taken a few so far, so we can't judge if they are doing her good; the doctors say she won't really get well until she has a change of air! Perhaps Brusú is not far enough, so we are thinking of taking a house on Lake Como, but nothing is settled yet and until Papa has really finished I think we won't leave Town. We have had dreadful weather and the heat is beginning to make itself felt. Papa says he must not, dares not, and cannot ask you to write, but for all that he wants, waits for and in short, asks for a letter; he says if you write to me it will be justice, if you write to him it will be mercy.'

Manzoni to Fauriel, a few days later: '*Respice finem*, dear friend; it's a real relief to think I can talk to you about something else now, instead of this tedious story, which is as boring to me as to its ten readers; I say I am bored; as for you, I hardly dare to think. Well then, to end all discussion, here are the last pages of the last volume, which you will be so good as to pass on to Monsieur Trognon. . . I am really put out that I can't reproach you for your silence; I want to, but I haven't the impudence. So I shall be content to beg you, from the heart, to write me a really long letter soon, to talk at length about yourself, since we are not to see you, and of the *Provenciales*, since we are not even to see them [*Les Lettres Provenciales* was the title of the work Fauriel had been engaged on for some time]. . . Giulia has told you that our Enrichetta is troubled with ringworm around her eyes; it is not serious, and can't possibly become so; but it is distressing to her, and to us for her sake, as you can imagine. They have recommended sea-bathing, and we have almost resolved to try this; we will probably go to Genoa for the purpose next month, and it is equally possible that from there we will go and spend some time in Tuscany. . . You are ever in my heart, and I do ask you to write to me. Until then, goodbye.'

In Tuscany, by listening to people talking, Manzoni would be able to give the style of his novel the liveliness, freshness, and purity of accent which he feared it lacked. The novel was already at the press, but he intended to revise and correct it for a new edition.

By the middle of June the novel had been printed in full, in three volumes. A first volume had been printed some years before in 1824, by the same publisher, Ferrario, with the title *Gli sposi promessi*; but the final title was *I promessi sposi*. Vincenzo Monti, who had been seriously ill for some time, received one of the first copies. Manzoni sent it to him at Monza where he was living, with a letter: 'The story was to have been presented to you there without a word and with many blushes by my Giulietta, whom I may also call yours in her admiration and gratitude: and it was a joy to imagine her dear modesty confronted with a fame which is just as dear to us. But a most ill-timed inflammation of the throat has kept my poor girl in bed for two days, and, although there is some improvement, it threatens to keep her at home for several days more. So for now you have only the story: not that I mean to condemn you to read it; but you must accept it from me. And as soon as the illness and the doctor permit, we will come and thank you for accepting it.' Monti had heard from friends that Manzoni was preparing to leave, but thought he was going to Rome. He replied: 'My dearest friend. . . fearing that your imminent move to Rome will rob me of the consolation of ever seeing you again, since each day I feel my end draw nearer, I have to say in writing that I go to await you in Heaven, where I am certain I shall see you in God's good time. Meanwhile, before my own Don Abbondio intones the *Proficiscere* for me, I want to thank you for the precious gift of your *Sposi promessi*, of which I will say what I said of your *Carmagnola*; "I wish I were the author." I have read your novel, and on finishing it felt my heart uplifted, and my admiration increased. Yes, my dear Manzoni, your talent is admirable, and your heart an inexhaustible fountain of the most tender feelings, which makes your writing so exceptional. . .'

Giulietta to Fauriel, 7 July: 'Next week we set off for Genoa, Leghorn and Florence; seeing Mama is still in such poor health, and moreover that the freshwater bathing has brought her some relief, the doctors have urged my parents to go to Leghorn for her to try sea-bathing. I think Mama will take about fifteen baths, and immediately after we will go to Florence, where I think we will stay to the end of October, or thereabouts. . .' They were all going except Filippino; fearing the journey in the hot weather would make him ill, they had decided to leave him at Brusuglio with the servants. 'He will be well cared for, the little darling; he's walking and saying a few words, and seems even more lovable these last few days as if to make us even sorrier, or perhaps it is we who are making more fuss of him! His nurse is leaving him tomorrow so that he can gradually get used to being without the people who are most dear to him. Mama had been a bit better just recently, but the day before yesterday she went out when she was hot, and as it's natural for the rheumatism to go to the weakest parts, one of her eyes is all swollen and redder than usual; she has put an ointment on it today. . . *Bonne Maman* has not been very well for some time either, she feels very weak almost every morning, as if she were going to faint. . . The children are all very pleased that they are going to see somewhere new and be out of doors a bit. Pietro especially is as happy as a sandboy. So I am going to see another part of our beautiful Italy, more beautiful than the part I know, but it couldn't be more dear! not as dear, for sure! I won't tell you how much your stubborn silence hurts us. . . I have been quite ill, and for quite a long time. I've been able to get up for the last fortnight but I still don't feel very well; for more than ten days I had quite a high temperature and a very swollen cheek, for a week I could only drink because I couldn't open my mouth properly, I think it was partly because of a big tooth coming through. . . I've just been to Papa, who is there doing corrections in the midst of all those gentlemen [she probably meant the usual friends], he says he hasn't time to tell me even half the things he'd like me to write to you; that's how he always is! . . . I must say that we have been delighted with the success of Papa's book, it really has surpassed not only our expectations but even our hopes; in less than twenty days six hundred copies

93

have been sold, it's a real furore, everyone is talking about it; they queue up to be sure of buying a copy. Papa is besieged by men and letters of every kind and every class, there have also been very favourable articles, and more are expected.'

They set out in mid-July, thirteen of them in two carriages, pausing at Pavia where they had luncheon with Bishop Tosi. As they continued their journey, they were caught by the rain. They had an accident: the carriage the children were in was overturned. Grandmother Giulia wrote to the Bishop from Genoa: 'First of all, please accept our most affectionate and respectful thanks for all the kindness and cordiality you showed us in that happy half-day we spent with you. You are and always will be our dear Father. After leaving Il Gravelone, we crossed the Po and those endless Sabbioni, and, because it was getting rather late and still raining, we were obliged to stop at Casteggio in a horrid inn, and to sleep badly, or rather not at all because of the bedbugs that were more in charge of our wretched beds than we were; we set off at 5 o'clock, but it was still raining, and when we got to Torrona there was a storm. We stopped quite a while to allow it to pass over, and to have something to eat. The postillions are enough to make you wild, they keep making us pay for ten fresh horses. After Arquato it was raining quite a lot, and as we were coming down along the edge of a precipice in La Scrivia, the harness of the children's carriage broke, I heard shouts, Giulietta looked out and saw the carriage completely overturned. You can imagine our terror. It was a matter of a moment, four steps and they would all have been lost, but the good God, the Blessed Virgin, the angels and saints we invoked caused the carriage to overturn just in a sort of cleft in the precipice which was full of mud. So it stopped, the horses in front, the postillion, Giuseppino, Enrico and all of them underneath. Giuseppino extricated himself, took Enrico and tossed him up on a mound nearby. . . all the others got out of the carriage, safe and quite unhurt apart from the terrible fright. You will see just how the good God helped us: they had difficulty in righting the carriage which was quite undamaged. Truly it was by the grace and the dear charity of the Lord, his Holy Mother, and our intercessors. I repeat, two steps further,

94

and then. . . Oh, thank the Lord for us! the boys didn't want to get back in the carriage, Enrichetta had to go with them. We continued our journey safely, and at 7 we arrived in Genoa. We are well housed at the *albergo delle quattro nazioni*, we have a terrace overlooking the harbour. We were supposed to leave the day before yesterday, but we were put off by the heat, the uncertainty of finding proper accommodation in Leghorn where we know nobody, the need of rest after such a shock, my need of purging, finding sea-bathing here without being obliged to go on up there, and such a cordial welcome from everyone, and from so many acquaintances, all this decided us to do our bathing here, and in fact Enrichetta is really enjoying the first one, I think. I'm sure we are doing the right thing; it's true that we are hearing Genovese instead of the beautiful Tuscan dialect, but we must be patient: 15 to 20 days, and then we'll leave for Leghorn and Florence, if we can find a good coachman, we would prefer it to the stage-coach. . . the purpose of the journey is for us to see the lovely Tuscan towns more comfortably, and for Alessandro at last to hear the beautiful language of the peasants that he believes to be the "non plus ultra".'

Manzoni also told the episode of the carriage in a letter to Tommaso Grossi, written from Genoa: 'The carriage with all our little chicks overturned on a bank, by God's grace, because behind it was La Scrivia at the bottom of a cliff. And also by God's good grace, no one was hurt, and it all ended in "puia" as, we understood from the speech of the good folk who ran up, that unhappy passion or sentiment, whichever you choose to say, is called in these parts. In the evening, or even somewhat before evening, we were in Genoa, no more, no less; and we are still here. And if you don't know how this change in our plan came about, I am just going to tell you. Some old acquaintances we found here, and the new ones we've made, began to inspire in us such *puia* of Leghorn, and the heat there which they say is outrageous, and a certain kind of mosquito which can change the whole shape of your skin and give you a fever, and various other things, all of which they discuss with such courtesy, cordiality and charm that, between the fear of going there and the attraction of staying here, we looked at each other and said: let's do our bathing in Genoa.'

The old and new acquaintances in Genoa were the Marchese

Gian Carlo di Negro, brother-in-law of Ermes Visconti, who had a delightful little villa where they spent very pleasant evenings, Doctor Carlo Mojon and his wife, and the Marchese di Saint-Réal, an octogenarian, superintendent of the Sardinian navy, married to a sister of De Maistre. Grandmother Giulia wrote to Bishop Tosi: 'You cannot imagine how the Piedmontese ladies and gentlemen lionize Alessandro, I think it is almost too much.'

At last they decided to leave for Leghorn. Manzoni wrote to Rossari, on the eve of their departure: 'My dearest fellow, between the noise of young and old, the former up to their pranks and the latter up to their packing, activities which may be dissimilar in their ultimate effects but which, above my head at this moment, produce a similar, even identical effect of irritation on my nerves, I take pen in hand to have a long chat wih you on paper, a good bellyful of talk with my *Noi*. . . And now let's imagine we are on my sofa by the fire, and let's jest the time away.' A young Genovese told him he had found in his novel 'many expressions which he had hitherto thought were pure Genovese. I almost threw my arms round his neck and kissed him on both cheeks. Give Ferrario [the printer] my regards and tell him that this Signor Gravier [a bookseller] counted out the price of the 12 copies in so many shining new 5 franc pieces, one after another. And that it gives me quite foolish pleasure that there should be only 36 of those copies left, and I shall be even more foolishly pleased when those too are disposed of. . . I must not omit to tell you that my Pietro is a consummate swimmer; he plunges headfirst from the boat, dives under and surfaces again at will. . .'

From Leghorn, Manzoni to Grossi: 'Oh what a dear letter, what a dear, sweet, honeyed letter I have received from my Grossi! Just the letter to make up for such a long silence, and I take up my pen to reply without delay – and you must be prepared for me to talk of almost nothing but my affairs, what we are doing and seeing, how we are and suchlike, for this is the way of travellers. I think I have just discovered (unless others had discovered and said it before me) why travellers usually speak ill of the people they meet and the places they visit; it is because they do not find the rooms, the furniture or anything they are accustomed to, and what is worse they don't find their friends; they have to think of packing and unpacking, always with their purse in hand, and, in order to lighten it as little as possible, they have to argue with people who would like to empty it altogether, and so on. . . But I have also observed that this annoyance and ill humour is extreme at first, but then gradually diminishes. . . So that if I had written to you from Genoa the day after our arrival, that is, after the fatigue and tedium of wandering from room to room to work out how best to fit in six or seven or eight beds, and after spending the first night on those beds and not our own, my style would have been that of a veteran of the Moscow campaign; but because I have delayed a little, you now find a certain note of festivity in my letter. . . now I can tell you that in Genoa we spent three weeks that were as happy as may be (for us) away from home, and that we were really sorry to leave. . . After leaving a week Tuesday, as I said in my letter to Rossari, we took four days to move or be moved here. On the first we passed continually from one beauty to another, with an almost constant view of the sea and of beautiful mountains, through groves of oranges, laurels, olives, figs, vines and charming villages, a real delight. And we thoroughly enjoyed it; although there were places – I won't say dangerous, but calculated to alarm my mother, who, as you know, is afraid of plunging over the edge at points where someone intending to commit suicide would be hard put to it to find a spot, yet even she enjoyed it, because for love of us she kept her fears to herself, and fear, when it cannot speak, gets bored and goes away.' On the second day, 'horrid mountains, with nothing beautiful to be seen, far or near, and with worse precipices'; on the third they arrived at Pietrasanta, 'the first patch of Tuscan soil you reach on that side, and there began the pleasure of hearing with my own ears this language which was a delight to me then, as it is here in Leghorn; so what will it be to hear it in Florence? I will write from there to tell you how wonderful it is.' During the journey, when they stopped at an inn for a meal, they were served a vegetable they called *cornetti* [beans] in Lombardy: 'so I turned to the waiter politely, and taking care not to stammer [Manzoni stammered], I asked: What is this dish? not as one who does not know the name, but who does not know what thing it is. Fagiolini, sir, pronounced this academic with the napkin over his arm. . .' On the fourth

97

day they stopped for an hour or two at Lucca, and again at Pisa, where they intended to return; and at last they were at Leghorn. They found there was no room at the hotel that had been suggested to them and they had to look for another, it was dark by now; the hotel they finally found was dreadful, 'and when we woke the sleeping children, who were probably dreaming of food, to give them a meal, some began to grumble and some to cry. . . In short, next morning we decided to go in search of another hotel since, with the best will in the world on the part of the owners, we could not stay in that one without considerable discomfort; we called on Monsieur Guébhard, a banker, to whom we were recommended by my cousin [Enrico Blondel]; and this was a real change of scene: off with the wild wood and on with the beautiful drawing-room; away with all problems. . . The hotel they found with the help of the banker was good, even excellent 'as far as bed and board were concerned', but it overlooked the main street of Leghorn, via Ferdinanda, also called via Grande, which was always crowded and noisy. 'But you will say: do all your rooms overlook the street? No; in part they overlook an enclosed space that you would call in writing a "cortiletto" and in speaking "on cortinett"; but do you know what goes on there? Below here is the El Greco Café, the best in the town, and the courtyard is part of it, and for much of the day and all the evening, there are adventurers from every nation, and they talk and shout and smoke and read, in fact it's like a magic lantern show. And then above us we have Goodness knows whom getting up to Goodness knows what when we are in bed; Pietro's guess, and I don't think he's far wrong, is that they play at jumping from one chair to another ten feet away; and winning this game must be a matter for great pride and joy from the row they make.'

At Leghorn they met Antonio Benci, a Tuscan littérateur and an acquaintance of Fauriel; Benci wrote to his friend Vieusseux in Florence: 'Manzoni has been here for some days now; I have read his novel, and it was a great pleasure to meet him again: he suffers with his nerves, pays no calls, and has no wish to do so: he is travelling with his mother (daughter of the famous Beccaria), his wife (from Vevey) and six children; he will spend two months in Florence: he may be leaving here tomorrow [it was the 25th August], the health of one of his daughters permitting, and will spend a day or two at Pisa.' The daughter who was unwell was Sofia; she had taken to bed shortly after their arrival at Leghorn.

The same day, 25th August, Giulietta was writing to Fauriel for the first time since their journey began. 'I am writing all in the dark, not knowing if my letter will reach you, not knowing if you are in Paris, or if you are inclined to receive it.' As usual, Fauriel had not written for a long time. 'We have been told that you too are thinking of travelling this summer. . . Mama has done some sea-bathing, but had to give up because of some boils that developed under her arms. Papa is continuing to bathe. . . We were intending to leave Leghorn today, we've been here sixteen days and Bonne Maman can't stand the din, the confusion, the continual crowds below our balcony, the endless traffic; but our poor Sofia has been seriously ill these last days with a bilious fever, and it's only today that her temperature has gone down; the poor little thing is very run down. However, the doctor says that if things proceed as he expects, we can leave next Tuesday, 28th. . .' They had met the De Maistres who lived in the country outside Pisa; they had gone to call on them with a letter of introduction from their relative Saint-Réal. Giulietta had liked them: she had read De Maistre's *Voyage autour de ma Chambre* and other books. 'I am sending this letter to Paris, and Heaven knows where you are! In a month and a half Papa has sold the whole edition. . . This success has really exceeded all expectations.'

When they reached Florence at the beginning of September, Sofia's fever returned. Manzoni was invited to the house of the Grand Duke of Tuscany, who said he was delighted to meet him; he received the following note: 'The Marchese Corsi presents his compliments to Count Manzoni, and has the honour to inform him that tomorrow morning, Thursday, at eleven o'clock he will call to accompany him to the residence of H.R.H. the Grand Duke, who will receive him without any sort of protocol, and therefore he is asked to come in frock-coat, trousers and top hat as the writer will be, and to bring his son.' The Grand Duke had heard that he always had his son beside him. So Manzoni went with Pietro.

Then he wrote to Tommaso Grossi: 'I am half ashamed, and I'm afraid you will think vanity has turned my head to have

99

wished to be presented to the Grand Duke. Oh, now the cat's out of the bag. But I must say it was not an impulse of vanity on my part, but an excess of kindness on his. . . Suffice it to say that in the end I had almost lost all sense of embarrassment, and felt free to enjoy the conversation of a most cultured and amiable man, of excellent understanding and heart. His Highness spoke of you and of your Ildegonda and the Crusades with great esteem. . . I know that those who speak with princes always exalt their genius and their heart, especially their kindness, because this suggests one was well received. But what is that to me? That's just how it was. . . I have said nothing yet of the health of the family. Sofia, who had had a relapse, is convalescent again, thank Heaven, and this time we feel more confident that she is making a real recovery. But you can imagine how the poor little thing has enjoyed Florence. My mother is not at all pleased wih the effects of this climate: she has lost her appetite, and feels that sort of vague indisposition that is everywhere and nowhere in particular, in short she longs for Milan; and to see her like this, as you can well believe, greatly diminishes the satisfaction the youngsters and I get from our stay. Poor Enrichetta has gained nothing from it, at least as regards her most obvious trouble, unfortunately her eyes are in the same state as they were, and sometimes she says they give her even more trouble. . .' Meanwhile he was revising his novel, which consisted of seventy-one great folio sheets; at his side as advisers on points of language were Gaetano Cioni, a Florentine, 'a learned, amiable man, author of those novellas which were thought to be sixteenth-century works', and Giovanni Battista Niccolini, from Pisa, author of many tragedies. 'You know how I am occupied; I have seventy-one sheets to launder, and I wouldn't find water like the Arno or washer-women like Cioni and Niccolini anywhere but here.'

Cattaneo wrote, complaining that Manzoni did not write to him. 'If I began to count up all the miles I've covered to get your news from the various people who have the privilege of receiving it, they would perhaps come to such a total that it would have paid me to come to Tuscany myself to get it. But I am not complaining of the distance I've walked: I would go ten times the distance on such an errand. I am bemoaning the fact that I never hear: *All are well and send their love.* The persistence of Enrichetta's trouble; that intrusive gastric fever of poor little Sofia; the gloominess that seems to underlie dearest Giulietta's last letter to Giacomino, such things are not at all calculated to reassure those who love you – I almost said: more than you deserve. You will say that I too have my good share of gloom. In truth, I have no great reason to be cheerful, with the foolish life I lead. With constant lumbago into the bargain, accompanied by a delightful sore throat etc. and goodness knows what else, you will see I deserve your sympathy if I seem a bit morbid today.'

And Manzoni to Cattaneo: 'You can expect family news from me soon in person, no later than next month. Unfortunately you will see Enrichetta in the same state of health as she left home: however, although there is no outward improvement, she has gained a little strength, and I hope this will help her to overcome the local problem more quickly. Sofia is convalescent. . . Only I can claim to have benefited, which almost embarrasses me; the sea-bathing, the movement, the mental idleness, and being in Tuscany have all revived me considerably. Everyone sends their love, as you must know; but Vittoria has been pestering me for some time that she wants to write to you: I've promised to leave a space for her, so I'll pass her the pen and we'll see what she can do: *Dear Cattaneo, love, Vittoria.*'

Now Manzoni was beginning to want to return home; in the letter to Cattaneo, encouraging him to go and see Monti, he concluded: 'Will you go? I'm afraid, I really mean afraid you won't. Model yourself upon me who have become a visitor, I might almost say a vagabond. But in Milan, a nook, sofa, hearth with or without fire, my dear friends, and that's all I ask.'

Giulietta had felt homesick and unhappy in Florence; she couldn't wait to return home; her nature was melancholy, and she did not make new friends easily; she found Florence odious, the Lungarni odious, and Lamartine's daughters who called on her sometimes boring. She did not write to Fauriel from Florence; she had written to him only once from Leghorn during the journey; for too long now Fauriel had not written. Instead she wrote many letters during the journey and their stay in Florence to Cousin Giacomo Beccaria; he was the Giacomino

101

mentioned in Cattaneo's letter. This cousin was many years older than Giulietta, son of an uncle of her grandmother, and a contemporary of her father; he had a villa at Coprena, and Giulietta had often seen him when they had stayed there. From far away she thought of him with great nostalgia; he seemed the only person in the world who understood her. Cesare Contú mentioned him, when talking of the Manzoni family: 'Giacomo Beccaria was their cousin, a man of culture who moved a great deal in society, who was secretary, then counsellor to the government of Lombardy in the department of eduction. As such, he found himself in contact with men of letters and artists, he felt the importance of the name he bore and of his relationship with Manzoni, to whom he was helpful in business matters, and many times he had all the family staying at his villa of Coprena, between Milan and Como.'

Giulietta wrote to Cousin Giacomo from Florence in September: 'Oh! how this Florence lacks precision! The streets are narrow and dirty. . . It's a real undertaking to go to the Cascine. Where can you walk? On the Lung' Arno, that's to say on the bank of yellow, almost motionless water where there's nothing to see. A short, narrow space, a dirty, uneven pavement, that's the Lung' Arno. . . This morning I saw the Church of Santa Croce where there are monuments of various famous people and I quite liked that. . . Grand-Maman thinks of nothing but Milan. . . Enough! we hope to leave this so-called Paradise of Italy on the first of October if the weather is fine. The mountain we have to cross prevents Grand-Maman eating or sleeping in peace, and she talks about it all day. . . I don't know why I am so eager to get back to Milan! . . . But these beautiful things seem so sad to me, it must be a tinge of melancholy in me that I ascribe to the things I see. . . I will write to you again on Saturday, you have to enjoy these insipid, boring letters of mine to the very last! In fact, you're bound to be pleased to see us come back to Milan as at least it will bring this burdensome correspondence to an end; if I have any regret, it is that I will not receive any more of your letters which really did me good, but it has been selfish of me to force such constant labour on you, forgive me, you've finished now. . . as for me, I sometimes feel a bit embarrassed about it but I do enjoy them so much. . . We still hope to spend a few days at your delightful Coprena and

102

enjoy the sweet peace it always affords!'

So they began to prepare for the return journey. They asked the advice of Count Alessandro Oppizzoni, Chamberlain to the Grand Duke, regarding the choice of a coachman. Oppizzoni was lavish with advice. 'The journey from Florence to Bologna with the whole family, all expenses paid, with a remittance for the Hotel at Bologna, would come to 18 *zecchini*, that is 36 ten-*paoli* coins, without the gratuity for the two men; including the tip, 40 *francesconi*. . . The service includes lodging, breakfast, and midday meal; breakfast according to your choice, either coffee, and milk, and butter; or two cooked dishes of your choice. Luncheon whatever the guests like or prefer. The stop could be at Conigliaio, which is about half-way, and there's a better hotel there. It takes 11 hours including the pause at breakfast-time. From Conigliaio to Bologna 10 hours. If you want to continue your journey by carriage, you can leave Bologna at midday or one o'clock to get to Modena by evening, the second day at Parma, the third at Piacenza and the fourth at Milan.'

The return journey went smoothly. Manzoni wrote to Cioni to give him their news and to express his thanks: 'Our journey went as happily as could be; I mean there was no inconvenience except that at every step we were moving further from Florence. All those shadowy dangers which so tormented my mother beforehand, vanished the moment they took shape; the devil of the Apennines, not only was not as ugly as she had imagined him, but, by contrast, proved to be almost beautiful; and at the terrible Futa Pass, the earth, the air, and everything was so smooth and quiet that even she joined in the laughter about it. The rest of the journey also proceeded without obstacles or accidents as far as the Po, which, being in spate and having broken the bridge of boats, held us up for a day at Piacenza. We reached here on Sunday. . . What can I say now that will equal or make up for those delightful discussions in Via Campuccio and on the Lung' Arno? Nothing; nothing, unless that the desire, or the regret, or the longing I feel for them will stay with me all my life.' Cioni lived in Via Campuccio; on the Lungarno was the *Locanda delle Quattro Nazioni*, where the Manzonis stayed; it was here that Cioni and Manzoni had devoted themselves to the revision of *I promessi sposi*.

103

So it was to Cousin Giacomo that Giulietta had written so much, and he wrote friendly letters in reply. But when she saw him again in Milan perhaps she found him cold and indifferent; he had seemed close to her on the journey and during their stay in Florence, like an understanding and affectionate ghost; and suddenly, seeing him again, she did not recognize him. After all, Giacomo Beccaria had a life of his own, and it never entered his head that it might include a sentimental attachment to this young cousin. And so for Giulietta even the return was sad; her solitude increased without the tender ghost that kept her company in Florence, and with no more letters to write, for in Milan Giacomo Beccaria called on them punctually once a week, no more, no less.

Grandmother Giulia too had suffered from melancholia in Florence, but for her it was a happy return, and she could hardly believe she was in via del Morone again, among their faithful old friends, Grossi, Cattaneo, Rossari, and Torti who now came every day to give lessons to the girls. 'Do tell me if you have completely recovered from the melancholia which made your absence from home so vexatious to you and caused you such distress?' the Contessa di Camaldoli, one of their acquaintances at Florence, wrote to her several months later. 'Has the excellent Signor Alessandro felt any benefit from his journey? Are his nerves a little stronger? Is his health somewhat improved? And how is his good lady wife? Are her eyes cured? Has she got over the other troubles she was suffering from? Is dear Donna Giulietta pleased to be back in the home she so longed for, among her friends? And that fascinating little Vittoria, what is she doing? does she miss us sometimes? We often miss her and repeat all the pretty things she said. . . To tell you what we have been doing – we left the beautiful city of Flora with great regret on the 7th November. . . But we had to yield to the tyranny of circumstances. . . And now our travelling is over. . . We are living in our country house at Vomero. My husband divides his time between books and plants. I busy myself with domestic duties. . .' Now that it was all so remote the journey seemed to Grandmother Giulia a beautiful memory, rich in people, friendship and experience.

In France *I promessi sposi* appeared with the title *Les fiancés*. The translation was not by Trognon, but was signed with the initials M.G.: it was Pierre Joseph Gosselin (the initials stood for Monsieur Gosselin). When he had already translated a third of the book, Trognon had found out that the novel was in the hands of another translator and a different publisher, since there was no protection then for authors' rights, and anyone could translate or print a book without any authorisation whatsoever. So Trognon had written to tell Fauriel he was giving up the task. Ten years later Gosselin published a new edition of his translation, revised with Manzoni's help, and this time his name appeared in full.

I promessi sposi had an enormous success, whose echoes reached Manzoni from every side; he had his work cut out to answer all the letters he received. There were letters expressing admiration, emotion, and happy amazement; conferring honours; requesting his opinion of works published or to be published; asking favours; offering favours. Count Valdrighi di Modena wrote begging him to send some verses for a volume in memory of Maria Pedena, killed for love: the volume appeared with the title *Poems and autographs by learned Italians to the indomitable virtue of Maria Pedena, a virgin of Modena of great chastity who was murdered on the 1st July 1827*; in the end Manzoni had declined to contribute. Contessa Diodata Saluzzo di Roero wrote most urgently, begging him to give his opinion of her poem 'Ipazia' ('you are the greatest judge of all things poetical') and then of her collection of novellas, which Manzoni suggested she should have printed by the publisher Ferrario. Francesco Gera, an expert in botany, wrote sending him some eggs of Chinese worms, that Manzoni had heard of and that he wanted to take to Brusuglio. Manzoni wrote lengthy answers to them all. He was in good health, even if with some – with Contessa Diodata Saluzzo and the botanist Gera – he discussed his ailments and his 'weak and peevish' state of health; for her part, Contessa Diodata Saluzzo descanted upon her own nervous troubles. He had a letter from the poet Lamartine, whom he had met in Florence: 'Reading your book has restored my need to write,' and 'I assure you it is one of the 4 or 5 books which has afforded me the greatest rapture in my life.' He had a letter from Cesare Cantú, who would later become a friend but

105

whom he had not yet met; 'The book is the author. Your immortal pages make me enamoured of the extraordinary intellect and heart you certainly possess. . . It feels like a century before I can come and avail myself of your generous permission to call on you,' and he begged to be allowed to dedicate to Manzoni a 'poetic novella' he had written. He had a letter from Zuccagni Orlandini, Royal Censor of Drama, asking his permission to produce his two tragedies in a theatre in Florence. Permission was granted, and the *Adelchi* was put on; it was attended by the Grand Duke of Tuscany (with whom Manzoni had remained on friendly terms, and who called on him once when he was passing through Milan), but it was a resounding failure, as Niccolini said in a letter to the actress Maddalena Pelzet. 'For three acts people just laughed and yawned; the chorus and the fifth act met with some approval, but the actors with a deal of derision. But not a word to the Milanese about this. . .'

'My dearest Rosa,' Counsellor Somis wrote to his daughter who had been a guest of the Manzonis for a long time many years ago, and who was now married and living in Turin. 'I am sorry about the life you are leading which cannot be good for your health [apparently her married life was a fairly wretched and laborious one]. Possess your soul in patience, and commit yourself to God, but in all love, and do read *I promessi sposi*, which you will enjoy, whatever others have said, and do not choose to be mad with love for a madman. . . [obviously the father did not like the husband she had chosen]. Your sisters embrace you, as I do, praying that God will send you His divine blessing.' 'My dearest friends,' he wrote to the Manzonis, recommending a priest he had met at Susa at the house of another daughter. 'The reason I have not written to you, or to others, is that I am losing the little sight God gave me, which I have so abused. . . Last year Contessa Sclopis was more fortunate than I in seeing you and embracing you, and she talked to you about me more than she should have done. She gave me news of you, which delighted me; especially of the glory Don Alessandro has earned with his *Promessi sposi*. . . My daughters Rosa, Paolemilia, Teofila and Veturia send you their warmest greetings. . . Pray God for me as I draw to the close of my life, and love me as I love you, Donna Giulia, Donna Enrichetta and Don Alessandro, my dearest friends.'

106

Manzoni did not write to Fauriel until March 1828. Fauriel had
not written either. 'Dear friend,' wrote Manzoni, 'why was this
letter not written last year? why was it not dated from Florence?
How can it be that, thinking of somebody all the time, and feeling tormented by the need to write to him, still one does not
write? I put the question to you, as I think you know something
about it. For you know that one of the reasons for my long
silence was the uncertainty whether to begin with an apology or
a reproach.' He sent the letter by some acquaintances, Count
Taverna and his wife whom he wished to introduce to Fauriel,
and a eulogy of the couple took up a great part of his letter.
Then he listed the people he had met at Florence the previous
year who all remembered Fauriel: Niccolini, Capponi, Gior-
dani, and 'that dear, good Cioni'. Then he sent his regards to
Mrs and Miss Clarke; the latter had recently written to
Enrichetta, severely blaming Fauriel and Manzoni for never
exchanging a word of news. 'Addio; I have found a moment to
write: not as I intended, but it's time I lack at present. Would
there be any point in asking you to write? Why not? Stranger
things have happened. Addio, I press you to my heart.'

'Mon cher parrain,' Giulietta wrote to Fauriel a year later.
'My dear godfather. The other day Marietta passed on to me
your dear, kind note (for I hope you would not in all honesty
expect me to call it a letter). . .' Marietta was Maria Trotti, sister of Costanza Trotti Arconati; she was twenty, and a contemporary of Giulietta. The Trottis had a villa at Verano, near
Carate, and not very far from Brusuglio, and they were friends
of the Manzonis. Costanza Trotti Arconati and her husband,
who lived in Belgium, were friends both of the Manzonis and
of Fauriel. Maria Trotti travelled a great deal between Paris and
Milan. 'You tell us only the vaguest things about the future. . .
You know that Milan, Brusú and Coprena exist, you know the
peaceful life that goes on there, and you know the place you
hold in the hearts of those who live in them alternately, what
more can I say? You say it's impossible, so we are left longing
and regretting. . . For some time poor Papa has been more
unwell than usual, because apart from his stomach and nervous
disorders, which remain the same as ever, he has had violent
toothache which he endured for a long time, and after having
the tooth out at last, he is still suffering from neuralgia and

inflammation. Mama, too, is never well, in fact only Grand-mama always *sings a triumph song* as we say in Milan because she enjoys perfect health, and she is still as fresh and young as ever. All the children have such bad coughs that we can't help fearing whooping cough, though the doctors assure us that it's only a heavy catarrhal cough. . . We still don't know when we'll go to Brusú and whether we'll go to Genoa for the sea-bathing or elsewhere; in short, summer is drawing near and we're still not thinking about it – which is all to the good, because I hate all changes, I would always like winter to last two years, we have quite frequent storms and even hail. What a joy it would be, dear godfather, if we could see you, and you could see us all! I think you would find the grown-ups pretty much the same, but the children very different; my brother is now quite a handsome young man, taller than his father; he studies moderately and enjoys himself a lot, and spends his time with such lively youngsters that they manage to make us lively too, whether we will or no; Pietro is still mad about horses and hunting – especially horses. I really hardly know what to say about Ermes, because he has become so strange that one scarcely knows not only what to say but even what to think of him. All the other gentlemen are well except Cattaneo who suffers quite a lot from rheumatism. . .'

She wrote to him again from Coprena in October of the same year, 1829; Fauriel had written to Giulietta from Gæsbeck in Belgium, where he was the guest of the Arconatis; he had put a flower in the letter. 'I cherish the flower you sent me, you wouldn't believe the pleasure it gave me,' wrote Giulietta. 'Papa has been working hard for some time, which means he suffers much less from his stomach and nervous troubles, so he is almost always cheerful; I feel he is adopting a more youthful way of life, so he seems younger than before. . . He feels better in the country, so he can take more pleasure in everything. I am telling you this without him knowing it, because he never wants to be talked about. If you knew his friendship for you!' – Marietta was at Gæsbeck too. Giulietta liked her, but felt envious because she was there with Fauriel, helping with his correspondence and acting to some extent as his secretary. 'It takes all the friendship I feel for Marietta not to envy her too *bitterly* for all she is doing for you; I share her happiness with all my heart

108

but not without a stab of jealousy; it's true I wouldn't be such a good secretary as Marietta, but I would try so hard! . . . I said to Papa: I have given your regards to Monsieur Fauriel, as you told me to do – you've done wrong to write to him today without telling me – but I haven't closed the letter yet – ah! that's all right then, in that case tell him. . . you must tell him such a lot of things, but I wager you don't write even half of what I tell you to say. . . – the fact is, you may think a lot but you tell me nothing. . . – what? first of all, tell him everything affectionate you can think of, tell him how I wish and how I beg that he will not break his word, and will do what he promised, that I am *avid* to read what he is writing, that he should make haste for love of me, and for love of all. . .' Manzoni was referring to the *Lettres provinciales*, the book Fauriel was working on but never finishing. 'That's more or less what I remember of what he said.'

She wrote to him again in the spring of the following year. From Marietta who had returned to Italy she had heard that Fauriel was working too hard. As always, she begged him to come to Italy in the summer. She gave him news of everyone. The condition of Uncle Enrico Blondel, who had been ill for many years, was now very grave. Enrichetta was pregnant. 'Mama is having a rather difficult pregnancy, and the distress she feels continually for the appalling illness of her brother makes it worse. We would rather anything than see my uncle in such cruel spasms; for four months the most famous surgeons confess they have never seen anything like it, I am so afraid it must come to a bad end. His poor wife is more dead than alive and at times seems to be going out of her mind, so you see what a picture this unfortunate family presents.' There followed more cheerful pictures. 'I think my brother is one of the happiest young men you could meet, he sings and enjoys himself from morning till night, studies as cheerfully as others enjoy themselves, and enjoys himself desperately, like one who leads a solitary existence, which is certainly not his case. It's a different matter with the young ladies, what one does the other does, like a clock ticking quietly and regularly, which means we have no cause for complaint. Enrico is beginning to come out of his shell, his temperament is quite the opposite of his brother's, he is more concentrated and quiet, although in fact he makes more noise. . . Summer is coming, which means it's time to go to Brusú, but we haven't fixed the day yet, however, I think it will be towards the end of May to supervise the silk worms. Afterwards Papa intends to spin the cocoons in the house, which requires a lot of attention, so we'll have to stay there for Mama's confinement, which I think will be early in July. Grossi is in the country too for his silk worms. . . I don't expect you to answer this, or at the most just tell me you are well and haven't forgotten me, but two lines will do for that.'

Fauriel was preparing to set off for Provence. With Giulietta's letter went a brief note from Manzoni; both were brought by the mathematician Guglielmo Libri, who wanted to meet Fauriel, and Manzoni said in his note: 'In introducing to you a man in whom Italy takes pride, and who will give her more cause for pride each day, I am sure of doing you a particular favour. . . I am pleased and proud to be an intermediary between you; I say no more, except that I envy you both the time you will spend together.'

Before leaving, in June Fauriel also received a letter from Gæsbeck where he would not be going that year; it was from Marietta and her sister Costanza. Marietta wrote: 'Perhaps you do not know Signor Blondel is very ill, one cannot imagine worse suffering. . . Signora Blondel is desperate; she never leaves him, and her delicate health is impaired by so much anguish and fatigue. Signora Manzoni has not been well, they had to bleed her. The whole family was to move to Brusuglio at the beginning of June; Giulietta was rather upset to leave her beloved Milan. . . Poor Giulietta looks rather gloomy, surrounded as she is by so much suffering, her thoughts must be very sad. She seems especially anxious about her mother, she ends up saying: "Anyway, I hope all will turn out for the best." I hope so too, but like her cannot help feeling sad and anxious at present. I am sorry to give you these painful details. . . And you? what are your plans? Lucky you to be going to the south and seeing those beautiful places. . .' Costanza: 'Until now we've had more rain and cold than last year. . . Everywhere I turn here I find some souvenir of you, we often say on our walks: we did this walk with Fauriel, or else, just here he left us to go and work. But who knows, you may come back one day? Addio, I leave you, hoping it will be so.'

110

In July 1830, Enrichetta had a baby girl. She was called Matilde. *Cette pauvre Julie*, as Marietta called her, that poor Giulia was sent after her mother's confinement to the Grigioni to take the waters, but also because they hoped the distraction would lift her spirits. She went with family friends, Peppina Frapolli, the Marchese Lorenzo Litta and the Parravicinis. During the journey she wrote long letters to her sister Cristina: 'Andeer, 2nd August. My dear Cristina. . . After I wrote to you the other evening, we slept in the little room that Signor Litta let us have and he slept in the sitting-room on a table; there were two beds, a chest of drawers, tables, all our things and Signor Litta's, you simply couldn't move, small windows without blinds or shutters and bare new walls. Next morning we went to Mass at half past six, there were only peasants beause polite society attends the ten o'clock Mass, it was a bit of a climb to get to the ugly little chapel. . . We set off immediately after in splendid weather, arrived at the top of the San Bernardino in a fresh wind, with snow on the mountain and magnificent sunshine, there's a beautiful lake with very limpid water, we came down again very rapidly; there are about 60 hair-pin bends, but the horses here are strong and so used to it that you couldn't be afraid even if you wanted to; you go on like that for three hours down the most enchanting road. We passed through Val di Reno; words fail me to describe the imposing nature of this landscape which is sometimes really the reverse of picturesque. We thought Splugen was a lovely spot; from Splugen to Andeer the road gets more and more beautiful, we reached Andeer just as they were sitting down to luncheon, and as it was midday we did so too. The hotel here is all you could ask in size, order, cleanliness, elegance, even luxury, it presents a strange contrast with everything we've seen hitherto; during the meals a young man in a blouse, with great side-whiskers, played the harp; it was really very fine. . . I was very amused by all the serving-women here who don't even understand the signs we make to them; they just go on laughing and answering in German; when they speak proper German I understand a little and necessity has forced me to find a few words to make myself understood, it's really funny, but the local language is "Romansh", I think they call it, and you can't understand a thing. At half past three Baron Busti, who had heard you could do the whole Mala road and

111

get to Thusis and back in four hours, suggested we should go there to save a day, and we set out just as if we were going on an afternoon outing to Porta Renza, but it's a strange expedition, I assure you! I had never imagined anything so horridly beautiful. . . My heart is with you despite the mountains that separate us. . . . We eat well everywhere, the potatoes are always excellent and the butter, we have delicious strawberries, and we've even had excellent cream ices, which were a *sporgiment* [an offering, in Milanese dialect] from Signor Battaglia, who does a great deal for this place. . . We always travel in an open carriage so we don't lose any of the view or the air which often makes you open your mouth to gulp in as much as possible.' '3rd August, San Bernardino. This morning we left Andeer at five, the journey went quite well, though we did have a bit of a storm on the San Bernardino so that I was quite stunned when we got out of the carriage. Signor Litta was the first to bring us your letters which gave me more joy than I can express! I could think of nothing else, to such an extent that I hardly greeted Signor Litta or the other people around me; it was midday, so we were sitting at table, and I put your letters under the tablecloth; we were about 50 at table, and three musicians were playing: you can imagine how wretched I was; some familiar tunes, indeed the whole thing, brought tears to my eyes so that I had to hide my letters altogether and come and read them and cry my fill in my room! San Bernardino is really very dreary, and it's terribly cold.

'Tomorrow I intend to start taking the waters. I am feeling more or less the same, that's to say I haven't time to think of my health, and I can't eat just what I fancy; today I'm *dog-tired*. But Cristina, please write so that I can at least guess what you're trying to say! You reproach me, I don't know which of us is justified, it really is maddening, I want to devour your letters and I can't even read them. Tell my good Mademoiselle Burdet that I was more than grateful for her note. But most particularly tell Mama I'll write to her Saturday, it's impossible today because if I want to say all that's in my heart in answer to her letter, I need to devote myself to her entirely; say I'm sure she'll understand. . . and *bonne Maman*; and Papa! Dear Cristina, there are no words to express what I feel for these dear people! Give my love to everyone at home, and the doctor. My cousin has written, I am truly grateful and I'll send him a line in haste to tell him so; he says the Lodonio girls are getting married, I'm very pleased to hear it. . . I can't wait to be with you, however hard I try to enjoy myself. . . Don't let Mademoiselle go, for goodness sake!' The cousin who had written was Giacomo Beccaria; this letter from him and the line of greeting she sent him from the Grigioni marked the end of a relationship which perhaps had brightness and intensity in her heart only.

Giulietta did not write to Fauriel, and he had news of her from Costanza Arconati who sent him a short letter from Brussels. In France the last of the Bourbons, Charles X, had been deposed in July, and Louis Philippe d'Orléans had succeeded him. It was a great event for European Liberals. Costanza wrote: 'I feel I must tell you how happy we are and rejoice with you at the great happenings in your country. We have been living a new life for the last few days, we first heard the news on the way back from Germany when we were still a day's journey from Brussels. Peppino [her husband] would like to set off at once for Paris with Berchet. Tell me if this is wise. I am more than eager to return to France, in two months perhaps. You will have heard of Enrichetta's safe confinement, but you won't know that Giulia has gone to take the waters at Saint Moritz with Signorina Frapolli, or that Alessandro, Pietro and Grossi were to leave for Geneva at the end of July, I hope they are there to rejoice freely in the happenings in France.' Fauriel replied: 'You know the facts as well as I do; I can only repeat what millions have already said everywhere. I need not tell you of my immense joy: that would be as unnecessary as to tell you all the rest. All that remains is to proceed to the consequences of this great and just event, and everything justifies the hope that they will be as happy as possible. I see not the slightest objection to Peppino and Berchet coming here when they like; they need take no particular precautions except to make sure their passports are in order. . . Everything is calm and peaceful here as if nothing had happened. . . Do come, as soon as possible! I heard Enrichetta's baby had arrived safely; as for Giulia's journey, I knew nothing of that, but I am pleased. I am also very pleased that Grossi and Alessandro are appearing, it will be a great pleasure for them to breathe on this side of the Alps; I only pity them the moment of return. . . Young Count Libri, whom

113

I met recently when he brought me a letter from Giulia, bore himself admirably in our recent events. . . I wish Italy many men like him. Other Italians also gave an excellent account of themselves. Some Englishmen were magnificent. I think all the nations of Europe were represented in this victory, which is as much European as French.'

Manzoni, Grossi and Pietro did not go to Geneva. The Manzonis remained at Brusuglio. Enrico Blondel died in Milan on 4 September, and his wife, *tante Louise*, tried to poison herself. In October, Enrichetta became ill with bronchitis. She could not shake off the fever. 'I wanted to write to you about the distressing news I have heard of dearest Enrichetta,' Bishop Tosi wrote to Manzoni, 'The Marchese [Parravicini] was so kind as to give me more precise information, and to reassure me.' In December a friend of Manzoni, Abbé Giudici, wrote to Bishop Tosi: 'Do you know that Enrichetta has had a recurrence of the bronchitis she had in October? They have bled her six times. But now there is reason to hope that the remaining slight fever will be passing over. But such a weakening illness could be fatal to a feeble constitution. It's lucky that Alessandro and Donna Giulia have the gift of seeing everything through rose-tinted spectacles.' Manzoni to Diodata Saluzzo in December: 'When I received your very kind letter, my wife had succumbed to a tracheal inflammation, which yielded only at the seventh bleeding. Now, thank Heaven, the illness is past, and there remains only the problem of a long and weary convalescence.'

In March 1831 Massimo d'Azeglio appeared in the Manzoni household. He was then thirty-three. He had recently lost his father. Manzoni had corresponded with the father years before on literary topics. He came with a letter from his brother Roberto, whom Manzoni had met for a few minutes in Genoa. Cesare Cantú wrote of the d'Azeglios in his *Reminiscences:* 'Alessandro had had a literary correspondence with Marchese Cesare Tapparelli d'Azeglio (1763-1830). . . Cultured, pious, a monarchist like most of the Piedmontese aristocracy, Cesare was editor of the newspaper *L'amico d' Italia*. . . Of the three sons, whom he brought up strictly in honour and piety, Luigi became a Jesuit, and distinguished himself in jurisprudence and philosophy; the first-born, Roberto, was an artist, and upheld the honour of the family in Turin; Massimo devoted himself to landscape painting and led a free, artistic life in the Romagna and in Tuscany.'

Massimo had also lived in Rome for a long time, where he had had an affair with a lady, Contessa Morici, by whom he had a daughter, little Bice; then the Contessa had left him; this hurt him very much, and he had left Rome and lived in his father's house at Turin for some time; on the death of his father, he had decided to settle in Milan. 'In Milan I found the Germans,' Massimo d'Azeglio recounted in *My Memories*, 'which was not appealing; but was Carlo Felice any more appealing, *felicissimo* as he was to rule on their behalf? I wanted to apply myself to the study and exercise of the arts, and I felt one might die of consumption in Turin, where the arts were tolerated about as much as Jews in a ghetto. In Milan, on the other hand, an artistic movement had arisen from a combination of many circumstances, and of many distinguished men who had come together there.'

Besides being a painter, Massimo d'Azeglio had been writing for some time. He had begun and got quite a long way with an historical novel, but he did not mention it to Manzoni at that time, as he had been intimidated by some of the ideas Manzoni had expressed to him on historical novels. He was tall, slim and strong, with well-marked features, a large nose, large moustache and large eyes. Cantú said in the *Reminiscences:* 'Manzoni admired in d'Azeglio that all-round ability he lacked: he played, sang, danced, rode, fenced, played billiards and cards.' Perhaps Manzoni did admire him at their first meetings, but with a vague uncertainty and reserve; but Grandmother Giulia liked this visitor enormously and at once, because 'he played, sang, danced'; this worldly self-possession, boldness and ease of manner and bearing took her back to figures of men who had fascinated her in her youth.

Massimo d'Azeglio, in coming to call on the Manzonis, had two precise purposes: to talk about his historical novel, and to see what the eldest daughter was like, possibly with a view to matrimony. He did not dare talk of the novel, as has been said; but he did write asking for Giulia's hand in marriage; it was the 9th of April, not many weeks after his first call.

115

'May I say I have come to Milan expressly to make the acquaintance of your family. I wanted to meet you and you cannot fail to understand my motive and all that it means to me. Then I wanted to know your daughter of whom my family had spoken highly, and this was confirmed by all I saw and heard on coming to Milan. Without more ado, may I say from the heart that I should consider myself only too happy to be your son-in-law.

'My income is 21 thousand francs, which I do not yet enjoy in full, as I have to pay annuities to my mother, some uncles and other family pensioners, but I shall do so when I have the misfortune to lose the former, whose heir I am. . . I shall be disposed to spend the winter in Milan, and the summer at d'Azeglio or elsewhere. My work has borne fruit hitherto, and may bear more fruit in the future: and I do not think this is contrary to your way of thinking. Which means, this income may also be calculated among my possibilities. As for myself, in part you already know me, but you may easily make further enquiries in Turin.

'For now I have little to add. . . The matter speaks for itself. I can not flatter myself that I deserve the most important consent, that of your daughter, but I cannot renounce all hope of obtaining it.

'If she had reasons to reject my proposal, having placed such trust in her, I feel sure the whole matter will remain buried for ever. I would leave Milan, and I do not think my conduct would give rise to gossip. After being received into your house in such a friendly manner, it would be a great grief to me to cause you one moment of displeasure.

'If you feel we can enter into discussion, please write me a line, suggesting a time when you are free, and I will call on you. Any time suits me, as I have no other business in Milan.'

Manzoni was certainly pleased with this letter. He talked about it to Enrichetta and his mother. He weighed up the advantages: he had known the father well; he knew the brother a little; he knew they were a family of sound principles. Giulietta was questioned; she seemed doubtful. She asked for a week to think it over.

Manzoni answered the letter, expressing his own consideration, and that of all his family, for d'Azeglio: 'You cannot fail to have seen in us the high esteem which your character and talents must inspire in all who know you. I am only doing justice to my daughter's feelings in saying she is included in this "we". But will it seem strange to you that she asks for a week to reflect? . . . My daughter has always felt a difficulty which has hitherto seemed insuperable to her, that of uniting herself to someone who is not from her own part of the world; as it seems equally painful to her to think of moving away, or to impose, in such an important matter, upon the delicacy at least of the person in whose will she must submerge her own.'

D'Azeglio sent Enrichetta a small painting of his (he had already sent some of his lithographs) asking her to give it to her daughter. The note was in French, and was signed 'Maxime de Zey'. In fact, it had been his mother and his brother Roberto who had jointly encouraged him in this marriage plan. Now his mother was anxious. She had asked for detailed information 'about this girl and the family'. 'I know it's a good name, the mother was not well-born, she has passed on, she was a lady of exceeding virtue and brought blessings upon that House, especially upon her husband, who abjured philosophism and turned to a godly life. To tell you the truth, I think some leaven of his old maxims remained in him, especially as he has been ensnared by Jansenists. If this is so, I do not know to what extent or how much it may have influenced the moral upbringing in the home. [Perhaps her information was incorrect or unclear, because she seemed to think Enrichetta was dead.] I think of you a hundred times a day, my Massimo, of your affairs, of the important knot you are about to tie, and I pray, and urge other good souls to pray, that all will turn out for your eternal salvation, and for your peace here below if it please the Lord to grant you happy issue in this.' Then she heard that they must wait a week for a decision; she was pleased 'at the importance the young lady accords to such a step, and if the answer is Yes, you will have good grounds to hope that Heaven has ratified this decision.'

D'Azeglio wrote to Manzoni: 'Though the heart finds the delay long, reason must bid it be silent, and I am deeply grateful that your daughter did not deny me all hope, and that she fixed upon a term so reasonable. The feelings she cannot fail to inspire show me that her happiness is a necessity to me and always will be, and for this reason I want her to reflect upon the proposal, and not to delude herself in the slightest on my account; if I were to obtain my heart's desire by fomenting the smallest delusion, I should feel everlasting remorse. I think you all view me too indulgently; I have many faults that I know, and perhaps more than I know. To name one, despite my strongest efforts my temperament is not always equable, perhaps because my nerves are very sensitive. Then, as you see, I am not and never will be rich: for myself I am most happy and thank God for it, for I have found that the desire to possess more than a just and modest competence is a bottomless pit; but I cannot speak for others. And from now until the time when it shall please God to take from me the person who loves me most and whom I have loved most in this world, not only am I not rich, but our circumstances must be somewhat straitened: for the first time in my life I wish for riches, but I have none, and I must say so. The modesty of my present income would perhaps make it advisable to spend some months in the summer at Azeglio, to do as the ant does and enjoy more ease in the winter. The countryside at Azeglio is the loveliest in the world, but the castle has no real beauty, only good air and beautiful views, and local people who feel great affection for me and my family. Then, regarding the problem of my not being Milanese etc., I think I have solved that in advance. If I announced that I have just resolved to settle here, I should be claiming a false merit. But I tell you in all truth that this was my intention in any case. Having striven for many years to learn the principles of my art, I have perhaps reached the age when I may hope to produce some fruit: in all Italy Milan is the place most suited to my purpose, so that your daughter's delicacy, truly worthy of a noble soul, may be set entirely at rest. . . I therefore await the end of this week, during which I hope you will not forbid me to come and spend a few moments with you all in the evening. . .'

Manzoni: 'I can give no better answer to your amiable request than to tell you it was my intention to assure you yesterday evening that you would do us a great favour by calling on us during this time. I was only prevented by the fear of forcing your kindness in some way. You will not be surprised to fnd a certain person a little embarrassed.'

In the course of that week, Giulietta tried to imagine her own future existence beside this being who was strange to her in every way. She must have compared him with the image of Cousin Giacomo, familiar to her from childhood. Cousin Giacomo was for her like the clear, still water of a lake that had always existed in the landscape of her thoughts, in which she could see her reflection, and whose shores and shades she had always known. With this calm, reflective temperament, Cousin Giacomo was an older, reassuring presence. Perhaps she had never seriously thought she might marry him. He had proved cold and distant towards her, at a certain point, and she had been hurt. But the suffering was more in the nature of idle melancholy than bitter pain. Anyway, it was a closed book. But she could not help knowing her heart needed quiet and abhorred adventure. This evening caller who was manifesting such a hasty desire to marry her, that nose, those whiskers, those eyes, that dazzling ease did nothing to reassure her. That figure would never assume, at her side, the lovable strength of a father figure. And this was what she needed. Perhaps because her father was too self-absorbed to listen to her. Perhaps because there were so many children, and her father and mother could not give her the attention, time and availability she secretly wanted. She wanted someone who understood her, as she had imagined Cousin Giacomo did when she was writing to him from Florence, or as she had imagined Fauriel understood her when she was writing to him. How many letters she had written to one and the other! Both Fauriel and Cousin Giacomo were familiar, friendly figures, and at the same time remote, because they wanted nothing specific from her. The newcomer, on the other hand, said he wanted to marry her.

Less than a week after the proposal, Giulietta said no. Manzoni had to convey her refusal to d'Azeglio: 'I must tell you that my daughter has been unable to decide upon a step which, truth to tell, was very far from her thoughts.'

D'Azeglio to Manzoni, 14 April: ' I could not answer your letter immediately, as I was about to leave for a dinner-party which I could not decently fail to attend. You can imagine whether I enjoyed the occasion!

'I pray that God will turn the affliction which your daughter's final reply has caused me to as much good and happiness for her! God knows these prayers come from my heart: and if they are granted she will have nothing to wish for in this world. As

119

for me, it is God's will, all I can do is bow my head.

'Your lady-mother has shown such kindness towards me, and such concern that my desires should be fulfilled that I shall remember her with eternal gratitude.

'So I thank you all for the amiability and concern you have shown me on this occasion. Perhaps I will not find it in my heart to come in person to say my last goodbye; I am sure you understand my motive in that it would not enter your head that there could be the slightest trace of bitterness toward you in my heart. Indeed, if I knew at what moment I might find you, it would give me real satisfaction to take my leave of you before setting off.'

Manzoni to d'Azeglio, the same day: 'The distress you are so kind as to express is for me an added reason for gratitude: and you must know that we share it. This is one of those painful situations in which everyone suffers and no one is to blame. . . As for me, you can imagine how eager I would be to take advantage of the friendly readiness you express to see me; but I must tell you that a strange nervous disorder has for many years prevented me from going out unaccompanied. Therefore I am encouraged by your kindness to say that I am at home, usually in a little study on the ground floor, until two, and that you are more likely to find me alone after midday.'

Grandmother Giulia had insisted that Giulietta should accept. She was her favourite grandchild, and it hurt her to see her always so sad, pale, listless, and apparently resigned to a solitary fate. This d'Azeglio seemed to her a most attractive figure; she could not bear to think of him disappearing; she thought Giulietta would regret it bitterly later. She did not give in; she went on insisting. She was the most authoritative member of the household, warm, impulsive, incautious, even reckless in her propositions; Enrichetta, on the other hand, was prudent, cautious and discreet. As for Giulietta, she probably felt, together with the fear of marriage, the fear of growing old in the rooms of this house; she was twenty-three; seven years older than her mother when she got married. She made up her mind. So it fell to Manzoni to write another letter to d'Azeglio in which he begged him to discount the refusal which had gone before: 'Your way of proceeding with us inspires me in such confidence and prompts me to such freedom that the very doubt

120

that one word can produce an effect so much desired by you and by us is sufficient for me to want to say that word to you, however strange it may seem. You will understand that I refer to a reopening of yesterday's conversation. If you feel it is still possible to speak on that subject, be so good as to suggest a time or simply to come, and ask them to call me to my study if you don't find me there; if you feel otherwise, I shall at least have the satisfaction of having hinted at something other than what I was mortified to say in my last letter to you.'

D'Azeglio sent his mother a portrait of Giulietta and the news that all had gone well. His mother replied: 'And so, my dearest, sweetest Massimo, let us thank God. . . I confess, my dear, I had no peace last night, thinking all the time, who knows what news the post will bring me? My Massimo will be consoled, or a prey to bitter pain! I resigned myself, but in my heart of hearts I was saying if the Lord grants my wishes I shall indeed be happy; and so it went on till morning and the moment when this letter of blessing came into my hands. . . I should like you to send me a copy of the latest edition of Don Abbondio. I read it too hastily last time, and all I remember is that he was an honest fellow.' She liked the portrait: 'You have certainly shown good taste, the character of the face is gentle.' And to Giulietta: 'Yes, my dear Giulietta, I love you already, because the Lord has chosen you to be the wife of my son. . . My prayers are fully answered; I was longing to see him united with someone who would know how to discern his qualities, and the beautiful soul within the young man. . . My consolation will be complete when I embrace you and call you my daughter. With all my heart I am your loving mother.'

Meanwhile Costanza Arconati was writing to Fauriel from Brussels at the end of April:

'Not knowing whether or not you have heard what I am about to announce, I am writing the very moment I have heard it myself. Marietta has had a letter from Giulia saying that she is about to get married to someone she loves and who loves her. It is Signor d'Azeglio, a Piedmontese, a friend of Collegno [this was Giacinto Collegno who would later become a brother-in-law of the Arconatis, by marrying one of the Trotti sisters, Margherita] and worthy to be so. He has spent the winter at Milan, attracted by the reputation of Manzoni, and has fallen in love

121

with the daughter. Poor Giulia seems by every word in her letter to be at the zenith of happiness. Signor d'Azeglio is settling in Milan, not to take Giulia away from her family. I imagine Enrichetta and Alessandro and *donna* Giulia are very pleased about this marriage (Giulia forgot to say) because it also represents what the families wanted, but it was decided by mutual affection. I take great pleasure in this happy event myself, I have heard a lot about d'Azeglio from Collegno; he really is a distinguished man. The choice he has made proves it, don't you think?'

Massimo and Giulietta got married on 21 May. They went to the Castello d'Azeglio where they spent part of the summer. Pietro was their guest at the castle, as well as Cesare Balbo, cousin of the d'Azeglios and friend of Massimo. In July Giulietta wrote to her father. It is a letter that reveals a determination to be a happy wife and to seem so. 'Now I must tell you something that requires the permission of my husband but a smile was his only response and this is sufficient to absolve me from the bond of secrecy. . . For some time Massimo has been working on an historical novel. . . He wanted to mention it to you and in fact one evening, before our marriage was discussed, he introduced the subject of historical novels, perhaps you will remember what you said to him then; . . . this so discouraged him that he put away his papers and did not confess his secret to me till we were betrothed, on condition that I would tell nobody. It cost me a great deal, but I obeyed him, I tried to persuade him to talk to you about it but his courage always failed him. In Turin his cousin, Count Balbo who knows his work reproved him strenuously for neglecting it like this, Massimo told him the reason for his discouragement and Balbo said he should chance all to win all and that he must complete a work composed with such care, seeing that he has already planned some lithographs illustrating the most striking passages. Massimo had always promised to let me see his manuscript but now that he has regained a little courage in Turin he has been reading it aloud in the evenings. As they say, I don't know anything about it and I ought not to speak of it because I am persuaded in advance that everything Massimo does must be done well, but I still maintain that I understand enough to be able to say that anyone who was not Massimo's wife would be very pleased with his work. I find in it a very clear, fluent style, facts well related, a very well contrived plot, and descriptions worthy of a skilful painter. . . However, you will judge for yourself, so I shall say no more. . . The battle of *Barletta* is the dénouement of the novel, Cesare Borgia plays an important part in it, but all this is more sketched in than described. Pietro is delighted with it. I look forward eagerly to a word from you, but do not imagine that I expect a letter, dear Papa; just write a word on the back of the letters the others write to me, so that I can encourage Massimo to work. . . I have written this hastily and very badly, and I do beg your pardon. My mother-in-law sends you her most sincere greetings. Addio, my dearest Father, remember that the affection you show me brings happiness to one who is so proud to call herself your daughter, and who combines with the general admiration the most profound devotion and filial love.' Giulietta seems suddenly to have realized the public importance of her father, or rather she now views it from outside, warming herself at his fame in the strange landscape she has come to live in.

Besides, she must have realized that d'Azeglio had married her because she was Manzoni's daughter. Awareness of this gave her, in her marriage, both unhappiness and strength.

Manzoni informed them that he was willing to hear the novel. D'Azeglio himself should read it aloud when they met again, after the summer. So d'Azeglio wrote to him:

'I think that in principle your arguments against the historical novel cannot be refuted; certainly not by me. But I also doubt if the time will ever come when your opinion will be adopted by the masses, and in the meantime I feel this genre, although imperfect, might be put to use for the general good. . . Comparing what has been written, painted and engraved by the French in particular about the glorious events of their nation, with what the Italians have done to illustrate theirs, I feel there is so much pride on one side and so much modesty on the other, that I could not help wishing that we too might learn to boast a little of things that are true. . . Then thinking over the Italian events that might form a series, I hit upon Barletta's challenge and tried to paint a picture of it. When I had finished the painting, I thught one might enliven it (you will say spoil it) with some sort of a plot, and so it went from one day to another and

123

I found myself filling five or six notebooks; and Balbo kept me at it by goading me like an ox whenever I stopped.

'Dear Papa, please kiss the hands of Mama and Grandmother for me, and give them my fondest greetings; you must take my opinions in good part; from Mama's letter I see they are disposed to digest my story. It takes some courage to arrive in the Manzoni household *un gros manuscrit à la main*, and start reading as if it were nothing at all! But I say to myself 'Vouran minga coupam'. [They won't want to kill me'] – God knows if I am right – . . . Tomorrow we are going to the Baths: our address Aosta by Courmayeur.' His mother added at the bottom of this letter: 'Our dear young people set off yesterday morning for Cormaior in good health: I hope the air will restore Giulia completely; her departure caused me a pang at heart: I love her so much and every day I see more clearly that she will bring happiness to Massimo.'

The novel was read aloud to Manzoni in the sitting-room at via del Morone, at the end of the summer; Enrichetta and Giulia, Grossi and Manzoni were there to listen to it; when it was finished, Manzoni said: 'A strange profession, a man of letters, anyone can take it up from one day to the next! Here's Massimo; he takes it into his head to write a novel and lo and behold, he doesn't do at all badly!' He found some stylistic negligence here and there, especially in the last pages; he offered to revise them, d'Azeglio said 'please go ahead'. (The novel appeared two years later. It was called *Ettore Fieramosca*. It had been revised by Manzoni and printed by the usual publisher, Ferrario of via San Pietro all' Orto. It was a great success.)

Massimo and Giulietta went to live in an apartment in via del Durino, that Enrichetta had prepared for them.

In August Enrichetta wrote to her cousin Carlotta de Blasco, to whom she had not written for many years. Her cousin had married a Signor Fontana and lived in Savona.

'I cannot reproach myself for one moment of indifference or forgetfulness, indeed I cannot, my dear cousin; you will have heard how I have often had long periods of wretched health, you will have heard that for several years I was quite incapable of reading or writing a word because of my sight, which, although a little better now, still does not allow any prolonged concentration, and if I can write, it's partly force of habit and always with difficulty. . . . What changes there have been since we met, dear Carlotta! It seems a century!

'You must know what a big family I have, I must tell you a bit about my children, 8 in number, although I had 12 births, but the children God deigned to preserve to me are robust and quite well endowed by nature, all having, thank God, good characters and intelligence. As you have heard, my daughter Giulia had the good fortune last May to marry the Marchese Massimo Taparelli d'Azeglio, a most accomplished young man, and it would take too long to tell you about her surpassing happiness. After Giulia comes my son Pietro who is already a full head taller than his father, he is 18, then comes Cristina who is 16, Sofia 14, Enrico 12, Vittorina 9, Filippo 5 and a half and my little Matilde who is only 13 months and so dear to me, she is as fascinating to us as if she were our first baby.'

In August she wrote to Costanza Arconati, who had come to see her parents on their country estate at Bellagio but had not had time to see the Manzonis before returning to Belgium. Her sister Marietta, however, was still in Italy with their parents. 'I am sorry about you, dear friend, but I can't help feeling pleased at the idea of seeing her sometimes in Milan [Marietta]; Giulia will be delighted. I also heard from our dear son and daughter today [Giulietta and Massimo], letters that convey nothing but happiness and love for us. . . . We have heard nothing from Monsieur Fauriel, we read in the newspapers about his post [Fauriel had been given the chair of foreign literature at the Sorbonne], thank you for giving us news of him; and we shall be most grateful if you will give him our news, and assure him of our sincere and constant friendship.'

In August Vittoria, who was then nine, was sent to Lodi to the College of the Madonna Delle Grazie, run by the The English Ladies; her mother was too tired and too poorly to take charge of her education. Signora Cosway, the painter who many years ago in Paris had painted the portrait of Grandmother Giulia as a young woman, had settled in Lodi some time ago, where she had founded *The House of the English Ladies;* Vittoria was recommended to her, and she gave regular news of the little girl.

125

Enrichetta wrote to Vittoria, on the last day of August:

'How many times since you left, my little darling, have I looked all round for you, how many times have I thought I heard your voice! . . . and when my motherly solicitude questions instinctively where you can be, my heart answers: "she is in a safe place, and in good hands. . ." And then the pain your absence causes is partly relieved. Yes, I think you will be better there than if you were still with your Mama, who is prevented by her poor health and the occupations inevitable in such a large family from taking such care of you as her duty and mother love would wish.

'Your sisters Cristina and Sofia are with you in heart and mind, and I often hear them saying to each other: "Vittorina will be having breakfast now, now it's her dinner time. . . now her playtime. . ."; or they wonder: "what is our Vittorina doing now?" and I say: "she will be good and happy. . . she promised me. . ."

'Your brother Pietro, your sisters, Enrico, and even little Filippo send their fondest love. Filippo just said: "Why hath Vittoria gone away, Mama? I wis' she hadn't gone; tell her lots and lots of kisses from Filippo." Your little sister Matilde gets sweeter every day, and I pass on a little kiss from her. Your sister Giulia and her Massimo wanted to come and see you yesterday, but they were prevented. . . . Your Papa and Grandmother give you a big hug, and so does your Nanny, who is so sad not to have her Vittorina with her any more.'

Grandmother Giulia to Vittoria:

'My dearest little girl! Your letter gave me so much pleasure, dear Vittorina! I thank you for the consolation it brings to my old age. It seems the Lord is blessing the sacrifice we made in sending you away like this to put you in that sanctuary where virtue and learning are drawn from the holy faith that ennobles all things and consoles for all things. Oh my dear Vittorinetta! you are with a friend I value so highly, Mme Cosway: a happy instinct made you love her as soon as you met her – so what must your affection and obedience be by now? One is so willing to obey those one loves! . . .

'So you still remember my impatience, little *espiègle* [tease]? Unfortunately it occurs rather often, and I think a little patience may be better than a prayer. Our Divine example was so gentle, especially with little children! . . .

'My little pet, I hope we shall soon be able to come and see you; but you know that when we are at Brusuglio there are always so many things that make it difficult for us to get away. Giulia is here with her husband, but today they've gone to Milan for the exhibition of Massimo's paintings; people are mad about them. You will understand that I am *bien charmée* about it: an old grandmother has to be forgiven for a little vanity. . .

'Papa, Mama, your sisters and brothers, your Nanny all send lots of love. Your Filippo sends you lots of kisses; he is such an engaging little pet, and loves you so much.'

Enrichetta to Vittoria some time between the autumn of that year 1831 and the winter of the following year 1832:

'As Sunday was Massimo's feast-day, your sisters sent him beautiful bunches of flowers, and I decided to send him one in your name, so that you should not be forgotten. . .'

'Yesterday your poor father came home quite upset, because he had seen a little girl who looked just like his Vittorina, and he couldn't help embracing her. . .'

'The day before yesterday was Papa and Mama's wedding anniversary, and Giulia and Massimo asked us all to dinner to celebrate it; oh, how we missed our Vittorina!'

'Today is Papa's birthday, and the d'Azeglios want us to celebrate it at their house. We will go, but in my heart I will be feeling all the time the absence of my Vittorina; but Filippo and Matilde won't be there either, they will stay home and have *leur petit dîner* with Nanny; Filippo thinks this is a real treat, as he'll be *master of the house*.'

In the spring Enrichetta went to see Vittoria at Lodi. Then she wrote:

'My dear Vittorinetta! I am still drowned in the joy of seeing you yesterday. You can imagine how eagerly the whole family surrounded me on my arrival here, to know how you were, and if I had found you happy and *potelée* [dimpled]. Your dear Papa, in particular, couldn't stop asking me questions. . . In short, my good little girl, though we are obliged to send you away for your education, our hearts and our loving care are with you always.'

And again, Enrichetta to Vittoria in May:

'I know your heart is loving and good, you have always been

127

so sensible and well-behaved, wishing for everything that can uplift the soul to God, that I can have no fears on that score: but I do fear that you may be less than whole-hearted at your studies, which is quite natural at your age, but which may easily be corrected by making an effort, tackling your work zealously, and making up for lost time.

'Always try, my little one, to behave so that no one should ever have cause to reprove you, if you do not want your poor Mama to feel distressed at the thought that you might be upset. Oh, you don't know what it does to a mother's heart to think of her little girl shedding a tear far away! . . .'

Towards the end of May, Matilde became seriously ill. For a few days they were afraid they were going to lose her. Then she began to recover. Enrichetta to Vittoria:

'I won't conceal the fact that our dear little babe has been very ill, but God deigned to answer our prayers and to allow the medicines to produce their salutary effect; and so our dear baby was preserved.

'The poor little thing was suffering from severe inflammation of the chest: we had to apply leeches twice, and draw off a great deal of blood. Now little Matildina is breathing regularly in her sleep, and takng her medicines and broths like a good girl. She is very weak and does not move from the position we put her in, we take the greatest care to make no noise around her, now and then she opens her eyes, recognizes us, smiles and says our names in a tiny voice, and she often makes me put my face close to hers and gives me lots of little kisses. You can imagine the joy we all feel, after the fears and anguish of these last days.'

Enrichetta to Vittoria, from Brusuglio, in the summer:

'Matilde is recovering like a flower: the colour is coming back to her delicate cheeks, and her little legs are starting to carry her around again.'

The doctors told her it would do both her and Matilde good to go to the sea. So some of the family set off for Genoa. They stopped for a few hours at Pavia where they lunched with Bishop Tosi. From Genoa, Enrichetta to Vittoria: 'We travelled all night. At 6 in the morning we stopped for a while at Ronco, to shake off the dust, and drink coffee, and at half past 11 we reached Genoa, stifled with the heat and dust. We are staying at the same hotel as last time, when you were with us – do you remember?'

Enrichetta to Vittoria, from the Castello d'Azeglio, on her return from Genoa, in August:

'We reached Azeglio on the 18th, after a good journey. The dear inhabitants of the castle were not expecting us until nightfall, and we took them by surprise at 11 in the morning: you can imagine our mutual delight! We are enchanted with this beautiful situation. The castle, which is very old, overlooks lovely hills and a charming little lake. My days are very peaceful here. We share the happiness God has granted to our Giulia. Her Massimo is loved and venerated by everyone around, and he is considered Lord of the district. . . . My heart beats so fast at the thought that in a few days I shall see gathered together around me, at our dear *Brusú* all my dearest children, my riches and my happiness!'

Grandmother Giulia gave a lively description to Uncle Beccaria's wife of that same visit to the d'Azeglios:

'When it was morning we set off for Azeglio, which we reached about midday. I need hardly tell you what an affectionate and demonstrative welcome we received from these dear people: Giulia is a bit thin; on the other hand she is getting bigger (three months), she is in good health, eating well and has a good colour etc. And her Massimo still the same charming fellow. The good Mama [Marchesa Cristina] looking younger, quick as a bird, cheerful and happy, she walks, plays bowls, and in the evening tombola, her favourite game. There are elegant ladies here, who call in the evening; I could give you so many details, but I'd never finish.'

From Brusuglio, in September, Enrichetta to Vittoria:

'Everyone likes Massimo's paintings very much – he has put four big ones and several small ones in the Exhibition in Milan: we are delighted to see how much this new style of painting is appreciated, and how our Massimo is esteemed for all his rare qualities. . . . You are still too small to understand these things properly, but I wanted you to know that this brother of yours is a joy to us, and that you can join us in thanking God for the happiness He has granted dear Giulia. . . .'

Vittoria spent October at Brusuglio; then went back to the college. Enrichetta to Vittoria:

'My eyes followed the coach as it carried you out of the gate-

129

way until I could see it no more. . . My heart follows you all the time. Later I went to church with Enrico, and you can imagine with what a full heart I offered up to God the pain that oppressed me that day. . .

'Everyone loves you dearly. Our chubby Filippo cannot be consoled for your departure, and sends you a thousand kisses, and Matilde often calls *Vittodia Vittodia!*'

Enrichetta to Vittoria:

'My dear Vittorina, continue to be loving, compassionate and gentle with your companions at all times. . . it is so sweet to be loved!'

Enrichetta to Vittoria, the 26 December:

'You gave me a treat on *your* feast-day on Sunday, as you managed to make your little letter reach me that very day. . . . I received it in the evening, and it answered a real need. It was the first time since your birth that I have spent Saint Victoria's Day without hugging you in my arms. . . I hope you had a happy Christmas. . . We spent it quietly together. Giulia and Massimo dine here and spend the evenings with us, together with the usual friends who come to visit us, and who all ask after you. . .'

Enrichetta to Vittoria, on New Year's Day:

'Our little Vittorina must have some of the New Year *crescenza* [a sort of 'panettone', or large Milanese cake]: it was made by *Jean* [the servant] who made one like it for us, and we want our Vittorina to share in all our little pleasures. – My dear Vittorina, I send the loving wishes of everyone in the family that the new year which is beginning today will be all happiness, holiness and gaiety. . .'

On the 10th January that year, 1833, Giulietta gave birth to a baby girl. Enrichetta to Vittoria:

'I am writing in haste to tell you that you are an aunt. Last night, beween 3 and 4 o'clock, your sister had a lovely little baby girl. But God does not wish our happiness to be complete, for this poor little mite was born before her time; and she cries continually and is so extraordinarily small that we feel she may not live. I am writing to you from the sitting-room which is next to the bedroom, and I have the poor little mite with me, crying all the time so that it breaks my heart. Your Nanny is holding her on her lap, and trying to make her swallow some drops of sugared water. There are moments when we hope our cares may succeed in keeping her alive, but we must always say: "God's will be done! . . ." I was happy to be a grandmother as you to be an aunt; so let us go on hoping, dear Vittorina!'

Enrichetta to Vittoria, ten days later:

'Unhappily we are very much afraid this poor little mite may not live. I don't want to hide our fears from you, so that your little heart may learn to be resigned to what God wills for us; meanwhile we pray, my good little daughter. . .'

And about the same time, his mother the Marchesa Cristina to Massimo d'Azeglio:

'As for the little creature, I think like you, that if the Lord chooses to take it to Himself, it is a kindness; in the state it's in it can hardly make a sturdy constitution, which is very worrying for parents. . . It was good of you, poor Massimo, to let me know so quickly, it would be even better if you would tell me if Giulia is feeding it, or if it has a nurse, which would be better in the circumstances. I heard that you felt the earth tremor and I feared the upset was the reason for Giulia's premature confinement, but from your letter I see I was mistaken.'

And again to her son, some time later:

'My dear Massimo, I must say (without meaning to give offence) that you are not much good yet at giving news of confinements, you leave out the most important part, which is whether the mother can feed it, and is doing so, and if the baby sucks and takes nourishment; in this case there is cause for hope, otherwise God's will be done. . . However, I am inclined to think I shall see this little grandchild only in Paradise where it will be well and there will be no crying.'

The general forecasts were decidedly bleak for this baby girl, who had been named Alessandra, and everyone was already resigned to her death. They were wrong. Alessandra, or Alessandrina, or Rina as everyone called her in the end, survived. Giulietta was feeding her.

Enrichetta to Vittoria, when the baby was twenty days old:

'I have good news to give you of your little niece; we are really beginning to hope that God will let us keep her; she takes only her mother's milk, and grows a little stronger every day. . .'

Enrichetta could not often go to see Vittoria at Lodi. She

wrote:

'You cannot be more impatient to see me than I am to come and hold you in my arms; but my dear, good little girl, I need not repeat that my love for you could never be diminished by distance, which would be slight in the miles that separate us, but which is unfortunately immense by force of circumstances, the most insurmountable being my poor health which imposes many privations upon me. . . So we must continue to have patience. . .'

And again the same winter:

'Sofia sends you the Baby Jesus you asked for; Matilde is here beside me, scribbling with tremendous concentration with a pencil on a great piece of paper, to write to *my deawest Vittodia;* to tell you the truth, she won't let me put two words together, either she breaks her pencil, or no sooner has she settled herself than she wants to get down again, or she wants another piece of paper. . . and she keeps on saying she wants to write *loth of fings to dear thithter in Lodi.*

'Our little Rina is very delicate, but they assure us that if she can reach three months, she will grow strong and healthy. God grant it, for the sake of our poor Giulia who is utterly absorbed in the care of her little babe! . . .'

And again: 'Spring is coming, the season is growing milder, the distance separating us seems less great, and I hope I shall soon be able to come and hug you.

'Everyone here is well, and they all send you lots of love, especially your Papa. Not an afternoon passes, when we are all sitting round the little fireplace in the drawing-room after dinner, without us saying: "What a pity our little Vittoria isn't here!" I don't say this to increase your regrets, but to persuade you that your share in our love is undiminished.'

And again, in April: 'Your sisters were waiting for your letter so impatiently that they jumped all the steps at once to see who would get there first and snatch it from the hands of the *porteur.* Enrico thanks you very much for what you said to him. He had the joy of taking his first communion.

'There is nothing more solemn or more intensely religious than the service of First Communion in the church of San Fedele. It fell to me to assist my Enrico, and the memory will always be uplifting to me. The evening before we had a very happy surprise. The Rector came and told us to prepare our hall very quickly so that he could offer us some music. At half past seven he returned, accompanied by Maestro Neri and the twelve little boys who were to sing next morning the Hymns for the first Communion, composed by your Papa, and they wanted him to hear Maestro Neri's beautiful music. We all enjoyed it very much and our joy was marred only by the regret that you had left that morning.'

'Con che fidente affetto / vengo al tuo santo trono / m'atterro al tuo cospetto / mio Giudice, mio Re! / Con che ineffabil gaudio / tremo dinanzi a Te! / Cenere e colpa io sono: / ma vedi chi t'implora / chi vuole il tuo perdono / chi merita, chi adora / chi rende grazie in me.'

['With what trusting love / come I to Thy holy throne / prostrating myself before Thee / my Judge and King! / With what ineffable joy / I tremble before Thee! / Ashes and guilt am I: / but Thou seest the one who implores Thee / who seeks Thy pardon / who deserves and adores / and who in me renders thanks.']

Thus sang the twelve little boys; these were the 'Strofe per la prima comunione', which Manzoni wrote at that time for Enrico's first communion. The Rector was Giulio Ratti, formerly canon at San Babila, and now rector at San Fedele.

From Brusuglio, Enrichetta to Vittoria, in June:

'Matilde is so happy to be at Brusú. We have a girl to look after her during the day, as your Nanny has to go to Milan with your brothers all the time. Poor little Matilde is so good and so reasonable, and accepts with such good grace all the changes we keep having to make! . . . She gives us nothing but pleasure and is no trouble at all: she sends you a *gweat bid tiss*.'

From Uncle Giulio Beccaria's villa at Gessate, Enrichetta to Vittoria towards the end of June:

'Goodbye now, my darling little daughter, be good and strive zealously to do your duty. Cristina and Sofia hug you and send you all their love. Your Papa and Grandmama hold you close to their hearts. Everyone here sends loving greetings. Your Mama has no need to talk of her love for you. . .'

No other letters from Enrichetta to Vittoria were found, this is the last; she must have written again in the ensuing months, but any later letters have been lost.

The Manzonis often went to Gessate, to Uncle Giulio Beccaria's villa. He had married when he was no longer young; his wife was called Antonietta Curioni de' Civati, and was usually called 'la zietta' in the family, 'little Aunt'. The Manzonis were very fond of him and his wife.

Cousin Giacomo saw Enrichetta at Brusuglio when she got back from Gessate. He wrote to Uncle Beccaria: 'She seemed to me much diminished. However, the doctors have not given up hope of a cure.'

In August, Giulietta and Massimo came to Brusuglio. Giulietta's mother-in-law, the Marchesa Cristina, came for a few days too. Enrichetta was very ill and could not get up. Manzoni wrote to Vittoria:

'You will have heard from Sofia that your dear Mama had to be bled twice. To cure the inflammation (which, however, was never very bad) two more bleedings were necessary: now things have taken a much better turn; and I can tell you to be cheerful, as we all are.'

And to Cattaneo who had asked for news, from the region of Canzo where he was spending the summer.

'Enrichetta scolds me because I have been so long giving you news of her: she knows perfectly well how much you love her, the minx! But I delayed on purpose, as we were going through some ups and downs, and I was certain that it would all turn out well, so I didn't want to upset you with gloomy news. Now things have taken a turn for the better: there's no more talk of fever; the cough has not gone altogether, but it gets better from day to day, and soon it will be just a matter of building up her strength again.'

To Cattaneo again, a few weeks later:

'The condition of my – and to you I can say our – Enrichetta continues to improve, very slowly it is true, but definitely to improve.

'I wish you better weather because I can see from my hill that the horns of Canzo are all shrouded in clouds.'

However, they thought fit to leave Brusuglio and take the invalid to Milan. In September, after nine bleedings, she seemed convalescent. But her fever returned. Her breathing was laboured, she had a cough, and convulsions. Cousin Giacomo wrote to Uncle Giulio Beccaria almost every day with news:

'Yesterday Enrichetta was feverish, and as it was the eve of the feast-days, she wanted to observe her devotions and to take the Eucharist, which made the family very sad. But today she is a little better, and Alessandro, Giulia and the children are less distressed. If things improve, as the doctors flatter themselves, by the administration of muriate of barytes, we may still hope to see her restored.' 'She is responding well to the muriate of barytes and can tolerate it in large doses, having taken 32 grams.' 'The course of the illness seems to be intermittent, that is, one bad day and the next calm. Doctor Casanova, who had moved to Milan and was staying in the Manzoni house, the better to supervise Enrichetta's treatment, has fallen ill himself. You see this is another misfortune for the patient, and a trouble for the family. . . The doctors cannot hold out much hope.'

Before that summer, writing to Vittoria, or cousin Carlotta, or Costanza Arconati, Enrichetta had always spoken joyfully of Giulietta's great happiness. Perhaps she was trying to persuade herself. That summer, during her illness, she probably saw how unhappy her daughter was.

After the birth of their baby girl, Massimo and Giulietta had left the house in via del Durino to move to an apartment in via del Marino in what had once been the Palazzo Imbonati and which had then been bought by the Blondels. Enrico Blondel had died in an apartment in that same palazzo. His widow, Louise Maumary, or *tante Louise* as the Manzonis called her, lived there now. She was still young and very beautiful, slender, with black hair. Giulietta was jealous of her. Her relations with her husband deteriorated. In fact, they had never been either simple or serene. That radiant conjugal felicity had existed only in the words of the family and in Enrichetta's letters. Perhaps he found her cold. Perhaps she found him fatuous. At any rate, their relationship became embittered in the new house, where jealousy was added to it.

In October Giulietta received a long letter from her mother-in-law, the Marchesa Cristina. After the first conventional smiles, there had been no love lost between them. This letter, which arrived when her mother was ill and when she was already wretchedly unhappy, must have hurt her cruelly. In any

135

case it was a pitilessly cruel letter. We do not know if Giulietta answered it.

'My dear Giulia,' wrote her mother-in-law, 'This letter won't reach you very quickly; no matter, if you accept it willingly I shall have achieved my purpose.

'In the first letter you wrote me before you married Mass., you said such nice things, that you were so pleased to have him, that you would think only of making him happy, and thus of pleasing me, for you knew that Mass. meant everything to me: you said flattering things to me too, which I certainly do not deserve: that you would always look on me as a mother, you begged me to help you with advice etc. Then before coming to Turin, you repeated all this, and begged me not to judge your heart by a cold exterior etc. etc.: I leave out the rest which is unimportant.

'Giulia, my daughter, you must not take it amiss if I dwell a little on what you wrote then. You had and have good reason to love Mass. and to esteem him: never mind that he's my son; you know as well as I do how much he is loved by his friends, by your father and all the family, in short by anyone who really knows him; you love him in a way, but do you make him happy? The first days we spent in Azeglio, from the 31st, I doubted it but said nothing; the second summer my doubts increased, but I forced myself to be silent; but hardly had I got to Milan this year than I felt confirmed in this heart-breaking thought; Mass. is not happy. . . the three months in Cernobio (apart from a few days in August) and then in Brusú. When I got there I would have taken the mail-coach and left at once, if the pain of abandoning Mass. had not robbed me of my courage. The hope of supporting my son made me drain drop by drop the bitter chalice you prepared for me. Sadly this is the simple truth. I never spoke to you because you were then in such poor health that I preferred to remain silent, rather than harm you or that dear little creature; I resolved then to write to you at length, and to avoid painful discussion which would have achieved nothing, persuaded as you are that you are always right.

'There are many kinds of lawful love established in God's order, the love of a wife is very different from that of a mother, brother, etc., however, all these loves demand sacrifices, sometimes greater, sometimes lesser. To be strong and constant, the love between husband and wife must be based on mutual esteem (and this you have) and requires a continual sacrifice of will and temperament, in order to establish that fine harmony, that true and solid love that consoles us in every circumstance, a love that lasts.

'If love is shown only in kisses and simpering etc. etc. it's like a baby who if you refuse him the breast, turns from sweetness to rage, sulks, makes faces, etc., and all this is purely and simply egoism; we may accept it in babies, but at the age of reason, no. Mass. has faults, who has not? I did tell you he was a lamb, and very patient, but in the long run the lamb will turn into a lion, and who makes him do so? He is not God, he's a man, but such a man that, if for your part you did only what was reasonable, he would be in a position to envy nobody. If the beaker overflows when one drop is added to it, who is to blame?

'Everyone is born with particular inclinations, good, bad, indolent, gentle or fierce, etc., a good upbringing modifies these defects; as the reason develops one understands things better. . . . If, with the capacity for thought God gave you, you had persevered when Mass. sought you out, you would already be what you ought. You would have subdued your lofty pride, the egoism which seeks to bend everyone to your will and makes you sulk if you fail. You would have simpler and more solid tastes which would be more pleasing to your husband who sacrifices everything to satisfy them, but without ever managing to please you. As he told you, he is not rich, but you see how his *true* love strives to content you, and his only reward, when I was there, was to be upbraided by you when he had been 4 or 5 hours in the sun, panting and weary, and then more than once (I heard this in casa Manzoni) to be told you had moved into his house to be worse off. Oh Heavens! I shall never forget the pain I felt.

'Giulia dear, I have had no reason to complain of your *procédés* towards me (even if it happened once, the next time it did not touch me) but have I not more reason to complain since you have hurt me by your behaviour towards one who is the light of his mother's life? I who have done everything for you, yes, for you – since for Mass. I have done less than was necessary – neglecting no opportunity to give you a nice present, etc. and

137

this is how you have rewarded me! but I repeat, if Mass. were happy, I would even accept blows from you. Oh dear Giulia, how many times did my heart reach out to you with love, then this idea would loom before me, this woman is torturing my Mass., and I felt a stab of bitter pain.

'I could say more on this matter, but I do not want to be overly tedious. I pass to the matter of filial affection and at once I ask, would you be content if your daughter at 24 displayed the same affection as you do to your parents and grandmother? The latter, you say, with her excessive and ill-conceived love was the cause, etc., etc. Admitting that she spoiled you (and I must agree), do you therefore have to make her pay for it, now that perhaps she weeps for it in her old age? Unfortunately she sees everything and feels acutely. And what can I say of your mother? I assure you I should not like to be treated like that by my daughter, or by my Mass. How half-heartedly you have assisted her in all the time that I have been an onlooker. You were in the next bedroom, yet you were capable of staying away for hours, without putting in an appearance for a moment? Good God! she saw, watched, felt profoundly, I can tell you: perhaps her illness is partly due to your behaviour, and you? you were content with four or five hasty visits. They did not want us to talk, I know, but I went 10 or 12 times just to look at her, rejoice if there was any improvement, etc., and she is not my mother. . . Cristina was quite jealous. . . a kind word can win her round. There is no excuse; it was quite simply negligence, and nothing else; when the spirit is willing, everything is possible. Remember, my daughter, this is bread cast upon the waters, pray Heaven you are not thus treated by your own children. I have not observed any particular negligence towards your father; certainly you are not very demonstrative towards him, but he seems not to think much about it, luckily.

'And what is the cause of all this? I'll tell you. It comes from having almost abandoned the good practices you told me you observed as a girl. You go to Church like Protestants to their chapel, once on Sunday and that's all: I've seen it in Azeglio, in Milan, in Cernobio. All good things come from God. If we do not pray, He is not obliged to grant us that higher grace to prac- tise virtue. If you had an irreligious husband I would say to you, just do what is prescribed, refrain from anything further to avoid upsetting him; but this is not your case: why not attend holy communion sometimes, or a short act of worship if you can't get to Mass: why stay away from the sacred fount of every grace for 4 or 5 months? At least for the chief festivals: pause to consider what you read, the society you surround yourself with every evening at your home, which *I entirely disapprove of;* the cutting things I have so often heard you utter. You waste so much time, when you could be cultivating the talents you have, to your husband's great satisfaction, and acquire a store of sound instruction for your daughter.

'I told your family you were a good housekeeper, but to you I can say you have not been so this year. I have observed what has been spent in the house, and it is far too much. Enough furniture to fill two more rooms: a carpet that couldn't have cost less than 500 or 600 francs, when a clean drugget would have been sufficient: then all those trinkets on the tables, they must be yours, why not save your money for more solid things? When you showed me your account books, I saw one said liveries; and 25 lire or francs for 5 little dresses for the baby, I never dreamed I would see such a thing in an account-book. The material must be bought but made up at home. Lenin has other things to do. . . but you can sew very well, my dear; instead of spending so much time at your embroidery frame making costly things that damage your health, busy yourself doing what a woman does best. I have calculated roughly what you have had this year – certainly far more than I from tenants at Cal.na – and now I don't know how you stand. You have certainly put nothing aside. And since we are on this subject I warn you you can expect little from me, with all the expenses I have; so you would really be advised to be sensible. I give you this advice regarding your budget.

'It remains to say a word about the servants. The nurse is not what she was; more than once I've seen her up to unseemly tricks. At Cernobio she gave the baby to someone else, then escaped to the kitchen or to the harbour to chatter with boatmen, and I feel she has too much to say for herself in the house; I am not saying she is vicious, but too frivolous, which won't do at all when Sandrine is 4. Too much gossip arises from her chatter, and you encourage her.

'My dear Giulia, I have touched upon all the main points I

had chosen. I have spoken the truth, I have tried to speak frankly, but not in a spirit of offence, but the truth is often painful; I hope its effect on you will not be sad or unavailing, but that it will serve to make you examine yourself, and profit by the advice of a mother who truly loves you and is not afraid to make painful incisions for your good, and for the good of our Massimo.

'If this letter arrives when you are in a disturbed state of mind, postpone reading it so that it may be as medicine to you, and not poison; this is the wish of one who writes to you with painful effort. If it does you good, if God blesses my words, all else is as nothing. Keep this paper, perhaps it will be the last so prolix and from a heart so full. I have not long to live, but I shall have the consolation of having given you this proof of my sincerity and love.'

Together with the preaching, moral judgements, recollections full of bitter rancour, angry reflections about expenditure, and furious rage at the idea that her beloved son should have to live with a woman 'who does not make him happy', the Marchesa Cristina's letter also reflects, albeit painted in the acrid colours of anger, the figure of Giulietta as she then was. No longer the melancholy girl who wrote tender letters to Cousin Giacomo who did not take much notice of her, or tender letters to Fauriel who never answered. No longer the melancholy girl in the Grigioni, consumed with home-sickness for her sisters and brothers, her mother, her home. No longer melancholy, but desperate. She listened to the gossip of the nurse which may have touched on *tante* Louise and her jealousy. She was buying furniture frenziedly. Apparently she demanded to be called Marchesa (though the only true marchesa was her mother-in-law). She despised her husband's relatives ('*la cousinaille*', she called them in a letter home, written in a scrawl that was almost entirely indecipherable) and felt humiliated and that she had come down many degrees to an ambience inferior to her own. But above all, she saw nothing around her resembling her girl-hood dreams. She fled from her sick mother's room, and would not stay and nurse her like the others; she fled because she knew this time her mother would not survive the winter, and her own unhappiness was too great to stand this approaching separation. She fled so that her dying mother should be spared the sight of

140

her unhappiness and the evident failure of her marriage.

Massimo must have been, like her, disappointed in the marriage, and found their life together extremely uncomfortable; but perhaps this did not completely destroy his happiness as it did hers; he had other resources, work, friends, and probably other women (whether or not it really was already a question of *tante* Louise, as Giulietta thought, we cannot know). His relations with his wife's family, however, remained warm and affectionate. In the winter he wrote to his cousin Cesare Balbo, telling him about Enrichetta's illness:

'Poor Manzoni faces the likelihood of losing his wife soon; she seems to be wasting away. You would have to know, as I have done, their hearts and their life together, the love they have borne each other for twenty-five years, the angelic life they have spent together, to have any idea of the blow of this separation. Moreover, when you think that three boys, two little girls, and two girls of marriageable age will remain motherless, the whole family without a guide, that the grandmother is turned seventy and not fit to run the house; because of his health and his habitual way of life, Papa is more in need of others to look after him than the reverse: you see how many misfortunes greater than words can tell are contained in this one. I wish you could see Papa these days. I thought I knew what man he was, but I did not know: I have discovered that his talents are as nothing to his life. If you heard the things he has uttered! The other evening, for example, when all the family were gathered together in a moment of terrible stress, he said to the children: let us say an Ave Maria for your mother. When they had said it: let us say another for the people who have hurt us most, so God will more gladly accept our prayers.'

In early December Vittoria came from Lodi. On the twelfth she was sent back. She would not see her mother again. Cousin Giacomo wrote to Uncle Giulio Beccaria: 'This morning I saw Grossi. . . he confirmed that Enrichetta was not in danger for the moment, and may be said to have improved a little. In any case, we have taken the necessary steps, if the worst comes to the worst, and arrangements would be made by me and by Grossi for the family to come to you at Gessate at a time of their choice, and Grossi would be very willing to accompany them. But let us still cling to the hope that such a tragedy may not occur or at least not so suddenly. . .'

And the Marchesa Cristina wrote to Massimo:

'Just a line, Massimo dear, with Christmas greetings to you, Giulia, Sandrina and all the Manzonis and friends. My dear, this is a very sad Christmas, but I offer my greetings in a Christian sense, that is, I pray for you all with the courage and resignation which makes profitable for the soul those afflictions that the Lord visits upon His children. You cannot imagine how grief-stricken I am at the griefs of a family with whom I feel at one as with my own. From the moment I heard that angel had taken the last rites, I have known no comfort, and my stomach is upset all the time.'

Enrichetta died on Christmas Day, at eight in the evening. The funeral took place on the 27th at the neighbouring parish church of San Fedele. The body was taken to Brusuglio. Manzoni wrote the epitaph for her tomb. 'To Enrichetta Manzoni, née Blondel, incomparable daughter-in-law, wife and mother; her mother-in-law, husband and children pray with bitter tears but in living faith that she may enter into the glory of Heaven.'

Then they all went to Uncle Giulio Beccaria's at Gessate. On 31st December Grandmother Giulia wrote from there to Vittoria:

'My darling Vittoria, God has taken from us the angelic creature He had given to us in His mercy – to you as mother, to me as the dearest daughter, to your father as an incomparable companion. Oh! Vittoria dear, the pain and desolation are indeed great, and we will feel the loss of that angel in every minute of every day.

'What a life and what a death was hers! You had to leave her before she left us all: offer up to God your sacrifice, and hers in sending you back, which cost her very dear! She made a like sacrifice in not seeing her dear Matilde again, saying: "I have already sacrificed her to the Lord".

'I will not go into many details now, although they are sacred and precious; I will just tell you that for several days she was longing for Christmas Eve, and indeed on that day she received the Holy Eucharist and extreme unction for the second time. She spent the day until evening in a gentle agony, conscious and praying all the time. Our good Rector was with her all the time. The moment came. She was supported by Pietro and Massimo; everyone was praying; a faint sigh told the Rector she had passed to Heaven, and he announced it to us in these words: *We are praying for her, now she is praying for us.*

'Then I saw the angel again: a heavenly smile had formed on her lips; everyone came to see her with love and veneration; she was taken to Brusuglio amid the tears and prayers of all. . .

'Your poor, desolate father is resigned to the will of God, but submerged in the most profound, I might even say unimaginable grief; and us? . . . Oh, dear Vittorina, may the Lord help us! I say no more. We went to the Beccaria house, and now we have come here to Gessate. Excuse my bad writing: I am writing in the evening and I can't see very well.

'My Vittoria, dearest girl, if we would die like her, we must live like her. Oh Vittoria, remember that you are Enrichetta's daughter! – This name says *everything* – *everything* that is good and holy on this earth. Vittoria, my little one, I can't write any more. Your Papa presses you to his poor heart; everybody sends their love, including Uncle and "la zietta" . . . Oh Vittoria, remember the life your mother led! As long as I live, I shall always be your most loving Grandmother.'

She wrote a long letter to her friend Euphrosine Planta. The Falquet-Plantas lived in Grenoble. They were old friends of the Manzonis. One of their sons, Henri, had spent a few days at Brusuglio that summer when Enrichetta had fallen ill.

'Alas! my dearest Euphrosine, your tender heart spoke true when it presaged some misfortune, for the greatest possible has befallen us. Our angelic Enrichetta is no longer in this world of woe. Alas! I have very painful details to tell, but let me say a word about us, poor, unhappy creatures that we are. Our pain reached its peak, but in the end it has to lose some force to be bearable at all, but the deprivation, day by day, minute by minute, of one who was the soul, the counsel, the pillar of the whole family, one who was for 26 years our model and our joy, no! my friend, no, one cannot grow accustomed to such a loss. I have, so to speak, lost my daily bread, and as our grief is continuous, it is all the more scorching and hard to bear. If I say this, judge for yourself the state of my unhappy son; his lamentations (oh! they come from the very heart!) follow wave on

143

wave, grief engenders grief, he lives on pain and resignation, resignation and pain, for her presence is everywhere with us. All our children have felt this irreparable loss, and feel it still. Each day they pay their tribute to her of veneration, love and grief. But let me speak of her, not us. A few days after your Henri left us, she felt worse than usual, but without taking to bed. Our two girls were staying with their sister at the lake and we were to go there too for the 24th (July) to celebrate Saint Cristina's day, but Enrichetta was not well enough for that short journey. Alessandro and Pietro went on their own. They all came back together two days later and found Enrichetta in bed; gradually she began to suffer very bad pain in her intestines, so she was bled a great deal, and so two months passed, her illness fluctuating all the time, in the most alarming way. On top of all this a dreadful catarrhal cough, chest infection, and her sufferings endlessly renewed by endless remedies, but with such patience in face of every trial! Fortunately the season was clement, but winter was coming on and our house is no good at all for the winter.

'To bring my story to a close, on the 23rd November we were able to take her to Milan. She did not suffer at all on the short journey; everything had been prepared to receive her. After a few quieter days in which she wanted to take the holy sacrament, she began to suffer greatly once more, and consultations were arranged, etc. . . . Our good doctor from the country moved in to be with her day and night. She was gripped by frequent convulsions, and her poor body was wasted away. She knew she was dying, but she did not want to talk about it to us: "Oh! they get too distressed!" She consoled herself by gazing at a little picture of the Holy Virgin, saying "*She is my consolation.*" Not a word of complaint; her resignation was complete. She only asked her women: "Tell me, when is Christmas Eve?" Hearing her ask this, the women and I were anxious. Alas! it was on Christmas Eve that she asked for her confessor again. She wanted to take the holy sacrament again, since she had received it not many days before, he told her that if she were well enough, the parish priest would certainly bring it. Her poor husband, who for some time had talked to her of nothing but the bliss of her eternal life, kept saying to her: "I offer you to God and beg you of Him." Oh, God! what a time

144

that was! At last came that Christmas night. About midnight a strong convulsion gripped her; at once we called our good priest, a young man but full of doctrine, virtue and deep spiritual feeling; he gave her the holy oil, and since she was calm and in her right mind, he brought her the holy sacrament. We were beside her bed, we asked her blessing. she held my head in her hands, saying: "Oh! my poor *nonna!*" She said to Alessandro: "I commend my little babe to you." But she did not want to see her, saying: "I have already sacrificed her to God." Not a complaint, no sign of weakness, but loving and grateful for any little service done to her. She was as if already absorbed into God, and consoled herself with a little picture of the Holy Virgin she held before her. The priest did not leave her, she did not want him to go, he was praying all the time. Her son Pietro and her son-in-law were supporting her. The whole of Christmas Day passed in this way; we wandered from one room to another, stifling our laments and sobs. Alessandro was in a desperate state, but always at prayer. At eight in the evening the children and I were in the other room, Alessandro prostrate at the end of his wife's room, his head on the ground, seeing and hearing nothing, the priest was commending her soul, when d'Azeglio said: "Her pulse has stopped beating." The priest turned to seek Alessandro; he found him on the ground, knelt before him and said: "We were praying for her, now she is praying for us."

'This was how we heard of her *blessed passing*, as she called it, but so deadly for us. I need say nothing of us, for you can imagine and feel for the state we were in. My sister-in-law had come from her country estate, where she had left my brother. She took us to her house that night, and in the morning we set off with her. Before leaving, we went back to my house to see our beloved once again. An angelic smile had taken the place of those lines of pain that such a cruel illness had imprinted on the face, now young and beautiful again. Oh! Euphrosine, I kissed her hands, but dared not touch her, My poor Giulia, who was ill in bed, got up to come with us; after a few miles she had to turn back; her husband, who also returned, rendered every possible office to that holy body; no one touched her except her women and Massimo who placed her in her last resting-place. People came to see her; they prayed for her; at last two days later she was taken to the church, and in the evening to our country estate. A grave had been prepared in the cemetery. The peasants came to meet her with lighted candles. They kept vigil all day and in the morning they wanted the local priest and several others to say the funeral service again there. Oh! can you forgive me all these details? my poor head is so confused. I don't know how you can follow all this scrawl, but it is all so alive in my memory that my pen goes on and on, without my knowing what I'm writing. We stayed with my brother for about a fortnight; now we are at home to feel each day the loss of her who was *our necessity*.

'Dear Euphrosine, I want to tell you that I share with all my heart in the loss of your good mother. Such a holy and precious death should console us, our faith tells us; but our hearts are flesh and always there to torment us. Do not worry about us; we have had no material worries at all. . . . Goodbye, my dearest friend; I feel I still have some bond upon this earth if you love me.'

This was Enrichetta's will, which she dictated a week before she died:

I, Enrichetta Blondel, wife of Alessandro Manzoni living in Milan, dispose of my belongings in the following way:

Regarding my dowry, I wish it to be divided into equal parts between all my children, both male and female; regarding my possessions outside my dowry, I leave half to my three sons Pietro, Enrico and Filippo, and the other half to be divided equally between all my children, both male and female; I wish my husband to hold everything in usufruct during his natural life.

I wish my above-mentioned three male heirs, and likewise my husband and usufructuary, to pay once only by way of legacy to my five daughters Giulietta married d'Azeglio, Cristina, Sofia, Vittorina, Matilde one thousand five hundred Milanese lire each.

This legacy to Giulietta, wife of the Marchese d'Azeglio, shall be paid once the will is proven, the other daughters may not demand it during the life of their Father unless in the case of their respective marriages.

The witnesses to the will were don Giulio Ratti, Provost of San Fedele, Tommaso Grossi and an accountant called Casti glioni.

'Our friends have had the greatest misfortune that could happen to them', Constanza Arconati wrote to Fauriel. He had not written to the Manzonis for a long time. He had not even sent a line when Giulietta got married. Costanza Arconati begged him to write. 'My dear Fauriel, will you not write them a word? Your silence, justified or not, I do not know, at the time of Giulietta's marriage, upset them so much that I can imagine what they must feel now. I beg you, do write.'

Fauriel did not write. Manzoni wrote to him in February 1834, recommending to him Niccolò Tommaseo, who was going to Paris. For his part, Manzoni had not written to Fauriel for a long time. 'A sacred duty forces me to break a silence which will not have surprised you. . . [the "sacred duty" was to introduce Tommaseo, who was so eager to meet him]: you know that at times there are words bitter to pronounce, even impossible to find, for the simple reason that they are in vain. . . Goodbye, dear, evermore dear friend; what remains of this poor family embraces you; one day I shall be able to communicate with you more fully.'

Fauriel received Niccolò Tommaseo most cordially. They became quite good friends. He did not answer Manzoni's letter, and never wrote to him any more. Neither did Manzoni write to him again.

In the summer of 1834 Mary Clarke was in Italy. She saw the Manzonis in Milan and and gave them news of Fauriel. She knew he was preparing for a journey to the South of France, but did not know when he was leaving.

Mary Clarke to Fauriel:

'I am still filled with emotion after leaving the Manzonis so that I can think of nothing else. . . O Heavens! if you could come and spend a fortnight here during your trip, how much good you would do Manzoni; he loves you with all the love of which his noble heart is capable. How pleased I would be if I could persuade you to give him this pleasure! How he spoke of you! his friendship is not in the least diminished, nor the fascina-

147

tion he feels for you. Think how easy it would be when you are in the south of France; think how short life is; think of the happiness of having a friend like him; remember that for so many years you have thought of nothing but work and that this dries up the heart, and that it is not time wasted to spend time with one like him. . .' Here the letter broke off, and besides, Mary Clarke did not know where to send it, because she did not know if Fauriel was still in Paris or if he had already left.

That summer, at Brusuglio, Giulietta took to her bed, never to rise again. As usual, Cousin Giacomo wrote to Uncle Giulio Beccaria:

'The Manzonis did not leave Brusú yesterday because of Giulietta d'Azeglio, who has succumbed to a fever for which she had to be bled.' 'When I was going to see the Manzonis, I saw the cook Giuseppe on the way and, when I asked after Giulia, he told me that he was going to fetch her confessor, as she had wished to perform her devotions this morning. . . So, not to disturb her religious practices, I saw fit to delay my visit to Brusú. . . From what I heard, however, it seems things are not going at all well.'

Giulietta died on the 20th September at Brusuglio. On her death certificate was written 'tuberculosis of the abdomen'.

All the Manzonis went to Gessate, to Uncle Giulio Beccaria's villa. Cousin Giacomo wrote to Uncle Giulio:

'When I got to town yesterday evening, I went immediately to casa Manzoni, but heard they had all gone to you. I hope that, in spite of the distress of mind, they are all reasonably well. I beg you to express my condolences to them, and to d'Azeglio. I shall arrange in the coming weeks to come to Gessate to embrace them all.'

The author of these laconic notes was the Cousin Giacomo with whom Giulietta had been in love.

Giulietta was buried at Brusuglio. Manzoni wrote the epitaph for her tomb:

'To Giulia d'Azeglio, née Manzoni who died in the peace of the Lord / on the 20th day of September 1834; / her husband and her desolate relatives / commend her to His mercy / and to the prayers of the faithful.'

148

Manzoni wrote to the Grand Duke of Tuscany in October 1834:

'It has pleased the Lord to take from the world my eldest daughter, in the flower of youth, at the beginning of a very happy marriage and ardent motherhood. Mindful as I shall be as long as I live of the pity Your Highness deigned to show me for the cruel blow which struck me at the end of last year, it would seem to me almost ungrateful to remain silent about this other cruel blow, so soon after.'

Mary Clarke to Fauriel, from Lille (about a month and a half had passed since her last letter, and passing through Basle, she had heard that Fauriel was at Marseilles):

'I would have written without waiting for your letter, if I had known where to send, because I dearly wished to speak to you about the Manzonis while my heart was so full of them, and while my impression was more happy than sad; now what I have to say can only give you pain. They have lost Giulietta, and during my stay she was so much better that they hoped to save her. It is all the more horrible in that, as far as I am persuaded from enquiries I made, it was her own folly that began to destroy her stomach, and a year or two ago she could have been saved if she had consulted the doctor who did me so much good; she did not die of any illness, but of a serious wasting and general, slow inflammation. The fact is that she had destroyed her digestion over a period of years, eating almost nothing, and then was not sufficiently well cared for, and all the fatigues of her confinement and nursing aggravated her weakness. . . If you could have the courage to write to Manzoni, I assure you it would do him good: just a few lines; this grief will be much less than the first, only it will reopen the wound; how I pity the poor grandmother! Signora Arconati wanted to suggest you go to Milan with her. . . She wanted you to join her at Gaesbeck. She would take you in her carriage, you would be very comfortable; I have nothing to say about this plan, because if you wanted to go, it would be quicker to go from where you are now; as for me, I should be happily resigned to see you later if Manzoni were to reap the benefit. The impression he made on me was like nothing I've ever known, at times I couldn't look at him without tears coming to my eyes and I was obliged to go out of the room several times, his face seemed to me as Christ

149

must have looked to his disciples, I wanted to kneel down before him. He has hardly aged at all, only his hair is all grey, he was almost cheerful the two days I was there, but it's not insensitivity as Signora Arconati thinks, but his nature is so tender and so gentle that he cannot bear grief too long and seeks to elude it from time to time; grief is so ugly that it proves antipathetic to extreme beauty, but there are traces of tenderness and suffering in his face that bear witness to what he has been through; he shows supreme grace.

'I would have liked to curl up before him like a cat in the sun; the three days spent at Milan have been a great event in my life; I was drowned in melancholy yet the pleasure of seeing Manzoni was so great that the melancholy was dear to me. He still has the same candour, takes an interest in everything, seemed much amused by all I told him of Paris, judges people there and knows them as if it was scarcely six months since he was there; he does me so much good, he restored my faith in disinterested intelligence, so that I want to return to Milan in a year or two to retemper my mind and faith. . . . The two boys look good lads, quite nice-looking but without any fascination. Pietro has a certain grace and presents himself well, although they say he's a great idler. Matilde, the youngest, who is four, is a little jewel of grace, coquetry and vivacity, I've never seen such a charming little creature. Signora Giulia is still as affable and affectionate, looks a little older, but apart from this I thought she hadn't changed at all. "And our Fauriel!" she said to me with the same tenderness as ever. Oh! you don't see their like anywhere, and I set them in my heart again as in a reliquary; the more people I've seen, the more I love these, there's nobody to compare with them. Signora Giulia talked to me a great deal of Enrichetta, she told me she feels her loss more keenly every day, that she could never leave Alessandro, that he was like a child, that she was very old and trembled at the idea of leaving him alone when she died. Enrico has grown quite handsome, he doesn't look like his father, he says nothing and looks rather a wild spirit, I rather liked him. I didn't like Azeglio over much, I don't know why. I've nothing to say against him, he has great moustaches that look pretentious, but I didn't see any ostentation in him. However, every individual is like a work of art. There are very passable paintings which have nothing noticeably wrong with them

150

yet nothing pleasing either, and in that family where so many can capture your heart with one glance, anyone who lacks real grace has no success.'

Fauriel neither wrote nor came. He seemed deaf to the pleading of Signora Arconati and Mary Clarke. He preferred silence and absence. Perhaps he did not come because it seemed too painful to see the Manzoni family as they were now. He and Manzoni might have found themselves face to face with a burden of memories too heavy to bear. He did not write because a few lines in a letter seemed a miserable offering. As Manzoni had said, 'at times there are words bitter to pronounce, even impossible to find, for the simple reason that they are in vain'. Fauriel died ten years after Giulietta, in 1844. Giulietta's letters (*Mon cher parrain*), her portrait and a drawing by her together with letters from Manzoni and Giulia, were found in his apartment in Paris and returned to the Manzonis by Jules Mohl, an orientalist who had been a friend of Mary Clarke.

Why did the friendship between Manzoni and Fauriel die away? And when did it die? What happened between them? Why did what was only negligence on both sides in their letter-writing become over the years such a strange and profound silence? Perhaps there is no precise explanation. The day Fauriel left Milan, in autumn 1825, abruptly and without a word of goodbye, perhaps the relations between the two men had fractured, or were on the point of fracture. Perhaps Fauriel had things to do in France and did not want to be detained; perhaps he had run out of money; he was known to dislike goodbyes; there are so many hypotheses. But perhaps fundamentally he had realized that what had been a friendship was becoming something else: a cold, formal connection which it would be sad to continue. Perhaps Fauriel had lost all faith in himself; and felt he was going downhill while Manzoni was climbing, so that their steps could no longer be directed towards the same places. Or perhaps the explanation lies elsewhere, in the nature of Fauriel. Sainte-Beuve said he loved 'civilisations at their birth and the springs of rivers'; he loved dawn, not midday or dusk; so, in human beings, he loved the search, promise and expectation, not fulfilment. Perhaps Manzoni had understood this too and felt the other becoming ever more distant and strange; and so there was nothing more between them, no letters; they never

151

wrote or met again. And when Manzoni was stricken with grief, Fauriel felt incapable of sending him a simple word of pity and affection, because the pity was too great, and affection fell silent in contemplation of so many vicissitudes, so many contrasting, interwoven and scattered emotions.

> Sí che Tu sei terribile!
> Sí che in quei lini ascoso
> In braccio a quella Vergine
> Sovra quel sen pietoso
> Come da sopra i turbini
> Regni, o Fanciul severo!
> È fato il tuo pensiero,
> È legge il tuo vagir.
>
> Vedi le nostre lagrime,
> Intendi i nostri gridi;
> Il voler nostro interroghi,
> E a tuo voler decidi;
> Mentre a stornar la folgore
> Trepido il prego ascende,
> Sorda la folgor scende
> Dove tu vuoi ferir.

[Yea, Thou art terrible! / Yea, concealed in those swaddling clothes, / in the arms of the Virgin / on that merciful bosom / as from above the whirlwinds / Thou reignest, stern Boy! / Thy thoughts are fate, / Thy will is law.

Thou seest our tears / Hearest our cries; / Thou dost search our will, / And it is Thy will that decides; / While to ward off the thunderbolt / Our prayers rise in trepidation, / Deaf the thunderbolt falls / To wound where Thou wilt.]

These are the opening lines of a poem, 'Christmas 1833', which Manzoni wrote on the first anniversary of Enrichetta's death. He wrote only a few, fragmentary stanzas. God is remote. His dwelling, in dark skies furrowed by lightning, inspires terror. In that remote dwelling God sees and hears tears, cries and prayers, but His will remains immutable. After a few stanzas the page remained blank. It was impossible to continue.

How can one invoke or address a God who seems so distant, lofty and inexorable? One can only say how He acts, and bow one's head. 'Deaf, the thunderbolt falls – to wound where Thou wilt'.

Giuletta's baby, little Rina, was taken into the Manzoni household and entrusted to Giulia.

D'Azeglio said to Cesare Cantú, going with him to Gessate to visit the Beccarias one day that autumn, shortly after Giulietta's death, and feeling the first breath of winter: 'I can't feel it without thinking how cold my Giulia must be there in the open country'. Cesare Cantú remembered these words with some astonishment, for d'Azeglio uttered few words of tenderness and commiseration for his wife. His memory of Giulietta must have been opaque, heavy, anguished, devoid of light. Her image evoked difficult days, mutual incomprehension, disharmony.

His mother, Marchesa Cristina, thought again of the harsh letter she had sent to Giulietta. She wrote to Massimo in March 1835:

'My scant virtue, and a touch of ill humour caused me to make that complaint, which I so repented. My dear Mass., I should have remained silent, knowing your heart as I did, but what can I do. . . you too must forgive me; I don't expect every letter from you to be an epistle, but every 4 or 5. You give me new life when you tell me what you are doing. . . I don't know why, for some days Giulietta is on my mind in such a grievous way; I have renewed my prayers for the dead, if ever they were needed.'

In April 1835, at Lodi, Vittoria took her first communion. She wrote home, and her grandmother and father both replied.

Grandmother:

'Oh, Vittoria, half a year has already passed since our Giulia turned her gaze away from life's tribulations to go and join your saintly mother in Eternal Rejoicing. . . But I, poor old sinner that I am, cannot obtain from God that resignation that makes grief sweet to a Christian soul, and of which your father gives me such an edifying example. . . Pray the Lord at this holy time to grant it to me: your innocent prayers will certainly be more

153

acceptable than mine. . .

'Our little Rina, whom Massimo has entrusted to my care, is such a pretty dear. . . Poor little mite, for whom a *great-grand-mother* must take the place of a mother. . .'

Father:

'Your letter affords me that living consolation that the Lord reserves sometimes, in His mercy, for those He has most sorely tried. Yes, my little Vittoria, your sense of the ineffable grace you are preparing to receive gives me the sweet hope that it will be for you a principle of constant grace and unbroken blessing. May the joy you already feel, and the greater joy still before you, teach you now and throughout your life that there is no real happiness except in union with God, and in the hope of a more perfect, intimate and indestructible union with Him. Love and gratitude, confusion and courage! Trust all the more when you feel yourself frail, because the Lord never fails those who know themselves and pray. Promise to be ever faithful in all things to His holy law: promise it unhesitatingly, since He who ordered it promises His help. In strong hope, ask Him what you feel you need most; ask beforehand for those things you will need, when the world, with its flattering and false doctrines proposes, enjoins and demonstrates a law opposed to the one which must be your salvation. Learn now to fear this world, because it can be stronger than you: accustom yourself to despise it, since He who so loves you that He comes to be with you, is stronger than it. At this happy, holy time, feel a more lively gratitude, a more tender affection, a more humble reverence for the Virgin, in whose womb our Judge became our Redeemer, our God became our brother: ask and pray that she may protect and teach you all your life. Your angelic mother looks on you from Heaven with happiness, and with you offers up supplication, thanks and promises.'

In summer 1835, less than a year after Giulia's death, d'Azeglio married again. The speed of this new marriage outraged the Manzonis. Moreover, he was marrying Louise Maumary, *tante Louise*, and there were rumours in the town that d'Azeglio had had a relationship with this lady when Giulietta was still alive, and that her jealousy had been well founded.

Niccolò Tommaseo, who was in Paris, commented:

'Azeglio is getting married again, and he's taking the Widow Blondel, of whom they say Giulietta was jealous. Wretched business!'

And Costanza Arconati commented:

'And does not this prompt marriage, following upon a love which had already existed for some time, perhaps arouse the suspicion that poor Giulietta was never loved?'

On the other hand, these are the kindly, discreet comments of Giulio Carcano, writer and man of learning, who later published a correspondence between Massimo and Louise:

'He had sought a second marriage within the domestic circle that was so dear to him, an intelligent companion, a mother for his orphaned baby girl.'

Shortly after their marriage Massimo and Louise came to take back little Rina who had been living in Giulia's care in the Manzoni household since Giulietta's death. They took her to their home for good.. This was a bitter blow to Giulia, and seemed a fresh and bitter offence to her and to Manzoni.

Uncle Giulio Beccaria and his wife, 'la zietta', found nothing contemptible in d'Azeglio's behaviour, and they remained on good terms with him. For this reason, in that autumn of 1835, the Manzonis refused their invitation to go to Gessate, and went instead to spend a few weeks at Monticello with acquaintances, the Navas. Cesare Cantú wrote to 'la zietta':

'Yesterday I saw, guess whom? the Manzonis. I went to Monticello to the casa Nava expressly to see them. He and the Nonna are in excellent health, looking cheerful and happy, and the Nonna said she felt 10 years younger. As for him, he looks like a schoolboy, and you know he doesn't lack masters.

'But Giulia took me aside and opened her heart to me about the griefs she had suffered, and the need she felt for immense, warm-hearted courtesy such as the Navas practise. . . She recited to me more or less the letter she had written you; that if they had come to Gessate, they might have met d'Azeglio with that woman etc. . . . . She found it quite right and proper that he should marry again, but thought the manner of it horrible, and strange that you should approve. Here she got into an endless maze of talk, but Alessandro, who had noticed, interrupted the conversation asking her: "Will you never have done with your

Odyssey?"'

Cesare Cantú and 'la zietta' were great friends. It was said later that they were lovers.

Manzoni opened a law-suit against d'Azeglio. Giulietta had died intestate; in her last weeks, she was 'incapable of speech', according to the documents relating to the trial. Manzoni and especially Giulia thought the interests of little Rina should be defended in a court of law. When Giulietta had got married, Giulia had made her a donation, and now wanted that money to be pledged to the little girl. The suit was argued in the court at Milan, and went in favour of d'Azeglio; the Manzonis lost their case.

As the years went by, relations between Manzoni and d'Azeglio became affectionate once more. Manzoni was fundamentally very fond of d'Azeglio, because 'he could play, sing, dance', because he was different from him in every way.

Louise, like Giulietta before her, wished to be called 'marchesa', and this annoyed the real Marchesa, Cristina di Bianzé.

D'Azeglio soon got tired of Louise, and a few years later they were already living apart.

In 1836, Vittoria was removed from the school at Lodi, and put in the Monastero della Visitazione, in Milan.

In January 1837 Manzoni married again. He married donna Teresa Borri, widow of Count Decio Stampa, who had been left a widow young, with one son whom she had brought up on her own. The son was then eighteen. It was Tommaso Grossi who had spoken to Manzoni of Teresa Borri. It seemed to Giulia quite right that Alessandro should marry again. At first she liked Teresa Borri very much. But immediately after the wedding differences arose. Teresa had a brusque temperament and was used to giving orders. Giulia took a strong dislike to her son, Stefano. Bit by bit Giulia tended to withdraw to her own rooms, and began to live like a stranger in the house where she had reigned. In the summer Tommaseo wrote to Cantú from Paris:

'They tell me D. Giulia is more or less alone in the country, her son all wife!'

'Is it true that D. Giulia bears something of a grudge towards her daughter-in-law? She used to hold such sway!'

Meeting Fauriel in Paris, Tommaseo spoke to him of Manzoni's new marriage. Malicious things were being said about it. Fauriel said: *'Qu'on s'arrange comme on veut; il a besoin d'être heureux'* ['Let them suit themselves; he needs to be happy].

Tommaseo continued to muse about the Manzoni family, whom he had not seen for some time. In summer 1838 he wrote from Nantes to Cantú:

'Donna Giulia is rather left out; not ill-treated, I hope; give her my best regards. The girls must be over twenty by now. Quite different in appearance from Giulia who died. At least, they seemed so as little girls. Nothing of the father's genius in any of them. He is just an accident of destiny.'

In 1839 Cristina married a young man called Cristoforo Baroggi, a love match long opposed by his parents.

In February 1840 Giulia was writing to Rosa Somis (Counsellor Somis had died the year before):

'Oh my Rosa, could I forget you? you, the loving daughter of that good man for whom I have always felt the most profound veneration and esteem and warm sincere friendship? And gratitude that still lives in a heart that should be crushed by the years, but which on the contrary feels every hour of every day the pain of so many fatal losses. Dear Rosa, I cannot, I do not know how to resign myself. After the irreparable loss of my angelic Enrichetta whom you loved so much, oh Rosa, Rosa, everything is changed for your poor old friend, absolutely everything. . . When you came to Brusuglio the last time I saw you, I urged you to write, to keep me informed of your circumstances, you promised to do so, yet I have always been in the dark about your life: I heard of your change of state only a few months ago – is it I who am at fault, or you who have forgotten the poor old woman? Oh Rosa, your forgetfulness has hurt me!

'I hope to hear you are happy, you were always such a dear, good girl. Pray for me, for my needs are too great, and may that dear saintly man who in his life, always tried to do good to me remember a poor unhappy old woman. Rosa, I press you to my heart with the most sincere and heartfelt effusion of love and emotion.'

At Brusuglio that summer Cristina had fallen ill. She had recently had a baby girl, whom she had called Enrichetta. She was ill all winter; in April Vittoria left school – she was eighteen now – and came to live with her and help her. Cristina died in May.

Vittoria went to live with Sofia (but Sofia too was to die a few years later, in 1845, leaving four children).

Giulia wrote to Vittoria on 20 June 1841 (she herself would take to bed with inflammation of the lungs and die a few days later on 7 July):

'Oh my beloved child, your *povera poverissima Nonna* hugs you tight, and thinks of you and Sofia all the time, my dearest girls! Write to me, and *whatever happens* you know you can always open your heart to me. May God be always the driving force and guide of your every action. Never, never forget your angelic mother.

'Yesterday I went to the Visitazione and found dear Matilde still sad at your departure and the fresh test God has chosen to send us, but resigned and serene. Write to her, Vittoria dear, write to her rather than to me.

'Then I went to pay my tribute of tears and wretched prayers at the tomb of our beloved and lamented Cristina. Oh holy God! Decrepit old woman as I now am, to be preceded by so many darlings of my blood!'

Part Two
1836–1907

Teresa Borri I

Teresa Borri was born at Brivio, in Brianza in 1799, daughter of Cesare Borri and Marianna Meda. Both parents belonged to the aristocracy. When she was born they were not rich; the French occupation had destroyed family fortunes, and the father, an *assessore di tribunale* [one of the citizens called upon to sit, together with two judges, in a criminal court] in Milan, had been deprived of his office. He was made a stipendiary magistrate at Brivio. He lost this post, too, after the battle of Marengo. He held two minor offices, until, with the return of Austrian rule, he was made master of ceremonies at court. He moved back to Milan, and bought property at Torricella d'Arcellasco. Teresa had two brothers, Giuseppe and Giacomo. Giuseppe took a degree in law, and was a sculptor and writer. Giacomo was a priest.

When she was seventeen, Teresa met a friend of her brother Giuseppe, Count Stefano Decio Stampa, and at nineteen she married him. Stefano Decio had grown up in France, and had studied medicine at the Sorbonne. His mother, Julia, lived in Paris. The Stampas owned many houses in Milan, and many country estates. Teresa and her husband were living at Lesa in one of the Stampa villas, and had been married for only a few months, when Stefano Decio coughed blood. Neither he nor his wife chose to take it seriously. He treated himself with a diet and bleeding. Teresa was pregnant. In November 1819, in one of the Stampa houses in via Meravigli in Milan, she gave birth to a boy, who was called Giuseppe Stefano.

Stefano Decio was still unwell, but they decided to go to Paris to see his mother. In Paris, the painter Deveria did a pencil sketch of Teresa as a very beautiful young woman, with delicate features and cheeks, her large eyes lowered. Deveria also drew

161

husband and wife together, sitting side by side, she in profile with her hands in her lap, he turning to look at her, with a sort of resignation in the set of his shoulders, his features and his smile.

They returned to Italy; he got worse. He went to Lesa with the baby for the fresh air. Teresa remained at Milan with a throat infection. She was always to be plagued with throat infections and inflammation. 'I am better here than in Milan,' her husband wrote to her, 'I cough at night, but I cough it up easily, and then I still dream a lot, and always about food. I am sure I would be much better if I could ride. . .' But he was not even strong enough to walk. The letter is in French apart from a sentence in dialect; Teresa was also in the habit of writing partly in French, partly in Italian and partly in Milanese, a habit perhaps acquired from him, which she never lost. 'If you could see the baby,' he wrote, 'he's splendid, he tries to move everything he touches, however big. He is cutting his canines with no trouble at all'. People in Lesa made a row at night because it was the feast of San Martino; he felt like letting his pistol off at them. 'A real cat orchestra at five in the morning, just when I am enjoying my best sleep.' *Maman Mimi* (Teresa's mother, Marianna) had returned from the country estate at Torricella and was in the house the Borris owned at Borgo Gesù, but she was sleeping in a damp room, which was sure to bring on her rheumatism, and he was worried about it. He tackled his brother-in-law Giuseppe, 'Pepino', who was not bothered. Then he asked them to send 'a half dozen birds' because he liked making experiments on animals. The servant could get them from those bird-sellers on the steps of the Cathedral. He also wanted 'a few yards of cheap muslin, the most ordinary sort, and some pieces of green gauze, as fine as possible, for my butterfly nets'.

Teresa joined him at Lesa when she was better. By now Stefano Decio was taking only rose-hip jam, a Genovese sweetmeat. He died in December.

He had made a will and divided his estate equally between his wife and son, assigning a pension to his mother, Julia. But the mother was not content with this allowance, and claimed a vast portion of his estate. She had made Stefano Decio sign a paper, when he was still under age, promising her an annuity. In the last days of his life, her son had written to her in Paris asking her to send back this document. Julia did not move from Paris and did not send it. When the will was read she began legal proceedings against Teresa and her grandson.

The law-suit lasted many years. Teresa had to cope with tiring journeys, discussions with magistrates, attorneys and lawyers, examine documents and make all the financial calculations; her brother Giuseppe helped her, but she wanted to investigate and supervise it all herself. The baby was delicate. Teresa was always worried about him. In the summer she would send him to Torricella to her parents, Marianna and Cesare; she did not go, either to keep an eye on her case, or to avoid putting her parents to too much expense. 'Goodbye, my big little Stéphany, goodbye my angel, my life,' she wrote to the little boy. 'Goodbye, my Stéphany, most beloved of children.' Stéphany was terribly capricious, and his grandmother complained to Teresa that she found him tiring. Teresa begged her to have patience 'for the love of Stefanino, of me, and of all of us'. She had another throat inflammation which she treated with tamarind and with bleeding; then with emetic tartar, and with a vegetable juice that was like swallowing 'squash made from mould'.

In 1822 part of the legacy became available to her. She sold the house in via Meravigli, and she and the little boy went to live in an apartment in the same street, with her mother and father, and Giacomo, the priest: Giuseppe had his own establishment. In the summer she and Stefano could go to the villa of Lesa, part of which, however, was still used by relatives of the Stampas, the Marchese Caccia-Piatti and family; they were noisy and disorderly and prevented her enjoying the garden. Stefanino wanted to spend the whole day by the lake throwing stones, he kept slipping out of the house and running down to the shore, and she was in a perpetual state of anxiety. She preferred to send him to grandmother Marianna at Torricella. At Torricella there was a boy called Cesarino whom Stefanino hated and used to kick. 'Stefanino, my darling,' wrote Teresa, 'your dear Mama who misses you very much, asks you a great favour: don't be nasty to Cesarino, who is so fond of you, although you don't like him! Even if you don't like Cesarino, remember God loves him, for He created him; my darling Stefanino, I think of you all night; you are always at the centre of my heart and mind; I'm sure you will listen to your Mama, because I know you love

163

her so.'

In 1823, as soon as she had some money at her disposal, she ordered a 'family portrait' from the painter Francesco Hayez, paying for it in advance. It showed her mother, Giuseppe, herself and Stefanino. When she had the painting at home, she did not like it. She wrote about it to her mother. 'I am not very pleased with Peppino's portrait. I say nothing of my own; one is not allowed to judge one's own portrait; everyone agrees it is perfectly painted. For myself I can only say he's given me a most impressive double-chin, and I have a very slight one. But how fascinating and charming Stefanino's portrait is, and how like him!' She asked Hayez to make a few alterations. Hayez refused, and offered to give the money back and keep the painting. She did not want to. She sent it back for the alterations. Hayez made none. Years passed. She and Hayez exchanged furious letters. Finally Hayez kept the picture and gave her another one of a different subject. They resumed friendly relations.

In 1825 an uncle died, brother of grandmother Marianna, and the Borris inherited property, money and houses. They left via Meravigli and all went to the Bigli district.

Teresa was looking for a tutor for Stefanino. She found one Ghezzi who had been, she was told, tutor to the Manzoni boys for three years. She had heard of the Manzonis, but never seen them.

Stefanino had grown more robust in time, and was quite a pretty little boy. His mother thought he was extraordinarily intelligent. Grandmother Marianna felt some anxiety about him, he was so spoilt, and Teresa reassured her. 'You are anxious about the little lad,' she wrote to her at Torricella in summer 1827, 'but I see him night and day and I'm not anxious at all; what a difference! Can two mothers who feel the same concern and the same love for such an enchanting little angel, find themselves at two extremes, one quite secure and the other fearful? This is impossible, so rest assured, like me. . .'

'Her son slept beside her bed until he was a little boy, and until he was a young man in the same suite of rooms.

'She played with him almost as if he were a little sister, without ever losing his respect. . . As tender as the most devoted mother, she became more severe and terrible than a father, if her son gave her cause. Although she took excessive care of his

164

health, for fear he might become consumptive like his father (and as a result of his cossetting he developed habits of laziness which he never managed to shake off), yet she told the peasants with whom he played to hit him if he hit them; and she made him apologise to the servants if he offended them with some boyish insolence; and she asked him, with withering sarcasm, if he thought he was little Count Ciccin, described by Porta.'

This is how Stefano Stampa remembered his mother, when he evoked his childhood many years later. He spoke of himself in the third person. His mother had been dead for some time. These memories were gathered into a volume which he published in 1885, and which bore only his initials, S. S.

In 1827 Teresa read *I promessi sposi*. She wrote about it to her mother. 'I'm reading Manzoni's novel. Oh, Mama! how fine it is; he really is a man after my own heart. He depicts everything in such a natural way, and how beautiful and perfect that nature is! You will say that this implies that my nature too is beautiful and perfect; and why not? Was I not created by God and for God?'

She heard of Luigi Rossari, and wanted him to be Stefano's tutor. Through Rossari she met Tommaso Grossi. She met Giovanni Torti and shortly after d'Azeglio. As Stefanino drew and painted, d'Azeglio let him come to his studio. Stefanino's admiration for d'Azeglio was boundless.

When the law-suit was finally settled in court, Teresa was reconciled with her mother-in-law, Julia Stampa. They wrote to each other; the mother-in-law came to Milan to embrace Stefanino. The memory of their long legal quarrels was buried.

Teresa and Stefanino left her people and went to live in a house in the Monti district.

It was Grossi who spoke to Manzoni of Teresa. He described her as a cultured, intelligent, sensitive woman, devoted to her son and to her domestic responsibilities. He introduced her to him one evening at the theatre. Grossi knew Manzoni was tired of living alone, and that his mother wanted him to marry again. Stefano Stampa reports: 'It seems that Manzoni sent or let Donna Giulia, his mother, go to call on her, and this lady was delighted, indeed quite enamoured with poor Teresa. She called on her again, and a few days later Manzoni came in person, and after a few more calls asked her to be his wife.' The words 'poor Teresa' arise from the fact that later there were to be, between Giulia and Teresa, bitter disagreements, which caused pain to Teresa; but in any case, Teresa liked to have this adjective of commiseration added to her name.

Teresa hesitated about this proposal. Whether her hesitation was real or simulated is hard to say. The objections she put forward concerned her own poor health – she so often had bad throats, and other troubles – the thought of her own inadequacy for such an honour, and the fear that her son might not be happy. Perhaps the last was the only sincere objection.

Stefano was then seventeen. He said later that his mother came into his room one evening and said to him:

'You know I have devoted my whole life to you. Everything I've done has been done with your good in mind. Now I have to tell you that Manzoni has asked me to be his wife. If I were to accept, it would be only in the hope that such a connection would be beneficial to you. But if you prefer us to live together on our own, apart from the world as we have done until now, tell me frankly and I shall reject this proposal.'

The son replied:

'You are the best judge of what is good for me. Do what you think best for both of us.'

Then Teresa wrote to her own mother:

'Don't tell anyone except my brothers, promise faithfully not to tell anyone else that in one month I believe I shall be the wife of Alessandro Manzoni. I shall come to see you as soon as possible, I hope, but it may be as late as possible, as from one to four Manzoni is here, before one I am in bed, and after four it is too cold for me with my poor health, which has not been poor enough to put off Manzoni who wants me in all my physical and moral poverty. I need hardly tell you that, first of all, I wanted to know not only if this would hurt Stefano, but if he would like to have Manzoni for a father. It was Grossi who did everything for me. . . Alessandro will not pay calls; he never calls on anyone all year: not even his uncle Beccaria, although he spends weeks with him at Gessate. So when I come to see you, you will see in me both a daughter and a new son: Alessandro never goes out with a lady, but is always accompanied by his closest friends, though he never calls on them either.' Then she wrote to a sister of her mother, Aunt Notburga, a nun: 'My dear aunt, I have been considered capable of fulfilling new and sacred duties! Poor trampled wretch that I am, I have been sought out for the highest possible place! But pride will not find wings to reach me, and, though wife of Manzoni – of ALESSANDRO MANZONI – in my own eyes I shall still be poor Teresa.' She also wrote to Giuseppe Bottelli, a priest at Arona, whom she had known well at Lesa; he replied: 'I offer Your Ladyship my congratulations, although nothing can add to the summum bonum of soon being wife to Alessandro Manzoni. Placed on this most sublime height, the too-humble expression of a *poor trampled wretch* must be forgotten. . . Dearest Countess, take all diligent care of yourself that your health may become ever more precious.' And Aunt Notburga to her sister Marianna: 'My purpose in writing is to rejoice with you in Teresa's marriage: Jacob's prayers for her have been granted [Jacob, that is Giacomo, the priest]; in this marriage I see such a radiant sign of divine mercy towards your daughter, that I leave the talking to others, and thank God in the depths of my heart for His goodness. . .' She enclosed Teresa's letter: 'She shows in it a great deal of respect for her husband, humility and piety; in short, she is already quite changed, and is preparing to undertake a happy career; I am very pleased, but let Jacob go on praying. . .' The aunt's letter breathes a sense of relief: Teresa must have caused the family considerable anxiety.

Tommaseo wrote to Cesare Cantú, who had written to him: 'Thank you for the secret you confided in me, but don't blame me if others are already talking about it. When I first heard it mentioned as an uncertain rumour, I feigned ignorance. When it was then presented as news, I could no longer pretend, especially as they now say it is a *fait accompli*, and as for the details, they know better than I do. All women's gossip. As for me, I'm delighted; and his mother will no doubt be pleased; the family will gain fresh life, and his talent will be stirred. Here they say she's an unbeliever, and *galante*, too. Do tell me the truth of the matter. . .'

We do not know what Cantú replied. We know only that, later in his memoirs, Stefano Stampa wote pages and pages on that 'galante, too'. Cantú, in his *Reminiscences*, included

Tommaseo's letter without comment.

The wedding day was fixed for 2 January. Teresa ordered lots of clothes. She was a fragile, slender, graceful woman, small in stature, with thick, curly hair. She was then thirty-eight.

Manzoni's sons and daughters came to meet her. She said she wanted to be a big sister to them.

The Provost of San Fedele, don Giulio Ratti, came to meet her. He probably spoke to her about the most suitable way of comporting herself in the household. She wrote to Manzoni: 'I was in full agreement with everything he said. . . I am perfectly happy about it, and we parted in complete accord. Alessandro, will that Alessandro have a good night? There is one who would have stayed awake all night asking herself this question if she had not indulged in writing these few lines, in which is included the most tender embrace for a certain incomparable mother.'

The wedding took place on 2 January 1837. Teresa and Stefano moved into via del Morone. Disagreements with the 'incomparable mother' began at once.

Stefano Stampa, in his memoirs:

'When she entered the house, donna Teresa left donna Giulia in complete charge. Needless to say, she did not interfere with the three sons, two of whom, as young men, were always out, and the last was at school; neither did she attempt to influence the girls: two of marriageable age, the third at school, and the fourth a little child, cared for in all material things by the French nanny, and educated, then later sent away to school, under the direction of her grandmother and her sisters. It did not cost donna Teresa to abdicate all influence in this way, as it was her own carefully considered choice, for she thought there was no need for anyone to interfere in the Manzoni family; and if there had been any need, any attempt to break old habits would only have led to disagreements.

'Besides, her poor health would have been an insurmountable obstacle.'

Cantú:

'When Enrichetta died, it was thought that *Postquam primus amor deceptum morte fefellit* ['After my first love failed me, cheated by death. . .', *Aeneid* IV, 17], in the autumn of life Alessandro must resign himself to a widower's solitude, and be content to watch over Pietro's family. But he felt the curse of solitude and the need of a companion. He chose Teresa, daughter of Cesare, one of the Borri counts (2nd January 1837), who had been wife to the nobleman Stefano Decio Stampa, and had a son in the prime of youth and hope. We wished him that repose which is often called happiness, and that he might find the domestic support customary in such marriages in the winter of life, where warmth is replaced by reciprocal help and common memories.

'It is rare for a stepmother to bring comfort to children already adult. The newcomer, while feeling the great worth of possessing such a man, and without wishing as some claimed to wean him away from importunate friends and isolate him in order to absorb him, claimed more wifely authority than the meek Enrichetta had done. This was hurtful chiefly to donna Giulia, accustomed to being regarded as the mistress of the house. The change led to bitterness, which was bound to affect Alessandro.'

The 6th January, Costanza Arconati, from Bonn, to her sister Margherita (who had meanwhile married d'Azeglio's friend, Collegno):

'I haven't heard a word about Manzoni's marriage; it is no surprise because his mother's letters indicated how keen she was on it. Yet this decision makes me sad. It takes away something of the aura of sublimity that surrounds him. When I consider all the particular circumstances, it seems an act of weakness. What does Fauriel say about it?' And a few days later: 'I was surprised to hear that a son of 17 was appended to Manzoni's imprudent marriage. The girls have every right to grieve; and it's natural that the public should judge Manzoni more severely than another. Tell me what Fauriel says. . . It's a calumny to suggest Manzoni did not treat Enrichetta with every kindness. I am also convinced that he does not love the wife he has now as he loved Enrichetta, but he could not manage without a companion.'

Fauriel said: '*Qu'on s'arrange comme on veut. Il a besoin d'être heureux.*' This was reported by Tommaseo, who saw him in Paris at that time. These sentiments are placid, sensible, affectionate and certainly true. Manzoni could not stand grief for long, he wanted to be happy.

But Teresa made all the others unhappy. She made Giulia unhappy, slowly pushing her out of the space she had occupied till then. Perhaps she did not exactly contest the running of the house, but her place in the house. Above all, she contested the place she occupied in Alessandro's thoughts. She made the dead Enrichetta's children unhappy. In the whole world she loved only herself and her own son, and she partly loved her own close relatives, as an extension of herself. Everything else was shadowy. When she married Manzoni, she installed him in the spotlight of her own world. She devoted herself to a cult of his greatness and glory. She did not look upon his children with aversion, but with indifference. They were shadows, useless shadows, grey and uninteresting. She looked at them as one might look at strangers, outside the windows, who have chanced to wander into the garden, and will soon, thank God, go away.

When Enrichetta died, Filippo was sent away to school at Susino on Lake Como. He was eight. He wrote little letters to his father, full of zeal and melancholy. They discovered later that the school was dreadful, and he had had unhappy experiences there.

'I always pray for my Dear Mummy and my Dear Sister Giulia. I will do my best to study with good will. Come and see me soon. Be so kind as to send me a little drum and a ball and a mouth organ.'

On 27 January 1837, after his father's new marriage, he wrote his first letter to his step-mother:

'Carissima mammina. I know I have another Mother who will take care of me, so this is for me a piece of good fortune for which I shall be most grateful. I promise her all the respect and all the love that a son owes his parents, and I will keep my promise. I have written this letter from the heart, and I am resolved to be ever your obedient son Filippo.'

And a few months later:

'Carissima mammina. As soon as the Headmaster rang the bell to go out to play, I sat down at my little table to write you these few lines. Last Thursday we did our exams, and I hope I have done myself credit. I wait anxiously for you to come with all the family and with aunt and uncle Beccaria, but you never appear. So I beg you, o cara mammina, to come Wednesday. I beg you to bring me my summer clothes, a straw hat, some pencils, a box of brushes and paints, the *Magasin Pittoresque* and some other nice books, a little drum and a ball. . . Now I come

170

to the chief thing. I hope you are well, as we are. I promise you to study and be a good boy so that I may be a source of consolation to you one day. . . Goodbye, dear mother, please give my love to all the family, and remember your aff. son, Filippo.'

For many years – since 1822 – Tommaso Grossi had had two little rooms on the ground floor of the Manzoni house in via del Morone. In May 1837 Grossi left those rooms and went to live elsewhere. According to Cantú, Grossi left the rooms as a result of Manzoni's new marriage, and for some reason connected with Teresa. Cantú: 'He [Manzoni] had to dismiss some friends. Grossi gave up living in the same house, and here we must just make a sign, for history must show a certain discretion.'

What Cantú meant by this we cannot know.

It seems that Grossi intervened in a discussion between Giulia and Teresa, seeking to make peace.

Many years later, Stefano Stampa explained that Grossi 'had given up his rooms in the Manzoni household because he had decided to get married himself'. In fact, Grossi did get married not long after. He became a solicitor and began to practise. The friendship between him and Manzoni remained unchanged.

The discussion between Giulia and Teresa apparently concerned Stefano. Giulia was in charge of the house-keeping. Stefano was supposed to pay towards his keep every month. They quarrelled about money, about what should or should not be included in that monthly contribution.

From Paris Tommaseo wrote to Cantú:

'I am really sorry about don Alessandro. Can Grossi and others not prevent the worst of the gossip?

'And how does he pass the time if he's not writing?'

And in another letter:

'What's this? Manzoni no longer receives his close friends in the morning? Well, when do you see him?'

Gino Capponi to Tommaseo, still in the spring of 1837 (he had heard Manzoni wanted to reprint a revised version of *I promessi sposi*): 'His wife is making him work. Poor man, that's just what he needed! *Cessi ogni ria parola.*' [No more wicked words.]

Tommaseo to Capponi:

'Manzoni, my good sir, is doing nothing. The daughter-in-law is most capricious, the mother-in-law full of complaints.

'The stepdaughters in a huff.'

Manzoni had never reprinted *I promessi sposi* with the corrections made during the trip to Tuscany; he proposed to do so. He had the idea of an illustrated edition, thinking the illustrations would be a defence against pirated editions, of which there had been an enormous number over the years. At that time there was no protection of authors' rights, so Manzoni had made very little out of *I promessi sposi*, in spite of its immense success.

He wanted to publish the illustrated edition himself. He, Teresa, and his friends were absolutely certain it was an excellent idea. They called upon Francesco Hayez, an old acquaintance of Teresa, to attempt some drawings. But these were not considered satisfactory. They called upon the French artist Boulanger, but his drawings too were viewed unfavourably. Then d'Azeglio came up with a painter called Gonin, whose drawings Manzoni thought very beautiful. He started writing to Gonin almost every day. 'Mio Gonin.' Engravers were brought from Paris. A small printing-press was set up in via San Pietro all'Orto.

Giulia was strongly opposed to this project, not to the illustrated edition, but to the idea that Manzoni should become his own publisher. It seemed to her vastly imprudent. Cousin Beccaria shared her fears. So disagreements arose between Teresa and Giulia, in addition to all those already existing. In time it became clear that Giulia and Cousin Giacomo were right.

Giulia detested Stefano, and for his part Stefano detested Giulia. Perhaps this detestation dated from the very first day they lived together. Giulia thought Stefano spoilt, disorderly, lazy, overbearing and proud. He used to remain shut in his room painting, taking no part in family life. Stefano thought Giulia an unbearable old woman. He refused to call her grandmother. When they went to Brusuglio in the summer, he thought it was the most boring place in the world. He fled to Torricella, Lesa, Morosolo, to the many houses and villas belonging to the Stampas. Writing to his mother from afar, he never put greetings for Giulia in his letters.

In fact, Giulia detested Stefano above all because he was Teresa's son. She had hated Teresa ever since she had seen her

172

in their house. She hated her euphoria, exuberance, excitable effusions, loquacity. She hated her delicate health, the thousand attentions she devoted to herself, which seemed to her a way of usurping the centre of the stage. She also detested the way she idolized Alessandro. She thought Teresa's feelings for her husband were nothing but inordinate vanity.

Teresa, from Brusuglio, to Stefano, who was travelling: 'How I could love the lady for being A's mother, B's daughter, or simply an old lady, a state which has fascinated me since I was a child! But for days now she's been standing on one leg, with her head under her wing; God forbid that she's just getting her breath back, because in the process Alessandro is losing his breath for study, his health, his well-being and everything except his amiability, and his divinity. His friendship and love for me take the place of a whole world of happiness, but you're not here, and I long for you. . .'

Teresa's brother Giuseppe came to visit them in July, and commented on his visit: 'So I bowed to Manzoni's mother, before whom one is tempted to say: *benedictus fructus ventris tui*. But if in Manzoni I felt I recognized the philosopher Rousseau would like to find in his democracy, to dictate a code of laws to him, in Manzoni's mother, on the other hand, you feel you are seeing Monna Aristocrazia in the flesh. Her manner is magisterially proud, her words, even when they flatter, keep you at a great distance; she is not the daughter of Beccaria the teacher, but of the Marchese. Her speech is sparing, considered and sententious, and never does the slightest smile appear to smooth her brow. In short, her face, her manners, her words shed a mortal chill in your heart. . .'

Filippo came home from school in September: 'Filippo has arrived,' Teresa wrote to Stefano, 'he's a dear, sweet boy; he's like Alessandro in every way, you met him this winter, but you will get to know him better now.' And in another letter: 'Poor Filippo will not go back to Susino, to that ferocious imbecile of a Sig. Longhi'; Filippo stayed home, and they found a tutor for him, don Giovanni Ghianda.

Tommaseo came in October. He wrote in his memoirs: 'I've been to see Manzoni who invited me to Brusuglio. They disturb me. He is good; his mother unhappy; his wife artful; his son Filippo without affection.'

173

Stefano tried to spend as little time as possible at Brusuglio. 'He loves the mountains,' Teresa wrote to her mother about Stefano, 'and won't go to the country if there are no mountains or lakes, or a lake; you can't *blame* him for this, in fact, I think he's quite right.' The word *blame* is underlined, obviously there had been a quarrel, and Giulia had *blamed* Stefano, who scorned Brusuglio, a place without mountains or lakes. He spent his summers at Lesa, or Torricella, or Morosolo where he had a villa. Teresa had wine sent from Morosolo, and Giulia refused it, and when she saw it brought to the table, she pushed aside her glass angrily. In the first summer of her marriage, Teresa had written to Antonio Maspero, steward at Morosolo, mentioning the possibility that the whole Manzoni family might descend upon the villa, a fairly improbable event: 'Who knows if one day you will find us descending on you for a week or ten days! but perhaps there are too many of us: there aren't enough beds; because, even counting only one male head of the household, with three girls, the grandmother, Stefano and myself, that makes seven beds for a start, and then we'd need ten more for five women and five menservants. So that I wouldn't know, not just where to house them, but where to sleep them. And then how would we manage for linen and crockery? . . . If ever the grandmother decided to come to Morosolo for a few days, I will let you know well in advance; we would all like to except the grandmother, so it will be very difficult. Stefano will come, if no one else. . .' Later, in the summers that ensued, the idea of getting the grandmother to Morosolo or Lesa never arose: relations between her and Teresa had so deteriorated that there was not the remotest possibility of taking her to either place.

Stefano loved going to Lesa. The Caccia-piattis were still there, but now they were inoffensive; the villa belonged to Stefano; the Caccia-piattis were relegated to a small apartment and caused no annoyance. Sometimes they were asked by Teresa to keep an eye on Stefano. In the summer when Stefano was far away, which was almost always the case, Teresa was consumed with apprehension, and her worries and her low spirits weighed upon the whole family. Alessandro had more than ever to surround her with attentions, distract her and console her. Giulia thought Stefano was given too much freedom. Moreover, in all his comings and goings, she had to see to his

174

dirty linen, and she complained about it. Teresa decided to put an end to these tedious complaints: henceforth Stefano would make his own arrangements for his linen. Or rather his valet, Francesco, would see to it. If he came to Brusuglio, Francesco would go to dine 'at his own house, or at the small ale-house'. Teresa wrote to Stefano: 'Write to tell Patrizio you are resolved to ask only for room and firewood at home; you should have done so already.' Antonio Patrizio administered the property of Teresa and Stefano. Cousin Beccaria, the Councillor, was also informed of all this. He helped Giulia with the household management.

Teresa's father, Cesare Borri, had died in 1837, the year she married Manzoni.

When Stefano was away at Lesa, or Torricella, or Morosolo, Teresa urged him not to forget, in his letters, 'his compliments to the grandmother'. But Stefano sent Giulia neither compliments nor greetings; and to avoid sending them to Giulia, he did not even send them to Manzoni. Yet Stefano was fond of Manzoni. 'I do not send my greetings,' Manzoni once wrote to him at the bottom of one of Teresa's letters, and she added: 'No, Papa is not obliged, not only to greet you, but even to state he does not greet you! Unworthy as you are of the good wishes that he feels for you, and that he has sent you! not even once to say: give Papa my love and best wishes. – Shame on you! shameful and shameless as you are; I am not joking, I am in earnest. I hope and believe it is because of a certain recommendation Papa told me he made to you, and which I did not hear about until today, but if you did not choose to obey, you could have sent him love and kisses and said *I ask your pardon on my knees*, without it being or seeming a jest, you could have done anything, even disobeyed him, but surely you could not have forgotten the noble brow and hair of that divine Alessandro who is so fond of you.' This was Alessandro's recommendation: as Stefano was about to leave, Manzoni had whispered to him jokingly: 'greet the person you don't want to', that is, remember always to put a greeting for Giulia in your letters. These joking words, whispered in his stepson's ear, show how far Manzoni now was from his mother, so far as to joke about her anger. Indeed, Giulia's anger could seem petty – dirty linen, absence of greetings – but they came from very real and bitter suffering, for which the boy Stefano was not to blame. Giulia knew that Alessandro had moved away from her, to stand, with Stefano and Teresa, on another shore.

In 1838 d'Azeglio's mother, the Marchesa Cristina, died. D'Azeglio hastily sold his houses in Turin, as well as the castle of d'Azeglio. He found a governess for little Rina, called Emilia Luti. He came to see the Manzonis at Brusuglio, with the little girl and the governess. Giulia was more cheerful when she had little Rina with her.

Emilia Luti was a Florentine. She supplied Manzoni with invaluable suggestions about the Tuscan language, and was a great help to him in his revision of *I promessi sposi*.

Teresa wrote to Stefano, preaching the Tuscan language to him:

'Note that Papa says *novamente* and not *nuovamente* as you are so fond of saying with the *u*: you're always saying *buonissimo viaggio*, for example, which is quite unsuitable; the *u* is hardly ever said or written. Have you seen that *finir gli anni* is said for *compir gli anni*? and *dar una capata* for *fare una scappata*? We have noted and learnt this from signora Emilia Luti, together with many other fine things. . . do remember that *cosicché* is not Tuscan; they say *sicché, di modo che,* but not *cosicché*. . . Papa is here and greets you.' 'I certainly do! Do you know who it is?' Manzoni added in dialect. 'I embrace you most affectionately. Without saying who! . . .'

A young man called Cristoforo Baroggi, son of a solicitor, had fallen in love with Cristina, and she with him. They wanted to get married, but the Baroggi family were hostile to the marriage. Cristoforo's father, lawyer Ignazio, thought that Cristoforo, who enjoyed spending money, should marry a girl with a large dowry, and that Cristina's dowry was insufficient. He felt he could not help his son from his own income, which was why he opposed the marriage.

In the summer of 1833, just before Enrichetta fell ill, they had received a visit at Brusuglio from Henri Falquet-Planta, son of Euphrosine and Sébastian Falquet-Planta; he had fallen in love with Cristina and wanted to marry her. Euphrosine would have been pleased, but grandmother Giulia was not taken with the idea of Cristina marrying this Henri, and had opposed the idea. Henri lived in France, which was too far away. Cristina was still so young.

Years later, she received a proposal from a merchant in Cremona, twice a widower. She rejected it.

In love with Cristoforo, she was hurt to find herself repulsed by his family. Uncle Beccaria and Cousin Giacomo intervened to persuade Lawyer Baroggi, but the latter refused to hear of the marriage. Cristoforo and Cristina prepared to marry in spite of this. There was a lengthy correspondence between Manzoni, Uncle Giulio and the cousin. Finally, after a long period of uncertainty, the lawyer yielded and gave his consent. In September 1838 Cristoforo Baroggi came to the Manzoni house as a fiancé.

In October of that year Sofia married Lodovico Trotti, brother of Costanza Trotti Arconati, Marietta, and Margherita. He had been a captain of the Uhlans in Moravia and Bohemia, but had resigned from the army and returned to Italy a few years before. Teresa wrote to Stefano, who was at Lesa as usual:

'Papa has asked me if I have written to you about Sofia's marriage. Lodovico Trotti will be much better off than we thought; and he's so good, affectionate, brave, proud and gentle that Sofia really is a lucky girl; as you know, he's a very good-looking young man, strong but kind, and all his relatives are such excellent people, respectable and respected that it's a great joy to Alessandro to have them related to his daughter. The father, the Marchese. . . is delighted with this marriage, like all the Trotti family. . . Poor Cristina, too, has had a chance to show her affection for me; Pietro and Enrico are making a fuss of me. . .' Pietro and Enrico behaved cordially towards her.

Cristina and Cristoforo got married in May 1839.

In June 1839 Enrico set off for Lyons, where he spent a year, to gain experience of the breeding of silk-worms and of the silk trade. Cristoforo Baroggi had recommended him to his acquaintances in the town; he had founded a bank there. 'My dear Enrico,' Manzoni wrote to his son, 'you can imagine what comfort I got from your letter, and from the intentions it conveyed. . . My satisfaction in you, as in all of you, depends upon your well-being. So continue to prosper; indeed, go swiftly from strength to strength in the career you have embarked on, in which your father will do all he can to help you. Always bear in mind that fine maxim, the truth of which you must already have learnt from experience, that to go to sleep happy one must say, not: I've done what I wanted today, but: I've done what I had to do. Work and boredom are the choice before us in this world; the first, apart from the other reasons for embracing it, brings its own reward: in the second all is punishment. But you know that even good things are not entirely so, unless they are subordinated and directed to the one absolute good. Think often, dear Enrico, of the angelic mother from whom you chiefly learned this lesson. . .'

Writing to Stefano, Teresa continued to complain not only that his letters never contained a greeting for the grandmother, but even greetings for Manzoni or the rest of the family. This absence of greetings was deeply distressing to her. 'Your letter. . . without a shadow of affection, thought or greeting for Alessandro has left me quite turned to stone, but to stone burning with shame. . . Papa who was there said (we were alone) *oh well, if that's the way it is, and the young lord doesn't send his regards, I won't go to Lesa any more. . . he was such a good friend, and all of a sudden he doesn't remember, doesn't even bother to send his greetings.* Think how this pierced my heart for your sake! it seems impossible just because he said to you: *greet the person you don't want to. . .* If he had said just as you were leaving, remember to greet the guinea-fowl in your letters and the geese and ganders, you ought to greet the fowl and the geese and the ganders, and then greet him. I know you don't like the person he asked you to remember; and I know it's just because of the suffering she costs him; if she adored him, you would love her from the heart, I know; but he not only accords this person who is his mother the respect required by human and divine law, but he also lavishes upon her the feelings that can only spring from a heart like his. . .'and then how improper not to send your regards to Enrico, who always mentions you in his letters from Lyons; nor to don Giovanni [Ghianda] who called specially to greet you the morning you left; nor Cristina, who always remembers to send her regards to you and ask for news of you when you're away!'

Teresa often spoke of Filippo in her letters to Stefano; she thought he looked like Alessandro; he was her favourite stepchild at that time. 'Filippo wanted to add a few words at the end of this; he gets more and more attached to me; he doesn't come

178

into my room out of discretion, which he had to learn at school, but he makes up for it with his caresses, and his pretty ways, and affectionate expressions for you and me; he urged me in his open, insistent way to send you all his love: *you will send him my regards, mama; don't forget to tell him that I love him very much and that I always remember him; that I hope he's well and having a good time; but do you think that he'll remember me? is it really true that he sends me his regards?'* Filippo must have been full of admiration for Stefano; he saw him coming and going, free, cheerful, having a good time, with his palettes and brushes; Stefano had money, independence, a mother to scold and love him, and everything he did not have. As for Stefano, always so miserly with his greetings, who knows if he really remembered to send his regards to this little boy, entrusted to a priest, whom he occasionally met in the avenues of Brusuglio or at table.

Teresa and Alessandro went to Lesa in the summer of 1839; Stefano was there and greeted them very effusively; they planned to return in the autumn, although the thought of the Cacciapiattis bothered them a bit. Stefano wanted to meet the expenses of this first visit to Lesa by Alessandro; he was twenty now and the court allowed him control of his own income; but he was not yet allowed to buy or sell, or to incur debts. Teresa felt well at Lesa, all her indispositions vanished; whereas, in the heat of Brusuglio the summer months seemed tedious and heavy; but they had to spend the summer and a good part of the autumn there, none the less, to take care of the estate. 'You'll see how well I am!' Teresa wrote as she left Lesa, to Stefano who was still there. 'It's Lesa, Lesa all the time, Lesa which delights Alessandro, who is still talking about it with his mouth watering.' It must have been painful for Giulia to hear them talking of the wonders of Lesa, to see at table the wine from Lesa that Alessandro liked, and see Alessandro and Teresa setting off for Lesa, while she remained alone at hot, despised Brusuglio, with Filippo and don Ghianda and the others who were excluded from Lesa.

In 1839 Sofia had her first baby, Antonio. In 1840 Lodovico's father, the Marchese Antonio Trotti Bentivoglio, died. When the will was read out, Lodovico discovered that his share of the inheritance was much less than his brothers'. His father had been angry with him when he had abandoned his military career, and had chosen to punish him in this way. Manzoni wrote a bitter letter to Costanza Arconati, Lodovico's sister, asking her to intervene with the older brother to make the terms of the will more favourable to Lodovico, 'husband and father'.

In 1840 Cristina had a baby, Enrichetta. Then she became ill. She developed a sort of erythema on the face. In the summer, at Brusuglio, her condition was very bad. She was bled. Teresa wrote to Stefano at Voltri (where he had fallen ill himself and Teresa, in a panic, wanted to join him, but they had soothed her, and in fact it was nothing serious): 'Cristina, after being bled three times and cruelly bitten by leeches several times, and put on a very strict diet, silence, darkness, etc., after having lost a lot of weight and all her colour as a result of the remedies, has now been sent to Doctor Casanova, who has taken the precaution of making her husband the first recipient of his diagnosis, adding that it would soon be over, but that in the few days that remained to her they must remove lots and lots more blood. You can imagine the laments of poor Cristoforo who had never dreamed, not only of taking a black, but even a cloudy view. They immediately went to Piantanida, who changed the treatment together with the name of the illness, which is no longer a "slow-fast inflammation", but shingles, as Caramella said last year when she saw the tremendous eruption she had in the face. Just think of shingles being treated all winter and spring and half the summer with sulphur baths, morphine and opium in those quantities! So, no more bleedings, no more opium, she has been put on a simple diet, but with meat, and encouraged to get up; which she did at once and post haste to Milan, away from that doctor who would have it his own way, in spite of the result of the consultation. Now she's been in Milan for three days and made great progress, because she gets up, eats, receives friends in the drawing-room, and is doing very nicely; apart from that pain she has [in the temples] which has come back dreadfully and continues, sometimes more, sometimes less, but by what her doctor says, who is now Piantanida, she shouldn't take any more remedies for it, as unfortunately there aren't any.' According to Piantanida she was in no danger. 'So as far as that's concerned dear Alessandro can breathe again. . .'

180

Manzoni wanted very much to go to Lesa that autumn, but it was not possible, first because Teresa was ill with a 'phlogosis' in the head, and feared 'to encounter rude air' on the journey; then in October Pietro became seriously ill. Teresa wrote to Stefano: 'After various lapses due to his excessive and unfortunate drinking, Pietro is in bed with severe inflammation of the brain and the intestines, which causes delirium night and day. . . imagine poor Alessandro, who had begged and prayed, coaxed and constrained him to give up that drinking!' And Manzoni to Cattaneo: 'At last I can take up my pen to tell you of a danger, which, thank Heaven, has passed over. My Pietro had succumbed to a violent attack of meningitis, and after sixty hours of delirium, has now recovered, thanks to the prudent but determined application of bleeding and of tartarate of tin. Yesterday morning the deadly symptoms began to diminish; during the day he improved steadily; finally last night of blessed memory, at about two o'clock he went into a wholesome sleep. . . the doctors are very pleased, so you can imagine our feelings.' Teresa to Stefano: 'In four days they bled him profusely nine times, applied 24 leeches, and administered a load of emetic tartar.' But Manzoni was always an optimist: in November Pietro was ill again, and 'they had to go back to the bleedings, leeches and three blister-papers'.

When Pietro recovered, there followed a brief spell of peace; Giulia was in a good mood, pleased about Pietro's recovery; Cristina too, although very thin and pale, seemed better. Enrico had come home. Giulia finally agreed to taste the Lesa wine; 'All in all, I might call it a *honeymoon*, please God it may last!' Teresa told Stefano, 'not for me, but for Alessandro, who was losing his health, his studies, and years of life!. . . Poor Alessandro. . . *It's true that even before, if the conductor was different, the music was the same.* [By which Teresa meant that even with Enrichetta, Giulia must have been unbearable.] We hope that now that deadly orchestra will cease or hold its peace somewhat! Who knows if God, or time and her 77 years may partly change her, at least in the ways most necessary to Alessandro! As I've never written so explicitly about this matter, you would do well to burn this letter, after reading it, I mean. . .' Stefano did not burn it.

I promessi sposi began to appear in instalments, in the new revised and illustrated edition. Teresa exulted in it. But it very soon became apparent that things were not going too well. The printer Guglielmini proved to be untrustworthy. Subscriptions rapidly declined. Unsold copies piled up in the rooms of via del Morone. Giulia and cousin Giacomo had sensed that the undertaking would prove ruinous. They were right.

Teresa's brother, Giuseppe, came to stay at via del Morone that winter. Giulia did not speak to him. There had never been any sympathy between them; and now Teresa's family – and of course above all Teresa herself – seemed to her most to blame for that unfortunate publishing operation: they had strongly urged Manzoni to become his own publisher. This visit of Giuseppe Borri to Manzoni made her more than usually gloomy. Giuseppe made this comment on his visit: 'His mother was reading, and went on reading, or at least turning the pages of her book, all evening.'

A page which Tommaseo wrote many years later tells about Manzoni and this edition, and the facts that preceded and ensued, in a few rapid, dry words:

'He was correcting, even recasting proofs, and, regretfully, reprinting sheets. And one day when he had some spread out to dry in his room, he said to me with a smile: "You see I too have something in the sun." Indeed, he had estates in the sun; Carlo Imbonati's legacy had enriched his mother, who had her friend's body dragged from Paris and from Milan, but she diminished that inheritance by many charitable works and by the troubles impatiently borne, inflicted by the second daughter-in-law, made all the more grievous to her by the memory of the first, a lady of incomparable gentleness. And the mother herself had chosen this second wife for her son, who took her almost unknown, and did not know how to keep peace between the two ladies, and was always so resigned as to seem unconcerned. But then his sons' irregularities diminished his wealth; and his writings, which outside Italy would have enriched him, not only brought him no profit, but financial damage in the end. Self-inflicted harm, more or less asked for, because he decided to reprint the novel with vignettes, as if such reading needed such distractions; and they brought an artist from Paris, and spent time and money and trouble; and the printer secretly produced extra copies and sold them at reduced prices, perhaps to make up for the trouble of having to alter the proofs all the time with fresh corrections, and hold up a sheet until he had recast it in his own way.'

Early in the spring of 1841 Cristina became ill again. It was the same illness and nobody knew how to treat it. Violent headaches, and that eruption on the face. They stuffed her with opium again. Her face was swollen, deformed, unrecognizable. Once she had been pretty. *Ma petite noiraude*, Enrichetta used to call her. She was the only one in the family with black hair.

The course of the illness was rapid and terrible. Soon they all realized she was lost. Her husband tended her lovingly. She lived to the end of May. She did not want to die. She had a little baby girl, a happy marriage. She thought death was unjust and rebelled against it, refusing the sacraments. Her father had to intervene. '(6 o'clock, after dinner) I lie awake at night,' Teresa wrote to Stefano, 'thinking of poor Cristina. . . at that moment they came to call poor, adorable, broken-hearted Alessandro to poor Cristina, who cannot overcome her shrinking from the sacred oil; her confessor cannot convince her, she will only believe her father. . . Poor Alessandro! It has fallen to him to prepare her for confession and the last rites; now. . . Oh, God, what a cup my poor Alessandro has to drink!' And later: 'Alessandro returned broken with grief, after preparing Cristina for extreme unction: so that she told him to go, for she was content; then, when he had gone, she called Cristoforo, embraced him and said: *I am content*. You see how she will be in Heaven. Oh Lord! Put some black crêpe on your hat.'

Teresa to Stefano again, after the funeral:

'Sofia looked quite dreadful; Thursday evening you had to feel very sorry for her; now she's a little better, but her face is horribly drawn; I mean, it makes you fear for her health. Vittorina will come out of the convent to go to Bellagio with Sofia; you can imagine her state, too. Poor Alessandro couldn't even go to Brusú, because yesterday evening they were taking poor Cristina there; she was received by peasant schoolchildren with lighted candles, and they insisted on carrying her on their shoulders with great solemnity to the cemetery, where she was placed beside her mother and her sister! I am in a very weak state. . .'

This is the epitaph her father wrote for Cristina's tomb:

183

'For Cristina Baroggi Manzoni / who, with uplifting patience / through a long and painful illness / with Christian resignation / crowned an immaculate / pious and charitable life / and a death precious in the sight of God / offering to Him in sacrifice / a beloved baby girl and husband, / her sorrowing relations / implore your prayers / and His divine mercy.'

Filippo to Stefano:

'My dearest Stefano, oh! you will say, what has happened to Mammina that she is getting Filippo to write to me? Nothing has happened to her. She is not writing because she is sitting chatting to Papa on the sofa; forgive her for being so frivolous as to chat instead of writing to you; she is excusable because Papa has only just returned from Bellagio where he accompanied Sofia and Vittoria. The next time you write to her, give her a good *refilé* [scolding], because it's a shame the way she always trembles for fear of thieves, though the roads Papa was using are quite safe. But she's a woman, after all! We are all indebted to you for sharing in our grief for the loss of poor Cristina! It was truly a very hard blow for Papa, but Mammina is always there to console him with her gentle words. I am plagued with rather bad toothache; I shall have to have two out. Brothers, sisters, brothers-in-law all send you boundless greetings and thanks for your kind thoughts. Papa tells me to give you all his very best regards; you know how fond he is of you. . . Goodbye, dearest Stefano, remember you have in *Filippo* a brother who loves you like a precious friend.'

Cristina's baby had been taken to Verano, to the villa of the Trottis.

Teresa had commissioned a portrait of Manzoni from Francesco Hayez. Writing to Stefano, she expressed her disappointment that she was too weak to accompany her husband to every sitting: 'I should say that I am recovering from my weakness by eating two beef-steaks a day, and tasty broths; but the improvement is so slight that I am scarcely aware of it, and I despair of being able to accompany Alessandro to Hayez tomorrow, even in the carriage. This time, however, I am not writing from bed, but from my magnificent table, which Cecchina contemplated with great admiration yesterday; together with my little bookcase. I get the impression that Grossi is not feeling too well these days, but he came to take Papa for a walk; I think he works too hard, poor Grossi. It upsets me to see him so thin. For a Grossi to be reduced to working as a solicitor! Oh! it is a disgrace to the Italians in general and the Milanese in particular.'

Towards the end of June, after fourteen sittings, the portrait was finished. At that time, Giulia took to her bed. Teresa to Stefano: 'The Nonna is very ill, and I am very distressed for her (you will think I am exaggerating! but it's true) and for Alessandro. Just think! that another blow should strike him after the last. However, I hope not, but I am afraid, because she has a sharp pain; yesterday she went to bed, and was bled at once, and twice today. . . If only I could write to rejoice in the successful portrait of Alessandro! . . . Oh Heavens, how I wish for my sake and Papa's that you were in Milan, if the Nonna, poor lady, should get worse! Worse, you must understand, means, *fatally*. Papa does not know how bad she is, and I don't know what to do. I feel that if you were here we could change the subject a bit, and relieve the gloom; and to tell the truth, reluctant as I am to suggest it, if things went badly, you could do a great deal for us; enough! even I don't know what to say! . . . I assure you I am as distressed about her condition as if she had never once upset me. . .' Stefano did not come. He answered: 'I'm sorry about the Nonna too, for her, for Papa and for the family; but what good would it do you to have me in Milan, if she got worse? What good could I do? I have no idea how to comfort people, I can only keep them cheerful when they want to be. . . So! . . . Enough, please write at once, and if I really could do any good, tell me straight out, and I'll come to Milan to do what I can; in any case, if you wanted to go to Lesa, I could go and arrange the passports.' Passports were required to go to Lesa, as it was in the kingdom of Carlo Alberto.

Sofia, her husband, Vittoria and Emilia Luti were at Giulia's bedside. On 28 June Teresa wrote to Stefano:

'She was given the sacraments in great haste; she was almost given the holy oil at once, and none of the doctors thought she would live to the morning; all yesterday evening and all night they were praying for her soul and nobody imagined she would see the light today; but in the night she roused herself and this morning she greeted Alessandro and recited, in a laboured way,

185

it's true, but quite intelligibly, part of his hymn which tells of the Blessed Virgin going to Saint Elizabeth; because today is, in fact, the day of the Visitation; and she sent them all to mass for her, including Alessandro; poor woman, how lucid she is! But she wants to die because she is suffering too much, but you would hardly know except by her face. I've been twice to receive her blessing and her pardon, poor woman! However, this morning there's a faint hope in the quinine, seeing her miraculous resistance to her illness, and the miraculous waking, speaking and being aware of the slightest thing. All this so upset me yesterday and the day before that I can't eat or walk, but I get up a bit.' The next day: 'That poor woman sent for Alessandro last night, and he flung himself down on the bed to ask her forgiveness, and she blessed him, and asked after me, saying: "And your wife. . . my daughter-in-law. . . where is she? Tell her I commend the children to her." Imagine how upset I've felt last night and this morning, not to be able to get up and go upstairs! My heart would not and will not allow it. I am keeping to a strict diet; I am drinking a lot of fresh water; and since yesterday I've been taking laurocerasus water every two hours, which has steadied my heart and given me a bit more strength. . . The other evening Pietro came and hugged me tight, crying, and so did all the others.' The 6th July: 'The Nonna is still alive but in such a wretched state that all the time she is longing for the end. . . Just think how many days and nights she has been in extremis. Three times her soul had been commended, poor woman! Oh Heavens! to see poor Papa, who can't stay still for five minutes; up and down, up and down, from the top of the house to the bottom all day, and in the night!. . . Nobody can speak of yesterday, because it already seems far, far away, with so many ups and downs, so many things said, given, things to be done, things done, said again, thought again. . . Sofia and Vittoria sleep upstairs and are at her bedside every moment, they look like ghosts as you can imagine. That this should happen to Papa a month after the shock of poor Cristina, and so long drawn-out, yet so short! . . . God forbid he should fall ill! Please pray to Him! and pray for the Nonna, for your Papa, Stefano, and for poor Cristina, invoke that very Father Cristoforo [of *I promessi sposi*], who is, after all, our Alessandro, as well as once being called

186

Lodovico. . . This morning the poor Nonna wished to be bled again. . .'

Giulia died in the night between the 7th and 8th of July. She was buried at Brusuglio. Manzoni and his family went to Verano to stay with the Trottis.

Manzoni wrote this epitaph for his mother's tomb:

'To Giulia Manzoni / daughter of Cesare Beccaria / a matron revered / for her lofty intellect / her liberality to the poor /her profound and active piety / commended / to the mercy of the Lord / and all the prayers of the faithful / by her inconsolable son / and all her sorrowing family.'

Teresa Borri II

Giulia had made a will on 10 January 1837, that is a few days after this new marriage of her son's. She left everything to her grandchildren, with a life interest in everything to her son. In favour of her grandchildren she had raised a mortgage of a hundred and ninety thousand lire on the estate at Brusuglio: she had overvalued it, because years later the estate was valued at only three hundred and ninety-five thousand lire. Obviously she already distrusted Teresa; and her son seemed to her, from a practical point of view, improvident. The will was judged by many to be lacking in sagacity, and to be the cause of the serious financial troubles which were to occur. But it is difficult to say if this was really the case.

So after Giulia's death the whole family spent a few days at the Trotti villa. Stefano was at Torriggia to supervise the building of a boat; then he went to Lesa, where Teresa and Alessandro joined him, and they stayed there until the beginning of October.

In August Pietro, Enrico, Filippo and don Giovanni Ghianda were in Milan in via del Morone. Sofia went to Pré-Saint-Didier with her older boy, Tonino, who needed the mountain air; she left her second child, Sandrino, with the nurse at via del Morone. From Pré-Saint-Didier she wrote to Enrico, who had sent news to her; Enrico was her favourite brother. She usually wrote in French, and when she wrote in Italian, she made mistakes in spelling, and sometimes in syntax.

'First of all I must thank you with all my heart for getting my Alessandro to write me a few words. . . Poor Sandrino, I can't wait to see him. You did make me laugh when you said he was shaking, I could just imagine him like a wobbly *blancmanger*. . . I will simply say I am most grateful, as I know you are more annoyed than otherwise by *salamelech* (dialect for clumsy salutations). I can just hear you saying *Oh, what a bore!*. . . But I wish your letters were a bit more detailed, especially about your brothers. . . Do you not know how long Papa intends to stay away? and where will he go when he returns? when is don Giovanni leaving? how is Filippo behaving? what will happen when don Giovanni isn't there?' In fact the tutor had expressed his intention of going away. 'Tell Nanny that my Tonino is completely better, and I think he has started putting on weight again. As for his big tummy, my Cousin Trotti who knows about children assures me it's caused by that touch of rickets, which makes him twist his legs a bit, and that it will all pass as he gets stronger. I make him take the baths which I am assured will do him a lot of good: he stays in a half an hour with me, and thoroughly enjoys it, I don't know what's come over him because you will remember it was impossible to get him in the water in Milan. Forgive these tedious details, but they are for Nanny, and they come with lots and lots of love to her. I say nothing about my health, because I'm really well. Of my state of mind, I have made it a rule to speak as little as possible, because I bore other people, and do myself no good, so *glissons* (let's pass over that), which will be better for everyone. We'll be almost alone here soon, as the company is all leaving bit by bit. . . We will stay a bit longer so that I can take at least 20 baths. We went by mule to the Piccolo San Bernardo, which I enjoyed, and I continue to go on various excursions.'

When she returned to Milan to collect her little boy, she felt sorry for Filippo on his own, bored and sad, and she took him with her to Balbianello, to the Arconati villa. Before leaving Filippo wrote to his father:

'Dearest Papa! I am truly most grateful to you for the pleasure you have afforded me by allowing me to go to Balbianello: but gratitude is shown more by deeds than words, so I shall try to repay your kindness by the best possible behaviour, and by attending to my studies. . .'

And Sofia to her father, from Balbianello:

'Filippo has been here since yesterday, he is so happy, poor little chap, I really felt sorry for him cooped up in Milan all alone, with no company and no amusement, and in the holidays! His letters were pitiful, you could see he was dying of boredom. How long do you think he can stay here? Tell me, dear Papa, and I'll send him home whenever you think. . .'

Sofia to Enrico from Balbianello:

'I see that Mr Enrico will not break the ice, so I will – why do you never write? you may think you can say the same of me – but it's quite a different matter, I have so many letters to write, three or four every day – I'm in the country, I spend a lot of time walking and going for trips on the lake, and my little boys take up a tremendous amount of time – But what are you doing? there is not a soul in Milan at this season! – I wrote to Pietro quite a while ago and I've had no reply, so one way and another there seems no way of getting news of you. . . What will you do this autumn? if you came to spend a little time on this beautiful lake, I promise you you'd see what a good time can be had in the country at this lovely time of year. It's not too hot and you can go for long walks, there are so many people out of doors you'd think you were in Milan. . .Filippo seems to be enjoying himself, Lodovico has asked the younger of the Tegia brothers, who is more or less Filippo's age, to spend some time here. . .'

The Beccarias, Uncle Giulio and the 'zietta', were staying nearby in their villa of Sala Comacina, but Sofia was not keen to go there because Cantú was staying with them. Manzoni and Cantú had not been on very good terms for about a year. Manzoni was writing *La Storia della Colonna Infame*, about the 'untori' or plague-spreaders, which he intended to publish with *I promessi sposi* in the new revised and illustrated edition of which the first instalments had appeared. Suddenly a book by Cantú came out, *Il processo degli untori*, on the same theme. Cantú had not mentioned it to Manzoni, although he knew what he was working on. Manzoni felt bitterly about it, and had to make cuts in *la Colonna Infame*. Moreover, it was said that Cantú had become the lover of the 'zietta', the young wife of elderly Uncle Giulio Beccaria. So when Sofia and Vittoria called on their uncle and aunt, they had the impression that 'someone' was hastily 'imprisoned', that is, that Cantú was obliged to remain shut in a room and requested not to show himself, and that the 'zietta' was 'gênée'. However, Sofia and Vittoria often went to see d'Azeglio, who had bought a house at Loveno. But it was a rather inconvenient house. Sofia to Enrico: 'Today we were supposed to go to lunch with Azeglio at Loveno, but it is drizzling, so we'll stay home; we've already been to see him, and I must say I don't know what possessed him to buy that house on the top of the mountain, there's such a poor road to get there, and the house is in a dreadful state and he's having to build to make it habitable, so it would have been just as well to build on the shore of the lake. . .'

Teresa and Alessandro went back to Milan, Stefano stayed at Lesa; Teresa had been reading d'Azeglio's novel, *Niccolò de' Lapi*, which had come out that year; she did not like it at all, and wrote to Stefano: 'At last I've finished the *Lapo, Lapone, Lapaggione de' Lapitti*. With all due respect to you, that's not love of the fatherland, it's love of the municipality! Does he call that a novel? It's just history, almost all history taken up here and set down there, mixed in with the possible captivity of Troilus and with endless male and female genuflections, such as to nauseate the most beautiful Helen, let alone Niccolò, if he had some sense in place of his 91 years. But what an eternal babbler! what a bore! what a foolish fellow! He thinks he is talking of the fatherland, and he's always talking about the city of Florence, like Massimo, as if it were the only Italian fatherland! And those congresses he constructs with no threads or glue to hold them together! And it's all so disconnected, the true and the false! Oh dear me! people will never, never be interested in all the confused tangle about that wild woman, which is more romantic and impossible than the love stories of Don Quichotte! oh, I could go on like this! Don't be cross!' But Stefano's worship of d'Azeglio could not be dented by any words of his mother's.

Teresa to Stefano:

'Gonin has arrived, and now they're working full speed ahead at the vignettes of *la Colonna Infame* which Papa hopes to finish by the end of July. So be it! It will make a great stir. . .'

In the spring of 1842 Enrico got married. He was twenty-three. His wife was called Emilia Redaelli. She was noble and extremely rich. She brought a dowry of three hundred thousand lire and a magnificent villa at Renate. The two settled there. Sofia was delighted about the marriage; she liked her sister-in-law very much; but the others were perplexed. Enrico was involved in business; he sold silk-worms; he had grandiose

191

notions, and his wife seconded them. Neither Enrico nor his wife had any idea of the value of money, she probably because she was so rich, he by temperament. And it soon became clear that, instead of urging caution upon him, she encouraged him in imprudent ventures. Enrico immediately began to ask for advances on the legacy from Giulia, and his father and Pietro were not at all happy.

In that summer of 1842 there was an eclipse of the sun; Teresa and Alessandro went specially to Brusuglio to see it; Teresa described it to Stefano:

'So on the morning of 8th July 1842, having made our preparations the previous evening, we got up at 4.30. We saw the beginning of the eclipse from the avenue of plane trees: half and then the total eclipse from the hill. Papa had had a great swathe cut in the wood that surrounds the hill on the left, to see the Monte Rosa properly, which (if the sky had been clear) should have had its summit lit up even during the total eclipse: they massacred those poor dear tree-tops, amid general rejoicing: but the Monte Rosa and all that chain of mountains *Se prirent à bouder la lune et le soleil et nous tous aussi; ils se drapèrent dans une écharpe de nuages*, and goodbye mountains! [they began to sulk at the moon and the sun and all of us; they draped themselves in a scarf of cloud] – When total darkness fell, Alessandro shouted out without knowing it: Oh! great God, in light as in darkness! Then when the light reappeared, he began to clap and shout: Beautiful! Oh how beautiful! Oh, magnificent! – But he had no recollection of all this, it was so spontaneous: I say that Alessandro was the mouthpiece of a whole population, of Milan at least, some of whom had gone into the squares on foot, in carriages, on horseback; others were on the roof-loggias, on the campaniles, on the Cathedral, the roofs, which were full of men, women and children (just think, the roofs crowded with women and children!!). They all burst out shouting and clapping at the full eclipse and when the light returned. In the country people were on their knees, saying it was the end of the world. At Brusuglio the boys who were watching their cows, began to weep loudly, shouting: – It's an earthquake!! an earthquake!! The black-cap went on singing, but the nightingale made the *cruu-cruu* that it does when it's alarmed. I heard them; (give him my best regards, Manzoni had said to her in dialect, while she was writing –) but it's he who sends his regards! the dearest he!'

That summer of 1842 Sofia's health began to give cause for concern. She was bled. In August she had her third baby boy. The confinement went well, but anxiety continued. She had chronic pleurisy. Grossi's wife had a son too. Teresa to Stefano: 'Grossi had a fine fat boy this morning or last night. Anyway an excessively *grosso* Grossi has been born, fulfilling their wishes. The day before yesterday Sofia had another boy, not fulfilling their wishes. Sofia wanted a girl; Grossi wanted a boy. However, both got through it very well, I mean the two ladies, apart from the strong pains, which were short and sharp for both of them.'

Emilia Luti was travelling with the Littas, and Manzoni was waiting for her to come back to do a last revision of the text with her; meanwhile he was working with intense concentration – that summer they did not move from Milan except on the day of the eclipse – and Teresa, in one of her little notebooks, was writing Milanese words with the corresponding Tuscan words alongside. Stefano was at Lesa, expecting Rossari. Teresa to Stefano: 'Rossari needs a lot of cheering up! do see to it, and don't drag him round all over the place. . . Try to guess what he wants, and don't drag him off to do what you want, however much you fancy it's for his good, his entertainment and his delight; believe me, my dear Stefanone, do as I say.' Two of Sofia's children, Tonino and Sandrino, were with them; Teresa to Stefano: 'Tonino Trotti is with us here, and Sandrino has been with us for a while too; so Tonino put a kiss on the paper so that *unca Tepa* shall have a *tiss from Ninon.*' Again, Teresa to Stefano, on the 19th August: 'In four days *la Colonna Infame* will be finished!!! Ah!!! we can breathe again, expand our lungs and heart, what a delight!! a week or a fortnight of pagination and proof-reading, and it will all be finished! oh, che *gust!* che *guston!* che *gustononon!*' [A joking dialect expression of mounting joy.]

After her confinement, Sofia went back to Verano with her new baby Giulio and the other two; the Trottis sometimes stayed there even in winter; Vittoria, who had left school, was with them almost all the time. Sofia exchanged frequent visits and affectionate letters with her brother Enrico and her sister-in-law, who were living at Renate. Toys and sweets arrived at

Verano from Renate for all the name-days and birthdays of the children; at Renate there was a park, an orchard and a big kitchen-garden, and Emilia sent Sofia strawberries, flowers and vegetables in season; once she sent a little lamb, a lambkin Sofia called it; the children acclaimed it joyfully and took it everywhere with them. Sofia to Emilia: 'Tonino has taken advantage of a bright spell to go out in the garden with his lambkin; if you could see how he loves him; he follows him everywhere, even into the rooms.' Sofia to Emilia: 'I assure you I am quite confused by your kindness, and in spite of the plea-sure your lovely strawberries give me, I am sorry to see you deprive yourself for me. You can be sure that they are very wel-come, we all have a big helping, and the boys think they are a great treat.' 'My Tonino sends his Aunt Emilia a hug. I advise you to try the *arrowroot* in milk or in broth, because it's really disgusting with water.' Sofia to Enrico: 'I haven't the courage to send this ribbon to Emilia myself, I hope my impudence will be pardoned more readily by your intervention. I am sorry Vit-toria sent it to me *roulé* so that it's all *gaufré* when you unroll it. I hope it will be all right if it's ironed (with a lukewarm iron, otherwise you'll lose the ribbing).' When she went to Milan, Sofia busied herself with little errands for her sister-in-law, a hat, feathers, cuffs. But she was often very tired. Sofia to Emilia: 'I haven't been very well, I've had an abscess in my mouth that has been very painful. But I would have liked to have better news from Enrico, I am very sorry you are still not well, poor Emilia; have courage, what can we expect, everyone has their troubles in this world. . .' Emilia was pregnant; she suffered from nausea, anxiety and low spirits. Her mother, who lived with her, donna Luigia Redaelli Martinez, had health problems and Emilia worried about her. Sofia suggested they call Doctor Piantanida. But, in fact, Emilia's worries were chiefly financial; Enrico needed a lot of money to further his many complicated commercial enterprises; he was asking everyone for guarantees and loans: Sofia's husband Lodovico, Uncle and Aunt Beccaria. Sofia to Enrico: 'I'm sorry I can't give you a definite answer from Pietro, but I have never been able to get anything out of him, and he says that if you don't go to Milan to talk to him, he can say nothing. But he said it is only right and proper that you should reveal the state of your affairs even if it is not required of you, because you might regret it, and anyway a man of honour cannot do otherwise; however, do go to Milan yourself and talk to him; Pietro sends these accounts with a note of the expenses you have incurred, he advises you to keep accounts because you know how things go all too often.' Sofia to Enrico: 'I have spoken to Lodovico about that matter and he said that, if things stand as we agreed yesterday, he will be pleased to do this for you. I am very pleased I can give you this answer, I was almost sure of it yesterday because I know from experience that my Lodovico is always ready to oblige. I hope you will soon be able to bring this matter to a close. Give my love to your dear Emilia and say I'm very sorry to hear she has headaches, I can sympathise all the more as unfortunately I know what it means. Goodbye, your affec. sister Sofia. I asked you to send me those books of the annuities and you forgot.' Don Giovanni Ghianda was sent to ask Uncle Beccaria and his wife for money; but the 'zietta' categorically refused to help. Sofia to Enrico: 'Egoists, all of them, and I advise you not to trust their fine words any more. I'm very sorry, dear Enrico, to have to give you this bad news, but you can believe I do it with the feelings of a truly affectionate sister: apart from this, I was very pleased to hear from Lodovico that Emilia was well yesterday, keep up her spirits, and do try to keep up your own strength. You can't imagine how desperate I feel that I can't be with you both . . .'

In spring 1843, as usual, Stefano set off for Lesa, and as usual his mother worried about him all the time. She wrote to him almost every day and Stefano wrote to her too, but there were long delays in the post between Lesa and Milan and sometimes the seals on the letters were broken; Teresa was convinced the police were opening their letters to find out what was happening in the Manzoni family. 'The postal police want to see with their own eyes why you went to the country outside your state to your house, by boat with your servant Francesco from Brusuglio all alone and no one there, with dark thoughts of going by boat perhaps even by night not to catch fish, to do what? that's the point!!! But let him who knows tell. . .' Teresa intended to join Stefano at Lesa in the autumn with Alessandro, and she asked .

Stefano to go to Stresa to visit Abbé Rosmini who lived there, enquire if he was well and if they might meet him. 'So we may or may not go to Brusú this afternoon, depending whether it rains or not. And we must go, because we should have been there before this. It is understood that we are coming back to Milan on the last day of August to prepare for Lesa and to see the *Exhibition*.'

That summer Uncle Giulio Beccaria became seriously ill. He recovered, but they had thought he was dying. Teresa to Stefano: 'In weather that became quite fiendish half an hour after he left, Papa has been to Gessate, where the Marchese Beccaria is in a very bad way. I am sorry, because in his heart of hearts he was fond of us, and he is Alessandro's only close relative. Apart from my distress about the Marchese, I am worried about the weather, and about Alessandro who has gone off in a poor cart, the laundry cart, with two country horses, the steward's Peppo as a coachman, and Filippo to support him. There's been a hurricane that nearly made me cry, not for the hurricane, but for Alessandro travelling like that.' A few days later: 'Papa came back the day before yesterday without experiencing the horrid mishaps I was imagining might happen to him (I am speaking as you or he might do against myself): the Marchese Beccaria was still making good progress yesterday after, I think, the sixth bleeding.'

Teresa and Alessandro went to Lesa in October, and stayed there more than a month; then Teresa wrote to their administrator, Antonio Patrizio, that for their stay Alessandro wanted 'to pay the whole journey both ways and two thirds of the expenses'. Manzoni saw Abbé Rosmini at Stresa; they discussed questions of language; Manzoni had submitted to him an essay, 'Della lingua italiana'. That autumn, at Belgirate, Manzoni found a shoemaker who made him some comfortable shoes; and as soon as they got back to Milan, Teresa wrote asking Stefano to order three more pairs, one pair *col legnazz*, that is, with cork soles, and two without. Manzoni had left his blue umbrella behind at Lesa; since Rossari was still at Lesa, Stefano gave him the umbrella to bring back to Milan; but either Rossari did not understand or did not want the encumbrance; Teresa was offended with her son, for she thought he had not treated Rossari with sufficient respect. 'What on earth possessed you to

196

entrust Papa's umbrella to Rossari, when we could have brought it in the carriage so very easily!!! Rossari's passport to Arona! Papa's umbrella to Rossari! Didn't you realize it was putting him out to have to come via Velocifero! We should have brought something for him in our carriage, rather than load him with extra things! Oh, what a muddle! Meanwhile Rossari, not believing or not realising he was supposed to bring that umbrella (I mean Papa's), passed it to Pendola, and Pendola must have taken it back home, so you will bring it to Milan, or send it.'

In the spring of 1844 the Arconatis arrived in Milan: Costanza, her husband and her son Giammartino. The older son, Carletto, had died in 1839. The Arconatis had left Belgium – Giuseppe Arconati had emigrated to Belgium in 1821, because he was condemned to death by the Austrians; his wife, Costanza, had followed him; now he had been pardoned – and they were living in Pisa. Teresa to Stefano: 'I've seen the Arconatis to whom I was very gracious, and so were they. I shall see the little boy, but meanwhile I know, as far as one can judge at present, that he is a marvel of grace, of *bons mots*, health, beauty, and everything. I am delighted and pray the Lord to keep him precious and well for those poor people, the poorest in the world since they lost a young lad who was the same age as you.'

Emilia's confinement was drawing near, and she was still anxious and depressed, either from fear of the birth or about money. Sofia was in Milan at the time, and her father asked her to prepare a layette on his behalf for the baby that was expected; Sofia busied herself to get the layette ready in time. She wrote to her sister-in-law trying to cheer her up: 'Dearest Emilia, you can't imagine how I felt yesterday as I read your letter thinking I could be of no use to you, I wished I had wings to fly to Renate! poor Emilia, how I should like to be near you! If I were at Verano, I'd move in with you for a few days (would you want me?) and do all I could to help you or at least soothe you; I would have seen to Enrico and to the dear little baby you will soon have; would you have trusted me? But my health too prevents me making plans, otherwise believe me even being in Milan would not stop me flying to Renate to join you. But yesterday for example I was fine, and today I feel dreadful, so that my head is all confused and my hand is shaking. I'm hurrying to send off this stuff I've managed to put together. . . I hope you'll like it, I've done my best. You'll find the baptismal clothes in the carton, you're welcome to have them because I don't need them now, in the same box there's the veil and mantilla you left here, and the bracelet; I'm sending you one of the caps you asked me to get: and I've thought about the others. The hat is ordered.' She had also arranged a nurse for her, the one she had for her baby Sandrino. 'I've talked to Sandro's nurse and we agreed I should tell you to send for her on Easter Sunday, and she'd be ready to leave before noon. But if you can't wait, send for her Thursday at the same time, I'll let her know and I'm quite sure she'll be ready. I haven't forgotten the wool-muslin but I haven't found it yet – thank you for the flowers and the lettuce, it was excellent.' And to Enrico: 'I must say I am still so unwell that I simply cannot do what I long to do. I assure you, my darlings, that I think of you all day, and do what I can for poor Emilia, by commending her to the Lord. – Please tell me honestly if she's pleased with the layette. . . When you write to Papa abut the *happy event*, you would do well to say a few words of thanks for the layette, he doesn't know that you were told about it. I've looked for the wool-muslin but haven't found it yet, perhaps you'd send me a tiny piece of fringe to match the red. . . would stripes do? If I can't find wool-muslin, should I get some other material or *percale? Percale* does very well in the country. Goodbye, dear Enrico, I think you'll already have Sandro's nurse there when this letter gets to you. . .'

Emilia had a baby girl whom they called Enrichetta. Sofia to Enrico: 'You can't imagine my joy last night as I read your letter, I rejoice with all my heart for you and dear Emilia, give her all my love, tell her to take great care and be sensible, and not to indulge the very natural longing to see and know everything that's happening to your baby, tell her to trust Sandro's nurse, she can rest assured she's practical and intelligent, and I recommend you to see there's no noise in Emilia's room; peasant women have a mania for standing chattering in sick-rooms, tell them there's to be only one woman or two at the most in Emilia's room, and that they should be silent, the most important thing at this time is quiet, don't let Emilia talk. . . Tell her to put the baby to the breast even though she seems to have no milk because that will bring the milk on. . . Tell Sandro's nurse to keep the baby warm, to cover her up well especially her legs and feet: she ought to put a hot water bottle in the cradle when she's sleeping to keep her feet warm because these poor little newborn babies have so little vitality that one has to supply what they lack. One of those beer bottles would be best because the earthenware is thicker and keeps the water warm longer, for now it's best not to put the lacework caps on her but the night ones perhaps with two *beguins* (bonnets) underneath for warmth. Have a fire lit in the room, and see they don't expose your baby to the open air, try to see she stays in the same ambience, especially in this bad weather it would be best to go to the baptism in the carriage otherwise well covered and have them put warm water in the font, this is done in Milan, they always did it for my boys. . . the broth for Emilia's *pancotti* (bread soup) should be veal for the first few days, beef broth is a bit heavy, keep her well covered especially her head. . .' To Emilia: 'I meant to write and thank you and *scold* you for your lovely long letter but I've felt so poorly the last two days that it was quite impossible. Goodbye my darling in haste kiss your dear Enrichetta for me, I'm going to bed.' To Enrico: 'Please *deign* to write me a line with detailed news of Emilia; you haven't even answered the letter I wrote you; tell me if Emilia has any trouble breast-feeding, if she still has plenty of milk, if she has any appetite, how your baby is etc. etc. . . . I can't wait to see her, I don't know if Lodovico told you of my plan of going with him to Renate and not coming back until the next day; but just at that time I felt even worse than usual, and today has been a bad day too. I've had to wait till the evening to write to you because I couldn't have done so earlier; enough, I mustn't think about it too much or I get too depressed. . . Goodbye dear Enrico, urge Emilia to be careful, tell her that in her situation if she wants everything to go well she should take care of herself, look at Virginia Dal Pozzo, she was fine all through her confinement and on the 43rd day she went to pay a call; there were lots of flowers in the room, the smell made her so ill that she had to stay in bed for two days and take purgatives, and she still hasn't quite got over it. Take care what she eats too, only bland things, plain cooking and no salt, and be careful of the air, she shouldn't be tempted because it's warm – be patient – has she started to get up? how did she get on? when her milk weighs on her get them to give her a little warm sugared water; it will do her a lot of good. Please write me a note and answer my questions. Goodbye I'll close now because I'm too tired to write any more. I hug you, Emilia and your baby girl. Sofia. Nanny sends her regards, she is delighted for you and sends her love. At last I am able to send the hat.'

That summer Marianna, Teresa's mother, became ill. She had gone to see Aunt Notburga and had caught a chill walking in the damp convent garden. But perhaps it was not only that, because her limbs were swollen. Teresa from Brusuglio to Stefano: 'Today if I had been able to, if I had had a good night, I would have got up to go to Milan; but I'll go tomorrow instead; and Alessandro will come too for my sake; and as Alessandro is coming Vittoria will come too, so that will mean all the women and the menservants. So if for the sake of your grandmother even people who are not related to her are moving and putting themselves out, just imagine if the *petit-fils* were not to bestir himself! So I'll be expecting you in Milan: Papa is of the same opinion. . .' But Stefano did not stir. Again Teresa to Stefano: 'I have heard by express delivery that Mama has had a slightly better night! how does she manage! it's a wonder she does not die from the continual lack of sleep! but unfortunately today she is bad again! Yesterday Domenico brought a message that the swelling had greatly increased! Just imagine! Swelling and difficulty with breathing! May the Lord help and comfort her, because I can do nothing; when I arrive tomorrow I don't know if I'll be able to go there at once or if I shall be obliged to go to bed for a while! however, today I'm quite well: but the looseness is not over, so I'm still on a diet; which makes me very weak.' Again, Teresa to Stefano: 'Yesterday I spent some hours with Mama, and she was a bit better, but unfortunately the swelling is much worse; but she still looks smiling and cheerful. She had a good night last night, and is a bit better today. It's midday and I'm getting up to go there.' Stefano did not move from Lesa and the Manzonis left Milan and returned to Brusuglio, because it seemed that Marianna was recovering.

Still in that same summer, in July 1844, Sofia had a baby girl and they called her Margherita. It had been a difficult birth.

Manzoni was told of these difficulties only when they seemed to be over.

On 15 July Fauriel died in Paris. He was seventy-two. The year before he had had an accident when he was knocked down by a carriage. He died alone. He and Mary Clarke still wrote, but had not met for some time. He and Manzoni had not written to each other for very many years, and had never met again.

It took about ten days for the news of his death to reach Brusuglio. Teresa to Stefano: 'I've had a very good day today by my standards; it's true it was nearly lunch-time when I got up, but I did the avenue of plane trees before lunch, then ate well: then I walked all round with Alessandro *sans être rendue* [without being too tired]: and now I'm writing to you in the late evening, and I'm writing without any difficulty: and I'm writing to you from the table, on the table which was used to write *I promessi sposi*, and in the study which was, and still is used to enclose Alessandro among his papers and books. But I can say, as De Fresne said in that witty letter to Reboul: I search all around, look aloft, rummage, dip the famous pen in the fortunate ink well over and again: I fail to find one phrase of the *Promessi sposi*, not a line or a thought from the *Adelchi* or *Carmagnola* etc. etc. So I'll tell you that someone who was with Alessandro at Milan and Brusú for perhaps three years and in this very study in the evenings, at the time when M. Cousin was also in Milan and at Brusú, M. Fauriel, such a friend of Alessandro, died some days ago in Paris, which has made Alessandro very sad; the said dear Alessandro himself prepared pen, paper, pencil, lamp and everything for me to write to you on his table; then told me to send you his very, very kindest regards.'

Jules Mohl, friend of Fauriel and Mary Clarke, wrote to Manzoni, sending him a drawing and a miniature which he had found in Fauriel's bedroom. The drawing was the work of Giulietta, 'the daughter you had the misfortune to lose', wrote Jules Mohl. He thought the miniature of a little girl might be Giulietta, but he was not sure. At any rate, Cabanis' daughter, to whom Fauriel had left all his works of art, had given him permission to send them both to Manzoni. Mary Clarke was in England; Manzoni had sent her a portrait of Fauriel he had; Jules Mohl said she must be too distressed at that time to thank him.

201

Then he gave a few particulars of Fauriel's death.

For some time Fauriel had been suffering from a polyp which caused a rush of blood to his head and made him sleepy. So he had had an operation.

This polyp was in the nasal cavity. Many years before, in Italy, he had already had an operation at Mary Clarke's insistence: she thought it deformed his nose and spoilt his looks. But it was obviously not cured and he still had the polyp. So he had another operation. We do not know whether the polyp really troubled him or made him torpid, or if he was again obeying the aesthetic whims of Mary Clarke. From what Jules Mohl wrote, the operation was necessary. All went well. The next day Fauriel was feeling well, and went out to the Louvre. He caught cold, got erysipelas and died within a week.

Of Manzoni's feelings at the death of Fauriel we have only the word 'sad' in a letter from Teresa to Stefano talking of various other matters. In the years that ensued Manzoni rarely mentioned Fauriel in his letters. 'A friend ever dear and ever lamented. . .', 'My illustrious and lamented friend Fauriel. . .' This is how the image of Fauriel surfaced, not more than once or twice in the course of years, among other topics, names and themes, in Manzoni's letters.

On 15 August, Teresa's mother died.

Teresa and Alessandro decided to go to Lesa. They were to be joined there at the beginning of September, by Sigismondo Trechi, who was convalescing after a 'terrible pernicious fever'. Teresa had ordered a chest of drawers to put in Trechi's room, and it did not come and she was in despair. Manzoni had had a letter from Abbé Rosmini, who was impatient to see him. 'I live in hopes that this year will satisfy my most eager desire to see don Alessandro again on the shores of this lake of ours. . .' And Teresa to Stefano: 'I've been waiting and waiting and waiting for them to send a *cantarà*, a *trumo*, a something or other with drawers, old but good, already made and finished a century ago for us to have it in the future for the 7th or 8th or 9th as Trechi is coming on the 9th or 10th, I think.'

So they were preparing for their departure. But at the beginning of September Teresa fell ill. She had been unwell for a while, she felt 'extremely weak and shattered into fragments and tiny pieces'. Manzoni wrote to Rosmini: 'Unfortunately my wife's health makes it impossible for us to travel to Lesa.' Teresa sent for Doctor Mazzola, who had operated on her for tonsilitis years before. Then other doctors were called. A tumour was diagnosed. Stefano Stampa told the story: 'and so the poor lady was treated with frictions of mercury and with iodine; but the tumour grew instead of diminishing, and her health deteriorated . . .' The winter months passed and Teresa became more and more poorly. The doctors felt her hard, swollen stomach and perceived movements, which were, according to them, 'rumblings of the lower intestine which sometimes lifted the tumour and shook it'. In the night of the 7th to 8th of February she was gripped by atrocious pains. It was the tumour bursting, said the doctors. They bled her. They said it was the end. She believed them and announced it to her son 'with a sad smile'. Suddenly they all realized that they were labour pains. The first doctor, Mazzola, had at one time advanced the hypothesis of a pregnancy, but without conviction because of Teresa's age (she was forty-five) and besides, the others had immediately spoken of a tumour. Twin girls were born. In the night Manzoni had sent for an obstetrician, Doctor Billi, but he arrived when it was all over. 'He arrived in time to baptise one of the twins who lived almost till the morning, and to baptise the other *sub-conditione* because it was still-born, or died as soon as it was born. Then in a whisper Doctor Billi asked Manzoni (who was standing near the fireplace, behind a screen which was hiding the light and the fire from the patient) if he might take home the little dead body (I think it was five or six months) to put it with his collection of foetuses. Manzoni looked embarrassed; he made a movement of the head that looked like consent, and the doctor put the little body in his pocket and took it home. But Manzoni never divulged this fact to his wife, nor did the son to his mother, for they were both convinced that she would have been distressed' (Stefano Stampa).

When the first baby died too, they cut a lock of her hair, which Manzoni placed in an envelope; on the envelope he wrote:

'And you who have no name, but are the blessed daughter of the Saviour in heaven, look down from there in blessing on your parents, who wept for you and envied you. Teresa and Alessandro Manzoni.'

Vittoria was given the task of communicating the event to the family; she wrote to the 'zietta': 'Papa would like to write to Uncle to inform him of a *great event* which occurred last night; but as he feels rather tired after being up all night, he has asked me to write for him. Just think that our poor invalid, to everyone's astonishment, was delivered of all her tumours last night by giving birth to a beautiful baby girl, who, poor little thing, is already an angel, as she survived only nine or ten hours. We were all up all night, consumed with anxiety, as nothing like this was suspected so we thought the poor invalid was in a very bad way indeed. . . We passed from the appalling fear of an incurable disease (as the doctor had spoken an hour before of colic of the uterus) to the relief of seeing the trouble vanish in a moment! . . . Things are going well now, and the patient is doing quite nicely. Heaven be praised! Dear Sofia is better, but her pain has been quite severe these last days.'

On 31 March that year Sofia died. She had taken to bed in February. The doctors said she had developed an obstruction of the pleura. Like Cristina, she was happily married. She had an affectionate, kind, sensitive husband and four beloved little children. Before her stretched a happy, festive prospect, full of colour, friendly faces, solicitous relatives, and she lavished attention on others, her brothers and sisters, the babies that were born to her, the objects and the foods she received and sent. Yet this world which seemed to her so beautiful could not exclude the memory of the loved ones she had lost. She would be gripped by a fit of terror. She was always so tired! Then suddenly the beautiful lakes, mountains, villas, boat-trips, were all plunged into darkness. 'Of my state of mind I have made it a rule to speak as little as possible, because I bore other people, and do myself no good, so *glissons*, which will be better for everyone. . .'

Vittoria

In the summer of 1841 Vittoria was nineteen; Matilde was eleven. Vittoria left school; Matilde stayed there.

The adolescent Vittoria was different from her sisters, because she was stronger, healthier, more vital. She was not beautiful, but attractive, with fresh, healthy colouring, and a slim, robust, agile form; *le petit écureuil*, the little squirrel, Stefano called her. But she was at once beset by misfortunes: by the death of her sister Cristina, then her grandmother, and a few years later her sister Sofia, she found herself deprived of the only people who offered her maternal affection. She quickly lost her rosiness and her fresh vivacity and strength, and became a melancholy girl, easily moved to tears, often ill, without much will to live.

Cristina had died in the spring of 1841; Vittoria had nursed her, then returned to school; in the summer she came home, but found a very different scene: her grandmother was old; her stepmother reigned. Her brothers were ill at ease, as they had been since Teresa had come into the house: but now that their grandmother was so old and overwhelmed with grief, the unease weighed more heavily. Now it was just the house of their father, Teresa and Stefano: there was no room for anyone else. Vittoria went off to Bellagio with Sofia, Lodovico and the children.

'I commend our dearest Sofia to you: she needs comfort and support: help each other. . . Oh my Vittoria, I love you so. . . you will understand. . . Kiss my *Ninoni*, repeat Nonna's name to him, and kiss the other little angel too. Give my fondest love to my dear son, Lodovico; I feel ever greater esteem and affection for him, if possible. Your Papa sends you all lots of love too, and Donna Teresa sends her regards and Nanny sends lots

205

of hugs.

'My Vittoria, may God and the Blessed Virgin ever watch over you, and keep you always as you were on leaving that holy place.

'A kiss, my dearest darling, from your Nonna.

'P.S. I see I haven't mentioned my health; I am as usual – cough and no appetite.'

This was how Giulia wrote to Vittoria from Brusuglio in the summer: these are the last lines of her last letter. A few days later, Vittoria and Sofia were called to Brusuglio.

Vittoria wrote to tell Matilde their grandmother was dead:

'Oh Matilde mia, it breaks my heart to have to send this terrible news! . . . For you she really was the most loving of mothers, after *ours* had left us. . . how she loved you! and how she thought of you to the very end! . . . I at least had the painful consolation of being able to care for her and help her, close her eyes with my own hands and kiss her brow once more. I send you a lock of her dear hair in saddest memory.

'You must pray God to take her noble soul straight into the glory of heaven, and ask Him, after sending us so much grief early in our lives, to prepare a little peace and happiness for us in the future. . .'

Now that their grandmother was gone Vittoria felt that Matilde had only her. Their father was self-absorbed; their brothers full of their own problems. She felt that she and Matilde were two orphans. She felt it, but would not say it. Although she had become so melancholy, Vittoria kept a deep-seated, innate warmth through life's vicissitudes: and even in moments of bitter despair, this deep, conciliatory warmth led her to view the world as a place that was never entirely dark and inhospitable. Besides, at that time there was still Sofia; and then there was Pietro, whom Vittoria loved and thought of as her strongest support.

At that time Matilde still used the formal address to her father, as the nuns had taught her to do. She wrote to him in the autumn of 1841:

'My dearest, most esteemed Father,

'It was my duty to address myself to you before this, and such, indeed, was my wish, but an indisposition prevented me from fulfillng the desire of my heart, but now that I am completely recovered I cannot delay affording myself this satisfaction. I have heard from my dear Sisters of your excellent state of health, and of the happy issue of their journey, which gave me great satisfaction. The wise instructions you are so kind as to send me continuously, are really engraved in my mind and heart; I promise you, dearest, most esteemed father, to practise them better than I have done in the past.

'The last day of last month we did our examinations in the presence of His Eminence who in his great goodness, pronounced himself perfectly satisfied. Be so kind as to present my duty to dearest Mother, and accept the respectful filial affection which always affords me unspeakable satisfaction. . .'

About Matilde, we know that she had fair hair and complexion and blue eyes. It is not difficult to imagine this gentle, judicious little girl, brought up by the nuns, writing her little letter to her father in her beautifully neat, precise, uniform hand. How remote her 'most esteemed Father' and 'dearest Mother' must have seemed! And how remote and severe the 'wise instructions' that reached her from her father! The nuns had told her that her father was there to guide her on the right paths, and 'dearest Mother' was there to offer tenderness and motherly warmth. But from her father she received these 'wise instructions' which she felt she must learn by heart like school lessons; and from Teresa she had never received anything that gave her pleasure or that she managed to recall. And she had seen so little of both of them! However, she acquiesced in the nuns' teaching out of obedience, but saw no real sign of it about her. At eleven Matilde, perhaps more certainly and clearly than Vittoria, knew that she was an orphan, and admitted it to herself.

Vittoria went off to live with Sofia at Verano. Sometimes she stayed in her father's house, but uneasily, and for short periods. Writing her memoirs years later, she adduced a reason for this unease: Stefano. 'Dear Stefano, always so kind to me! yet it was chiefly because of him that, as a girl, I preferred to live in casa Trotti than in casa Manzoni. When I came home from the convent, I found this *new* brother; there was something in his show of brotherly affection that I did not care for. I discovered later that he had discussed with Lodovico the idea of making me his companion. When I heard this, I backed away so that he never revealed this notion of his to me. As I said, poor Stefano was so good, so upright, religious, and not lacking in intelligence, but. . . so dull! Lord, forgive me for never having been able to bear dull people! When I think *how* bored I would have been if I had married Stefano, I thank You for arranging a different future for me!'

However, even if he had confided these vague matrimonial projects to Lodovico, Stefano always maintained that his feelings for Vittoria were purely fraternal. It may be that, in thinking of marrying Vittoria, he wished above all to marry into his mother's ambience; and thereby please her. Mistakenly, no doubt, for Teresa, who so much wanted him to marry, would not have considered Vittoria a good choice. She would have thought her unsuitable for Stefano, delicate, and somehow unworthy of him. However, between Vittoria and Stefano there were never any precise words or acts leading to a sentimental attachment. And the fundamental reason why Vittoria did not like living with her stepmother and her father was probably that she felt herself a stranger in the house. Her relations with Teresa were not particularly bad, and they even became quite good later when she was far away in another province; but they posed problems and made life bitter.

When Sofia died, the whole family went to spend a few days at Niguarda. Teresa remained in Milan, with Stefano. Manzoni wrote her a short note from Niguarda. It was the first of April; Sofia had died the day before.

'My dear Teresa, get Stefano to send me detailed news of you. We are well.'

Teresa did not regain her strength after that birth. She lived like an invalid for a long time. She was up for only a few hours each day, and considered she was nearing the end.

Sofia was buried at Brusuglio.

At Verano, in the garden of the Trotti villa, Vittoria carved these words on the trunk of a tree:

'Dear Verano, where I have spent so many sweet, happy days: 1841 – 42 – 43 – 44. . . Then it all finished, forever!'

Verano, the Trotti villa, Sofia, Lodovico and their four children: there in those rooms, in that garden, among those people, she had felt loved and protected, it had become her home. Now that Sofia was dead, she had to leave. And nobody in the world could give her the generous affection that Sofia had offered, at once sisterly and motherly.

She went to via del Morone, where she did not feel at home, and where Teresa ruled with her querulous, invalid ways.

Then she succumbed to a serious attack of bronchitis. The family feared she would meet the same fate as her sisters.

At that point *tante* Louise intervened. Her intervention was precious and providential.

Tante Louise and her husband, Massimo d'Azeglio, had been living apart for two years. Even when they were in love, in the first years of their marriage, he was often away from home; he liked to roam the countryside, as he had done as a boy, with a little group of friends, in search of landscapes to draw and paint; he would spend the night in dirty little flea-ridden taverns, climb stony tracks on the back of a mule, venturing through woods and wading mountain streams; he sent affectionate letters to his wife, with minute descriptions of his days and the people he met; he bewailed the distance that separated them, and commended the little girl to her, little Rina, whom she was bringing up as if she were her own child; every letter ended with a loving sentence to them both: 'now I wrap you both up in a ball and give you lots of kisses.' Gradually, when they were together, relations between husband and wife became sharp and irritable, his absences grew longer, and his letters colder; finally they stopped living together, every now and then he would come to see her, for the sake of his little girl for whom he felt a great bond of affection; the child remained with *tante* Louise, who surrounded her with every care and affection, as she had always done, for which Massimo was grateful to her. Manzoni, too, regarded her with respect and gratitude for the same reason, and the times when *tante* Louise and the Manzoni family had been on bad terms seemed very remote.

In 1845 *tante* Louise was thirty-nine. She had a generous nature and liked to make herself useful to others. She considered her help was indispensable to Vittoria, and suggested to Manzoni that she would take her away somewhere, for a change of air and ambience. She was preparing to spend some time in

209

Tuscany with little Rina. Vittoria could go with them. Relieved and grateful, Manzoni accepted.

So *tante* Louise, Vittoria and little Rina set off. They went to Genoa, La Spezia, and then Pisa, where *la tante* had taken an apartment.

Costanza Arconati, in a letter to Mary Clarke, pronounced herself delighted that Vittoria had finally *sortie de ce taudis de sa maison paternelle* and affirmed that the 'Marquise d'Azeglio' was a second mother to her. Costanza Arconati could not stand Teresa. She felt that wherever Teresa was, everything became constricted, dreary and oppressive. The house in via del Morone seemed to her *un taudis* [a hovel], a black, airless, oppressive hole. It was certainly true that, at that time, the house was a rather gloomy place, with Teresa unwell, Stefano worried about her state of health, Manzoni anxious and tired, and sad memories wherever they looked.

Vittoria sent little presents to Teresa, from her travels, and asked her father for news of her, which was always bad. She wrote long letters to Pietro describing her new life. Just as Sofia had always been close to Enrico, Vittoria had always been close to Pietro from her earliest childhood.

Vittoria to Pietro, in May, from Pisa:

'*La tante* is making me take English lessons from an excellent lady-teacher here; and I'm having other lessons too. . . As Aunt is so fond of riding, and there is nowhere where this exercise could be more enjoyable than here, where there are extraordinarily beautiful rides in a place called *Le Cascine*, I thought I would go with her, and I am having riding lessons. We have very fine, comfortable rooms on the Lung' Arno: I have met some of the nicest people you could imagine: and yet, however I force myself, I can enjoy none of this; the slightest pleasure is always followed by profound bitterness. . .'

She confided her every thought to Pietro. He was both father and brother to her. 'My dear Pietro, you told me at a *tremendous* moment, that our poor Mother had commended us all to you in the last days of her life; only two little sisters are left to you, poor Pietro. . .' The idea that Matilde, some not-so-distant day, would have to leave school in her turn, filled her with anguish. What would become of her? how would she live in that house, now so different from what it had been? 'Poor Matilde! I pray

210

God may not reserve for her the sad youth He prepared for me! . . . From now on I may say mine is almost over.'

Yet it was Vittoria's natural instinct to look for something to afford her some immediate consolation, and reconcile her to life, when it seemed utterly dark and hostile; and in that first period in Tuscany, although she felt old at twenty-three, jaded in body and soul, unable to escape from her painful memories, yet the idea of her father's fame gave her great pleasure:

'They absolutely adore Papa here: I am never ten minutes in society without hearing his dear name ringing in my ears. . . I assure you that in spite of my physical infirmities, in spite of the even more wretched state of my morale, and the aversion and embarrassment I have always felt at being in society, I repeat I can assure you that these gentlemen manage in the end to make the time pass pleasantly for me; and they do it with a kind attentiveness which I certainly do not deserve. But it's all done not for me personally, but rather for the *name* I bear – so unworthily – and I receive all these demonstrations as proof of their love and veneration for our Papa, and I rejoice inwardly, much more than if it were for me – which, besides, could never happen. . .'

'These gentlemen' who made 'the time pass pleasantly' were Giuseppe Romanelli, the poet Giuseppe Giusti and Giovan Battista Giorgini.

Giusti was then thirty-six. He was born at Pescia. He had studied law at Pisa, but had never practised. He wrote poems deriding Austria, which were printed clandestinely and circulated throughout Italy.

Giuseppe Romanelli had introduced Bista Giorgini to *tante* Louise and Vittoria. Romanelli, a professor of civil and business law at the University of Pisa, was conducting a law-suit taken out by Manzoni against the publishers Le Monnier of Florence, who had published a pirated edition of *I promessi sposi* ('on me fait une avanie dans cette Toscane que j'aime tant' – they have insulted me in my beloved Tuscany, Manzoni had written to *tante* Louise, begging her to find someone to come to his aid, and she had put him in touch with Romanelli). Bista Giorgini was a colleague of Romanelli at the university. He taught canon law. He was born in Lucca in 1818. He was thin, with a black 'imperial'. In June, Vittoria wrote about him to Pietro:

'There is a person here of outstanding merit, who is highly

211

regarded in Tuscany, and who carries his adoration for Papa to the point of idolatry. This is Prof. Giorgini, who has begged me to get Papa's autograph for him. I couldn't possibly refuse, especially as it is he who makes the time pass so pleasantly for us, reading *I promessi sposi* wonderfully well, and speaking of Papa, to tell the truth, as I have never heard anyone do. . .'

In the summer Vittoria and *la tante* were to meet up with Pietro, Lodovico and the children at La Spezia. Vittoria was longing for the summer. She was eager to see Sofia's children again; they would play in the shade of the trees by the bay, 'breathing the balmy sea air'. She wrote a great deal to Pietro, fondly imagining this imminent meeting, and gradually became cheerful, and more curious about the things that were going on about her.

'Tuesday morning there was a solemn mass at the Cathedral, attended by the Court with all the ladies dressed in their ball-gowns. . . such *folly!* There was such a crowd I risked being suffocated in going there; I returned safely, but I wouldn't go again. In any case, we're better off at our windows than anywhere, because we are at the best point of the Lung' Arno, and we see a continual flow of people. The Grand Duke often passes under our windows, on foot, in the midst of the crowd, and he has more the bearing of a fine gentleman than of a sovereign. Mossotti told me he met him one day with his little girl in his arms, like a nanny. Poor Grand Duke, he is perhaps the only *digestible* sovereign there is. . . !'

The summer came and they met at last at La Spezia as they had planned. Vittoria had a letter from her father. She had sent him a little portrait of herself.

'I cannot and will not delay telling you how much the thought, the thing and your words touched my heart. The portrait is already in position, that is, in the only little place left in my den: between the two windows, under the Madonna, so that I can look at you from my nook. . . it will not move from there; your coming might cause it to lose the extra value it has in your absence, but not drive it away!'

Manzoni was writing from Milan. He and Teresa had stayed there, because she was too unwell to contemplate the slightest move. 'Why can I not give you absolutely and consistently better news of Teresa?' wrote Manzoni to Vittoria. 'There is now no trace of blood and the cough has more or less gone: but she suffers a great deal, chiefly from the erysipelatic inflammation of the skin. God grant you find her at least fully convalescent, as I am sure you pray. . .

'I am with you in thought; but since I cannot be there as I should like, at least make sure you return from this absence fortified in body and spirits. Give my love to Pietro, Lodovico, Tonino, Sandrone, the little scamp Giulio – give him a biscuit from *grandpapa* every day at table. . .'

Less than a month later, however, he was urgently calling Pietro back to Milan because Teresa's condition was worrying. So Pietro had to leave La Spezia before the others. Lodovico and the three children stayed on; Lodovico had not brought the fourth, Margherita, who was scarcely a year old.

When Pietro had gone, Giorgini and Giusti arrived. A letter from *la tante* inviting them to La Spezia had been delayed. It was now September, and Vittoria had to return to Milan with *la tante*; this had been settled.

Vittoria to Pietro, from Genoa:

'God willing, this time I won't arrive empty-handed. I am bringing a present worthy of you – something that will give you a lot of pleasure, and will certainly be unexpected: *I'm bringing Giusti!* – Monday morning, at La Spezia, we suddenly took a great decision. In spite of a host of things that might have prevented him accompanying us, above all (unfortunately!) his health, poor Giusti could not resist our pleas, and the mania he's always had to spend some time with Papa; so he decided to set off with us. You can imagine how delighted we are! We've travelled together, and now we're here, he and I using the same inkstand. . .'

Giusti obtained from Florence his passport to enter Lombardy, but Giorgini did not have a passport; besides it was forbidden for university teachers to leave Tuscany without a permit from the superintendent of studies, and the superintendent of studies at that time was Gaetano Giorgini, Bista's father, who had no idea his son was at Genoa, nor of the journey he was intending to make to Milan. So Bista was reproved by the superintendent 'as a son and a teacher'. However, in the end the permit and passport arrived.

Still from Genoa, Vittoria to Pietro:

213

'From your letter I'm delighted to hear you intend to put both our friends up at home. This was what aunt and I hoped, but we did not presume to ask. . .

'Poor Giusti, if you could have seen his pleasure on reading your letter, and how pleased he is that he decided to come! Yesterday afternoon, while we were on a boat-trip out of the harbour, he was suddenly seized by such a rush of joy that he grasped our hands, exclaiming: "Oh, these blessed angels who are taking us to Milan!"'

In the same letter, later (the question of Giorgini's passport had just been sorted out: the Austrian consul had intervened):

'This is splendid! Both our friends are so happy to come and stay in our house, and I am sure they will be delighted with the cordial and affectionate welcome that is usually given in casa Manzoni *(soit dit entre nous)*.

'On the whole Giorgini, too, has been quite cheerful during the journey, but he has Giusti beside him playing the *tutor*: when he's about to go into *raptures*, he gets a little shake and he has to steady up. . . It's curious how these two are absolutely in charge of each other, while neither seems in charge of himself. . .'

Giusti and Giorgini stayed in Milan a month as guests at via del Morone. They were given a very warm welcome. But Teresa was getting steadily worse; she was given extreme unction about this time. But she still wanted to meet Giusti. They took him to her room. Giusti stayed a while chatting beside her bed; he recited some of his poetry to her. As she said goodbye to him, Teresa said: 'Now I look up at him from below [that is, from her bed] but soon I shall look down at him from above [that is, from heaven].' Either Giusti misunderstood these words and saw them as an expression of disdain, or they were just not to his liking.

Tommaseo and Cantú did not like Giusti at all. According to Tommaseo, Giusti spoke derisively of Manzoni. 'That poor fellow thought he could mock "il Nostro" [Manzoni] and when he was staying with him in Milan thanks to Giorgini [this was not correct, it had not happened like that] he was careful to observe a cold, malign disrespect towards him. It's a sad thing for a young man almost to lie in wait to discover the weaknesses of an old man, of a great man; especially if he is seeking to find in him the wretched traits he himself presents. Giusti would

214

recount with a snigger how the wife of the worthy man meant to make fun of him and his faith by saying that she would die shortly and would be looking at him from *up there*: but it depends how she said it, and whether the poor fellow misunderstood. The wife is certainly a believer now; and certainly the desire of that great mind to learn from Giusti some words of his native Tuscan was a matter to inspire respect and gratitude, and to put to shame the Tuscan who, on returning home, said that he did not share the opinions of "il Nostro" about language. He told me how, when his wife happened to say she had had a bad night, Manzoni asked him like a schoolboy to his master: *should it be 'notte' or 'nottata'?* It's like when he says of Renzo in his novel that with the tongs *he traced stories in the ashes*, Giusti suggested that he should correct it in the Tuscan manner to *"made arabesques in the ashes"*.'

And Cantú wrote:

'Manzoni spoke rather ungraciously of Giusti, saying his characters were all caricatures like Alfieri's, and that he translated the latter's phrase-book into the language of chattering sluts; that he knew very little, he held the politics of cafés and the religion of gazettes. In conversation Giusti was more amiable and less caustic. Thanks to Giorgini and the Marchesa d'Azeglio he was introduced to Manzoni in September 1845, and even planted himself in his house. Supposing that his coming would alarm the Austrian empire, he was astonished when he went, according to the rule, to announce his arrival to the police in Milan, to find he was quite unknown to them.'

Looking back on his stay in Milan, Giusti wrote his famous poem, 'Sant' Ambrogio'. 'M'era compagno il figlio giovinetto – D'un di quei capi un po' pericolosi. . .' (I had as a companion the young son – of one of those rather dangerous thinkers): he was referring to Filippo, who was then nineteen.

Giusti was delighted with his stay in Milan. This is how he recalled it in a page of his *Ricordi*:

'On the 22nd August I set off for La Spezia, where I would have stayed for four, five or six days, as it suited Bista Giorgini, who took me there. The Marchesa d'Azeglio and Vittorina Manzoni were at the Baths at La Spezia: but unfortunately for us the season was far advanced, and these dear ladies had to return to Milan. They gave us so many good reasons for accom-

215

panying them to Genoa, and from there to Milan, that we could not refuse, and we stayed a good month in the house of Alessandro Manzoni, with that dear family. . .

'What a sad return journey we had! We rushed away, at considerable risk to ourselves and the horse, with the impatience one feels to lose sight of places and things that remind us of a treasure we are obliged to leave behind. A month before we were following the road from Genoa to Milan in the company of two delightful ladies who were taking us to meet a good man; this time we were travelling it alone, moving away from all our friends: you can imagine how the road burned our feet!

'In all honesty I never remember feeling such dismay, except in the days when I feared I must leave this world. . .'

Manzoni, too, must have remembered their visit with pleasure. Perhaps he later judged Giusti in the way Cantú described. But at the time he must have made a pleasant impression on him: and he particularly liked Bista Giorgini.

That autumn, after their departure, he wrote affectionate letters to Giusti: 'Geppino mio'. 'You must make haste to love me, because I am old, and there's no time to be lost.' It is true that Giusti wrote to him and he was slow to reply. 'I must say that I enjoy chatting, especially with friends, and most especially with friends like you, but not on paper,' Manzoni explained. '. . . you know me – don't you know I am full of modesty? and that consequently I am only reluctant to write, not to read? I can't wait to read anything of yours, verse or prose. . . When you have a moment to spare, write to your Sandro; and if he does not reply at once, think that it is out of modesty, not laziness.' The words are affectionate, but it may be that, in stressing the modesty of writing very little, he intended a dig at the other man, who wrote a great deal.

Vittoria had become ill in Milan. In December, as soon as she felt better, *tante* Louise carried her off to Tuscany again.

Manzoni wrote to Giusti as they were setting off:

'Where the inanimate letter is lacking, two living letters come to supply the need, and I am pleased indeed that they are going to Pisa, but not at all pleased that they are leaving here. The usual harmony of human desires.'

From Pisa Vittoria wrote to Pietro:

'So here we are at Pisa, but who knows if we will spend the

winter here, or if we'll go right down to Sicily, as Aunt would like. For myself, I have no wishes, and I live *au jour le jour*.'

Vittoria certainly liked living from day to day, in a capricious and unpredictable way. *Tante* Louise was sometimes in a very bad mood, and either Vittoria or Rina had to put up with her nerves; but in general she found life with her aunt pleasant and cheerful. For the little girl, perhaps, it was less so; Rina, or Biroli as they called her at home, missed her father. Massimo was travelling around Italy, his visits were infrequent and brief; he made up for it by always writing most affectionately to the little girl: 'Rina, my darling. I could see, perhaps more than usually, that you were sad to see me go; and though, on the one hand, this hurt me, it also comforted me, my pet. But, please God, we will not be apart for long this time. Meanwhile, remember what I told you when I held you on my lap in my study; I am sure I don't need to tell you to love the person who loves you so much, and does so much for you – But I know your heart. God bless you, my little one.'

Coming away from Milan, Giusti and Giorgini had quarrelled, and the quarrel went on for a while at Pisa, provoking a great deal of talk; 'I'm sick and tired, to put it bluntly,' wrote Vittoria to Pietro, 'of all the gossip I've had to listen to! – right from Milan Giusti began saying Giorgini had grown cold towards him. Giorgini said it was a fixation and that he had not changed. They stopped for four days at La Spezia on the way back from Milan, and Giorgini spent the four days at the house of the Marchesa Olduini, who, as you know, is a famous beauty, and it seems he was very happy there. To Giusti it seemed impossible that Giorgini, after enjoying himself in our house, could enjoy himself equally well in the Olduini house. For his part Giorgini maintained that they had been obliged to stop at La Spezia because the Magra was in full spate and they couldn't cross, and that anyway there's no law that says just because someone enjoys the conversation of a man of genius like Papa, he may not take pleasure in the company of a beautiful lady. . . Foolish talk, as you see, but when our friends got to Tuscany there was already bad feeling between them. It seems that Giorgini, who is sometimes too silent, and sometimes talks more than he ought, has talked a great deal about their stay in Milan in more than one drawing-room in Florence,

Lucca, and here. People were all ears to hear him, and tongues ready to repeat what he had said, often misrepresenting it, as will happen. Giusti kept hearing this one and that repeating remarks made by Papa, and it infuriated him. He said not everyone was capable of understanding what Manzoni said, and that in any case you don't repeat things you've heard a man say in his own home, and he sent word to Giorgini that he *begged him to shut up*. Giorgini took it very badly, said that Manzoni need not be afraid of making his opinions known to the whole world; then he let his tongue run away, saying not very nice things about Giusti. . . for example, that when Papa was talking seriously to him, he fell asleep, that Papa preferred to talk to him than to Giusti, etc. etc. – Aunt has always been on Giorgini's side, and the other evening I was present at a squabble between her and Giusti. She said if there came a day when he wanted to speak ill of her, he should do it openly, and be so good as to spare her those *reticences*, which are always worse than accusations. As I said, Aunt was defending Giorgini, whilst I must confess I inclined to Giusti, because I had allowed myself to be influenced by some gossip I'd heard about Giorgini. Then when I realized it was without foundation, given my character, I couldn't help confessing to him that I had at times thought badly of him, but he told me with a smile that *I was forgiven*. Well, thank Heaven, they've made their peace. – Giusti has good impulses for which you really have to like him; now, for example, as soon as they were reconciled, he wrote Giorgini a lovely letter, saying: "Let's forget these days of misunderstanding. . ."'

Manzoni wrote jointly to Giusti and Giorgini, when he heard they were friends again:

'My dear friends. It had to end this way! I simply could not believe that two people I had seen united so naturally, and who were so dearly united in my affection, could be parted.

'Thank you for not making me wait too long for this consolation, which I always hoped for, but with real distress that I should be reduced to hoping. I say no more, for what is the use of dwelling on a bad dream?'

During the quarrel relations between Bista and Vittoria had been clouded, too. Then peace and quiet returned. *Tante* Louise and Vittoria, and the little girl, did not go to Sicily and remained in Pisa.

It was said that *tante* Louise and Giusti were lovers. Vittoria
had not noticed, and later refused to believe it. Writing her
memoirs, she resolutely affirmed it was an idle tale. 'Enough to
make a cat laugh!'

According to Vittoria, *la tante* never thought of anyone but
her husband. But she oppressed him with her jealousy. He used
to call her 'the Spanish Inquisition', and 'avoided' her.

Occasionally he turned up in Pisa, but stayed only a few days
and left again.

Vittoria to Pietro:

'Massimo arrived here Tuesday evening, and will be leaving
for Florence tomorrow. The day before yesterday we dined
with him and Giorgini at casa Arconati; last night he dined here
with Giusti, Montanelli and Giacomelli, who made a tremendous impression on Massimo. He went so far as to say that as far
as he was concerned you could keep Giusti and all the great
men, even Manzoni, as long as he could enjoy a few hours with
Giacomelli. Indeed, I must admit he's *priceless*: he has a really
phenomenal talent for imitation, his facility is astonishing. . .
After dinner we went to casa Parra, where there's usually plenty
of good company, music and singing, and Giacomelli keeps
everyone amused. Last night he suddenly took it into his head
to mimic two porters from Leghorn squabbling over the suit-
case of *the daughter of I promessi sposi*, which had been lost. . .'

Vittoria was enjoying herself, the days flew by; she and *la
tante* received and paid many calls; they went for long walks and
drives; Vittoria was transformed, unrecognisable, they told her:
rosy, animated and pretty. From her sad period she still kept a
hair-style that was aging, two smooth bandeaux covering her
cheeks; *la tante* and Costanza Arconati recommended a different
style, with her hair gathered on top; she was not at all convinced
it suited her, she thought she looked impudent and like a witch;
'I thought my bandeaux were more suited to my face and my
nature,' she wrote to Pietro, 'but patience! . . . Poor Aunt! she
really is a loving mother and invaluable friend to me. . .'

Vittoria was happy: she thought everyone liked her, everyone
was kind, and Pisa was the most beautiful town in the world.

'On Wednesday we went for a splendid ride in the Cascine,
and went as far as the sea: we were a good party, and very much

enjoyed it. Giorgini, who always comes with us, rides as he walks and talks, with that careless, *absent* air quite peculiar to him. . .

'Aunt is very fond of him and regards him as a son. The other day he reminded me that, before he left Milan, I had promised to make something for him: he had understood from Aunt that I had made him a little purse. I'd never had the courage to give it to him; but on Thursday while he was walking along the Arno beside me, a poor man asked him for alms. Then Giorgini, with a meaningful look at me, answered: "When I have a purse to keep my money in, I can give alms, but not until then. . ." So when we got back, I told him I didn't want any reproaches, and I gave him the purse, telling him he had no excuse now for not giving alms.'

She was sorry for *tante* Louise: she was in love with her husband, and tried in vain to drive from her heart this feeling which caused her such pain. He was 'kind and considerate' towards her: but what was this to her, who loved him? 'I think she would be less hurt by ill-treatment than by the frosty correctness of this courtesy shown to her by a man who belongs to her, and who is always leaving her for such long periods, without even telling her when she might see him again. I don't think I could stand such torture. . .'

In December 1845 Bishop Tosi died at Pavia.

Manzoni dedicated *La morale cattolica* to him, with this epitaph: 'To the venerable and blessed memory / of the very reverend Luigi Tosi / I presume to dedicate this work undertaken / and executed with his paternal advice / now that he can no longer, / in his severe humility, forbid me to do so.'

In January 1846 Pietro got married in the church of San Fedele, without a word to anyone. He married Giovannina Visconti, a ballerina at La Scala. He told no one, because he thought his father would disapprove of his marriage to a ballerina, which was indeed the case. His father was told by Teresa and was shocked and horrified.

Pietro had always been the most sensible, docile and submissive of his sons. He had been accustomed to lean on his shoulder, since Pietro was only a boy, and they used to go out walking together. He had always been studious, and devoted to his father. He had studied philology and linguistics, economics and agriculture. And he had always been very helpful in the proof-reading and printing, seeing typographers, supervising the various editions of the *Promessi sposi*. After the death of the grandmother, he administered the family estate. He was constantly involved with the properties. Pietro had always stood beside him in any difficult circumstances, the only one of his sons who gave him a sense of security. And now, all of a sudden, he had married, without a word, and had married a ballerina!

But Pietro was both dear and necessary to him: he had to resign himself to this fait accompli. He received this new daughter-in-law, and put aside any resentment. Contrary to all expectations, he liked her. Not so Teresa, who, then and always, treated her coldly.

Vittoria, too, from her childhood had always thought of Pietro as a stable, infallible, secure support. When she heard he was getting married, she was pleased, but also fearful that this support would be taken from her.

Vittoria to Pietro:

'Remember, my dear Pietro, that everything that is yours is mine – so your Giovannina is my sister. I have always loved and esteemed her, both for what I have heard of her, and because she was dear to you and you to her: a person who has appreciated you above all others, and has preserved the precious treasure of your affections, will always be very dear to me.

'But listen, my Pietro, I beg you in the name of our mother, never to let this step you are about to take remove you in any way from your Vittoria, who loves you more than a brother, who needs you too much, who could not renounce the smallest part of your affection. I would never want, in any way, to cost you the slightest sacrifice, but tell me that if circumstances forced me to come to you, I would find you unchanged.'

In fact, when Vittoria was writing this, Pietro was already married, but she did not know. He wrote to reassure her: he would always remain her close and loving friend. Then a few days later Vittoria wrote:

'My dearest, best Pietro! I am almost too moved to express what I felt on reading your letter! Oh my Pietro, you cannot imagine what an immense comfort it is to me to think I am dear to you and belong to you. This certainty gives me a sense of repose and tranquillity, like a child taking refuge in its mother's arms. . .

'But you're too kind to me, you and my dear Lodovico: please God the comfort that you both afford me may never be a source of pain! . . . If Fate willed that, sooner or later, my situation should change, how could I be content in any other, after experiencing all that is most delicate and generous in this world? You have both spoilt me with your kindness – you have surrounded me with loving care, always guessed and forestalled my desires, and closed your eyes to my faults; and even in the terrible misfortunes which have befallen us, you almost forgot your grief to comfort mine. . . How can you think it a virtue in me if I have not responded with black ingratitude to all that you and Lodovico have done for me? If I share your joy now, after we have always shared our grief? I repeat, I feel I could hardly find anywhere else the feelings I have always found in you two, and I pray God that I may not meet on life's way anyone who is not like you. . .'

By March 1846, Manzoni had quite forgiven Pietro, and peace reigned in the family. Manzoni wrote to Vittoria:
'Things are going along quite nicely here too, and would be going very well indeed, if Teresa were not tormented by two ingrowing nails which will not heal. Today I had the pleasure of seeing Mossotti and I must say that I was more pleased to hear his good news of Luisa than of you; because I feel quite secure about you now, whereas I had heard that the dear, good Luisa, whom I can never thank enough, was indisposed.'

Teresa felt well enough to leave her bed; she wrote asking her administrator, Antonio Patrizio, to send her some money, and ordered some summer clothes. She was planning a journey with her husband, perhaps to Tuscany, or perhaps much further.

Pietro had settled at Brusuglio with his wife. Stefano was once again wandering from one place to another.

Bista asked Vittoria to marry him. She said yes.

She wrote to Pietro:
'I need your advice and assistance: remember *Who* entrusted

me to your care: I am confiding in you. . . I assure you I find
Giorgini so like those who are most dear to me that he seems
made expressly for my heart. . . I have always heard his father,
his grandfather, and all his family praised to the skies, and I
should be very happy to have to do with people like that. . . In
the few minutes I have ever spent with his father, I liked him
immensely, and Aunt too thought him extremely distinguished.
In short, it would be a great grief to me if, in my circumstances,
I had to renounce the support of a man like Giorgini. . .

'His family consists of: his father, who is Provost of Studies
to the Grand Duchy, and lives in Florence with his younger
son, Carlo, an engineer; his grandfather, who lives in his own
house at Lucca, where he holds a very high position as President
of the Council of Ministers, and where Giorgini's sister, who is
called Giannina, lives with him; the older brother, Giorgio,
holds an office. As for his mother, although she belongs to a
very respectable family, they say she's rather *eccentric*: she spends
some time at Florence and some at Lucca, but prefers to live
alone in the country; and if she gives no pleasure, neither does
she cause annoyance to anyone.

'Only you and Lodovico must know this for now, and until
Giorgini has come to an agreement with his father and grandfather, it's better not to upset Papa; if it did not work out, he
would have been disturbed unnecessarily. Nobody knows anything here, except Giusti and Costanza, who are delighted and
can't wait for everything to be agreed and arranged. God grant
it! I have suffered so much in my life, and sometimes I think the
Lord has chosen this compensation for me. His will be done!'

Vittoria was writng at the end of March, the time at which
Sofia had died the previous year.

'For some time my poor heart and mind have been beset by
such painful memories, such heart-rending images, and I did
not know how to escape from them; as I drew nearer the day
that was so sad and terrible for us, the bitterness of my solitude
seemed more profound and intense than ever. But the angelic
Sofia, who was my support, *my all*, for so many years, and who
remembers in heaven all I have suffered for love of her, has
come to my aid in these days of such atrocious memories, and
has set before me this man, so unusual and so *dévoué* that he has
offered to be my companion for life; and I consider, indeed I

223

feel, he was sent by *Her*, and I accept him from her hands.'

Meanwhile, Bista had written to his own father, to ask his consent:

'Dearest Father,

'As I advance in years, this bachelor life becomes more tedious to me. Obliged as I am to live far from my family, I find myself alone, and therefore driven to seek changing and often insecure relationships, to follow various paths without knowing where they will take me. So I cannot give a steady turn to my habits, a serious or constant direction to my ideas, or live in harmony with the position I occupy in the world. A state in which I might find at once employment for my affections, a serene conscience, the need for order, serious concerns, would satisfy the needs of my moral and material life.

'After telling you the *matter*, I will tell you the *name*, which plays a great part in the matter, and which you have perhaps already guessed. The more I know Vittoria Manzoni, the more the idea of making her my wife attracts me in every way. The qualities of her mind are such as one rarely meets, her habits simple and modest. After she left the convent, her life was spent tending her sisters in their illnesses, or in the very sad ambience of her father's house, with a stepmother who was also ill most of the time. Thus her character developed, naturally gentle and submissive, remote from any feminine frivolity or vanity. This is not to suggest that Vittorina is an insipid young nun: she is full of intelligence and sound judgement, and all necessary spirit and vivacity.

'In short, I believe that, even if one were to go out and search deliberately, it would be impossible to find a girl more suited to me, and less likely to cause concern to the family who are to receive her.

'I confess that the idea of being related to Manzoni, to Beccaria, to d'Azeglio, in short, to the most illustrious relatives one could aspire to in Italy, would be a source of no small satisfaction to me, and an addition to the principal idea of at last establishing order in my life, and to the other, even more fundamental fact that (apart from all the considerations I have stated up to now) I am immensely fond of the young lady. She is not beautiful, but is blessed with extraordinary *charme* and distinction, and has such a gentle gaze that will, I am sure, win your trust as

224

soon as you meet her.

'As for her health, she has completely recovered since she has been here, and there can be no difficulties on this score. As for her means, I have no precise details, but I am confident they are sufficient to enable us to establish ourselves respectably at Pisa, where my colleagues live on less than half what we, I think, will be able to put together.

'So I am quite clear and determined in my own mind, and the only thing that could deter me would be to encounter opposition in you, which would, of course, prevent Vittorina and her father from giving their consent: otherwise, I have reason to believe Manzoni would be happy to give me his daughter.

'Therefore, dear Father, be so kind as to let me know your will in the matter – but, in the considerations which must determine it, I beg you to remember that I am not speaking of a speculation, that the heart has a very large share in it, and that moral and sentimental considerations must be allowed to exert a considerable influence. Your judgement, therefore, must take *all* these things into account.

'Take all the time you need to reflect, dear Father. . .'

Gaetano Giorgini took a very long time to reflect, almost a month; then he gave his consent. Bista then wrote to Manzoni, who already knew all about it, from Lodovico or Pietro, or perhaps from *la tante*; he also knew there had been some slight controversies of a financial nature, which had been smoothed out.

Manzoni to Bista:

'Giorgini mio,

'You already know my attitude, and you have seen how my feelings for you began and how they have grown over a period of time, when there was no thought that something more intimate and sacred might be added to them; so my answer is naturally understood, like your question, and it remains only for me to say how happy I was to receive your letter which changed my hope to certainty. . .

Manzoni hinted briefly at the slight financial controversy:

'I confess, when I thought how little my circumstances permit me to give my daughter, this difficulty caused me some embarrassment: a quite different difficulty might well have arisen instead, and one reason for my gratitude is that this has not been the case. . .

'My dear Bista, I love you as a friend, and henceforth as a father.'

And the same day, to Vittoria:

'Vittorina mia,

'My letter to Giorgini is part of my response to the extraordinarily welcome letter from you: now I am answering you directly, but still only in part, for how could I express all I feel for you, now more than ever?

'I thank God, Who wishes you to be the companion of a man, whose rare talents would, in any other circumstances, be the first thing to strike me: but now it is his heart and soul. I feel this separation from you, my Vittoria, but let us see this too, as a benevolent design of Providence, choosing to remove you from places that hold so many dear, but too painful memories for you. In God's grace I know that, for the good Giorgini, and this most respectable family who are welcoming you with such loving kindness, you will be that sweet, sensible Vittoria I've always known, full of cheerful gratitude. . .'

Teresa assumed the wedding would take place in Milan. She heard, however, that it was to be held somewhere else, perhaps at Pisa: she was not told precisely. She was offended. She wrote to Vittoria:

'My dear Vittoria, I must say this decision of yours to get married so far away is not very civil, not exactly a well-bred thing to do! To turn your back on us, when we were on the doorstep, so to speak, waiting for you! . . . but I forgive you for the sake of the Pisan air which has done you so much good; I forgive you for the love you bear that young man, who is wiser than so many aged scholars; I forgive you for the sake of that carefree *je ne sais quoi* in his face, which I could recognize even in the near-dark: and if you said a *je ne sais quoi* had no appearance, I maintain it has a most significant one. And as *se raviser* (changing one's mind) is generally considered to be insincere, whether in Paris or in Milan, I want you to know that I spoke to Alessandro about that *je ne sais quoi* of Giorgini, so mature and candid, calm and open, as soon as I saw him, that is, a few days after I was given extreme unction; and when one is in that unknown region, between earth and heaven, one is not concerned with compliments, so it is not likely that I was resorting to hyperbole with Alessandro about his distinguished guests, however fond he was of them.' She sent her a present of a ring. 'And now, to *vegninn a vunna* [come to the point] and get round to speak of a certain poor thing, I don't know which way to turn or how to unfold my tale, so instead I will ask you, my dearest, to unfold this enclosure. . . I beg your pretty hand – which is now Giorgini's – to accept this humble ring, which to speak in the style of the seventeenth century, will bring you the colour of hope: hope and trust that every blessing will descend upon you and your Giorgini: but this is no longer seventeenth century talk. Addio, dear Vittoria! you must never imagine I could forget what I cost you when I was ill, with all the anxieties that I unwittingly added to all those already heaped upon your poor heart. If my poor prayers have been accepted by God, then I have made up to you for all the good you did for me. If you see Signor Giusti, remind him of the false prophet. I who, by the bathing season, was supposed to look down on him from above, still look at him from below. No more now to Giorgini. I am already tired, and I don't want to talk to him in a rush like this. Papa wants me to give his regards. . . but I won't! I do send you Stefano's regards, all the more since, if he has given up the idea of writing to you, *it is not that he did not have it!* Would you say something kind and nice from Stefano to Giorgini? you would be doing me a great favour, you know! I should like to send a most affectionate word to your dear new relatives, but I dare not begin just now. The dear grandfather who travelled specially! My most distinguished and friendly greetings to the Marchesa Arconati, and my compliments to the Marchese, if you see them, as I hope. We are expecting Lodovico, but he has not turned up yet. Probably he will arrive in a few days to give us news which is always such a dear consolation to us. Please give my compliments to the Marchesa d'Azeglio. I will say this to you, and to you alone – the Marchesa d'Azeglio has done you so much good in body and spirits by taking you away where the air has suited you, and showing you so many new things, that I am grateful to her as for a kindness done to me and to Alessandro, who is more important than I am. So you see how many times my gratitude to her is doubled! but as this feeling can be of no use to the person who inspires it, I do not like to express it. I am a little tired, so I must put an end to this pathetic play of the pen, which can never aspire to say all I feel in my heart, as you can guess.'

In this and other letters written by Teresa after her long illness, she appears less euphoric and excitable, and at times more natural and true; as if, after the illness, the temperature of her thoughts had changed, as well as her relations with other people, becoming more placid, with an undercurrent of melancholy.

In the summer Bista Giorgini went to Milan with Lodovico Trotti to fix the time and place of the wedding. Vittoria, *tante* Louise and Rina were at Leghorn for the sea-bathing.

Bista wrote to Vittoria from Milan:

'Yesterday my whole day was so taken up with the pleasure of being in Milan, in your house, with your family, that I didn't manage to find a moment to write to you; besides, absorbed in your family, seeking and finding in every corner, and every piece of furniture some memory of the time we spent here together, I felt so close to you, so much with you, that I really did not seem to be so many miles away. Papa's face when he saw me was one of those flashes of light from the soul that can never be forgotten! such a limpid, spontaneous revelation of love that it arouses in the heart an abiding trust that can never weaken. Certainly, whenever I think of Papa, I shall always see his beloved and revered face as I saw it then, and all the love this memory inspires will pour forth upon my Vittorina. . .'

One is a little surprised at the idea that, as he kissed Vittoria, Bista would kiss her more passionately, thinking of 'Papa'.

Vittoria to Bista:

'Don't forget to bring me a twig from the avenue at Brusuglio, where I spent such happy years in my childhood, and such sad ones after. And bring me a flower from Verano; and if they put you in the little room that used to be mine, go out on to the terrace where I stood so often watching the sunset, and give my love to the dear little valley of the Lambro, and the magnificent *Resegone*, which I used to think of as a real friend, because its majestic height so often inspired thoughts that instilled courage and comfort in my heart. . .

'Give Lodovico's little angels lots of hugs and kisses from me:

I used to think I should be a mother to them. . . find the most affectionate things to say to my poor Nanny, who saw me born, and who has spent her life caring for us. . . And kiss Don Giovanni's hand: think, my Bista, that his hand will give the blessing that will unite us for life, and *thereafter*: make him promise he'll really come to Nervi – I should miss him so if he didn't!'

The Arconatis were insisting the marriage should take place at Nervi, in their villa, and this was, in fact, agreed. Vittoria wanted it to be conducted by Don Giovanni Ghianda, Filippo's tutor, and friend of the family.

In August Matilde left school and came to via del Morone. She was then sixteen. She was delicate, and often ill.

Vittoria to Bista, who had meanwhile returned to Pisa:

'I've had a very sad letter from Matilde; and how could it be otherwise? I knew it would make a profound impression on her, when she came out of the convent to find the house *empty*. . . In what corner of the house could the poor girl take refuge without being assailed by such sweet and sad memories? . . . Our poor Nonna, who idolised the little creature, and was so grieved to let her go away, could never have imagined her return would be so sad. . . She was not there to witness all our miseries, to see our loved ones decline, then pass away as I did, so she did not anticipate the shock of returning home!'

Then Bista had a generous idea. He wrote to ask Manzoni if he would allow Matilde to come and live in Tuscany: either at Pisa, when he and Vittoria were married, or at Lucca with his relatives. According to *tante* Louise it was out of the question; she thought it was extremely bad form to take advantage of the Giorgini family: but Bista was adamant, and his family accepted the plan as the most natural thing in the world. It was decided that, for now, Matilde would live at Lucca with the grandfather and Bista's sister, Giannina.

Manzoni was preparing to go to Lesa with Teresa when Bista's letter about Matilde arrived. He also received news that he looked like winning his case against Le Monnier, that Montanelli was conducting.

In fact, the case went on for years and years, and later a lawyer called Panattoni took over from Montanelli.

Manzoni to Bista:

'Bista mio,

'However you arrange it, it cannot but be a great service and a great favour to me. Of course, it will be a dear joy for Vittoria to have Matilde with her for a few months: but it is not a question of sweetening her removal to a family where all is sweetness: nor of easing her arrival in a strange land, as this will pose no problem on entering such a family. To make a complete recovery, Matilde needed a change of climate for a time, and I, unfortunately, could not spend that time away from Milan; the fact is, the Giorgini family are welcoming my poor little maid with open arms, as if she were an old acquaintance. Please find the right words to express my heartfelt gratitude to your grandfather, who is as kind as he is distinguished, to your excellent sister, and to all your family: I can say no more than what I said to our dear, good Luisa: May God bless you all!

'I've had good news from the worthy Montanelli, and in my reply I mentioned the arrangement I have made with you. It remains, then, for you to be so kind as to reimburse him for his expenses, until our meeting in Genoa, which will be the greatest of pleasures to me. And I leave it to you to find the most suitable way of recognizing his noble and successful work. You see I've really got you embroiled in all this: that's what you get for falling for my Vittorina!

'You will know that Matilde is troubled with gastritis (a prevalent illness here), but it has never been serious and is now abating. But what have I said? I didn't stop to think that Vittorina will read this letter, and will worry about the word *serious*, even in the negative. So I'll say to her, and this must be taken as the truth, that it has always been quite superficial, and is now almost over. Matilde, too, does not know how to express her feelings at such extraordinary and spontaneous kindness.

'For some days my wife and I have been caught between going and staying, because of a return of her rheumatic pains which we thought had gone for good. Today she is better so we hope to leave tomorrow. . . Again, thank Montanelli for me: if you see Geppino, give him my warmest regards. To you the love of a father, a name dear both to him to whom I give it, and to him with whom I share it.'

Meanwhile Matilde was at Renate as the guest of Enrico,

230

where she had been sent for a change of air. Manzoni to Matilde:

'It is superfluous, but still a pleasure for us both to say how glad I was to hear you were better. Take care of yourself, and see that you come soon to spend some time with your Papa, whom you must leave again before long.

'Teresa, too, is making progress, but very slowly. An abscess in her ear, and an ingrowing toe nail complicate, and partly slow down her convalescence.

'Please thank Enrico and Emilia from me for taking care of you. . .'

In fact, Matilde was by no means cured; this gastric fever lasted the whole year, and she could not go to her sister's wedding, or to Lucca; and she stayed many more months in Lombardy.

So the wedding took place at Nervi on 27 September, in the villa of the Arconatis, called Villa Gnecco. Vittoria's sponsors were Giuseppe Arconati and Giacinto Collegno; Bista's were Massimo d'Azeglio and Berchet. Teresa had not been invited. The Arconatis excused themselves on the grounds that they thought she was too ill to come; she was at Lesa, waiting for the invitation which never came. Manzoni wrote to her from Nervi three days before the wedding:

'My Teresa,

'We arrived quite safely and found Vittoria and Giorgini, who also arrived this morning. Arconati, whom we met in Genoa, asked after you with tremendous concern, as did the Marchesa, and Louise: I need not mention Vittoria. The reasons for the *tremendous* is that he had been told you were ill, and that I too would have been prevented from coming. You can imagine how pleased they were when I told them it had been a passing indisposition. You'd like to know who was the raven of the bad news, but you shall not know, madam, till my return.

'Oh my Teresa! what a poor thing it is to write to you! but what a great thing when I can do nothing else.

'Take care of yourself, keep cheerful. . . I can see the face you're making, and I can even hear you saying: how typical! there are some emotions men simply don't feel or understand. But you are unjust.

231

'Goodbye, my Teresa; I commend Stefano to keep you *cheer-ful*: and he'll do his best, I'm sure, because he too is a man, and without feelings or understanding. Poor Stefano! he has certainly given you proof of the contrary.'

Vittoria wrote to her on her wedding day:

'Dearest Mama,

'Since I am denied the pleasure of having you here at this time when we are all gathered together, such a sacred and solemn moment for me, let me at least send you a few words of real affection. . . You can imagine what this moment means to me. . . the importance of the step I've taken! When I think of the state of profound and tranquil grace in being united for ever with my matchless Bista, the dear presence of my revered Father and the other members of a family that I am about to leave! . .
. all this combines to agitate my spirits, and I feel quite *ébran-lée*. . . So forgive these few confused words – and accept them from the heart of your Vittoria, who will ever remember with affectionate gratitude the delicate attentions you have always paid me and the kind concern you have shown for my health and misfortunes. I pray the Lord will repay you for what you have done for me. . .'

Vittoria had a conciliatory character, and liked to live in peace and harmony with everyone. She did not love Teresa, but always strove to accept her as she was; and she was more successful than her brothers at avoiding bitter disputes with her. So Teresa thought that Vittoria was the best of all her step–children, the one it was easiest to get on with. With Matilde, on the other hand, Teresa never had any kind of dialogue at all. Perhaps there were no difficulties, for Matilde had a gentle nature and she was rarely at home. There were neither difficulties nor kind words on either side, in fact, nothing at all between Matilde and Teresa.

After the wedding, Vittoria and Bista set off for Tuscany again; they were to stop at Ardenza for a few days and then continue to Florence; but they changed their plan, and went instead to Massarosa, a village on the hills of Viareggio where the Giorginis had a very charming villa, surrounded by lemon and olive groves and vineyards. Then they settled at Lucca.

Costanza Arconati sent Teresa a letter of apology. Teresa took a month to reply, but her answer was civil and placid, and showed no resentment. She pretended she had really been unwell at the time of the wedding. She thanked them for suggesting a certain German doctor when she was seriously ill; she certainly owed her recovery to the Boario water, but that doctor, 'sent by the hand of a benefactor and the heart of a friend', had given her useful advice. Teresa wrote to Vittoria: 'My Vittoria. . . I just want to tell you that the Marchesa Arconati has sent a very pleasant letter to say how sorry she was not to have sent me an invitation to Nervi, and other such kindly things that I felt my loss all the more keenly. However, when Alessandro set off for Genoa, I was recovering from a short but very severe indisposition. . . – So it was better that way. – And you, poor, dear, fortunate Vittoria, what have you been thinking of me all this time that I haven't answered all the sweet things that you found it in your heart to say to me to make up for my deprivation, while you were worn out with love and anguish in such a strange new moment of sunshine and storm. . .' She and Alessandro were at Lesa, and they stayed there until half-way through November. 'Alessandro is writing a lot, and every now and then sees his beloved and revered Rosmini; one comes or the other goes from Lesa to Stresa, and from Stresa to Lesa, alternating visits and objections, which – as it happens – if I hear them I mostly do not understand.' There was better news of Matilde, but they had not sent for her to Lesa, and she was staying partly in Milan, partly at Brusuglio with Pietro, partly at Renate with Enrico: for some unknown reason, none of the brothers and sisters ever visited Lesa. 'As you see, we have prolonged our stay at Lesa,' wrote Manzoni to Vittoria, 'because it really is beneficial to Teresa's health; and apart from that, I am more enamoured each day with the lake, the mountains, and the quiet. Here is her letter to you – oh shame on me! longer than mine will be. But you already know that a pen in my hand is just a goose quill and makes only very rare and very short flights. . . Stefano, who has just arrived, sends his best regards to the two of you, or the one of you; and Rossari, who is here with us, urges me to do the same on his behalf. You ask me to renew my blessing on you: dear Vittoria! it is continuous in my heart: so may God confirm it!'

Giusti had been unable to come to Nervi for the wedding; he wrote to Manzoni to apologize, and also to complain that

Manzoni never wrote to him. Manzoni replied:

'My dear Geppino,

'If I thought my unworthy silence might continue to procure me such letters, I'm afraid I would go on in the same way. Which reminds me of a little story, which in itself is funny, but for me has an undercurrent of sadness, like so many of my tales, unfortunately. Many, many years ago, in the country, we had gone to pay a call with my poor Giulietta, who was about seven or eight. She had remained behind for a moment in one of the first rooms of the house, when she saw a big dog coming towards her, a good creature, really, who just wanted to be stroked, but the poor little maiden was terrified. Then she saw a servant coming, took heart, and begged him to send the animal away; but he stopped and seemed not to understand, while she went on saying: dear such-and-such, dear such-and-such, help me, send this dog away. They heard her entreaties, ran up, banished the dog, and asked the servant why he had not rescued the poor little girl. And hear what a splendid answer he gave: she's so charming, I was so delighted to be called dear, dear that I couldn't bring myself to stop it. But your servant is not such a simpleton that he can't realize that in the end Geppino's voice will grow weary, and that he will be put aside as he deserves, certainly not for his heart, but for his inexhaustible and incredible laziness. . . I think you must often see a certain Professor Giorgini: give him my regards; and as they assure me he has taken a wife, charge him to pay my respects to his lady, who will accept them graciously, if, as they likewise assure me, she is a good little woman.'

In December 1846 Teresa made a will. During her long illness she must have thought a lot about death.

I, Teresa Manzoni, widow Stampa, née Borri, by this holograph – will nominate as my sole heir (both in Milan and Piedmont, in case this should ever be questioned) my dear Stefano (that is, Giuseppe Stefano) Stampa, my only son.

I wish everything I possess, either at Lesa, or in Milan, either at his house or here in Casa Manzoni, furniture, books, valuables, everything, to be for him: I repeat, for my aforesaid only son, Stefano Stampa.

It is my intention, however, that my dear Stefano should not be empowered to ask my revered Alessandro, my adored husband Manzoni, during the life of this same, for the restitution of the dowry drawn up in the Instrument of the 31st day of December 1836 in the deeds of the then Doctor Ignazio Baroggi, and that it shall remain intact; except for the receipt of the annual interests at the rate of 4½% (that is, four and a half per cent), which Alessandro my revered husband will pay to Stefano my son, reserving to my beloved husband Alessandro the right to pay the capital also, either in one, or two, or three payments.

It will not be necessary to state that the 20 thousand Milanese lire received one year and some months after the death of my poor mother Marianna Borri née Meda, shall be subject to the same conditions as I have imposed on the dowry which I established by the aforesaid Instrument of Dowry.

In memory of me I leave my adored husband Alessandro Manzoni my gold repeater, which I have always held precious since it has been worn sometimes by him.

In memory of me I leave my adored Stefano (G. Stefano Stampa) afore-mentioned, my church books and also my clothes; since my intention is not to give my things to the servants, of whom I intend to think myself before I die, if and when I can.

I commend with all my heart and soul my dear Stefano to my dear husband Alessandro. I hope he will continue his good will towards my son, as well as some of the good will he has shown me, by his amiability and indulgence.

Moreover (if I may be allowed to express myself in this way, and if my adored Alessandro allow and grant it to me), I commend my dear Alessandro to my dear Stefano, so that wherever Alessandro might need him in any way whatsoever, his actions, whatever they be, would be and shall be those of a son, for by his actions and his love towards me Alessandro has always been the hand of Providence to me, bringing me comfort in my every need, and delight at all times, without ever causing me pain, except when he was ill.

So my blessings fall upon these two, husband and son, Alessandro and Stefano, who have created for me a uniquely blessed life, by God's extraordinary mercy towards me.

This is my last will and testament.

To Vittoria, to Matilde, she left nothing: not a memento, not one small jewel. She left nothing to any of her step-children.

At the beginning of the next month, she was in good health and humour, so much so that she wrote to Doctor Bottelli at Lesa (the brother of the Abbé Bottelli she used to call 'il Bottellone', who had died several years before): 'I am well, and putting on weight incredibly; and I fall asleep quickly and sleep all night long so that it seems to me short; I get up before nine, after having breakfast; and I'm really pleased with myself, I can tell you!' But half way through January she had a severe throat inflammation, and Manzoni was very frightened; in February he wrote to Abbé Rosmini at Stresa: 'With my usual freedom, and my usual trust in you, I am writing to ask you and your fortunate children to pray for my Teresa who has been ill for a fortnight with inflammation of the trachea, and has already been bled six times, with no noticeable, or at least lasting improvement. She and Stefano join with me in this request. . .'

Rosmini and his 'fortunate children', that is, the beadsmen of the 'Istituto della Carità' which Rosmini had founded, said prayers. Teresa knew and was pleased. Slowly she recovered.

That spring Matilde was at Renate, and Enrico proposed to take her back to Milan. He now had two babies, and the second, Sandro, was not many months old. He wrote to his father. The letter is awkward, though what he had to say was extremely simple. He wrote:

'My dearest Father,

'A matter I could not foresee obliges me to be in Renate on Tuesday. As I am so desirous that we should bring Matilde back to you ourselves, I beg you to leave her with us until Tuesday instead of Monday, assuring you that we shall be in Milan towards the night, where I shall stay for two or three days at most with my little family.

'Matilde is really well. Dear Sandro has a slight cough, and it does seem like whooping cough, but it is very slight, thank Heaven, and doesn't seem to upset him at all, We all beg you to give our fondest love to Mama, and we hope to find her well on our arrival. Dear Father, forgive me if I have written to you so frankly, I am always so confused when I take up my pen to write to you, because I am always so afraid I won't manage to express properly what I would like to say, so without re-reading this scribble, I close it in great haste, persuaded of your indulgence, and I put down my pen because I am certain that you know the affection I have and must have for you.'

His father replied:

'My dearest Enrico,

'Although dear Sandro's cough is slight, naturally I am distressed to hear it is of that kind, both because the poor little fellow will be troubled by it for a while, and because I cannot fail to feel anxious for Matilde. I hope she will never carry him in her arms, or fondle him, but that she will stay some distance from him; but I am worried about the hours she would have to spend in the carriage with him. I am therefore obliged to propose something disappointing for all of you and for me, but which prudence demands, that is, that you come with Matilde on your own, if Emilia has not yet weaned the baby, or if in any case she cannot bear to leave him, even for a short time.

'Furthermore, though it is unusual but not extraordinary for whooping cough to be passed on to adults too, I confess I should also be anxious about the visit here, especially as Teresa has not yet recovered from an illness very like that.

'I have said nothing to her, not wishing to worry her unnecessarily; so she greets you all with a light heart, while I send Emilia a warm but sad embrace. I look forward to seeing Matilde quite recovered, and I embrace you with that love you know I bear you.'

Enrico:

'Dearest Father,

'I have told Matilde what you have written and she will obey your wishes and not carry Sandro in her arms or fondle him at present. I beg you not to worry because Matilde had whooping cough two years ago. I will come on my own on Wednesday to bring Matilde back, who continues in good health, and I shall return to Renate the same day. Emilia sends affectionate greetings, and thanks you for your messages to her. Dearest Father Wednesday I shall embrace you meanwhile accept my affectionate greetings.'

In the summer *tante* Louise came and carried Matilde off to Tuscany. They went with the Giorginis to Viareggio. Matilde

237

caught scarlattina. The Nanny was sent to Viareggio. Vittoria was pregnant.

Nanny looked after Vittoria in her confinement. She gave birth to a baby girl, who was called Luisa. Matilde went to Lucca to stay with Bista's grandfather, Niccolao, and his sister, Giannina, as had been arranged the year before.

In October Lucca ceased to be a state, and became a Tuscan province. Duke Carlo Lodovico left, to the great distress of grandfather Niccolao, who loved him; and Giannina wept. The Grand Duke of Tuscany, Leopoldo II, came in his place. Grandfather Niccolao was appointed Regent of Lucchesia. He was very old and very tired but he accepted the office for a while.

Giusti joined the Tuscan National Guard.

Teresa and Alessandro spent the autumn at Lesa, returning to Milan in November. Stefano had remained at Lesa, but because he was always worrying about his mother's health, Manzoni wrote every day with news of her. They were very short notes; the news was minimal, insignificant and therefore good. 'Teresa has had an excellent night, as she expected; a slight tickle in the throat, and a few twinges here and there cleared with six grains of quinine. . .' 'The tamarind and cassia have got rid of the irritation; she got up, drank some coffee, and later ate some soup and vegetables. . .' 'Excellent night – likewise breakfast.' 'Slept very well, breakfasted, and will get up what one might now call as usual.' 'Excellent night; also breakfast. I will say no more because, when it's a question of your health, you get so impatient if your mother asks you for minute details, and you produce endless arguments to us on that score, and then you go and do the same about her; in fact, the way the two of you busy yourselves each about the other's health is just like a scrupulous man's examination of conscience.'

Manzoni never, or rarely, wrote long letters to his stepson Stefano, always these brief notes, but they generally reveal an affectionate and ironic solicitude, a warm, cheerful relationship, and a sort of complicity. Even here, when Manzoni is depicting concisely for Stefano, in a few sentences, the extremely tedious days of his valetudinarian mother, a cheerful relationship is conveyed. Manzoni and Stefano were closely linked in their familiarity with Teresa's ill health, real or imaginary; closely linked and accomplices in the hope that the various remedies might relieve those ills: tamarind and cassia, Abbé Rosmini's prayers, Boaria waters, quinine and castor oil. While thinking a great deal about Teresa's health, Manzoni also thought a very great deal about his own; after all, he had done so all his life. But now he thought of it without too much anxiety, because the worries he had felt about his health as a young man had diminished with the years; somehow, since writing *I promessi sposi*, he had suffered less from the vertigo, the physical terrors which had earlier afflicted him, although he still did not feel equal to going out of the house alone. As for Teresa's ailments, they did not really worrry him, because they were too many and too slight; they worried him less as the years went by; he got used to them. She complained continually of her ailments, and had set them up in the very centre of their domestic life, the whole household revolved around them; these weaknesses were her strength, her way of imposing herself upon her fellows, her son who worried about her but often fled far away, her husband who said he was worried about her but shut himself away in his own rooms after enquiring briefly after her condition and scribbling a few hasty details to her son.

When Stefano was at home, Manzoni used to look at his tongue in the mirror; Stefano records in his memoirs, in which he speaks of himself in the third person. 'His tongue was usually rather whitish; but when it was clearer than usual, he saw this as a sign of stomach irritation. And sometimes when he made his stepson show his tongue for comparison, which was always clean and pink, he would exclaim almost enviously, in dialect: "Lengua de can!" (a tongue like a dog!)'

Manzoni envied Stefano. He envied him because he was young, healthy, free to flee from the house any time he liked; and whether near or far, the image of Stefano projected a cheerful light upon the house, his mother, and her tedious ailments.

Manzoni's own children never cheered him up. He did not see them as young people; on their various faces he traced no images of youth. From Pietro he constantly required services; against Enrico he defended himself: Enrico's humble, awkward tone probably aroused in him considerable irritation and equal awkwardness. Filippo worried him. With his daughters, he was either congratulatory, expressing his esteem, or apologetic, expressing his remorse. His own children aroused in him neither

239

envy nor cheerfulness. He did not envy them because they did not seem healthy, he had seen too many of them die; and they never seemed to him lucky; when a piece of good fortune came the way of one of them, for example, Vittoria, he was amazed, but fundamentally quite happy for that good fortune to remain at a distance so that he could admire it without being invaded by it. He had never been free, light-hearted or cheerful with his own children. His immediate response to them was to feel reminded of his duty to behave as a father, to provide sermons, or advice, or praise, or reproof, manifest confidence or misgivings, satisfaction or resentment: except for Pietro, on whom he was accustomed to rely so completely that he seemed not to see him any more. He was never natural and simple with his real children, except when he was quite desperate about their behaviour or the misfortunes that beset them. This habitual lack of ease and simplicity in his relations with his own children arose from the fact that he had never really had a father: he preserved no paternal image inside him: the memory of old Don Pietro, awkward and gloomy, aroused in his memory only a burden of perplexity and ancient remorse that he had never been able to bury.

In *I promessi sposi* Renzo had neither father nor mother. Lucia had no father. The Nun of Monzo had a terrible father, who ruined her life for ever. But Renzo and Lucia met on their way great father-figures presented by Providence: Father Cristoforo and Cardinal Borromeo. So Manzoni as a young man encountered father figures brought to him by Providence or change: the image of Carlo Imbonati, beloved by his mother, who appeared great and luminous from beyond the grave; and Fauriel; and finally Rosmini.

So to return to Stefano, Manzoni had with him a warm, affectionate, cheerful and entirely natural relationship. Stefano made less grey and gloomy his life with Teresa, which became ever more grey and gloomy with the passing years. Stefano amused him. Later, in her memoirs, Vittoria said he was boring. But perhaps he was not so boring. For Manzoni, he was a charming boy who, near or far, filled the house with his presence, and to whom, when he was far away roaming through villages and countryside, he had to write every day to say how much magnesia his mother had taken.

Matilde

At the beginning of 1848 Vittoria and Bista moved from Lucca to Pisa with the baby. Matilde followed them.

In March news reached Pisa that Carlo Alberto had granted the *Statuto* to Piedmont. Then came news of the uprising in Milan.

Bista left Pisa with a university battalion, consisting solely of teachers and students. Vittoria thought they would return immediately, since they were untrained. But some time later she heard that they had crossed the Po.

Stefano was at Lesa; Teresa and Alessandro were in Milan. On the morning of 18 March the insurrection broke out in Milan. Stefano arrived in Milan that very morning with his servant Francesco; he tried to enter the city and failed. The servant suggested they go to Brusuglio, which they reached by lanes and short-cuts. Teresa heard he was at Brusuglio, and wrote him a note: 'To Stefano, 18th March 1848. I am well. I have slept well. If you are safe, all of you, we are safe here at home. Your Mama commends your life to you, for her sake.' Manzoni added a line: 'We are in the midst of the crisis, but untroubled. Love to you all.' At Brusuglio were Pietro with his wife and Lodovico Trotti. Two days later, on 20 March, Teresa again to Stefano: 'I am well, and if I could be sure you won't come to the Dazi to try to enter, a great, an enormous weight would be taken from my mind. O, for the love of God, for the love of me, don't come and try to woo or force your way in! we will see each other soon, but meanwhile we must have patience. I am well: I get up now at seven a.m. Papa is well and in good spirits, but concerned to hear news of Filippo who was with

241

that French friend of his. . . O Stefano; I beg you, don't go trying to enter now, for Heaven's sake. In the evening, apart from the barricades there are traps on every side made of strong wire – apart from the fact that they were thinking of leaving the manholes open to obstruct movement – if they do it or if they've done it, it will be very risky for everyone. God's blessing on you, by my heart and my hand. Give my regards to Pietro and Lodovico, to whom your Mama commends you with that weakness she has and will always have. Papa is writing; he will tell you about Filippo for whom he has been praying last night and yesterday and today; and has asked others to pray. – But as he was with that Frenchman, I do hope he will still be with him. – However, I am distressed for him. For heaven's sake don't add to my distress by a lack of care for me, you who are the model of filial care. You need not have the slightest anxiety for me or for Papa. The steward is very well and is always with us. We have an excellent doorman, and an extra man at the door at night. Cormanino sleeps in the hall. . . and Domenico in the anteroom [these were two servants], which is quite unnecessary, anyway, as nobody is attempting to enter houses. I've written this on my feet to make haste. Not a half hour or quarter of an hour goes by without my commending you to your Angel, to the Madonna and to the Lord, with all my heart.'

At last they heard what had happened to Filippo. On the afternoon of 18 March he had gone to Broletto, with other Milanese nobles, to sign on for the Civil Guard. In the evening the Austrians attacked Broletto, and took twenty hostages. Filippo was among them.

On 23 March the Austrians left Milan.

Teresa to Stefano:

'What joyful tidings! What unforgettable, everlasting glory to the Milanese of the 22nd and 23rd March 1848. They have gone! And where is my Stefano? I need to see you to believe my own eyes. I am well in spite of the 15 battles lasting almost 5 whole days, but in my heart. . . The Lord receive our hearts for ever, may the Madonna and the guardian Angel receive our ever more tender affection. I embrace you. . . Will I soon embrace you? Your Mama. Filippo. . . will certainly come tomorrow.'

But Filippo remained a prisoner of the Austrians for several months. He had been taken by the troops of Marshal Radetzky, and imprisoned with the other hostages in the Castello Sfor-zesco; then, when the Austrians had abandoned Milan, the hos-tages had been taken on foot first to Melegnano, then to Lodi, then to Crema by stage-coach. At Crema they were visited by a certain Signor Grassi, who was selling arms to the Austrians; Grassi offered to lend them money, and take letters to their families. So Manzoni reeived a letter from Crema; Filippo was well, and suffering no hardships. Still by Signor Grassi his father sent him money, an overnight bag, linen and clothes. 'My dear Filippo, how can I explain the comfort we felt on seeing your handwriting?' he wrote '. . . Write at once to tell Pietro and Enrico your news, you can imagine how eagerly they await it. You can also imagine how Teresa and Stefano share in your misfortune, and long to see you. I trust in God that the exchange will soon take place, and I will have you in my arms. Oh, how we will thank Him!'

Filippo was twenty-two on the very day he was captured. He was studying law reluctantly, and spending a lot of money, and he was on bad terms with his father. But now all was forgiven. 'My ever dearer Filippo. . .'

Stefano, mentioned in Manzoni's letter as if he were in via del Morone, in fact, was not there, and had not put in an appearance there; he did not succeed in entering Milan; he left Brusuglio and went back to Lesa, then from there to Novara, then to Turin, and put himself at the disposal of the Piedmontese government. Teresa had no news of him; she thought he was 'either dead or wounded at some customs post, night and day these were always, always my visions!!!' she wrote to her administrator, Patrizio; then a friend, Don Orlando Visconti, came specially from Lesa to tell her Stefano was well; but when he came, she was asleep, and neither received nor thanked him. 'O what brave, heroic Milanese! unique in the world, a hundred times greater than the Parisians of the *trois journées*! Population of heroes, worthy of Roman Italy! But we. . . but my poor Alessandro whose Filippo. . . was arrested Saturday at the Broletto – poor Filippo, those poor young men in hands worthy of those who perpetrated the horrors of Tarnoff! – O good Patrizio! Will I see Stefano? will I see him alive? – He has been so good to me!'

Manzoni to Vittoria and Matilde:

243

'I have no heart to tell you about the wonders here, until I have Filippo in my arms. . . The house suffered no close shell-fire: only the street barricade was fired on, at the Corsia del Giardino end. . . Every minute there would be good news: one place taken, then another, until they held only the castle and the gates. In a word, the predominant feeling in Milan in those five days was joy, especially among those fighting.

'May God soon send our Filippo back to us!'

Stefano from Lesa, to his mother:

'I am very well. If I had time I would write about the political news of Piedmont, but it would take three or four pages. . . The name Republic has become generally not only unpopular but odious, at Genoa too, and even the students in Turin no longer talk of it. . . The army and the officers, too, are very uneasy about it, and God forbid that these brave soldiers should be overcome by discouragement or indifference. . . If we were to seem ungrateful, if the Republic were to be declared, there would be a grave danger that the Piedmontese would lose those feelings of friendship and brotherhood they've always had for us. . .'

In Milan a petition was circulated for union with Piedmont; many signed it; although Manzoni had signed a request to Carlo Alberto to come to the help of the Milanese, he refused to sign the petition for union with Piedmont. It was never clear why. Massimo d'Azeglio was furious. He said Manzoni was adhering to Republican ideas. But this was not so; Manzoni respected Carlo Alberto, he did not like the Republicans and he did not like Mazzini. D'Azeglio wrote to his wife: 'Tell Manzoni that, if he succeeds in making a republican of Carlo Alberto, he won't succeed in making one of Pius IX. It would be putting two ser-pents in the bosom of Italy, that would tear themselves and her. For the love of God, let's be content to make a constitutional State on the Po. . . If one is always in one room, talking to the same people, one cannot judge a country and the real world. . . Common sense, possibilities, not poetry, for Heaven's sake!'

Lodovico Trotti had rejoined the Piedmontese army. He had entrusted his four children to the Arconatis.

One evening, Manzoni was called upon to appear at the bal-cony. There were three hundred students in the street, 'accom-panied by another great throng', Teresa wrote to Stefano, 'and

244

even by ladies with their servants.' He did not want to appear, but Teresa and her maid, Laura, begged him. Flanked by his servants, Domenico and Cormanino holding lamps ('the lamps of the century', Teresa commented) he 'appeared at poor Filippo's little terrace or balcony and shouted: "Viva! Viva l'Italia!" Then they shouted: "Viva Manzoni!" and he called, "No! No! Viva! Viva l'Italia, and all who fight for her! I have done nothing! Mine is only a longing." And they shouted: "No! No! You have done a great deal! You have given the initiative to all Italy! Evviva! Evviva Manzoni, champion of Italy!" Then their leader pushed forward, banner held high, imposed silence and said: "I am the Leader of the University Battalion. Let us ask Manzoni for a hymn to the Liberation of Italy!" And Manzoni said: "I will do it! I will do it when I can!" . . . I did not move from my room, but I could hear the voices and the clapping. Alessandro was quite confused with modesty. But I hope they will have understood the reason for his: *When I can!* As long as those barbarians have our Filippo, you understand. . . will they have understood? . . . I hope so. . .'

Filippo had been taken to Kufstein, in the Tyrol. People said the hostages would soon be set free, but no one knew when.

Filippo to Vittoria, in April:

'My good Vittoria

'I am sure all the righteous indignation you felt towards me for going so long without writing will turn to compassion and love, when you receive this from the fortress of Kufstein in the Tyrol, where I am held hostage. The family must have told you of my situation. I assure you that I bear it with all possible resignation and firmness. My health is quite good. I'm only writing a few lines, but I want you to have news from me. Tell dear Bista that I am thinking of him too with the affection and heart of a true brother. Then give the biggest hug possible to my Matilde. Kiss your baby girl for me, and together with the names of Papa and Mama, teach her to say the name of Uncle Pippo, who loves her as he loves all his nephews and nieces. Please God the exchange of hostages take place soon, that I may once more be reunited with my family. . .

Filippo returned home in mid-June. From Kufstein he had been moved to Vienna, where he lived free under police supervision. He ran up many debts in Vienna, but his father did not know until later.

Bista had succumbed to pernicious fever at the front, and was sent back to Pisa.

Massimo d'Azeglio, who was field adjutant to General Durando, was wounded in the leg.

In July there was a serious fire at Brusuglio. The farm houses were destroyed. The financial loss to the Manzonis was enormous.

The war was going badly. In Milan they were afraid the Austrians would return. At the end of July, Manzoni made an inventory of the things in the house, locked the cupboards and rooms, gave the keys to Pietro, and set off for Lesa on 29 July with Teresa and two maids; Lesa was in the State of Sardinia. He left Pietro in charge of the house, and Giacomo Beccaria in charge of his interests. The same day Filippo too was leaving Milan, as a volunteer in the mobilized National Guard.

From Lesa, on 5 August, Manzoni wrote to Vittoria:

'Here news is slow to arrive, uncertain and contradictory. We scarcely know that Milan is free and on the defensive, that the king has entered with part of the army, and that the rest were on the way. Exactly what point the enemy have reached, we do not know. . . You can guess what is going on in my heart at this time, and it would be inopportune and pointless to talk of my anxieties. I'll say instead that both here, and from what one hears generally, from beyond the Ticino, there's bustle and agitation, but anything but sterile discouragement. I would almost say that faith in success has not even diminished, and this is a great good in itself, and a great presage of good.

'My Vittoria, Matilde and Bista, you know with what love I press you to my heart.'

On that very day, Milan was surrendering to the Austrians.

Vittoria, Bista and Matilde were at Viareggio. Massimo d'Azeglio joined them. The Arconatis and Collegnos were there. Here they heard Milan had surrendered.

In September, the Giorginis went to the Baths at Lucca, as there was cholera in the town. Bista's sister, Giannina, and her

246

fiancé went with them. Bista was translating Goethe's *Faust*. They went for long walks in the woods. It was a happy month, for Matilde and all of them.

Manzoni was invited to stand as a deputy in Turin. He expressed his thanks and refused. He wrote to Giorgio Briano, who had invited him to stand: 'A *Utopian* and an irresolute man are two useless subjects, at least at a meeting where the discussions are meant to reach conclusions: I should be both at one and the same time.' He was asked to stand as a deputy at Arona; he received a great number of votes, thanked and refused: 'In many cases, and especially the most important, the construction of my speech would be: I deny everything and propose nothing', he wrote, still to Giorgio Briano. '. . . Besides, there's something else. Speaking itself presents insuperable difficulties for me. The man you want to make a deputy stammers, not only in the metaphorical sense with his mind, but in the real, physical sense, so that he could not attempt to speak without putting the gravity of any assembly to the test: so in such a new and frightening situation, he would certainly get no further than attempting. I felt I could make these confessions frankly to you in private: when I have to write my letter of apology to the Chamber (since the College at Arona has been so cruelly kind to me) it will be a more complicated matter, since it is ridiculous to express certain ridiculous things in public.'

He wrote to Vittoria:

'You will have read in some paper, or heard from somebody, that the electors of Arona were so kind as to nominate me as a deputy; and you will have guessed at once that I excused myself.

'Indeed, it was like inviting a cripple to a dance festival.'

Costanza Arconati to Teresa, in October:

'Dearest Teresa!

'I've been wanting to write to you for a long time, ever since I was in Arona and had to renounce the pleasure of going to Lesa because I was suffering from an accursed rheumatic pain exacerbated by the journey. And this blessed rheumatism has been the cause of delaying writing for news of you and Alessandro. Today I'm taking advantage of a slight improvement to take up my pen, and beg for a long letter to compensate somewhat for this long deprivation. What are you doing? how is Alessandro? Is he still troubled with lumbago? We came to

Genoa because the Collegnos were here. . . . Then the need of rest and quiet brought us to the country, and we are in fact in a beautiful villa on the Riviera di Ponente [west of Genoa] . . . The catastrophe of the end of July and the ruin of all our hopes had so depressed me that I went more than a month without reading a paper, and I couldn't bear to hear anyone speak of our misfortune. Now although still distressed, I am less morbidly so. I think that if Italy has not achieved as much as our imagination assured us it would, none the less it has done more than ever before. As a protest against the foreign yoke, the last six months are honourable and extremely valuable. We were deceived on the one hand, in thinking Austria more decrepit than it was, and on the other in exaggerating our strength and worth.' Then she asked for news of Rosmini, and if he had returned to Stresa from Rome, where he had been sent by Carlo Alberto on a political mission to Pius IX; but Rosmini did not get back to Stresa until the next year.

Vittoria wrote to her father, inviting him and Teresa to come and spend the winter with them. On their return to the town from the Baths at Lucca, Vittoria had had worries and upsets: in the first place Matilde had become ill, and had had to be bled; then there had been a bitter quarrel between Bista and Romanelli: Bista was a monarchist; Romanelli a republican. Romanelli had fought at Curtatone, and had been taken prisoner; at Pisa they had thought he was dead, and had conducted a funeral service. When he got back to Pisa, he quarrelled with Bista about an article Bista had published in June: 'The Kingdom of Northern Italy'. They broke off all relations. Bista felt very bitter about it. The baby, little Luisina, was 'blooming', and full of health; but that autumn, because she was teething, even she had a cough.

Manzoni to Vittoria:

'Dear Vittoria! how touched we were by your invitation to spend the winter in Tuscany! If you knew how often we've talked of it, but unfortunately only as a beautiful dream! Even if there were not the probability of being able, and therefore having to, return to Milan soon, there is another difficulty, of money. We are living here as thriftily as possible, with money which Stefano has been able to borrow here for us. The contributions we paid willingly to our soldiers, the accursed contributions we were forced to pay to the Germans, the low value of the cocoons, the fire at Brusuglio have left us, as you might say, without a rag on our backs. And I must say that my face is red, not metaphorically but really, when I think of the debts I am incurring with you for Matilde. I have already spoken to Bista about it, and then I hoped that I would not be kept waiting so long: now, instead of improving, the situation has got a little worse. But I know who I'm dealing with, with my two children, and Matilde's brother and sister. So I am sure of your patience: it is mine that is causing me problems.

'Your letter from the Baths at Lucca comforted me with its news of Matilde's recovery; your last cannot give me the same cause for satisfaction. I hope to receive another very soon saying that the cough has gone. I am not so concerned that the bleeding did not immediately produce the required effect, because this remedy, unique and paramount in these cases, does, it's true, block the progress of the illness, but takes some time to remove it altogether. Now, lemonade, vegetables, total abstinence from wine, guard against sudden changes of temperature, and all's well. And poor Luisina, too, with her cough! But you'll have to resign yourself to something of the kind each time she's teething. Let's hope that the others will come less unkindly now the ice is broken. . . You can imagine how I'd love to see her and give her a kiss myself; I hope you'll be able to bring her to see me in Milan soon, since it seems the Germans are willing to make our residence there possible soon in the only way that depends on them, which is by going away.'

At Lesa, in August, Manzoni had heard he must pay a tax or fine of twenty thousand lire, as an emigrant. He had written to ask Leopoldo Maderna, the steward at Brusuglio, to let him have this money at once. There were also debts at Milan 'to the baker, butcher, pork-butcher and grocer'; the widow Tarlarini, pork-butcher to the household, wrote asking that her account should be settled, together with the accounts of Enrico and Pietro; they also had to pay the salary outstanding to the heirs of their servant Domenico, who had died at via del Morone a few days before they left. Then again they owed two months' salary to the Nanny, and they also owed her money she had paid to Vittoria. 'Ask her if she can wait a bit longer, until Providence enables me to do my duty.'

Alessandro and Teresa needed a passport to remain at Lesa, and it was not easy to get one. They had to draw up a declaration specifying that Teresa was in very bad health and not fit to tackle the journey to Milan, and her husband could not leave her.

They feared the Austrians in Milan were intending to sequestrate the possessions of people who had left the town. Teresa lived in terror of this. She wrote to her administrator, Antonio Patrizio:

'Alessandro has incurred the tax of twenty thousand Austrian lire by his absence, which he will not be able to pay. . . Now, since Alessandro is without the means to pay, and to tell the whole truth, also without means to go on paying our small household and food expenses, which for now, are being provided by a small sum borrowed from Stefano by means of a mortgage on the Nivolè, so as Alessandro is quite without present and future means, we shall have to allow the sequestration to take place. Now, if the furniture at the house in Milan were also to be sequestrated, I should like to ask you to be so good as to trouble Grossi for myself and Stefano about Stefano's three rooms (two of his, one of his servant's) which are two on the 2nd floor, and one on the ground floor; together with mine on the 1st, furnished almost entirely with my own things; I would ask you and Grossi to be so good as to save these from sequestration. . . Forgive me, my good Patrizio, for sending this infamous *spegasc* [dialect: a botch] and not rewriting this dreadful page. . . Our stay here is quite peaceful; to be brief, as far as our political cause is concerned, we hear nothing that could be said to offer any sort of indication for the near or the distant future. In my opinion, Italy *l'è on garbioz* [dialect: is a muddle], a tangled skein that it will take God knows how many years of educating to unravel. Meanwhile, (in my opinion, poor little old lady that I am) the present generation will all have time to grow old, and the old like me, will have time to move on to the next world. . .'

Thinking of her death, and imagining she was poor, she wrote the following declaration, in April 1849:

'I wish and beg my Alessandro not to spend more on my funeral than that minimum that is spent for the poorest, or at least for the lower orders.'

She had a cult of objects, and hoarded everything jealously, valuable or valueless. She pinned little tickets on everything, with a description or comment. Leaving Milan for Lesa, she had filled two trunks and a harpsichord case with her name written on them, and entrusted them to don Ghianda to be taken to his room in the Collegio Calchi, of which he was rector. Then Pendola, one time inn-keeper at Lesa and now an odd-job man, had come to move them from there to Lesa, where they reached her in September. She said those two trunks and the harpsichord case contained her dearest memories, things which she had received as presents or kept jealously as souvenirs. They were things everyone had seen in her rooms, with the tickets pinned on them. The jewels her mother had left her. A reliquary belonging to a great-aunt who was a nun. A gold filigree knife, in memory of her first husband, 'stupendous work, ancient Flemish'. The various editions of *I promessi sposi*. A 'quinter-netto', or five-page fold, with instructions written by Manzoni for Gonin concerning the vignettes. A 'lock of Alessandro's hair when he was young'. A glove of Alessandro's. A 'poor but faithful portrait of Alessandro Manzoni at 17, by Bordiga'. A miniature of the portrait of Giulia with Alessandro as a little boy, with an accurate description of the materials of their clothes and the colour of their eyes and hair. A few letters from Rosmini. Two portfolios of yellow leather with silver fastenings; two earrings with brilliants, a present from Giulia. 'A crystal *flacon* from Paris shaped like a marine chestnut.' 'Box made from shells. A work basket embroidered in chenille.' 'Three parcels of books with a beautiful little key.' A copy of Grossi's *Marco Visconti* in a de luxe binding 'with a note to me from the author'. But there were different opinions about the trunks and harpsichord case. Someone claimed there was something else in them. These rumours reached Teresa's ears. She wanted Alessandro to make a declaration about them. He obeyed. He wrote: 'Lesa, 1st May 1849. My dear Teresa. Since, for your peace of mind, you wish me to attest that the case and the two trunks with your name on, which were moved from Milan to Lesa, contain only your belongings; and since this is the simple truth, I bear witness to it absolutely and explicitly; and declare, equally absolutely that I do not admit the possibility that anybody of my acquaintance should ever have the remotest suspicion to the

251

contrary. Your Alessandro Manzoni.'

But it all led to bad feelings. It was apparently Giacomo Beccaria and Pietro who had voiced suspicions about the trunks; and Nanny, it seems, had affirmed that Teresa had taken things that belonged to the house. Teresa to Antonio Patrizio in October 1849: 'My trunks and my harpsichord case, marked with my name, entrusted to don Giovanni who is an acquaintance of mine, but a great friend of quite different people. . . these locked possessions of mine were secretly opened and searched by Cons. G. B. [Giacomo Beccaria]. I discovered this last January because the family Nanny, perhaps overcome by scruples, told Pendola. . . and then I heard it again this July when our chambermaid, who had gone to Milan to see her sick father, happened to meet the Nanny, who must have been overcome by scruples more than by shame, and said once again to the aforesaid chambermaid, Laura Boschetti, that my trunks had been opened by the Aforesaid Person. This poor lady [the Nanny] had proclaimed all through the house, high and low, (except to Alessandro and me) that in the trunks and case, which had still not left the house, I had put things, linen etc. belonging to the Manzoni household. . . When Laura heard from the Nanny that Cons. G. B. had opened my cases, to *check*, Laura said to her: "Well, what did he find?" "Nothing; *doma i so liber e i so strafusari* [only her books and her scarves]."' The Nanny, according to Teresa always spoke the truth, 'she would rather have her head cut off than tell a lie: except that she has spoken gross calumnies against me: but always because she believed it, or liked to make others believe it.' Since the keys of those famous trunks were at Lesa, Giacomo had opened them, Teresa maintained, with *picklocks*, 'I say with *picklocks*. God knows, and Alessandro and Stefano know too, if I could or would ever use or take advantage of their love for me to appropriate, either by art, or (let it be said) by cunning, one scudo, or a hundred, or one coin, or one book of theirs. . .' In October 1849 Teresa wrote some notes which she entitled 'Important memorandum. . . or rendered important by the conduct of Nanny, of Sig. Cons. Giac. Ba. and some others': she wanted another declaration from her husband specifying her ownership, since he had given them to her himself, of 'a mahogany *chaise-longue*', 'a white and blue *tricotée* blanket which has been on my bed for

252

three years of illness', and 'a linen-drum' that Alessandro had written to ask the steward at Brusuglio to send to Lesa, 'for the *sala à manger* at Lesa, so that we can use it in the winter'. The words 'some others' obviously allude to Pietro. At the end of 1849 Manzoni wrote letters to Pietro, which he later asked him to destroy. Brief fragments of them remain:

'You may expect only very sharp letters from me, because this wretched business is not over. I would have much more to say, but I am more troubled about R. and S. than you.' Manzoni was supervising an edition of his works, with the title *Opere varie*. R. and S. were Redaelli and Stella, the publisher and his assistant.

'I shall say nothing of the wretched matters I spoke of in my last. I am waiting with painful anxiety for you to speak of them. Embrace Giovannina and the two dear innocents who are starting their lives in the midst of woes they do not feel.' At that time Pietro had two little girls: Vittoria and Giulia.

Pietro had said he would come to see them at Lesa. Teresa to Stefano: 'So Pietro wants to call at Lesa? We've never seen him here yet, and if he comes he knows what poor lodgings he will find, but he is welcome to them.'

In January 1850, Manzoni wrote the new declaration required by Teresa:

'Dear Teresa,

'Since from an excess of delicacy you will not keep the English *chaise-longue* and the linen-warmer of tin which are at Lesa, without a declaration that you received them as a gift from me, I am making this declaration. But I have the right to add that they are trifles, not only in themselves, but still more by comparison with the gifts I have joyfully received from you, as a pledge of our immutable affection.'

A few days later he wrote affectionately to Pietro once again. Pietro's collaboration in everything was invaluable to him; in work; in disputes with Filippo, or with Enrico; in every difficulty. Now intent upon the supervision of this edition, he wanted Pietro's help as always: he used to approach him with requests for books, research, proof-reading. 'Tell me, Pietro, what is this silence? . . . I close, saying: do write; embracing you; and saying again: do write.'

Pietro did not come: he could not get a passport, which he

had requested for only four days.

Manzoni had registered a complaint about the tax, asking that it should be annulled. 'So far no news of that fatal tax,' he had written to Vittoria in the summer. 'Lesa and the surrounding area are full of Austrian troops. We have two officers in the house. I am waiting for a *very long* letter from you, with detailed news of you all, of Lodovico and his children, of Luisa: dear names! When will I see you again? And my Matilde? How can I thank you, when you keep her so far from me? How can I not thank you, when she is in such dear safe-keeping?'

In the end the tax was annulled. He gave the news in a letter, this time, to Matilde. He had good news of Matilde's health. 'From now on it's not a question of being better, but being really well; and you can enjoy it without having to make comparisons with the past, or to recall the ailments you have suffered. But how long must I hear of this wonder, and not see it? We live here with no fixed plan, waiting each day for the next to bring one ready-made; but our chief plan is to be able, and to have to, return to Milan at the end of the autumn. And then my Matilde too will return to the nest: if only I could go and fetch her! But there are too many obstacles. However, even if it can't be done that way, we still must be together. . . You too tell me wonders about this little granddaughter of mine; but I'm afraid you are not telling all. Beautiful, graceful, gentle, loveable, with a quick intelligence; but you say nothing about caprice. Goodness me! is she the only child to display none? Oh, my poor dear little granddaughter! If when they name *gran papà Sandro* she knew that this wretch counters the universal praise with imaginary criticism? she would say even at this tender age that human beings are poor things: but she will have to say it some day, anyway. . . A hundred kisses, and my apologies to the little granddaughter. To you the blessing of the Father of fathers.'

This prodigious little daughter of Vittoria's, at two years old knew all the characters in *I promessi sposi*, 'and if necessary would remind others of them'. 'Keep her in these good ways,' Manzoni wrote to Vittoria, and as soon as she can read properly, that's the book to make her read, for this is the way to make her enjoy it all her life. Old and sharp as I am, I can't look at the stories of Soave, the verses of Frugoni, the *Veillées du Château* of

Madame de Genlis of blessed memory, without a real feeling of sympathy, and a tug at the heart: why? Because they are things I read as a child. And now that these *Promessi sposi* have run through a good part of their allotted span, and are growing old at a terrible rate, there's a real need for somebody to be growing up who will perforce remember them. And if my own kith and kin won't do me this charitable office, who will?'

Vittoria to him:

'As time goes by, it becomes ever more grievous to me to have to live so far from you! Oh, it would be better, in my opinion, if, instead of maintaining the impossibility of Mama's undertaking the journey, you were to apply for a passport stating the need for her to spend the winter in a milder climate than Milan and Lesa. . . – I am convinced that it could only do Mama good to come and spend the cold months on the banks of the Arno where there's no such thing as winter. . . I will not and cannot give up hope of embracing you again this coming year, and one way or another I hope the good Lord will grant us this consolation and that I may at last throw myself into your arms, show you your Matilde grown up and in good health, put my poor little one in your arms, and hear you having long discussions with my Bista. . .'

In November 1849 the Capponi Ministry in Tuscany fell, Gaetano Giorgini, Bista's father, was Minister of Foreign Affairs. The Ministry of Guerrazzi-Montanelli succeeded the Capponi Ministry. Gaetano Giorgini lost his office and retired to private life.

In December of that year Bista's sister, Giannina, got married. Matilde used to spend a lot of time with her; they had two little rooms next to each other; they went to church together; sewed and embroidered together. After Giannina's wedding Matilde became melancholy.

Grandfather Niccolao sold the house at Lucca, which was too big for him on his own. Vittoria, Bista and Matilde spent Christmas at Massarosa; then they returned to Pisa, where they left their furnished apartments, and took a bigger house.

Tante Louise came to Pisa, Rina had been at school in Florence for two years. In February 1850, Massimo d'Azeglio was a guest at case Giorgiani. The government suspected he had come to Tuscany for political reasons, to spread the idea of a Piedmontese intervention to restore order. The Giorginis detested the Guerrazzi Ministry. Vittoria recalls in her memoirs: 'At that time the porters and the worst dregs of the streets were masters of Pisa: we saw these fine fellows come into our house and ask threateningly if *the marchese* was there, and I lived in a state of agitation. . . I told Massimo, and he jokingly showed me his seven-bore revolver, and his sabre, and glorified these *guardian angels* (as he called them). . . But I was far from serene. One morning a letter came from Florence from Tabarrini to Bista, telling him a warrant of arrest had been issued against Massimo, and that he should be sure to leave without delay. At first Massimo wouldn't hear of going; but Bista had to take a hard line, and then Massimo had his horse saddled and rode off secretly, straight to Sarzana.'

Rosmini's mission to the Pope in Rome had been unsuccessful. He returned to Stresa in November 1849. On his return journey he had spent a day at Massarosa, and he brought Manzoni news of Vittoria, Bista, Matilde and Luisina, or Luigina as Manzoni sometimes called her. The Pope had shown and expressed great esteem for Rosmini, and this won him jealousy and antipathy in the ecclesiastical world. Two of his books were put on the index. Manzoni and Rosmini met frequently in 1850: either Rosmini came to Lesa in his carriage, or Manzoni found a carriage to take him, accompanied, to Rosmini. When they could not meet, Manzoni was sad. 'I would never have thought I could feel such sadness for the sickness of a horse,' he wrote to Rosmini. 'Moreover, the absence of Stefano, who is in Milan for a few days, makes it more difficult than usual for me to go and avail myself of all the mental and spiritual benefit your words afford me.' And to Pietro: 'I still have the pleasure of seeing Rosmini. All is vanity, except the carriage, said Saint Filippo Neri. What luck for me that Rosmini has one! I see in him a great proof of how one's sense of deference may be preserved entirely, even when one's deepest personal emotions are involved.'

Stefano often went to Milan; his mother anxiously awaited

256

his return, as there were frequent storms on the lake in the winter; Manzoni sent him little notes with news, requests and recommendations of prudence: 'Please will you go to Radaelli to make a correction in the proofs. . . where it says "la pianta era morta dopo aver portato il suo fiore immortale", for "portato" substitute: "messo". 'Do me. . . the favour of going back to the printer, to tell him that if, in the correction of the proofs he finds some *buono* or *cuore* or *nuovo*, he should take out the *u*.'

In Milan Stefano used to go to see his uncles Giuseppe and Giacomo Borri, and Rossari and Grossi. 'Last night I went to Grossi's', he wrote to his mother. 'I also saw his ladies who had come from the country, and who charged me with so many greetings for you and Papa and *n'occor alter* (without fail). They looked well. . . Peppino had already retired to bed, but I saw little Lisa and thought she had grown and her hair is getting quite long.' His mother wrote: 'When you see Grossi's babes, take their little hands, and squeeze them for me.'

In February 1850 Manzoni wrote a long letter to Grossi. He enclosed summonses he had received from Vienna, from which he had learnt that, while Filippo was a prisoner in Austria, he had run into debt; and now Manzoni neither knew how to pay these debts, nor considered it just that he should have to.

'Dear Grossi,

'I knew perfectly well I would never stop being a nuisance to you as long as I live, but I didn't expect the nuisance to be of this kind. The enclosed summonses, apart from the effect they have had on my spirits, of which it is superfluous to speak, leave me entirely undecided what I must do or not do in response to them. It is quite impossible for me to pay these debts, which are nothing to do with me; moreover, if it were possible, I would not do so without thinking it over, and deciding it was right to do so, and how to do so. But since I have already received these demands, and there may be more, and a lawyer is appointed for me, I beg you to tell me what steps are necessary, and which might be dangerous.

'Seeing a young man forcibly removed from his home, kept hostage in another country, and, having a father, yet running up debts in that country, people might easily think: what was

257

his father thinking of? I am sure you will have no such doubts about me, but I must tell you how it all happened.'

When Filippo had been transferred from Kufstein to Vienna, Manzoni had asked a certain Signor Fortis, who had a business house in Vienna, to make arrangements for him to send money to Filippo, and asked if three hundred Austrian lire would do for a start. Signor Fortis 'thought it was a bit on the mean side', but Manzoni knew that Filippo had for years been inclined to spend in a grandiose, regardless way, and did not want to give any more; in the end he gave five hundred lire. Later he sent more. But Filippo borrowed money elsewhere; he ran up a debt of three thousand six hundred lire in the city. 'My distress at this and the many other similar instances will surely be increased in good measure by the judgements of the world,' Manzoni wrote to Grossi. 'What I have been doing for several years (for we are talking about years) to curb this fatal tendency of Filippo's to spend beyond his means, I have naturally done so that no one should know about it. . . So the world cannot know how, and how often, I have reproved him while paying his earlier debts; how I have intimated that, if it continued, I would be neither able nor obliged to heal his wounds; . . . how I have had, very reluctantly, to warn those who were giving him credit; how I gradually imposed such necessary restrictions as I deemed possible, and how I saw that they were carried out insofar as my situation, which you understand, permitted. I repeat, the world cannot know all this, and does not consider, indeed has never considered, itself obliged to wonder whether its judgement is based on insufficient information. So that it has the double advantage of condemning both of us at once, and saying: he did not keep a tight enough rein on him. But unjust judgements are, perhaps, the way the Lord teaches us a just knowledge of our own errors. And I pray He will grant my heart the strength to give Him the thanks I know in my mind I owe him on this score. But, as it is none the less permitted to seek comfort, and the compassion of true friends is a great and dear comfort, I have allowed myself this outburst to you. . .'

In this same month of February Manzoni received a letter from Vittoria (Teresa asked to keep it. She often asked her husband to give her letters he received. On this one she wrote: *Letter from Vittoria, which Alessandro gave me in response to my wish*

258

to have the words of his little girl). News of Matilde's health was not good. She had no appetite and was losing weight. 'I made her keep taking her lactate of iron tablets, sometimes combined with a little absinthe. . . This winter I've taken her out to some social occasions not to keep her hidden away all the time, and her pleasant, modest manner was generally found pleasing. In the last days of carnival she had a slight temperature, lasting a few hours. I immediately sent for a university professor, who prescribed an ounce of castor oil. . . This doctor found her rather lymphatic, and told me she had an excess of serum in her blood. He changed the lactate of iron treatment to iodine mixed with extract of walnut leaves; he also recommended her to take milk and roast meat, and to drink a spoonful of good wine every day and take plenty of exercise. Then we thought of giving her a change of air, and it was already arranged for her to join my sister-in-law who has just gone to Massarosa with her husband and baby. . . But *tante* Louise, writing also on behalf of the Arconatis, was so eager that we should take her to them in Florence, that we changed our plan. . . Thursday morning Bista took her to Florence, Aunt welcomed her like an angel, and although she has not been very well herself this winter, Bista says she was so happy to have Matilde with her that she's a different woman at the moment. Poor Aunt, she is so kindhearted; Matilde is already better since being in Florence. . . she's having a very pleasant time, going for beautiful rides and seeing a lot of people.'

That spring Teresa had an abscess in her ear which made her whole face throb and made it difficult to eat; she wrote to Stefano, who was in Milan: 'This morning I took my usual coffee and cream with a little soft bread, but although I had added some cold coffee, the tepid liquid felt so boiling hot that it set off terrible pains not where you filed my tooth, but further down where I think the enamel is damaged, which is not what you said. Can it be caused by the abscess in the ear? None the less, without even recalling the heroic Sancho Panza, who bit on a spoon while his mouth was being stitched up, for fear of not being able to bear it, unworthy Teresa di Sancho that I am, I continued my breakfast, alternating pains, coffee, soft bread and fresh butter which soothed me and gave me the courage for a renewed assault on my coffee.'

On Easter Day, Giuseppe Giusti died in Florence. Vittoria wrote to tell her father. Giusti was staying with Gino Capponi at the time. He had had lung trouble for years, and had recently seemed very poorly. 'They had brought his breakfast when at the first spoonful of soup he coughed blood more violently than usual; but he was not perturbed and even told the servant who was close by to pay no attention and not to tell anyone, but it happened again at the second spoonful, and in a few minutes his dear soul had left that poor body which had been so long tormented! He had told poor Gino Capponi, whose grievous misfortune it was that he should die in his house, that he intended to confess and take communion that week, and God who sees in our hearts will have taken note of this! The second day of Easter, an hour after the evening Ave Maria, a great number of friends of poor Giusti and Gino gathered in the latter's house, and they all accompanied the sad cortège!' Bista was one of the four bearers, and he returned home broken. 'Now he does not feel at all good and he looks wretched too because, apart from the moral anguish which was obviously considerable, it can't have done him much good to be out in the streets of Florence on a cold, rainy evening. . . Poor *tante* Louise, too, is very, very upset, as you can imagine; yesterday morning she wanted to go to church for a while! . . . and of course she emerged sadder and more disturbed than ever. . . Ah, dear Papa, I can't tell you how much this unhappy letter has cost me! . . . I am deeply sorry to have had to cause you such grief, poor dear Papa, I should like to find some words to soften the blow if possible, but you will find them in your heart!'

Giusti was buried at San Miniato al Monte.

Manzoni to Vittoria:

'Poor Giusti! in the prime of life and talent, and when that lively and original talent was steadily maturing! I am so grateful to you for telling me he had expressed the intention of confessing that very week! . . . I need hardly say that my second thoughts were for all of you, especially poor Bista, and our good Luisa, and Gino Capponi for whom the blow was so close. I see from the papers that there was general mourning in Tuscany; and such a loss is bound to be felt throughout Italy. But I think only the friends, not only of Giusti, but of Geppino, were able to appreciate fully the gentleness and goodwill concealed beneath that proud, sharp-edged intellect. . .'

'I must come to another sad thing,' he wrote in the same letter, 'because it is involved with so many sad things, that is, I must speak of my plans.' Teresa's poor health would not allow them to return to Milan, and they had had to renew their passports; the new passports ran out half-way through September. 'And Matilde? this is the thought that keeps me in cruel suspense.' There could be no question of sending for her to come to Lesa, because Teresa was ill so Matilde would have no 'company for walks' and would be bored; however, if she did not mind the boredom too much, he would send Nanny at once to fetch her. 'If not, I'll have to rely on you again for another five months, after which, barring serious illness, which God forbid, we'll go to Milan. . . I await a letter from Matilde, and, since you say nothing more about her, I assume she is quite well now.'

Matilde had returned to Pisa from Florence. She seemed more melancholy than usual. In fact, this was what had happened: in Florence a frequent visitor to *tante* Louise's house was a young Florentine aristocrat, a widower with a little baby daughter. A romantic relationship seemed to develop between him and Matilde, and Matilde had grown very fond of the pretty little child. But suddenly he disappeared and no more was heard of him. Vittoria learned from friends that doubts had been raised about Matilde's health. His wife had died of consumption. He took fright and left. Matilde must have realized why he had vanished, but she never said a word about it. She was inclined to be withdrawn and reserved. Vittoria and Bista felt that *tante* Louise had been rash to encourage meetings between the young man and Matilde, and did not conceal some slight irritation. There was some bad feeling, especially between Bista and *la tante*, but this soon evaporated. Matilde resumed her usual life, between Massarosa and Pisa, Bista's Grandfather Niccolao and his father Gaetano, Giannina and the whole Giorgini family. She was deeply fond of Vittoria's little girl, Luisina; she spent a lot of time embroidering, sewing and reading, and she used to write down her thoughts in albums, which she begged her sister to destroy or burn, if she died.

261

In May Manzoni wrote to Filippo. He had heard that Filippo intended to raise a loan by mortgaging the income from the shares assigned to him in the wills of his grandmother and his mother.

'Filippo! This is your father's voice calling to you; a voice which, whether gentle or severe, has only ever expressed concern for your well-being, as I call upon your conscience to testify. Filippo! turn back from a path which can only lead you to the precipice, and on which I am certain, thank God, that you are not proceeding with an easy heart. Think how you might feel one day when you remember turning a deaf ear to this plea.

'Must I speak of the many distresses you cause me, or rather of the state of distress I exist in on your account? I must, to make you reflect upon the grievous harm you are doing to yourself. Just think that an old man stricken by so many misfortunes and tormented by continual anxieties, cannot seek distraction without being plunged back into affliction by the recurring thought of a misfortune greater than all the rest; think that this old man is your father, and you are that thought.

'Remember how I have tried, as long as I could, to keep your first irregularities hidden, secretly making them good, and at the same time using all my authority over you, unfortunately in vain, to end them. And now what have you done, and what are you doing to your reputation? Are you not inflicting another severe punishment upon yourself by devouring your future means of existence? Disgrace and ruin! Pain for those who love you, encouragement for those who may be your enemies; oh, Filippo! is that your goal in life? . . .

'I have not spoken of God, but all the things I have mentioned are signs of His justice, as well as intimations of His mercy. I appeal to you in His name, with living faith in His grace which can give strength to the words that come from my heart. Your father's house and your father's arms are still open to you, if you return now to be henceforth what you should always have been. You can spend the few remaining months of my absence from Milan at Brusuglio with Pietro, with whom you have spent other months you must surely remember with pleasure. I am sure it will be a real pleasure to him to live with you again for a while as brothers. Consider that this return to your family

262

will in itself begin your rehabilitation, like the first step in a new life in which you will forget your transgressions. Ask yourself what your angelic mother would want you to do; can you hesitate to answer which would be more pleasing to that dear, saintly soul, who is surely praying for us all in heaven, which would do more honour to her blessed memory: to obey, or to harden your heart against this invitation. God forbid the latter! God grant that in the days He still wills me to remain here on earth I may call myself Your most affectionate father.'

Filippo did not go to Brusuglio. Where he was living, nobody knew. He turned up occasionally at via del Morone. His father wrote to him: 'I must remind you of the order I gave the steward some time ago that you should not come to my house with people I do not know.'

Grossi and Pietro had discussed together whether it was opportune to start proceedings for an interdiction.

Filippo wrote to Pietro in June:

'If you were not interfering in my affairs, why would you be plotting with the amiable Doctor Tommaso Grossi to dishonour me before society and the tribunals by seeking to impose an interdiction upon me? You cannot deny this, for word has come from the office of the same Doctor Tommaso Grossi, once so hated by you, but now, it seems, quite the reverse.'

In July, Filippo wrote to his father:

'I am obliged in conscience and in the certainty of happiness and tranquillity to take a step which, as the most important step in life, can never be sufficiently pondered, and which, for that very reason, after mature consideration and experience, I have decided I must undertake as the decisive factor in my happiness and my life and conduct. My dear father, I am married. I beg you to forgive me for proceeding to such a decision without your consent, but I swear it was for the best.'

His wife was called Erminia Catena. His father refused to meet her.

In September the father wrote a letter to Pietro of which only a fragment remains (again he had asked Pietro to try to get to Lesa):

'I pray the Lord to dispose me to receive all that may come to

263

me from that side or any other as His gift, that is, as a means of appearing before Him with some suffering well borne. Why must such cruel reasons be added to all the natural and dear reasons I have to desire your coming? Because it is God's will. This answer is more joyful and beautiful than any other, if only the heart can find such satisfaction in it as the reason is forced to find.'

The Arconatis had rented a villa at Pallanza. They invited Alessandro, and Teresa, to spend a few days with them. Teresa was not easily moved from home. Only occasionally had she gone, well wrapped up, for lunch with Abbé Rosmini, who had sent his carriage to fetch her. She was very frightened of the lake. But Stefano persuaded her to accept the Arconatis' invitation and to cross the lake to Pallanza. First he took her out in his boat on the lake a little way. He wrote to Rossari: 'The last few mornings, as Mama got up earlier than usual, I succeeded in taking her out in my schooner, and, wonderful to relate, in giving her breakfast on my schooner! And I breakfasted with her while they were raising anchor and setting the sails to receive the last breath of the dying north wind. Indeed, we were obliged to wait motionless for about half and hour for the first breath of the south west wind. . . the time passed and the wind came. The result of this trip was that Mama thought my craft comfortable and handsome, gained a little more confidence in my ability to sail it, and quite enjoyed herself. . .' So Teresa took heart, and the next day confronted the formidable lake again, and went to the Arconatis at Pallanza, not, however, on Stefano's boat but on the steamer. She stayed at Pallanza four days.

At that time the Arconatis' guests included Berchet, Ruggero Bonghi, a young Neapolitan friend of Rosmini, and Mary Clarke, who had come to Italy for a little while. Three years after the death of Fauriel, Mary Clarke had married Jules Mohl. She asked Manzoni to find her all the letters he had from Fauriel. She asked Teresa to help him look for them. Teresa promised to see to it immediately on their return to Milan, which would soon take place. Their exile in Lesa was over.

Manzoni had no desire to return to Milan, and would happily

have stayed at Lesa. From his meetings and discussions with Abbé Rosmini he had composed a dialogue, *Dell' invenzione*. He intended to write another: *Del piacere* [Of Pleasure]. What he wanted most at that stage in his life was to be with Rosmini.

Costanza Arconati to her brother:

'Don Alessandro is constrained by his wife and stepson to return to Milan when his passport expires, that is, half way through September, Donna Teresa to be near her doctors, and don Stefano to pursue his painting: but poor don Alessandro is dejected like a schoolboy being taken back to school.'

However, it is possible Manzoni thought it necessary to return. He had to discuss with Pietro many complicated and delicate family problems.

Manzoni to Vittoria and Matilde:

'Matilde mia, it is certainly a great joy to me that you are blooming, but the pleasure is spoilt a little by not seeing it with my own eyes.

'We have spent four days with the Arconatis, where Teresa dragged herself with difficulty, as she lacks strength and finds it difficult to stay up for a few hours each day; but she came home a different woman after being in company and having no time to listen to herself. My dear, dear, dear daughters, I must close, because tomorrow we leave at five, and there are so many things to do.'

They went back to Milan on 26 September.

At the beginning of October there was a tremendous cloudburst at Brusuglio with a hailstorm that devastated the countryside.

Teresa, from Milan, to Stefano who had remained at Lesa:

'The hailstones weren't stones, they were tiles, bricks, rocks, pebbles! It was dreadful! Don't tell your Francesco for the time being [Stefano's servant who came from one of the Brusuglio farm families] because the grain was already harvested and so far I've heard of no victims. . . Pietro got up at midnight, and they shut the children between doors for safety. The crockery in the cellar was swimming; water and hailstones were streaming from the damaged, almost collapsed roofs in the granary on to the grain etc. etc. There's not a leaf left in the garden, or a blade of grass in the meadows etc. It's the same at La Mojetta:

265

the poor Mojettas came early this morning to tell us of their distress [La Mojetta was a farmhouse and the Mojettas the peasants who lived there]. Pietro has just gone to bed to make up for his sleepless night. In short, wherever poor Alessandro looks, he sees damage.' '. . . plants, roofs, everything smashed, broken, torn, ruined. . .'

Stefano wrote to tell her Rosmini felt *lost* without Manzoni at Lesa. Teresa to Stefano: 'I read your letter out to Alessandro. . . Alessandro bowed his head on his clasped hands, and said *poor, dear Rosmini!* Pietro comes to Milan for a few hours every day, and Enrico's here today too. Nanny's been going to and fro between Alessandro and Filippo on money matters. . .'

Stefano had stayed at Lesa. In fact, contrary to Costanza Arconati's statement, he had not the slightest desire to be in Milan. He liked to feel as free and independent as possible, and when his mother and stepfather were in Lesa, he found excuses to escape to Milan, and vice versa. There was a very strong bond between him and his mother, and he was fond of his step-father; but he enjoyed those little trips from Milan to Lesa and Lesa to Milan, and he was always finding some excuse to go to and fro.

Teresa remembered she had promised to look for Fauriel's letters, but the commission irritated her and she kept putting it off. To Stefano: 'Today I hope to be able to get down to the search for things Mlle Clarke was asking for, and if not today, tomorrow, for I'll have to search in Alessandro's table when there are no visitors. . .' Then a few days later: 'I'm just going in search of the things Mlle C., now Mme Mauhl I think, is (rightly) longing to have; but I don't know how I'll get on, that's as maybe!' She misspelt the surname as if it were French, whereas it was a German name. Luisa d'Azeglio came to Milan from the Arconatis at Pallanza, and she too urged this search; Teresa did not see her, but Nanny passed on a letter she had had from Mary Clarke. Teresa to Stefano: 'She hopes I'll give her the letters of her dead friend. Till now I haven't been able to find time to go downstairs and spend a little while in Alessandro's study – either it was raining – or he had people – or he was writing – or I was writing – etc. etc.: today I'll see whether I'll have time, after seeing and talking to Patrizio about my business, to search in that table – I shall have to make up my mind

266

to it, and as soon as possible if she's leaving in 5 days.' And again, days later, to Stefano: 'See if you can find some way of letting Mme Mohl know that we're getting covered with dust, and looking through old stuff to find those old letters, unfortunately, between you and me, causing Alessandro a great waste of time and the greatest tedium and inconvenience.' And at last: 'Yesterday poor Alessandro did a great sorting out of letters with me, and has found only two to give to Mme Mohl. She'll be very pleased with them, because they are very literary, and one of them mentions Mlle Clark, who you know is the same person. Today or tomorrow I'll look in a little bundle, and in three or four satchels, now I know the handwriting; you'll understand that Alessandro is losing patience with such a tedious task.' In all, six letters from Fauriel were found.

On their return to Milan, Teresa and Alessandro had taken back all the servants dismissed when they left, together with one new manservant, and a cook; and Nanny was still with them as well. The cook was called Jegher. Teresa praised his cooking: 'He does his job well,' she wrote to Stefano, 'the soups he makes for me are always so good that I always eat them all up, and there's always a lot. But as for his own person, *l'è on strafojon, che no se capiss coss'el se sia* [he's an untidy fellow and one doesn't know what to make of him].' It was not very clear to either of them why they kept so many servants when they were both convinced at the time that they were very poor; probably each was persuaded it was the other's wish.

In February 1851 *tante* Louise had a miniature of Luisina painted by a Spanish painter, one Signora Leona Darro. *Tante* Louise wanted the little girl to pose dressed as a nun. She thought the habit suited the celestial sweetness of her face. But Matilde and Vittoria, when they saw the finished painting, were both seized with a sense of melancholy. 'The artist,' Vittoria recorded in her memoirs, 'had made a saint's halo around the head of the little nun. . .'

Cristina's husband, Cristoforo Baroggi, a banker, had gone bankrupt in January 1851, and shortly after was sent to prison. He had a passion for gambling and had run up enormous debts. His little girl, Enrichetta, was then eleven. She had grown up in

267

the house of some relatives of her father, called Garavaglia, who had taken her in when her mother died. Matilde wrote to ask Massimo d'Azeglio if he could come to the help of Baroggi, who intended to go to Belgium and make a fresh start. He needed some letters of recommendation. D'Azeglio refused. He was then President of the Council in Piedmont. He wrote to Bista that he had no intention of using his name 'for that wretched creature. . . Women's hearts often screen the light from their brains.'

Manzoni to d'Azeglio:

'State affairs may be scabrous and painful, but I don't think they have fundamentally the bitterness of private affairs, when, like this one, they are sad from every angle.'

He must have been thinking of the anguish Filippo was causing him.

In 1850 a son, Giulio, was born to Filippo. The next year, at Easter, Filippo had written asking to be reconciled to his father, imploring his pardon, and expressing his wish to send the 'poor babe' to receive his blessing. Manzoni replied:

'That you should remind me that, as Easter draws near, *men should be reconciled amongst themselves*, suggests you suppose me to be your enemy, since only among enemies can there be reconciliation. But for a father to be regarded in this way, and to need to be reconciled with his son, he must have done him some quite extraordinary wrong. Let your conscience tell you if I need to be reconciled with you.

'As for the pardon you ask of me, I have already assured you I felt no rancour towards you, and wished and prayed for everything good for you. . . But your telling me that, *if your courage had not failed you*, you would have tried to impose on me by surprise something I have never given you the remotest right to do [send the baby to him], forces me to declare that any such attempt would be an act, not of courage, but of violence. To forgive does not mean becoming a slave to the wishes of the person you have forgiven. . .'

And a few days later, sending Nanny with some money for him (this time Filippo had proposed bringing his wife to see him):

'The last words in your letter oblige me, against all my expectations and to my extreme repugnance, to declare again that I am, I wish to be and must be a total stranger to relationships you may have taken upon yourself but cannot impose upon me, and which I cannot allow you to impose on me. . . If, after attempting in vain to win your obedience, I am reduced to defending myself against you, I must make clear that, since, thank Heaven, I am moved to this by no passion, I shall and must be intransigent, conscious that I am doing nothing that does not conform to the duties of a Christian and a father.'

In the summer of 1851 Teresa and Alessandro stayed in Milan until half-way through August. Stefano was at Acqui for the mud-baths, and was waiting for them to go to Lesa with him. Manzoni was writing an appendix to a chapter of *La morale cattolica*. Teresa was making a list of all the furniture and objects that were her absolute and exclusive property. She wrote letters to Stefano with the usual lessons on the Italian language. 'Please note, my son, that *piano terreno* is not said, but *a terreno*, and not *coltre* but *coperta*. You don't say *coperta greve*, or *calzoni grevi*, but *coperta grave, calzoni gravi*.' The summer was sultry and they were plagued by mosquitoes. A doctor Vandoni had been murdered as a spy for the Austrians, and for a few days there was a state of siege in Milan, and cannon on the Dazi: Teresa wrote to tell Stefano not to be afraid on his arrival. 'Milan is peaceful and quiet, perfectly quiet, and as far as I know there's no shadow of trouble. . .' Rossari was suffering from the heat and could not accompany Alessandro on his walks. Teresa had news of Torti, whom they had not seen for some time. 'I've had news of the good Torti, but news that is "torete ritorte" [twisted and turned], as it came not from him but from someone who spoke with someone else who sees to his poor dear affairs in that tiny house of his. Poor, dear old man! and he is writing! and printing verses now, they say: I say *they say* because I haven't seen them. I imagine they will be *few and of worth like the verses of G. Torti*, as a certain poet said in *I promessi sposi*. Then the certain poet was Manzoni: now he is my Alessandro, and he's well, quite cheerful, looking rather better, and sends you his warmest greetings. As for his other old companions, poets, and half poets [Grossi and Rossari], I never ever so much as catch a glimpse of them, because I never go down to the ground floor: they never

269

come up where I am. . .'

They set off for Lesa half way through August, and stayed there till November. Alessandro saw Rosmini, but not as often as before, because Rosmini had got rid of his horses.

In September a letter came from Vittoria from Montignoso, another country property where the Giorginis had a house, with bad news: Matilde had been coughing blood. She had been bled.

Luisina had been alone in the room with Matilde when she had been taken ill, and running to fetch hot water for her, had scalded her arm.

Manzoni to Vittoria:

'You can imagine how upset, and I should add frightened, I was to hear of my Matilde's health problems. But the sequel comforted me, more perhaps than you might think, since the weakness that ensued, and that still prevailed when you were writing to me, is for me the most comforting of symptoms. Thank Heaven the bleeding was done at once, perhaps as quickly as it would have been done in Milan! Delaying this unique remedy is the only danger. . . I expect a letter from you announcing a complete recovery, or rather a continuation of good health.

'Oh poor Luigina! poor Vittoria! poor everybody! What a trial was set you! But what compensation in the affection, courage and patience displayed by your extraordinary little girl! . . . Thank God for it as for a most rare gift, love her still more if possible, and try not to tell her all that we feel about her merit.

'But the postman is approaching, and this letter must go. Poor Vittoria, how could I delay so long in writing to you? If your letter had been cold (an impious supposition!) I would have replied by return.

'I hug you all, and especially implore from the bottom of my heart the blessing of the great Father of all upon you.'

That autumn, while they were at Montignoso, Bista heard that he must leave Pisa and move to Siena, because a decree from the Grand Duke ruled that some faculties, including law, should be transferred from Pisa to Siena. Bista was enraged; it seemed that the Grand Duke was hostile to the university of Pisa, which in 1848 had been a nucleus for Liberals. Bista had to leave at once for Siena; Vittoria began sadly to arrange for the removal; they had so many friends at Pisa, and she was distressed to leave; she also feared the climate of Siena would not suit Matilde. They all left in January 1852; Bista had taken a small villa at Siena, and they moved in; they liked it there; the villa was outside the town, and they went for long walks in the surrounding countryside; Matilde seemed to blossom again. Their father wrote to say he would come to see them soon: 'I am determined to come, either with Teresa or with Pietro, to rejoice with all you dearest people in the little Sienese villa.'

Matilde to her father:

'I can't tell you what I feel when I think of your coming, and of the first moment I see you again! how could I explain such a feeling? . . . I have not seen you for five years; who would have thought it when I left Milan! Nothing could have been further from my thoughts! . . . How I long for you to meet all the members of this dear Giorgini family! – I can't tell you what they mean to me. The Grandfather is at Massarosa now, he very often writes me such affectionate letters, and says he loves me like his own grandchildren. I assure you there could not be a more loving Grandfather. I always call him Nonno, and call Bista's father Babbo [Daddy]: how could I do otherwise? they treat me just like their child. If you saw the love and concern they show for me when I am ill. . . I think it would be very difficult for me to find another Giorgini family – no one could be more affectionate, warm-hearted, affable, straightforward and delicate than they. I don't mention Bista because really *I can't find words to tell you what he has always been to me* – He has never faltered for a moment, and has always shown me the affection of a brother and care of a Father. . .'

Manzoni to Vittoria, in January 1852:

'I am writing in haste not to delay for one day sending the promissory note for Matilde of 353 Austrian lire 9 centimes for the half-year, and 68 lire for the interest on her holdings. And I fly from this topic of money which I so dislike, since I am so far from having available as much as I'd like: and not for myself, I assure you.

'Your dear letter would increase, if that were possible, my hope that I shall be able to carry out the precious plan of coming to see you next spring. The wish cannot fail, and I keep hoping.'

271

The planned trip, which seemed imminent, was postponed. Manzoni was relying on Pietro to accompany him, and in the spring Pietro had to stay at Brusuglio to look after the silkworms. Manzoni did not write to Vittoria or Matilde for some time; meanwhile, in February, Filippo was arrested for debt. At first nothing was said to Manzoni; he heard it from the Nanny. Vittoria, having no news from home, wrote to don Ghianda. Filippo had been arrested for a debt of four hundred lire.

Manzoni to Vittoria in April:

'Questioning Nanny in a general way, and receiving hesitant replies, I insisted, and discovered the disaster and shame they were trying to conceal from me, as they were sadly convinced that I hadn't the means to remedy the situation at once. . .'

There was only one way of remedying the harm already done, and preventing further occurrences, her father explained to Vittoria; this was by means of the interdiction. Grossi had already thought of it two years before, and had spoken about it to Pietro; but it was necessary to get Filippo's consent, and at that time Filippo had no intention of consenting. Now he promised to consent, if they helped him to get out of prison.

Acquaintances of don Ghianda arranged Filippo's release, which occurred on 15 April.

Filippo went to Enrico at Renate, with his wife and baby boy; they stayed in Enrico's villa for a few months; then he and Enrico quarrelled, Enrico sent him away, and he took rooms with his family, still in Renate, with an innkeeper called Radaelli. His wife was pregnant.

Enrico was now included, with Grossi and Pietro, among the people he hated most on earth. He considered him his persecutor and an impostor; the same went for don Ghianda. He saw Enrico and his wife going about the streets of Renate; he saw, or thought he saw, on their faces profound scorn for him and freezing pride. He decided to write to Teresa. He had insulted her years ago in a letter to Pietro, but now saw no possibility of help from any other direction.

'Renate, 14th December 1852. Dearest Mama,

'You will surely be very surprised to receive this letter, and at first sight may accuse me of impudence or even temerity; but as your first reaction will be succeeded by the thought that the person I am turning to in these extremities is the person I have the dear obligation, and holy, precious right to call my Mother, you will, I hope, feel moved to peruse it to the end and find in it motives for indulgence and charity. My present position robs me, in every way, of the courage to turn directly to my excellent Father, yet it is absolutely essential for me to summon him to my aid both morally and materially; to whom then should I turn but you?

'My turning to you will arouse in you a sense of disdain, perhaps almost of repugnance after a certain expression concerning you in a letter I sent to Pietro on 25 June 1850, an expression I know, unfortunately, rang painfully in my Father's ears. But for now I hope you will be satisfied with my word of honour that the expression was interpreted in a quite opposite sense to the one intended. Neither you nor Father can, I am sure, know its meaning, and to explain it I should have to unmask the cruel, slanderous utterances of a certain person, which are the real and the only foundation of that expression, and, unless I were driven to extremes, I should be ashamed to do this. . .

'Without bringing up the infamous and distressing vicissitudes I have lately suffered, without reminding you how I have been pitilessly deprived of everything, even the belongings of my innocent child; without dwelling on the seventy days imprisonment I suffered for a debt of 400 lire (which I committed to a rogue whom I trusted to give them to the proper person, and who instead ran off with my money, a notorious fact which should be remembered); imprisonment which apart from the shame, the grief, the abomination it brought upon me, was and always will be very damaging to my health, since my already poor eyesight suffered from it, and moreover, from the lowly tasks I was forced to perform like brushing and sweeping, making the wretched beds, etc. etc., and from having to sleep almost on the bare, damp ground, I contracted a serious ulcer which I feel acutely and will feel all my life; without, I say, going over such shameful, painful, but well deserved punishments, I must tell you what state I have been in from the 15th April, the day of my release, until now. Enticed both verbally and in writing by people who were surely abusing the name of my Father; ready, as I have shown in my letters, to do anything they told me was my Father's will, since apart from feeling obliged by nature and duty to do so, I will frankly admit I was also moved by the hope they gave me of his effective pardon; at the moment I thought was to fulfil all the aforesaid promises, I find myself – and why? – plunged into a worse abyss than before, abandoned and driven out by one who had received me and my poor little family with the most expansive demonstrations of affection, thrown out, I say, into the street, forced to live on the charity of an innkeeper who, trusting my word, and moved to compassion by the horrendous state I was reduced to, received me into his house, and is advancing food and lodgings on my current December allowance. Whether it is true that I did not in any way deserve that those people should fail in so many sacred promises, you might ask Radaelli [the innkeeper], to whom I owe a second life, and who also deserved the gratitude of my Father for the spontaneous solicitude with which he took to his heart my well-being and honour and that of my wife, who was tortured unimaginably by the person who had stretched out to me a hand I thought to be sincerely affectionate. He can give you the most exact information especially about my wife; he has no part in the matter, so he at least can, I hope, be believed. . . if for once in the world truth and charity are to triumph over imposture and malice. So I find myself at an inn, living on the charity of the proprietor, with my wife almost in the ninth month of her pregnancy, inevitably unwell since, apart from the usual problems of her condition, the fact that she has to iron, clean the room, make the beds, in fact do everything herself, undoubtedly damages her health considerably, with my poor baby boy who, thank Heaven, is wonderfully healthy and alert, but who shivers with the cold, and I have not twenty pence to buy something to cover him; and I too, lacking even shirts, oppressed by grief and humiliation, living on the charity of an innkeeper who is relying on my good faith, and continually seeing paraded before my very eyes the disdainful splendour and wounding sneers of other people, who had contracted the holy obligation to treat me with more Christian charity and good faith! . . . Now it is, indeed, charity I am constrained to implore from my Father! I recognize that my faults deserve severe punishment; but will your kind heart and my Father's generosity allow innocent creatures to suffer any longer, and for my fault? My good wife, in her present state of health, my poor two-year-old child? If, until I have obtained my Father's blessing upon the head of my good Erminia, it is decreed in Heaven that she must remain absolutely dead and despicable in the eyes of my family, I commend her to your charity as a pregnant woman. . .

I am twenty-seven; I am about to become a father for the second time; I have already savoured to the full the bitter fruits of heedlessness and obstinacy, so you can easily believe my words and my promises. My liabilities, thanks to the endeavours of Radaelli, are reduced to three thousand lire; and for this sum I am obliged to live outside the town. . . without occupation, useless to myself and my family, subjected to cruel gossip and mortifying observations. If I could once (as was so patently promised me in word and in writing) settle these last outstanding affairs of mine I would return to Milan; I already have an occupation waiting me, since more than one lawyer would willingly receive me in his office, and since, despite what certain people say who are no lovers of truth and justice, at least as far as honour is concerned, I still enjoy an unsullied reputation; I know I could earn a moderate amount there, apart from being occupied and making progress in my career and giving a good account of my time and conduct. If therefore my Father, as, no doubt abusing his name, was promised to me verbally and in writing, would turn a charitable gaze of pardon upon my sincere repentance and take pity on my situation, I should return from death to life, and would be enabled to demonstrate my repentance and redemption in deeds, and become a son worthy of the love of his Father, and a father worthy of the esteem and affection of his own children. For my children to grow up seeing me thus rejected and despised by my family. . . But oh God! God! take far from me this terrible thought! I have erred greatly, but you in your mercy cannot wish for the irreparable ruin and desperation of a repentant son.

'My good Mama, I commend to your charity, so manifest especially towards pregnant women, my poor wife and my innocent offspring. May her condition move you to compassion! . . . If your benevolent hand and my Father's heart are not moved to succour me, I shall be obliged, it breaks my heart to say so, I shall be obliged to take my wife to give birth in a public hospice in Milan. . .

275

'I have unfortunately always disregarded all the salutary advice I have received from you since my earliest childhood; unfortunately I have a thousand times responded to your affectionate gestures with irreverent actions; unfortunately I answered your cordiality with coldness and unconcern; but believe me, Mama, I give you my sacred word of honour, *all this did not come from my heart*. May this word be sufficient for you, at least until such time as I am constrained, as I said above, to tear a veil which I pray God may remain always impenetrable; . . . May God bear witness to the truth of my words.

'I dare not ask you to embrace my Father for me; I fall at his feet. . .'

To Stefano, the same day;

'I have always recognized in you the sincere affection of a brother who, though not belonging to me by blood, still loved me and always treated me with the attachment that should rather be the holy duty of brothers by blood! If you found me more than once remiss towards you, attribute it partly to my playing the *rascal* and believe that my heart, and indeed my entire will, were strangers to it. This is the moment to exercise to the full the fraternal sympathy you have always had for me; help me to obtain the charity of our mother, and then you can both unite to plead with my Father for me. If I could at least have the consolation of speech with you, you could be judge of my words. With what sincerity I would throw myself into your arms, with what trust I would move your excellent young heart. . .'

Teresa replied:

'The only thing Stefano and I were able to do on your behalf was to hand your two letters addressed to us to Alessandro so that he could read them; this we did and he agreed to do so. As far as we are concerned, no more can be done, since we have absolutely no wish to enter into family matters and intimate relationships. Do not imagine that any personal rancour could be the cause of this abstention, for it would already have been forgotten, *if there were any motive*, (even without need of Christian sentiments), towards one who has involved himself in such an unhappy situation. I pray God to spare you and your poor father any further troubles, and commend you to Him.'

It does not seem that Filippo had 'speech' with Stefano, or his

276

stepmother, or his father. His wife gave birth to another boy, who was called Massimiliano. Apparently the debt was paid, because he left Renate and settled in the town, with his wife and children. He lived and maintained his family by small expedients, debts, and with the money he received from his father each month, which came from the interest on the legacy from his mother and grandmother. Proceedings for the interdiction were abandoned. The thing he so much desired, to present his wife and children to his father, did not occur.

Manzoni decided to make the journey to Tuscany, with Pietro, in the autumn. He spent the summer at Lesa. He wrote to Vittoria at the beginning of August:

'However dear all your letters are to me, you will not be surprised to hear that the last was extraordinarily precious for the good news it gave of Matilde. O my dear Matilde who, by no fault of your own, caused me such grief as a baby, the time I feared to lose you, so I can hope to embrace you soon, and see you fit and well! As for Luisina, her Mama has no need to write, for I have heard wonders of her from so many others, and have come to expect them, whether you will or no.

'I need hardly say how much Teresa would like to see you all again, especially her Vittoria; but, in her valetudinarian condition, she could not set out on a journey without being afraid of falling ill, either on the way, or when she got there; and the thought of being ill away from Milan is an insurmountable terror to her. . .'

As Giovannina, Pietro's wife, was about to give birth and it might be difficult for Pietro to leave her, Vittoria wrote to ask her father if he would not like as a travelling companion not Pietro but Bista, who was prepared to come and fetch him and accompany him. But Giovannina had her baby in mid-August, a boy who was called Lorenzo. A nurse was found; 'a good nurse', Manzoni wrote to Pietro, rejoicing in the birth, 'is so important for the prompt and tranquil recovery of the mother, the father's peace of mind, and especially for the poor little creature. To wish for sons is normal at any time for those who have none; they come to fulfil the wishes of a good father. . . then when you hear them whimper and take them in your arms,

277

it seems unjust and cruel not to have wanted them always.' So all was well at Brusuglio, and Pietro could leave in all-confidence.

Then a letter came from Massimo d'Azeglio: his daughter Alessandrina, little Rina, was getting married at the beginning of September, and he asked Manzoni to act as witness. Manzoni accepted.

Rina was eighteen. She was marrying the Marchese Matteo Ricci, son of an old friend of Massimo's. The marriage was to take place at Cornegliano, near Genoa.

From Cornegliano, Manzoni and Pietro would proceed to Massarosa, where Vittoria and Matilde would be waiting for them; then they would all go to Siena together.

Manzoni sent Pietro a lot of instructions for the journey. Order a dress-coat. See to the passports. Prepare a sum of money – one thousand five hundred Tuscan lire – which he intended to give to Bista, to reimburse him at least in part for the expenses of Matilde's keep, which Bista had been providing now for many years. Prepare more money for the journey and their stay. 'An old, shabby, heavy surtout, in case it should be cold at Genoa.' 'I will buy a white tie at Genoa, or you can lend me one of yours: you know I want to observe the strictest economy.' Pietro was to come to Lesa, and they would set out from there. 'For the journey from here to Genoa, we must think whether, which is fairly certain, it is best to take the most economical means, that is, the mail. There will be no difficulty about you putting up here in Lesa, that is, in the house, as it can be done without inconvenience.' They left on 12 September.

From Cornegliano Manzoni wrote to tell Teresa they had arrived safely, and had been able to admire the work on a branch-line of the railroad from Arquata to Genoa. 'Gigantic bridges, very long, high viaducts with a series of great arcades, and pilasters that look like mountain masses and precipices. . . In short, I am astounded not to have heard of work of such magnitude, for, although we lead a remote life, their fame should have reached us. . . . I was delighted to hear what I imagined. . . that is, that there is no stretch of railroad in Europe till now that, for the qualities I have mentioned and the difficulties successfully overcome, can surpass this one.

'You can imagine how pleased I was to see Rina, grown and

blooming, and obviously as happy as could be. Her husband and father-in-law are as they were described to me, that is, amiable in a natural, spontaneous way that indicates other, more essential qualities. Massimo is his usual dear self.

'I think of you as you go about your daily activities, or rather inactivities: but as soon as you can, prove me wrong, and while I am imagining you sitting on the divan, get about in the carriage. Give my love to Stefano, and my regards to all. Goodbye, my dear Teresa, I shall be happier to tell you by word of mouth how much I love you and long to see you.'

On 17 September they were at Massarosa.

Vittoria wrote in her memoirs:

'Matilde and I, with Luisina who was five years old that month, were sitting on the flight of steps overlooking the meadow, trembling with impatience and joy, when the travelling berlin came through the gate. We flung ourselves into the arms of Papa and Pietro. . .'

Manzoni to Teresa:

'I found Vittoria and Matilde in excellent health; they immediately asked after you, as did Bista; I wish I could have said the same of you. I felt as if I had seen Luisina before, she was so exactly as they had described her. . . She has that quickness and grace that everyone spoke of. I will tell you a little reply she gave me yesterday. She came into my room while I was washing my face and preparing to dress again for lunch. I said: "Luisina, you will find I'm not a pretty object." "I didn't come for something pretty." "Why do you come, then?" "Because I love you."'

At Massarosa Manzoni met Grandfather Niccolao, who was fit and strong although he was eighty; he met Bista's father, Gaetano, and tried to tell them both how grateful he was for all their kindness to Vittoria, and especially to Matilde: 'But they show their kindness in a spontaneous, natural way that seems to rule out thanks.'

Everyone at Massarosa still remembered the day Rosmini had called on them. The strange thing was that Luisina seemed to remember it too, although it was three years ago. Manzoni asked her what Rosmini was like. She answered: 'He was of the right philosophy.' She had probably heard talk of philosophy of the right. One day when her mother had punished her, she said:

279

'Ever since I was *in mente dei*, you knew you wouldn't love the baby you were going to have.' And to her mother who would not let her go out because it was raining, she said as soon as the rain stopped: 'Mama, now will you take me to enjoy a bit of the air of God's creation?'

Walking in the countryside, Manzoni saw in a clump of pomegranates 'a *nestful* of cyclamen', a flower not usually found in those parts; he picked one and sent it to Teresa, who used to press flowers in the pages of books; he hoped to find it between the pages of a book, to remind him of those days in Massarosa: 'It will be a happy moment for me.'

From Massarosa they all went to Siena, which Manzoni had never seen; they stayed there ten days; they were all supposed to go to Varramista to see Gino Capponi, then return to Massarosa; but only Manzoni and Bista went to Varramista, because Matilde was not well; Vittoria mentions this indisposition in her memoirs; Manzoni said nothing about it to Teresa. He told her instead that Pietro, Vittoria, Matilde and the little girl were to take 'the railroad', and meet them at a station; but they did not meet; by some whim of the director of the 'railroad', only two wagons were sent off, and many passengers were left behind; so the four of them had to find some other means of transport, and arrived at Massarosa the next day. Then he wrote that he had not been well, and had had to take magnesia; so she wrote to Vittoria, full of anxiety. He wrote to her: 'I am writing, in Vittoria's name, in answer to your letter of the 25th, which I read with enraged affection, and vexed gratitude. Your anxiety would be very pleasing as far as I'm concerned, if it were not very displeasing as far as you're concerned; because I know perfectly well, unfortunately, that you make yourself really ill about it, as if there were any good reason; and perhaps you imagined me fettered to my bed, with the Lord knows what doctor beside me, while I was, and am, very well indeed.'

Teresa had had the cyclamen. She wrote to him:

'I received the longed-for letter. . . in which I found so many dear things; and I bless the poor cyclamen which made you say them. . . among so many dear words in your letter, I choose the dearest, as you would choose one cyclamen among so many flowers: the sweet and blessed word *always*, a word of fond memory and fond promise. I grasp it and hold it tight, and send it back to you.'

He preserved a precious, yet painful memory of their brief stay in Varramista: Gino Capponi was ill and had gone blind. They had walked in the park, a superb park: 'little hills with pines, holm-oaks, oaks, chestnuts, meadows and cultivated fields. . . and I can't tell you how oppressed I felt', he wrote to Teresa, 'to walk around it arm-in-arm with him and not to be able to talk to him about the things I saw, because it would only remind him that he could not see them.

'You know from experience, my dear Teresa, what a comfort it is to me to express and share my feelings with you; and I see that this possibility, even by the poor means of the pen, has brought from me more words than I would have thought.'

He was eager to get home, but he did not want to go to Milan immediately; he would have liked to stay on at Lesa a while and feared Teresa would have decided otherwise. 'I think it worked perfectly well last year when we left half way through November, and the weather must have been very reasonable. You know better than I how much better good weather is at Lesa than in Milan. Indeed, I should be very sorry to have to renounce this little treat of a holiday I was promising myself at Lesa, and some days with Rosmini. . .' 'I am still hoping to hug you *(until it hurts)* next week; and I hope hope hope that your letter will pronounce Lesa to be our destination. Till then goodbye, my Teresa; if I can't hurt you by hugging you from here, then I should like to do you some good.' 'I will bring you a letter from dear, good Vittoria, whose feelings about our departure you can well imagine, knowing her heart. Oh, why can we not have all our dear ones together! But I hope Bista will bring her to us next year, with Matilde and Luisina.' They left Massarosa on 12 October.

Manzoni talked to Tommaseo about Luisina. Tommaseo wrote: 'He often spoke to me about a little granddaughter of less than five, Giorgini's daughter, who is a *little miracle*; and who, when asked who the Pope was, replied: "He's the man who tells everyone to do good" – but she added (and certainly nobody had taught her to say it) – "he's a dirty man because he makes people kiss his feet." And because her grandfather used a word she didn't understand when speaking to her, she asked him to explain it, then said: "You're right, Grandpa, I'm very small." This same little child who gave such a good explanation of the ministry of the Pope, defined (if the word is applicable) the eternal God: after one of those series of childish questions and answers: who made the carpet? – the carpet-weaver. Who made the chairs? – the joiner. – Who made God? – nobody: He made himself.'

Manzoni's hopes were fulfilled: he and Teresa stayed at Lesa until the end of November.

Manzoni to Vittoria, from Lesa:

'How can the pen provide a substitute for the conversations we had at Massarosa and Siena? But what do I mean, the conversations, seeing each other, meeting up again after walks, coming face to face in the rooms, sitting quietly together? . . . I have to console myself with the thought of having you here with me next year. . .'

Matilde wrote back:

'Dear Papa, how sad we felt as we turned back into these rooms, everything we see and touch reminds us of days that were too beautiful, too happy to last! we were so touched by your letter, it made me cry, you have a way of saying things so that they go right to the heart. How I wish I could say what I feel as well as you do, how I wish I could speak of the gratitude, the love, the veneration I feel for you. Dear, dear Papa, you must read for yourself in the heart of your Matilde!'

They had recently returned from Massarosa to Siena, and Vittoria had had a threatened abortion from the fatigues of the journey. She had to stay in bed for some time.

In February 1853 Matilde was coughing blood again.

Matilde to her father, in April:

'I've been wanting and meaning to write to you for several days, but I put it off until now because Vittoria kept getting strong pains and I hoped she would soon present us with a little Giorgini, and I would have liked to tell you all the good news in one letter, but as I see things are taking their time I won't delay any longer, and that good news must wait till next time. I am keeping really quite well. . . After three weeks in bed on a diet, after the bleedings and all the medicines, I got up without feeling faint. . . If I can, I'll go out for a little drive today or tomorrow, I've already been down the stairs twice. . . I will never never be able to express what Bista and Vittoria have been to me, they have kept me company all the time, never leaving me in the day and staying with me at night till one or half past one, always waiting until the crises which occurred every night about midnight had completely passed. . . Dear Papa, now I must speak of something else, which demands all the trust a daughter can have in her Father for me to speak openly to you. I'm afraid my illness must be quite a shock to my sister's purse, because, according to my reckoning, it must have cost 20 or 22 "Francesconi" for the doctor here who has been to see me 50 times by now and will come a few more times, because he always had to come late in the evening when the gates are closed, and you have to pay to have them opened for the carriage to pass through. Then there's the doctor from Pisa they sent for when the illness seemed to be getting more serious, I don't know what they'll give him so I can't say anything about that; and then I went on taking a lot of medicines for a month so I'm afraid there'll be a sizeable bill from the apothecary. Dear Papa, I can't tell you how I feel when I think I cost you so much, without being able to be the slightest use in the world to you! Have patience, dear Papa, insofar as it depends on me, I promise never in all my life to displease you! If it is more than usually difficult for you to pay out money at this moment, allow me to say that I still have something left from my last half-year, and for now it would be enough to send me a quarter only. Please forgive me if I have annoyed you with all this talk. . . I must finish now and close my letter before Bista and Vittoria come, if they even imagined I was talking to you about these things, goodness knows what they would do! . . . I beg you to write me a line, it can't cost you so very much, and if you knew what it means to me to receive a little letter from you! Indulge me in this caprice this time, I pray, and brighten my convalescence. . .'

That same April Vittoria had a boy, who was called Giorgio Niccolao. Matilde wrote to tell her father the news.

Towards the end of May, one day when Manzoni had gone to Brusuglio and was talking to Pietro, 'and, of course, immediately talking about you all,' he wrote the next day to Vittoria, 'there emerged from the fond conversation the sad discovery that we had not answered Matilde's precious letter telling me of the safe arrival of Lao (or Giorgio?). . .' There had been a misunderstanding beween him and Pietro, and each of them thought the other was writing. 'I can't tell you how mortified I felt. . . I wish this letter could take wings. Poor Vittoria! so much suffering and such a reward, and then to be left to guess how we shared in both. . . . Tell Matilde that the coming month will not pass without her receiving a letter from me, assure her of this.'

In July Manzoni arranged for an order for one thousand Tuscan lire to be sent to Vittoria, 'partly for our Matilde's half-year allowance, and partly as a reimbursement, perhaps inadequate, of the exceptional expenses you incurred during her illness. . . . I have touched upon my mortification for the delay, but I must state it plainly, together with the mortification I feel in giving so little. May God improve my circumstances and send more prosperous years. . .'

Manzoni was about to leave for Lesa. The plan of sending for Matilde and Vittoria to come to Brusuglio was not mentioned again; in any case, perhaps Matilde's health would not allow it.

Manzoni and Teresa stayed at Lesa until December.

In December, on the day they returned to Milan, Tommaso Grossi died. He had been ill for some time. He was sixty-three. He left a wife and two children. Manzoni to Matilde:

'O my dear daughters, what a grievous and unexpected loss! Unexpected by me particularly, who am so much more advanced in years than he that I had never considered the possibility of having to weep for him. Rossari who was also completely at one with him, spoke at his funeral in words worthy of Grossi, and of such a friendship. . . . You continue to send good news of yourself, which is a great comfort to me in the midst of such distress.'

In February 1854 Grandfather Niccolao died at Massarosa.

In the summer the Giorginis went with Matilde to Viareggio; the doctor had ordered sea-bathing for Matilde; they took her to the beach in a sedan-chair; but there was cholera at Viareggio and they all left. They went to Montignoso. Matilde had been advised to drink a lot of milk; they sent for a she-ass – 'Pussy' Matilde called her in a letter to her father – which she also used for little rides. The summer passed peacefully apart from the cholera scare; there had also been a few cases in the surrounding countryside, so the 'Puss' and her 'baby-Pussy' had been brought from the Pisa district. *Tante* Louise who used to travel a lot between Lombardy and Tuscany, had quite a few problems with the various *'cordons sanitaires'*.

Tante Louise proposed to take Matilde with her to Pisa, where the winter was much milder than in Siena; the idea appalled Matilde, but the doctor said it was a good thing, essential even, and she had to resign herself.

Matilde to her father, from Pisa in November:

'Dearest Papa; here I am settled on the Arno with my kind aunt who overwhelms me with attentions. Dear Papa, I can't tell you how it hurt me to leave Vittoria, Bista, and the dear little ones, and how I feel their absence every moment of the day! The Lord requires this great sacrifice of me, let us hope at least it will not be in vain, and that I may really get my health back! Dear Papa, if you could have come to Pisa with us! . . . We had little hope of it for we realized Mama's health would be an invincible obstacle, and yet we flattered ourselves until the last moment! We will hope that Mama will pick up nicely in the winter, and that her health will allow you to leave her with an easy mind and come here in the spring; who knows? . . . but one must not cling to such dreams! . . . This morning I had a lovely letter from Vittoria, one from Bista, and one from 'Babbo': what an interest they all take in my health and how kind they all are to me! Vittoria tells me that when my name is mentioned, Giorgino starts to cry and calls for me, poor little pet, what it costs me to be far away from them, he was such company for me, and really entertaining, too. Here we just don't know what winter is, we never light a fire. . . Aunt has given me the finest room, it's beautiful, with the best aspect. For a few days I've really been feeling a *tiny bit* better. . . As it was fine this morning, I was able to go to Mass in a nearby church, which pleased me very much, because it was three weeks since they had let me go. Dear Papa, I have to come to something very tedious for you, please believe that I do it because I feel constrained to, but so reluctantly. I should like to be only a comfort to you and instead I am always a worry and a burden! – Since I've been ill like this, Bista has been put to a lot of expense. The doctor alone who looked after me all winter in Siena charged 38 francesconi. . . then there was another 12

285

for Prof. Fedeli for coming to Siena and for the consultation, I don't know exactly how much for the apothecary. . . Puccinotti would not accept payment for his consultation, and Prof. Almansi who saw me three times at Viareggio wouldn't hear of it, because they are both friends of Bista's and also because *I am Manzoni's daughter*. . . . then there are always a thousand other things when you have to move and we've had to move several times this year because of the Cholera, they have to find the most comfortable way for me, because the slightest fatigue on a journey makes me feverish. . . . Dear Papa, if you could send something to Bista, you would be giving me a great present too! . . . I know they have some unavoidable expenses just now; but they always have to think twice and do everything as economically as possible because they're not very well off! But when it's a question of me and my health they are quite regardless and would take the bread from their own mouths. . . . And now I also need you to tell me what arrangement I must come to with Aunt d'Azeglio here; I asked her if she had settled something with you, and she answered, you don't think I talk about money to Uncle Manzoni, you are my niece, I'd be ashamed. . . but on the other hand she has said at times that she's really quite short of money now. . . I started to pay for a few expenses, like the coach to come here, special mail, making a note of them, but I can't go much further because my half-year fell due at the end of September. Dear Papa! have patience and sympathy with me, I assure you it grieves me to be such a worry and a nuisance to you! . . . My poor health is really to blame; if I were well, I wouldn't have cost you much because I really never throw anything away; I always keep my things for years, so that even Aunt praises me for it, and I never make unnecessary purchases. But even I often find I have to spend my pin-money on little extras like tips etc. and I get through it quickly even though I economise on my clothes. Dear Papa, please write back to me at once. This time it's not a simple wish to have a letter from you, I really need you to tell me what I must do and what arrangement I must make! . . . I couldn't finish this letter yesterday or the day before, which perhaps is just as well as it means today I can tell you the result of the careful examination Prof. Fedeli gave me this morning. He says he can guarantee there is no organic defect of the heart, the left lung is perfectly

286

healthy, but there's some slight congestion of the right lung. If this congestion continues, they will have to try some vesicants – for now I must alternate cod-liver oil and Mialke syrup of iron iodide – go for a little drive along the Arno when the weather is good and be content with that for now and not go walking. I haven't been for a walk for nine months. . .'

Manzoni to Matilde, in December:

'My dear Matilde.

'I was sorry to have to delay sending this letter a few days more than I had said. This time I assure you it was not laziness. I was grateful for the page where you found room in the margin to give me better news again of your health, and if not of perfect health, at least of progress for the better. . . . God bless Pisa, and a dear name that rhymes with it! I hope your next letter will tell me that your rides on the Lungarno have grown longer, and God grant they will soon change to walks!

'Unfortunately my wife's condition does not improve, at least not appreciably. But, simply from the fact that there is no worsening, I can't help deriving hope of a happy turn. I've seen her before now languish for a long time, and then recover bit by bit; I've also seen her in a much worse state. God grant my prediction be fulfilled! She sends lots of greetings to you and Luisa.

My life goes on as usual: not cheerful, as you can imagine. I ask the Lord for grace to love all that comes from His will: but He replies: You too must do what you can. And this is the problem. I find work helps. Thank heaven, I have sent the end of the appendix to *La morale cattolica* to the printers. . .'

Matilde to her father, February 1855:

'My dear Papa,

'I have delayed sending you a letter from one day to the next in hopes of announcing my convalescence, but now I've lost heart, and feel too strongly the need to write to delay any longer. I am still feverish every evening, and it does not look like stopping for the time being; in the day, except for a slight headache which often troubles me and more or less acute chest pains, I've otherwise not been too bad for some time now and I can't complain; but in the evening I feel really poorly, sometimes I get very heavy sweats which leave me weak. Fedeli examined my chest again yesterday morning, and found no change, that is, the breathing is very laboured in the left lung because it is making up for the right which is still somewhat congested. Just think, dear Papa, I've been in bed 75 days today! I get up every other day to have my bed made and I sit for half an hour in an armchair that they bring up to the bed, all wrapped up in a woollen blanket; but if I stay any longer than the half-hour, I start to feel exhausted, and I go pale as if I were going to be ill. When I've been back in bed a few minutes I begin to feel better. But everyone keeps encouraging me, and even the Doctor assures me he can find nothing in my condition to arouse serious apprehension, and that I'll be better when the warm weather returns; and Bista, who was so kind as to come and see me at Carnival, thought I was looking no worse than last time. So let's hope they're right, and that I can really get better soon! I have had moments of deep depression, I confess, I was really discouraged, and my thoughts were so sad that I kept finding my face covered with tears. I thought so often: when I'm worse, I'll write and beg Papa to come, I really can't die without seeing him again and without the comfort of his words and his blessing! . . . Truly, dear Papa, if I were very bad you would come? Oh! but I don't think like that now! I hope I will see you again soon, but that we'll all be happy and I'll be able to run to meet you! . . . Aunt has shown me great kindness and concern, but I confess I miss Vittoria, Bista and the dear little ones so much that I long for the summer which I hope will allow us to go back to them. You can't imagine the love and affection they show me; they write me such long, detailed, affectionate letters every day that I really feel I am with them as I read them. They tell me even Giorgino is always talking of *auntie Tide*, and he often takes a piece of paper and a pencil and makes lots of strokes on it, saying he's sending kisses to auntie. The other day her Daddy brought me a lovely little straw basket from Luisina, bought with *her own pennies*. – Poor little pets, I always tell Vittoria and Bista I love them as much as they could do! – Vittoria will come to see me now in Lent, and Bista will come again in the Easter holiday. I see "Babbo" now and again because he spends part of his time in Florence and part in Montignoso, and he stops here on the way through. When he's here, he keeps me company for a long time and shows me such affection; he always tells me he loves me as if I

288

were his own daughter. Poor "Babbo" and I love him so very much, too; tomorrow is the anniversary of poor Nonno's death! . . . Sbragia comes to see me every day, and sends me everything he thinks I might like; when I was worse he stayed here for hours and has always done all he could for me. Dear Papa, when you write, do include a message for him. As for expenses, out of the 30 coins you sent me in addition to my half-year allowance, up to now I have spent 22, paying the apothecary for Nov. and Dec., and paying the servant every 8 or 10 days for various little daily expenses like milk, ice, candles, post, and lots of other little things, of which I can send you a detailed account at the end of my illness, if you want. So I have only 8 coins in hand. There will be the apothecary to pay for Jan. and Feb., and they've given me such a lot of medicines! If you think best, the Doctor need not be paid until I'm leaving Pisa. What seems most urgent to me at the moment, and I want to speak frankly to you about it, would be to think what I owe Aunt. I kept hoping Signor Finzi would come, but in vain. From all that Aunt says I can see she is not too well placed, a few days ago she even said quite clearly that she is going through a difficult spell and is really short, and I feel as if I could die when she talks like this and I think I am causing her extra expense. Poor Papa, have patience! it costs me dearly to talk of these things and to have to be asking you for money all the time! if only I could say that all these expenses had brought back my health! but God's will be done! . . . Give my love to Mama, and please tell me how you are. – Remember me to my brothers when you see them, Aunt sends you her regards, and please forgive this dreadful letter written in bits and pieces, as I've had to break off all the time from fatigue! Accept my warmest love, and send your blessing to your poor *Matilde*.'

At the foot of this letter Teresa wrote: *Letter which Alessandro let me have, or gave me 'à regret', because of the great interest he could see I felt for poor dear Matilde.*

Manzoni wrote to *tante* Louise. He told her he had sent her money on account for the expenses she had incurred; and said that the summer, and 'above all God's goodness', which he never stopped imploring 'for the health of that ever-beloved creature' led him confidently to expect 'more comforting news'. 'Unfortunately there is no improvement in Teresa's health either; but I think one can attribute the cause, at least in part, to this dreadful winter; which keeps me in hope that I shall have the double consolation of seeing her looking better soon, and of being able to carry out, in the spring or early summer, the plans so dear to the hearts of Matilde, Pietro and myself, and likewise to you, first because you are united to us by so many bonds, and then because you are you.'

And in a letter to Massimo d'Azeglio about the same time he wrote:

'I have at least had the consolation of receiving good news, which promises even better things for the future, about our poor Matilde. Luisa is a sister, friend and matchless mother to her.'

Matilde to her father, in March:

'They had to bleed me a little Monday evening because I coughed blood five or six times. . . . They treated me with ice and lemon as usual, and thank God, I've had no recurrence since then, and I hope it has passed over for this time because things have gone as they expected. Yesterday I was up for an hour, I feel fairly strong, and if it were not for that blessed pain on the right side which won't go away, I should be quite pleased with myself. Dear Papa, I hope to be able to give you even better news soon! I was so pleased with your letter to Aunt! What a precious hope it gives us! We haven't the courage to *hope too much*, because we are too afraid Mama's health will not allow you to leave her, but who knows if now the winter's over she won't be better in the warm weather? God grant it, dear Papa, and that you will be able to leave her with a quiet mind, and come for a while to your children here who so long to see you. Since you wrote such an exciting thing in your letter to Aunt, Vittoria's and Bista's letters are full of wonderful plans that cheer me up! . . . Aunt appeared to be quite mortified and astonished at the promissory note you sent her. There was no way of making her take it and I've had to keep it here myself. But we've agreed to do some reckoning together. . . . Oh, what a lot of money one spends when one has the misfortune to be ill so long. . .'

Vittoria and Bista had moved house. Their new house was in the centre of Siena, on the Lizza. Matilde hoped to be able to join them there in May. Manzoni to Matilde in April:

'I hope the advance of the fine weather will have advanced your convalescence. My thoughts run to the house overlooking the Lizza, and if they hurry there, they don't hurry away again. However, I really can't get there before July, as it is essential that Pietro should stay at Brusuglio until the cocoons are collected. . . . There's been a real improvement in Teresa's health. . . After reading your dear letters, one with grief and the other with consolation, she would so much like to write to you, and she is quite upset that she cannot do so yet. I tell her she must be content for now to pray for you, as she is doing.'

Matilde to him, in April:

'What tremendous pleasure it gave me yesterday evening when they brought me your letter, dear Papa; what a comfort it was to read it and think that in two months we will *really and truly* have you here with us! . . . Dear Papa, the thought makes me forget my wretched winter and all the troubles that have passed! . . . I go out for a little drive every day, so far they haven't let me try to do the stairs on my own, which depresses me a bit. . . Did you know, father dear, they've really fixed the day of my return to Siena, and it's quite near? On the 30th Aunt will take me to Empoli, where Bista will come from Siena to meet me. . . At last the long months of separation are over; how I long to see Vittoria again, the children who send me the most affectionate messages every day, and Bista. . .'

In May Abbé Rosmini became ill with liver trouble. Manzoni wanted his doctor, Pogliaghi, to see him. He and Teresa were in Milan; Manzoni had been slightly unwell. They received news from Abbé Branzini, who was caring for Rosmini, and from Stefano, who had gone back to Lesa at the beginning of the spring.

Teresa to Stefano:

'Please thank dear, good Abbé Branzini for us. I pray each night with all my heart that the Lord will restore Rosmini to us! . . . May God bless your visit with Doctor Pogliaghi, and illumine the mind of the Doctor, and put trust and obedience in the heart of the Illustrious and Venerable Patient.'

Doctor Pogliaghi offered no hope. Abbé Branzini to Teresa:

'I feel the greatest grief at the thought that soon the Reverend

Father will be with us no more. If D. Alessandro could make the journey without ill effects, he would certainly be doing a charitable deed for he would be so pleased to see him.'

Manzoni decided to go. Pogliaghi, who had returned to Milan meanwhile, set off again with him. Teresa to Stefano:

'Only Our Lord God can restore him to us. Tomorrow Pogliaghi and Alessandro will be coming direct by mail coach and boat, I repeat, they will travel direct as far as Stresa. . . remember the Boario water, which is there at Lesa. Morelli, whom I saw yesterday as you know, agrees that Recoaro water would not be right just now for poor, precious Rosmini, but that he should try the Boario water that he suggested to you for me, and which saved my life when I was swollen like a balloon on my legs and arms and everywhere, and I couldn't pass water at all, and when squill and saltpetre did nothing for the urine, but gave me terrible gasping spasms in my stomach. . .' and a few days later: 'I wrote you a long letter. . . please note that in it I spoke of the Boario water which is at Stresa and which might perhaps suit poor Rosmini's stomach!' Rosmini's illness had greatly excited her. As she spent her life thinking of her own illnesses, real and imaginary, when she was confronted with other people's she was in her element, and got almost intoxicated. Only Matilde's illness left her strangely silent, she made no suggestions. It aroused no ideas about medicines, journeys, doctors or waters. Stefano to Teresa:

'Pogliaghi doesn't recommend any ferruginous mineral waters, as he says while there's no temperature, they might actually do harm. And indeed I think he may well be right, because although iron does not *materially strengthen*, I did read in Liebig that it increases the vital part of the blood.' Stefano too, like his mother, loved illnesses; they excited him and roused his curiosity.

The doctors had prescribed certain special foods for Rosmini, as he needed to take nourishment. Stefano wrote to Teresa that he had to have a packet of *Racahout des Arabes* and a packet of *Tapioca del Brasile*. 'The first is a bottle of wrapped crystals, I don't know about the second. But write the names clearly on a piece of paper, because they aren't easy to remember. Then get Pugni, the packer, to make a little wooden box to hold the two packets, then send them by the mail-coach. . .' Teresa sent her chambermaid Laura to the luxury grocer Stefano suggested, and then to Pugni. She also set Jegher, the cook to work. 'It's all here, nicely sealed and written out by me and I'm sending Jegher. . . now Jegher's gone off to the Restellis with the little box, which I hope will arrive tomorrow by the Treasury mail, and which contains the *Racahout des Arabes* and the *Tapioca del Brasile*. Poor poor dear Rosmini! O Stefano dear! what a man we are losing! what a saint! what a sage! what a friend to my Stefano, and to all who had need of him! . . . Oh who knows, who can know, if the Lord God, an abyss of mercy, may not restore him to us, after having almost taken him away! . . . who can tell how good and merciful is the Lord God of Abraham, of Jacob, of Isaac, of Tobias! . . . O my Tobiolo Stefano. . .' Since either Stefano or Manzoni had expressed the fear that she would feel alone and be afraid, she protested: 'And you two (Alessandro and you, Stefano) whatever has got into your head or heads, that I might get agitated at the news that you are both staying on at the lake. . . both of you! what are you thinking of? I am waited on hand, foot and finger, better than before, because Jegher, Binzaghi, the women, Signora Teresina, are all at my disposal, and never leave the house by day or night. Then there are the Enricos, who are quite a *troupe* and keep me company, and ensure the house is safe upstairs [apparently Enrico and his family were in Milan at the time, occupying the top floor of the house]: then the Barni ladies, and all the Sogni menfolk, and all the people of all these people and, last but not least, Nanny and the door-porters. But I've never felt any fears, or doubts, or need of anyone, day or night.'

In May Matilde returned to Siena. She was received with great rejoicing; she had, in the house on the Lizza, 'such a lovely little room, with everything I could possibly need for my comfort. Bista himself saw to it that the furniture chosen for me should look well. . . At Pisa I had lost my appetite altogether, I had to force myself to swallow what little I ate. Now I'm even getting my appetite back. – I'd love to be well when you come, dear Papa, and be able to enjoy your company fully! We talk such a lot about your coming, and we think about it all the time! How lovely it will be to show you Giorgino, and really to have you here with us! . . . Dear Papa, I've kept all my accounts carefully. . . Of the 1200 (lire) you sent me, I've spent 1125. . . Now there's still the doctor! . . . For his visits I owe him 45 Francesconi, that is L300, but then there are the bleedings, the leeches, cupping-glasses, the dressings with the vesicants. . . 160 lire in all. I should be very happy if you could send me this, because Bista certainly can't lend it to me, and he told me only yesterday he was so sorry; and I'm afraid it would be a bit too long to wait until you come. . . Poor Papa! I cost you so much and am no use to you!'

In June Bista wrote to Manzoni that Matilde was not at all well. He offered to join him at Stresa and take him back to Siena with him.

Manzoni to Bista, from Stresa:

'The pleasure your kind letter gave me was considerably darkened by the news you gave of Matilde. But I choose to hope it is nothing more than you mention, that is, a slowing down in the progress of her convalescence.'

Then he gave news of Abbé Rosmini. 'About the incomparable man I am with. . . unfortunately the best I can say is that all hope is not lost. In the last few days his pains have diminished, even almost stopped; the dropsy is no worse, the bladder functioning better; but in spite of this partial improvement, the wasting continues, caused by the extreme difficulty or near impossibility of digesting even the blandest of food. . . What does remain constant in his condition, and you know what a lofty condition that is, is his spirit. The resignation, or rather the complete and natural acquiescence in God's will, the serenity which results from it, all this is apparent in his every word, every act, in the smile unchanged in such a changed appearance. . .'

'How can I thank you, dear, good Bista, for your willingness to come and meet me here?

'But I hold firm to my hope and determination to come there, or wherever you are in September, or after. . . Let Vittoria send the news to Pietro, who will send it straight on to me if I am still here. To you, to her, to our Matilde, one loving embrace from your unworthy but most loving father.'

One of the last exchanges between Rosmini and Manzoni is described thus by someone who was present:

'The patient, moved by extraordinary affection, squeezed Manzoni's hand more tightly, and pulling him closer, kissed him. Manzoni, surprised and greatly disturbed, bent down at once to kiss the hand of his friend which he was holding; but realizing, as he said then, that this was to do no more than the other had done, he became in some way still more disturbed and confused, and hastened to kiss his feet: the only way (in his words) remaining to him of resuming his position, though Rosmini protested in vain, by word and gesture, saying: – Ah! this time he wins because I have no strength left – And they clasped hands again.'

Tommaseo came to Stresa. He had been almost blind for some time. Teresa to Stefano:

'It was also a comfort to hear from you that poor Rosmini had the consolation of seeing his childhood friend again! – Tommaseo! – Poor Tommaseo! So poor in his purse! so rich in intellect and in heart! *Blind* as he is, to come from Greece, in order *not to see* his Rosmini! who will perhaps have suffered all the more to see him with his own eyes reduced to that condition. – O, for pity's sake. . . Tommaseo!' In fact, Tommaseo had been back from Greece for a year, and had just come from Turin.

Rosmini died on 1 July. Rossari came to tell Teresa. Teresa to Stefano:

'Poor dear Stefano! my poor Alessandro! poor me! poor us! poor everyone who loved him! I've known for *three hours* now. . . I don't know where you two dear ones are today – whether still at Stresa – or at Lesa – or on your way in this storm – but the Lord will be with you, because you went for His Saint – and you returned blessed in Heaven by his Saint, for whom there will be such rejoicing in Heaven! . . . But what of us! . . . of you! . . . of all his people! . . . what a desert! . . . here is Rossari come again from Stefano! Rossari from the Afflicted, – afflicted as he is himself, for the loss, for Alessandro, and for us! and for himself.'

Manzoni to Teresa:

'O my dear Teresa! this morning I heard in the Gospel for the Mass the words: *It is finished*, which were so close to the terrible feeling that filled my heart, that I was moved to offer it to the source of all consolation.

295

'The usual feelings which make me so happy to see you again, are increased by my need to share with you this great grief.'

That summer cholera had spread to various parts of Italy, and still continued in the autumn. Teresa could speak of nothing else in her letters to her son. She wanted to join him at Lesa, but Alessandro was reminded by Lesa and the lake of the happy times he had spent there with Rosmini, so that summer he did not want to leave Milan. But there had been cases of cholera at Brusuglio and also in Milan. Teresa persuaded him to leave, and they set off for Lesa in August. Then Teresa remained alone at Lesa, because he went to the Arconatis in their villa of Cassolnovo, and Stefano went off to Paris with his servant Francesco.

In October Manzoni was still with the Arconatis. They had invited Teresa too, but she would not move from Lesa, as she said she was not strong enough. Manzoni was very happy at Cassolnovo with the Arconatis, and from then on he got in the habit of going there often.

Over the years Teresa had increasingly adopted the habits and attitudes of a sick woman; she had done so all her life, but did so more and more. She dominated those about her with her infirmities. Constantly claiming to be ill, weak, indisposed, bit by bit she really did lose her health. And in the end this constant state of illness must have become tedious to Manzoni. He had supported her for years with extreme patience; he had believed in all those subtle ailments she claimed to feel, or had taught himself to believe them; he was profoundly attached to her, and her infirmities had been at the heart of their emotional relationship. In a sense, he even adopted her infirmities as a shield; they allowed him to isolate himself in a state of permanent apprehension, where any other preoccupations or apprehensions that filtered through seemed to lose their harsh reality and urgency. But bit by bit he had tired of this daily apprehension that had been going on for years, keeping the whole house in a state of alarm. He was beginning to show signs of impatience. From Lesa he fled to Cassolnovo.

Manzoni to Teresa, from Cassolnovo in October:

'Of the two letters you enclosed. . . one was from Matilde to Pietro. The news of her health would be quite good, if there were not a sad novelty, her cough. She expresses such a longing to see me, and talks in such a way of the grief she felt and tears she shed when she was told my journey would be delayed, that I feel most distressed at the idea of putting it off again until next spring. If the cholera dies out in Tuscany, as it seems to have done in the Genovesato, the approach of winter must not be seen as a sufficient reason to delay. You know how sad I would be to be separated from you for a period that cannot be brief: but it absolutely must be done, sooner or later; and you yourself want this comfort for my daughters and for me. Of course, all this depends on my assumption which, I hope, thank Heaven, is well founded, that your health is, I dare not say flourishing, but at least not a source of anxiety.'

Matilde to her father in October:

'I put off writing to you until today in the hope of receiving an answer from Pietro or a letter from you any day, but unfortunately I've waited quite a time and I am too eager to hear about you and my brothers to delay any longer asking you for news, *in all charity*. I wrote to Pietro on the 25th of last month, and we've been anxiously awaiting an answer, especially since Pietro spoke of some cases at Brusuglio where people have been suddenly stricken, which naturally rather alarmed us. . . I was encouraged by Pietro to speak to him of things that are on my mind. In these days when one can't help feeling rather agitated, it really is distressing never to have news of one's dearest relatives far away, having no letters from you after thinking for months we were to see you again! Forgive me, dear Papa, I'm afraid it is wrong of me to lament like this, I'm afraid of being tedious, but not of seeming demanding. . . do you know you haven't written to me for months, and can you not imagine what a line from you means to me? Every morning I wait for the post like one obsessed, saying to myself, I'll surely have a letter today, and every day there's nothing! . . .'

Manzoni to Matilde, still from Cassolnovo, still in October:

'Pietro sent on to me here the letter you wrote to him, and I've read it and re-read it with feelings I cannot express. My poor, dear Matilde! So the improvement, which certainly had taken place, in your tormented health, was not maintained in the way expected? But the fact that other distressing problems have at least diminished, even if they have not gone completely, gives hope that the new enemy, the cough, with the treatment you are receiving and all the care shown to you, and above all by God's mercy, may also give way gradually. May your sweet resignation, your tender, humble desire to perfect it, and the prayers of those who love you so dearly, obtain grace with Him!

'What can I say of the desire to see us again, expressed in your letter with words that are fixed in my heart. I think every day, many times a day, of your weeping at the Magazzino de' Marmi. Oh, why can I not tell you certainly that we will come before the winter? But since I was with you, I feel more strongly how the years have taken their toll, and I am no longer so hardened against the vicissitudes of the atmosphere. Last winter, as you know, I had one of those nasty inflammations to which I have been subject for some time. . .

'Enough, at the end of the month, or at the beginning of the next, I shall be in Milan, and there I'll make up my mind, according to the doctor's opinion, and how I feel. I hope to find a letter from you there which will reassure me about your health, and tell me that, if this plan so dear to our hearts has to be put off till the spring, you will not be too upset, my dear, good Matilde. . .'

In the letter Matilde had written to Pietro, which Pietro had sent on to their father, she said she had wept 'at the Magazzino de' Marmi', the name given then to the Forte dei Marmi, where the Giorginis had a house, and where they had gone with Matilde in September to escape from the cholera.

Back in Milan that autumn of 1855, Manzoni became aware of the disarray of Enrico's financial entanglements and general situation. The fact was that his affairs had never prospered, but there had been times when they seemed not to be going too badly. In December 1854 Manzoni had written to Vittoria:

'Enrico often comes to Milan about his silkworm contracts. His speculations in seed are very active this year, and would be much more so if he had capital, but I hope that this will come, even if he proceeds slowly, and then this speculation could be of real benefit to him. . .'

Next year Enrico was besieged by creditors. Obtaining nothing from him, they turned to his father. In December 1855, that is, exactly a year after that rosy forecast about Enrico's affairs, Manzoni wrote Vittoria a long letter, enclosing what he called the 'little promissory note', that is, the order for Matilde's half year allowance and the interest on the holdings, and telling her about his own anxieties and preoccupations: he begged her to destroy the letter, and she did so. But Matilde had read it. It had caught her eye when Vittoria was out, and seeing her father's writing, she had opened it: she had been appalled and had called Bista to explain some terms she found obscure. When Vittoria read the letter, she too was horrified. She wrote to her father on 13 December:

'My dear father!

'I am assailed by such a variety of emotions that I really don't know where to put my head, or what to say to you, dear Papa! The joy of seeing a longed-for letter from you! . . . and the painful news you are obliged to give us in it. . . the gratitude for what you have chosen to do for us, poor Papa! . . . and the bitterness of knowing that your situation perhaps makes a sacrifice of what you have done so generously [sending the allowance and interest]. Which all combines to embitter the comfort the Lord had sent us in the shape of your letter, and to add a painful sense of mortification and sadness to our gratitude which is so sincere and which I cannot find words to express! . . . Poor, poor Papa! what worries and griefs you have to bear! You can imagine that this has been a grief to us too, for although far from you, our hearts are always with you, and we live in heart and mind with our poor, much afflicted family! . . . Enrico's situation causes us grave anxiety and distress! . . .'

Her father answered on 18 December:

'I must say at once I was wrong to upset you all to no purpose by that outburst about my present circumstances. But I can also say at once in excuse that it never occurred to me you might see a "sacrifice". . . oh my Vittoria, thank Heaven I shall have enough for our necessities this year, while hoping for better things next year; and is not what you call a sacrifice a sacred part of these necessities?

'You must not expect news of Enrico's affairs, at least for some time. Trustees have been appointed for him and for his wife, but there is a chaos to be disentangled. I know they are both quite calm: an excellent sign if. . . it means they have good

299

reason to think there will be enough to settle their debts and still live decently, until they have what sadly little I shall leave him. . .'

Vittoria to her father on 22 December:

'It was a slight consolation to us to hear at least that poor Enrico *is quite calm!* God grant this calm is not feigned or illusory, and that it is really founded on the certainty that his affairs must shortly improve! What does worry me and what I should very much like to know is if he is in danger of losing Renate! . . . God forbid! I haven't the courage to write to him, but if you see him, embrace him for me, and please tell him I feel for his distresses and would remedy them if I could! . . . As I'm writing about such intimate subjects, I beg you to tell me, dear Papa, if you ever see Filippo and if he has caused you any further distress! If you see him and feel you can sincerely embrace him, do so from me too, for whatever has happened in the past, it is too painful to have to live estranged from part of my blood; and especially at this time, at Christmas when one needs one's family, and *memories of the past come back so vividly.* . . the only consolation we can find for the pain of absence is to be remembered by all the members of the family, and to unite in heart and mind to celebrate Christmas! . . .'

From Filippo, their father had received at about the same time a letter which he thought insolent. The letter has not been found, and perhaps Manzoni destroyed it. He wrote back to say he wished neither to write to him nor to hear from him.

Letter followed letter during the winter with news of Matilde's worsening health. At the beginning of March Manzoni wrote suggesting that Vittoria ask the doctor if he saw fit to 'try magnetism'. It was Stefano's idea. A girl, the niece of a chamber maid, who was seriously ill, had shown some benefit from certain experiments with magnetism. But a few days later Pietro had a letter from Bista saying that the doctor's prognosis was decidedly gloomy. Manzoni wrote to Bista telling him to decide if they should come: 'For the love of Heaven, don't let the word "decide" alarm your delicate sensibilities; I would cross it out, if I did not consider it to mean no more than expressing an opinion. . .'

300

On 15 March, Manzoni received a letter from Matilde:

'Caro Papà mio,

'I'm writing to you at night as a rather high temperature prevents me sleeping and gives me strength I entirely lack in the day; this is the 95th night! Now, thank God, the illness seems past its peak, but the excessive exhaustion and the really terrible aching in my poor bones never give me a moment's peace and I suffer day and night so that I sometimes see my bed surrounded with weeping. Dear Papa, I thought I knew all about illness and suffering! . . . I've been in this bed for four months. God, what I have suffered and what I am suffering! . . . Sometimes I weep in desperation but God has given me such comfort by the general confession I have made and the holy communion which has brought peace to my heart [a blank line follows].

'Dear Papa, the expenses grow distressingly and my purse is sometimes empty! I need such a lot of nursing, two women stay in my room at night and more or less all day because I can't make the slightest movement on my own however small, and the cost of an illness like this is unimaginable. Dear Papa and you are having problems this year! Believe me, I have cried many times! The idea of such an imperious need of money and such worrying straits! . . . What a misfortune Papa mio to have a wretched afflicted daughter like me! . . . In charity send me what you can to meet the first costs, when I'm better, God grant it will not be long, I will tell you what is needed, and how will you manage? . . . Oh, for pity's sake, have patience! . . .

'My head's *absolutely* dazed, I can't stop coughing and I must stop. . . I don't know what Vittoria and Bista will say about my wanting to write when they know. . . but the fever has kept me going. My dear revered Father! I beg you to send your blessing upon me every night to comfort me and help me to suffer and to get better, goodbye!

'I've said nothing of Vittoria, Bista, "Babbo", Giannina, may the Lord reward them! . . .'

Her father to Matilde, 19 March:

'My dear, ever dearer Matilde,

'My joy at seeing the address in your hand, my poor Matilde, gave way to grief to see how you are suffering! and to be able to do nothing but suffer with you, and pray and pray, albeit knowing how unworthy I am to be heard! But the One I implore is so good, and loves you, and I have commended so many loving souls to pray too.

'Father Piantoni Barnabita, rector of the College of Porta nova, has just left me, and said that his 141 pupils will pray for you, as they celebrate Easter tomorrow. . .'

Matilde died on 30 March, in the arms of Vittoria and her "Babbo" Gaetano. She was buried in Siena, in the Chiostro dei Servi.

Manzoni sent an epitaph for her tomb:

'Here lies Matilde daughter of Alessandro Manzoni consumed by a slow wasting illness on XXX March 1856 in the last year of her fifth lustrum [at the age of 25]; for a life beautiful in all the virtues that make her sex sublime she is greatly missed by her father, her brothers and her sister Vittoria wife of Gio. Battista Giorgini, who commend her to the prayers of the pious Sienese.'

That summer – at last and too late – Manzoni got to Tuscany. He went with Pietro and all his family. They joined the Giorginis at Viareggio where they were spending the summer. Manzoni went with Bista to Gino Capponi for a few days. They talked about questions of language, and planned to compile a trial vocabulary.

Then the travellers said goodbye to the Giorginis and set out on the return journey. They hired a private stage-coach because there were so many of them: the three adults, Pietro's four children, and a servant. They reached Genoa in twenty-four hours.

That year Lodovico Trotti died at Cassolnovo. He had been ill for some time; his sister Costanza was nursing him; he entrusted his four children to her.

In December Vittoria's little girl, the 'prodigious Luisina', caught scarlet fever, was ill for two months, then seemed cured, but became feverish again, her legs swelled, her breathing became laboured, and she died in May 1857. She was buried beside Matilde, in the Chiostro dei Servi.

Stefano I

In July 1857 Manzoni was alone in Milan. Stefano had developed a pernicious fever at Lesa, and Teresa had gone to him; it was nothing serious, and soon over. Manzoni could not get a passport in time and had to wait; he also wanted to be near Pietro, who was enquiring into Enrico's affairs and trying to alleviate the consequences. Manzoni had the company either of Rossari or Pietro, who came from Brusuglio every day; but Rossari suffered from the heat, and was also involved in the school; Manzoni went for walks with Pietro: he still found it impossible, as he had done all his life, to go walking alone. Indoors, he felt sad at the sight of the little flight of stairs leading to Teresa's room, 'and still more the little door at the top'. In his letters to Teresa he often mentioned those stairs. He wrote to her every day: he was tired by her presence, but saddened by her absence. He received letters from creditors, and news of Enrico's affairs, which seemed ever more complicated and alarming; he poured out his worries in the letters to Teresa:

'When I have the good fortune to be with you, and something painful occurs, you know what a relief it is to tell you: I am suffering. . . Although this is denied me at the moment, I still find it some relief to mention to you what is grieving me. So forgive me if I tell you I have been and am still disturbed by a letter from that person. . . he proposes I should become involved, and as you know, I cannot and must not do so; but the problem does not go away, and seems to instil a drop of poison into the holiday period, from which I thought all gloomy thoughts should be, if not extinguished, at least partly eclipsed. But these are laments, whereas I ought only to beg you to help me accept everything from the hand of God, especially as you show me the way. In any case (and this too comes

303

from His hand, but His all-merciful hand) seeing you again will afford quite different comfort from this poor writing. . . I want you to burn this letter, as I do not wish to leave any lasting trace of my feelings about this grievous business. . .

Teresa did not burn the letter, but she cut out some sentences where he spoke of 'that person': a creditor, or perhaps Enrico himself.

In 1857 Enrico was thirty-eight. He and his wife and children still lived in the splendid villa of Renate, with its park, orchard, kitchen-garden, and winter garden. He had seven children. The oldest, Enrichetta, was thirteen; then came Sandrino, Matilde, Sofia, Lucia, Eugenio; and that year Bianca was born. Enrico, according to Vittoria in her memoirs, had an inflated idea of himself; he thought whatever he undertook would succeed. He had flung himself into business without knowing a thing about it. His wife approved and abetted him. By now he was completely ruined. He had entirely devoured even his wife's rich inheritance. He and his wife had remained *calm* for a long time; that is, they had continued to spend immoderately. The creditors who were writing to his father were not just business creditors, but furniture and carpet sellers, shoe-makers and tailors. Enrico and his wife knew the splendid villa they lived in was quite lost, and that they would soon have to leave it. Swiftly, in the space of a few months, Enrico's complicated, intricate situation became extremely simple: he had nothing left.

As he left for Lesa in August, Manzoni knew that one of the creditors had started legal proceedings, and there was the risk he might draw the whole troop behind him; but at Lesa he received a reassuring letter from Pietro: the legal proceedings had been suspended. Manzoni to Pietro:

'You can imagine what a relief it was to read of the suspension. . . And as I assume from what you say that this was your doing, I thank you on my own behalf, since, as for the person directly involved, and his innocent children, your heart must have inspired you to it.'

Enrico to his father:

'My brother Pietro has made a sacrifice that only a heart like his could make. I do not speak of the delicate means he adopted to help me. These are things I can't possibly describe in this letter. Yes, dear Papa, I have asked God's pardon. . . Dear Papa, accept my assurance that if, sadly, circumstances may condemn us, when these circumstances are known I am sure we will obtain forbearance. . . Our whole lives will henceforth be dedicated to righting the wrong that has been done, and by the grace of God which I continually implore, I feel we will succeed. . . Forgive me, dear Papa, for writing so badly. I realize I have failed to tell you all my poor heart feels.'

That spring Teresa had made another will. Terrified by Enrico's doings, she had apparently sought to defend her own son against these financial landslips. In this will she cancelled the arrangements regarding her dowry; this time Manzoni was absolutely obliged to restore the dowry to Stefano on her death, immediately and in its entirety. 'To my most beloved husband Alessandro Manzoni,' she still left her 'gold repeater', that is, a watch, as she had already declared in the previous will. Stefano was the sole heir, and was absolved from any obligations 'that may have been indicated by me elsewhere'.

As she was once again preoccupied with death at that time, she grieved that Stefano, who was now thirty-eight – the same age as Enrico – was still unmarried. Years before he seemed to have been attracted by a beautiful girl from a wealthy family at Lesa: but in no time it had all come to nothing. 'Your most aff. Mama would dearly love to become a grandmother to a little Stefanello,' she wrote at the bottom of every letter, or 'The Lord Himself said: *it is not good that a man should be alone.*' Stefano, however, remained completely deaf to these exhortations. From time to time he started up some half-hearted matrimonial negotiations, to satisfy her: but it would all fade away quite quickly.

Teresa had not written to Vittoria after the death of Luisina. She wrote:

'Dear, dear Vittoria – I can hardly pluck up the courage to say anything but poor dear Vittoria! – Oh, how I wish I were near you, to hold your hand in mine, and squeeze it and kiss it, trying but not daring to say a word about the angel you have given back to God. . . Please forgive my silence, dear Vittoria! it is not the silence of the heart. . . I embrace you with a love that you can imagine, and I beg you not to write a word in reply so that you can rest your eyes. Have courage, dear good Vittoria! your Luisina is in an ocean of joy, in the arms of your saintly mother, praying to the Lord for you and all your dear people.'

Vittoria stayed in Florence for a long time with Babbo Gaetano. She returned to Siena early in 1858.

Since her adolescence she had never been very strong: she was always having headaches, backache, and she had trouble with her weak eyes. Grief made her still weaker. She could not see at all well. She was not to tire her eyes. Babbo Gaetano used to read aloud to her.

Matilde had told her, if she died, to burn the notebooks and albums in which she used to note down her impressions and thoughts. Vittoria obeyed.

However, a few pages survived, between January and March, in a diary Matilde had kept in 1851. Obviously Vittoria did not want to burn them. They were found many years later among Bista's papers.

When she was writing that diary in 1851, Matilde was not very ill. She had friends, amusements, pastimes. Yet she never stopped thinking of death.

Her mother's face which she could not remember; her sister's little girl who was growing up beside her, and who was as dear to her as if she were her own child; a few fleeting moments of happiness which she immediately thought of as a chance, fleeting light that her eyes would never see again. This was Matilde's youth, as she wrote.

'My dear saintly mother had to leave me when I was only two. . . Oh mamma mia! why could you not live to know my heart?

'This morning my Luisina woke me with her kisses: I put on my dressing-gown as fast as I could and ran into the sitting-room, to see the presents the *Befana* (white witch) had brought. The little darling squealed with delight to see her stockings bulging, but wouldn't touch anything until Bista got up too, to take part in her happiness. Later I was so happy too, seeing the portrait of Papa that Stefano has sent Vittoria [it was the Hayez painting, in a copy by Stefano]. Oh! if only Papa could come to Pisa too! What joy it would be to be near him, without having to leave Vittorina, Bista, and their little pet! – By now I am too attached to them, and I can't contemplate the remotest possibility of separation, without shivering all over!

'Last night a dance in casa Abudarham. . . I quite enjoyed it. I had a white dress with blue spots and three *volants* [flounces], little blue flowers in my hair, my *berthe di blonde* [flat hair-piece worn across top of hair] and a broad white and blue bow at my waist: my simple *toilette* was much admired. I wore poor Nonna's *rivière* of opals round my neck; and several people said the opals were the same colour as my eyes: that means eyes with no brightness, used to looking at dead things. . .

'Here I am, parted from Luisa, for goodness knows how many days! [Luisa Lovatelli, her best friend]. Her brother has German measles, and I must *exile myself totally* from casa Lovatelli, not to risk bringing it to Luisina. Oh! how I love the little pet! When she is grown up and I am no more, she will forget me, and she'll never guess how I loved her like a mother!'

Massimo d'Azeglio recalled a saying of Luisina's. When Manzoni and Pietro came to Viareggio that summer which was to be Luisina's last, and d'Azeglio was there too, one day they were all standing on the jetty looking at the sea. They were talking about Matilde. Luisina was listening. Someone said to her: 'Your poor aunt, who has left us for ever.' Luisina said: '*Ever* begins after – in this world we are just birds of passage – aren't we, grandpapa?'

In 1858, about the middle of May, Manzoni became seriously ill. It all began with a simple inflammation of the throat. But it soon became clear that it was serious. Teresa was terrified. Soon the whole town knew; people took up their stand beneath the windows. Prayers were said in every church. He was bled eighteen times. Two months later he was quite well, and went driving in the carriage with Pietro.

307

Uncle Giulio Beccaria had died in the February of that year. Manzoni received an annuity of four thousand lire a year; their uncle's wife, 'la zietta', said it had been the wish of the deceased to appoint this annual sum for him, but it seems it was, in fact, her idea.

In the summer Stefano fell ill; he had gone to Munich for an exhibition; he had to stop at Lindau, as he had a high temperature. Teresa heard and was terrified. She wanted to send her administrator Patrizio, Provost Ratti and Doctor Pogliaghi to Bavaria. In the end, she just sent Doctor Pogliaghi. But when he got to Lindau, Stefano had recovered.

So that was a year of terrors for Teresa. Then she became ill herself, not with an imaginary illness, as was so often the case: this time she was really ill.

She had been living the life of an invalid for years, so her life did not change. For years she had claimed that she ate very little. Nevertheless, she dedicated enormous attention to her meals. She used to describe them minutely to Stefano: 'Yesterday I ate a lot of fried brains, a little morsel of beef with onions, and two morsels of roast, with a small rice broth, and a small loaf of fine flour: afterwards I felt *hungrier than before*. – Now I've taken the two mouthfuls of Cassia and Tamarind I should have taken yesterday. . .' When they were at Lesa, Manzoni had to write and ask Pietro to send at once 'a large three or four pound loaf', 'breakfast for Teresa who, apart from her persistent lack of appetite, is reduced also by the state of her teeth to putting no more than the indigestible soft part of the bread in her coffee in the morning. To my surprise, at Arona they only make it at Christmas.' This time, however, perhaps she really lost her appetite: she really ate listlessly, but still with that supreme attention. For years she had lavished infinite attention upon her own health and she continued to do so. 'Castor oil! sunshine of invalids!' she wrote to her son in the solemn but jubilant tone she used to speak of medicines and purgatives; she was sure castor oil cured head colds. But no doubt her husband and son realised that something in her had changed and that she had suddenly become a real invalid.

She had a 'rheumatic pain' in her spine, which gave her no rest. She treated it with applications of *taffeta* material, leeches, *opodeldoch* rubs. She treated it by sitting in the garden with her back to the sun, while her chambermaid Laura shaded her head with one umbrella while she did the same with another. Stefano suggested they pour cold water on her spine from a watering can, seeing that she said this 'rheumatic pain' required cold water. Then she felt a great weakness 'in my legs, my thighs and stomach'. She went for little walks with Laura every day from via del Morone to the Case Rotte, near the Church of San Fedele, 'because it's absolutely essential to set those legs and thighs in motion: otherwise I'll lose the use of them'. But every now and then one of her legs gave way beneath her. She thought it was her age: she was fifty-eight. She had four chambermaids simply to look after her: Laura; Signora Teresina; a certain Luisa from Bruzzano; and Elisa Cermelli, from a quondam noble family from Campolungo. She was not satisfied with the one from Bruzzano: 'we'll be patient, we'll punish her, then if she doesn't improve, we'll turn her face towards Bruzzano again'. Each had a particular task: comb her hair, dress her, put her stockings on, carry out the suggestions of Doctor Pogliaghi and Stefano. To Stefano, who escaped to Lesa whenever he could, she regularly sent minute descriptions of her nights and her meals. She had abandoned Boario water in favour of Recoaro water. She was taking an electuary, a paste or powder sweetened with honey. 'Recoaro, electuary – always. Cutlet, soup and chocolate – always. A tiny drop of wine, very, very little but very good, white, 30 years old, that poor Sogni gave me. . . my legs and feet are not so swollen. But there's still that pain, though not so violent, in the middle of my shoulders and spine that demands cold water. . .'

In March 1859, as war appeared imminent, Bista wrote to Manzoni that he thought he should leave Milan. Bista and Vittoria feared Manzoni might be taken hostage, as Filippo had been. Bista offered to come and accompany him to Tuscany.

Manzoni wrote to him:

'*Fata obstant* [The fates oppose it]. I could neither bring my wife who, after a sore throat that required bleeding, leeches, decubitus and diet, is dragging herself through a sadly slow convalescence, nor leave her here in this condition. And there are other minor obstacles I won't talk about now. Moreover, I do not think that, even for an old man enfeebled by years and infirmities, Milan is likely to become dangerous. I know nothing about strategy, but I do know, in fact I remember, that the town has always remained outside the wars that have occurred in these parts.'

Then he added a few sentences about Enrico. 'In the midst of my painful worries, which have become more painful than ever (because the person who has so long been rushing towards extreme poverty has reached his goal, and I can only partly remedy his situation), the Lord has granted me a grace I could never have expected: that I can find, not relief but some sort of distraction in work. I have accustomed myself, in moments I might otherwise spend in useless affliction, to take my thoughts by the hair and fix them where there's something to be done, if not useful, at least not painful. That is why I am asking you to find out if anything has been done on the Vocabulary of Cherubini.'

However, he changed his mind about staying in Milan. He and Teresa set off with Stefano for Torricella d'Arcellasco. They would have had to request passports for Lesa. At Torricella, Teresa's brother, Giuseppe Borri, was expecting them. They stayed a month, from 13 May to 14 June.

On 20 May, the Franco-Piedmontese forces defeated the Austrians at Montebello, and again on 4 June at Magenta.

On 8 June Vittorio Emanuele II and Napoleon III entered Milan, to the acclamation of the crowd.

Manzoni returned to Milan the next week.

Vittorio Emanuele, on a private visit to Milan in August, heard that Manzoni was in financial difficulties. It was decided to assign him a life pension of twelve thousand lire a year, as a reward from the nation.

Enrico and family had left the villa of Renate, which no longer belonged to them. They went to Torricella di Barzanò, in Brianza. Having heard about his pension, Manzoni wanted to provide for Enrico's children: he wrote to two Houses of Education arranging for the older children to be accepted there; he sent a seamstress to measure all the children and make them some clothes. Enrico thanked him. But he had taken offence at these paternal initiatives; he wrote to tell Pietro he had other plans for his children's schooling and sent back the seamstress.

Then they heard he had nominated a trustee for himself and a legal representative for the children. His relations with Pietro, which until then had been good, became very bad.

His father wrote to him:

'Enrico,

'I could have overlooked the indelicacy and bad faith with which you responded to my charitable intentions towards you and your family, while it remained a matter between father and son. But now that you inform me you have, by a notarial deed, nominated a trustee for you and a representative for your children, thus changing a father's charitable intention into a legal controversy, I declare that, obliged by an action so injurious to me as a father and as a grandfather reluctantly to follow you along this path, I too intend to nominate a procurator to represent me in legal matters. . . the state of affairs you have brought about makes this a duty for me to which I am irrevocably bound.'

On 27 April Florence had risen in revolt. Bista was elected deputy in the Tuscan Council.

On 20 August he introduced the law proclaiming the union of Tuscany and Piedmont. He took part in the commission which transmitted this vote to Vittorio Emanuele.

In Milan, speaking from the balcony of La Scala, he was so tired and so excited that he fainted.

He devoted himself entirely to politics. The faculty of law was restored to Pisa; he was given the chair of History of Law. So he and Vittoria left Siena and went back to live in Pisa. But he was almost always in Turin, and did not spend much time at Pisa.

In Pisa Vittoria had many friends, and *tante* Louise and Babbo Gaetano. But her sight had grown worse and her health was poor. She spent long months at Montignoso.

There she sometimes met Bista's mother, Signora Carolina. She had been mad for years. She had not brought up her children, they had been brought up by their grandparents. For years she had been living on her own, here and there, in the various Giorgini houses. She was a bigot and lived surrounded by priests and nuns. She could not stand Vittoria. She said to her:

'What do you think you are, just because you're Manzoni's daughter? A fine thing! I've never been able to understand if he is a count, or if he isn't! And what would you think if you were the daughter of a *real* Count, like me? and of Count Paleologo, Grand Chamberlain of the King of Prussia! and if you had been held at the baptismal font, like me, by the Margrave of Brandenburg. That's a bit different from a Manzoni or manzetti [heifer], my dear girl!'

Vittoria became pregnant for the third time. It was the spring of 1860; in the summer Bista took her to Brusuglio, where she remained until October, with her father and Pietro. Teresa came too, for a few days.

That winter Manzoni had heard they wanted to make him a senator. He had written to Emilio Broglio:

'It is absolutely impossible for me to accept. I leave aside the fact that at seventy-five it is no small matter to travel, change one's residence and habits, be separated from an invalid wife and from a family who could not follow me. But there is more to it than this. There can be no question of my speaking in the Senate, as I stammer, especially when I am pinned down: so that I would certainly make people laugh behind my back if I simply had to respond, there and then, to the formula of the oath, I sw. . . sw. . . swear! To go to the Senate, even to remain silent, would be a major difficulty for a man who for forty years, as a result of nervous attacks, never dares to leave his house alone. . .'

Nevertheless, they made him a senator, and he accepted.

He received a letter from a lawyer in Como, who was Filippo's procurator. So Filippo, like Enrico, had nominated a procurator. Manzoni wrote to the lawyer:

'Ever since my son Filippo removed himself from my authority, that is, more than ten years ago, I have been forced to the resolution, after mature consideration, to take no part whatsoever in his affairs. Anything that has happened in the meantime could only confirm me in this resolution, if there had been any need of confirmation. Therefore I can. . . express no opinion regarding the procuration sent to you by him, of which you had the courtesy to speak to me in your letter. . .'

In this interval Filippo had continued to run up debts and to ask his father for money, money he solemnly promised to pay back in instalments and which he never paid back. Through his procurator, he protested because his father had sent his monthly order in the form of a hundred and twenty-five Milanese instead of Austrian lire. His father sent a further 25 lire. He wrote: 'I need not say that you should have left this L.25 until the repayment of a sum I advanced you. . . I need not tell you that I have lent you another sum of money that you were to pay back in several instalments, fixed by you, according to your most solemn promise; and you have paid me only one. These facts do not make your observations to me more unjust, but they give them a sadder and more painful character.'

In his turn Manzoni nominated his own legal representative.

Enrico and his family were living in Casatenovo, in Brianza, where a parish priest, don Saulle Miglio, seeing the family's pitiful condition, wrote to Manzoni. He suggested he send linen and foodstuffs to Enrico, seeing that Enrico squandered money. From then Manzoni addressed the money for Enrico's monthly allowance to this priest. He sent linen.

To Enrico:

'Heaven knows I should like, in your present circumstances, to spare you not only any reproof, but any observation at all; but I must point out that, precisely because of these circumstances, it would have been a considerable saving to leave your son at school in the holiday months.'

Vittoria went back to Pisa in the autumn. On 31 December that year, 1860, she had a baby girl, whom they called Matildina.

After the birth, she contracted miliary fever and for two months hung between life and death. Massimo d'Azeglio, who was in Pisa at the time, used to come and keep her company. He infuriated her by calling the baby girl 'raw sweetbread'.

Massimo d'Azeglio had been Governor of Milan between February and September that year.

That year Enrico's wife, Emilia, had also had a baby at Casatenovo; it was her eighth child. They called him Lodovico, in memory of Lodovico Trotti.

In February 1861 Bista went to Turin as reporter of the bill

313

conferring on Vittorio Emanuele the title of King of Italy. Manzoni went with him to record his vote. As he came out of the portico of the Palazzo Madama, between Bista and Cavour, Manzoni was applauded by the crowd. But he thought the applause was for Cavour, and he joined in energetically.

It was clear that Teresa was really ill, as, instead of lamenting her infirmities as had been her custom, she now maintained she was fairly well. To Stefano: 'I joined Alessandro at table to eat my pasta soup, and took my coffee and cream in my room with a fair amount of bread. I can't stand it for long in the warm dining-room, where there's the stove, as you know. So you will be persuaded that I am well, well for me, that is. But it's rainy, windy, damp, pouring, dark, it's night before evening, and evening before night, and I'm not at all melancholy, as you think, but *recklessly* cheerful for no reason. Poor Signora Emilia is always *reckless* with cheerfulness that does not cheer. . .' Emilia Luti had been to see her, and Teresa thought she had become old and fat; she had been in Switzerland, where she had taken a treatment for dropsy. Teresa wanted to try new treatments she had heard of: electric shocks; 'iron baths'.

The valet Clemente Vismara, who had been with the family for many years, detested Teresa, and she detested him. Later he gave his own account of the 'warm dining-room'. One day Teresa had eaten with her husband in the dining-room, which was a rare event, as she usually ate in her room. After eating she had started to rave, and made a scene to Clemente because the stove was giving out too much heat. She had gone off in a fury. Manzoni had remained alone with the servant, and said to him: 'Clemente, see that the stove gives out less heat.' 'I can't,' answered Clemente. 'Why?' 'Because it isn't lit.'

According to Clemente Vismara, the servants called Teresa 'Donna Stramba' or 'The Weird Woman', and they all hated her as he did.

It was a cold winter and Manzoni sent Enrico cartloads of wood, together with linen and foodstuffs. Enrico wrote to thank him, and at the same time asked for other things, especially money.

314

Enrico to his father, January 1861:

'My dearest Father,

'I can't tell you what a relief it was to me to receive the cartload of wood, the rice and the chickens. . . Please accept my warmest thanks, which come from my heart. God knows how it breaks my heart to have to ask you another favour, when I am just thanking you for your generosity. Since the excellent Priest has informed me that your generous quarterly allowance has not reached him yet, and that he therefore cannot let me have from his private account the money I need to pay for Alessandro's board which now falls due, as well as the house rent, and transport costs, all of which will come to about 500 Milanese lire, I find myself obliged (and God knows how it grieves me) to beg you to remove this great anxiety as soon as you can.

'May God grant me the grace I continually implore, that I may be, by my work less of a trial to you.'

Enrico had no work. And he had a strange relationship with money: he pursued it, begged for it, wasted it. For three years – ever since coming to Casatenovo – he had kept a rented piano, without paying the rent and without giving it back. The man who was hiring it out, a certain Signor Vago, wrote to Manzoni. He wanted the 'pianforte' back, and threatened to make trouble. Manzoni wrote to don Saulle Miglio.

In June Enrico asked if his father could increase his allowance. He also asked if he could send him some cherries from Brusuglio. Perhaps he was remembering with nostalgia the orchards at Renate; he was jealous of Pietro's children picking and eating cherries at Brusuglio. His father sent him some cherries with a letter saying he had bought them; they were finished at Brusuglio. Enrico to his father:

'Dearest Father,

'Cavallante Bestetti delivered your affectionate letter of the 27th to me yesterday, with the rice which I was so pleased to have, and the cherries which I certainly would not have asked for if I could have known you would be obliged to spend money to send me them. It really wasn't necessary. I expressed that wish, thinking there would be a little basketful for me too at Brusuglio; I must say I am quite mortified to have put you to that expense. Forgive me, my dear Father, perhaps I should have expressed myself better in my last letter. . . After you have

315

declared, with great kindness, that I neither could nor should count on any further help from you, to renew my request would show not only an unspeakable lack of delicacy but also stupidity on my part. Stricken by three different illnesses in my family, all requiring treatment. . . I have turned to you, who have always been so merciful towards me, begging you to help me in this painful emergency by allowing me a small increase now, which will enable me to meet these expenses, and which can be discounted from the next quarters. . .'

In August, Enrico to his father:

'Dearest Papa,

'How good you are to me! your affectionate missive has filled me with loving gratitude. Dear Papa, I thank you from the bottom of my heart, and cannot tell you what joy it gave to all the family and to my poor convalescents to receive those fine pullets, the ducks, and all those apples.

'Oh dear Papa, what will you say if at the very moment I receive a further token of your great kindness to me, I venture to ask another favour of you? I have done all in my power not to trouble you, but I have failed.

'Since the last load of wood you so kindly sent in April, which I have tried to use as economically as possible, for some time I have been without any at all. . . I would not dare ask you to send sticks, but just some faggots, some few splinters, in short, some of the sweepings from the wood-shed, anything would be good enough to boil a pan. This quarter I've been plagued by a thousand troubles; illnesses, and lack of water which involves me in daily expenditure just to have water to drink. . . Forgive me, I beg you, if I have ventured so far. . . Oh! if you could read my poor heart!'

Shortly after receiving this letter from Enrico, Manzoni received another from an innkeeper called Antonio Tettamanti. He was writing from Bizzarone, a village where Enrico's mother-in-law, Signora Luigia Redaelli Martinez, lived, also reduced to abject poverty. Antonio Tettamanti wrote:

'It's already some days since your son Don Enrico landed up in my house with all his family, and he goes frequently to Stabbio, not far from this township, to drink the waters. I am a wretched country inn-keeper and have not the wherewithal to continue to provide him with victuals, as he owes me about

316

three hundred Milanese lire. I've already asked him several times to settle my account and he says: today, tomorrow! but it's never the right moment. Not knowing how to proceed from now on I dared to consider turning to Your Excellency, as your goodness and kindness is well known, to ask you to rescue me from this predicament. . . if I do not hear from you, I shall be obliged to take steps which sadly it breaks my heart to think of.'

Manzoni to Tettamanti:

'I sincerely regret to tell you that I can in no wise stand surety for the debt you tell me my son Enrico has contracted with you. . .'

And to don Saulle Miglio:

'You must have thought, as I did, that the charitable burden you took upon yourself would bring only a succession of tedious, but simple and predictable cares. We were sadly deceived. The excellent D. Giovanni [Ghianda] had already informed me of his extravagant decision to remove his son from college, and the other, no less extravagant, of going, *with all his family*, to live in an inn, for no reason, at least no apparent reason, and with no idea how to pay for it. . .

'In this painful dilemma, uncertain whether to allow a scandal to occur, or to encourage other equally unthinkable schemes, it requires even more courage than usual, to turn to you for advice, and if it may be, for help.'

In that summer of 1861 Teresa's legs became completely paralysed.

Stefano went off to Lesa for a few days. When he got there he sent her a telegram. Teresa to Stefano: 'Hurrah for the face of the telegraph-boy! and hurrah for the filial love of my Stefano! . . . Oh, what a touching surprise! Praise be to God.'

She spent the month of July dictating long lists of Tuscan words, with the meanings alongside in Milanese. She dictated to one or another of her four chambermaids. *Some vocabulary collected in Florence*, she made them write at the top of the page. Then she wrote in her own hand: *'Brought to me by Stefano.'*

Sometimes she tried to write a few words to Stefano in her own hand. He had let her know he was about to return.

'I embrace you with all my heart and longing, and I beg you

317

not to come if you are tired, and if the weather is not good. I commit you to our dear Lord. Your Mama.'

This was the last letter she wrote to Stefano.

Manzoni thought she seemed better in August. It was very hot. Stefano had returned. Manzoni wrote to Bista on 11 August:

'There has been some improvement in Teresa's condition: the pains have stopped, and there is some flexibility if not movement in the lower limbs. . . It is unpleasantly hot here, and there has been a drought for some time, which will be a disaster, if it continues.'

On 23 August Teresa died.

Manzoni was at Brusuglio. When he heard of her death, he came, knelt before her, and went back to Brusuglio.

She was buried at Lesa. Neither Manzoni nor Stefano went. The mayor, don Orlando Visconti, presided at the funeral, and all the local people attended.

Massimo d'Azeglio confessed to Bista that he would have liked to write to Manzoni expressing his condolences, 'but when I tried, I found my inspiration in a state of absolute sterility, and the only idea that kept occurring to me was precisely what I could not put on to paper!' Massimo d'Azeglio loathed Teresa, and thought her death was a tremendous relief for Manzoni. This is what he would have liked to 'put on to paper'. Writing to Stefano, on the other hand, was an easy matter, because he knew his mother's death was genuinely a great loss to him.

For Manzoni, Teresa's death must have been at once a sadness and a relief, so closely mixed as to generate a confused anguish. He did not see her with Massimo d'Azeglio's eyes, nor Clemente Vismara's. He saw her with his own eyes. She was so many things at once to him, tedium and grace, tamarind and cassia, coffee with cream, the smell of *opodeldoch*. And they had spent so many years together, at Lesa and in via del Morone, tedious years at times, yet so encrusted in his existence that he could not detach himself from the memory without drawing blood. He did not go back to Lesa because it made him melancholy. He dictated this sentence to be put on the card announcing her death: 'Pray for the soul of Teresa Manzoni Stampa'. Some thought it too laconic. But he had written so many epitaphs, for so many tombs! He no longer had any taste for it.

318

Stefano II

After Teresa's death, Manzoni and Stefano went their separate ways. Manzoni asked Stefano to stay, but he did not want to, he said the house made him sad, and he left at once. Pietro, Giovannina and their four children came to live at via del Morone.

Stefano did not ask Manzoni for his mother's dowry. Every now and then Manzoni told him he would soon let him have it. But Stefano told him not to give it a thought. Only after Manzoni's death did he require it from the heirs.

Stefano spent some time at Torricella d'Arcellasco. From there he wrote asking Rossari to get the door-porter at via del Morone to give him two cardboard boxes, 'containing hats and caps' which had belonged to his mother, and some 'cushions, small cushions and very small cushions', which had also been hers. Then he asked him to find out from Manzoni the name of the author of a book he had once mentioned, *Of the hope of seeing our loved ones again after death*. Manzoni said it was a Dominican, one Father Ansaldi.

Rossari wrote Stefano letters full of fatherly advice. As Stefano complained of having 'a weakened ventricle', he suggested he was taking too much coffee with cream, like his mother. He suggested 'eating a little and often': 'a cup of chocolate', and an hour or so later 'half a small roll, with two fingers of wine'.

Stefano took a house in the Santo Spirito district. In the autumn he brought Elisa Cermelli, one of his mother's four chambermaids, back from Campolungo. He wrote to her: 'Lisa. I am writing this little note to tell you you can come to Milan immediately because by Tuesday I will have prepared a bed for you too in the new apartment. . . So carry out these instruc-

319

tions. Take a carriage for yourself, and get your father to accompany you to Seregno, or one of your brothers, so you don't have to do that part of the journey alone. Then take second class seats on the steamer so you won't have to be with all kinds of people. . .'

He also brought back Signora Teresina, to keep Elisa company and serve her, and a young manservant. Francesco was old, and had returned to his family at Brusuglio.

He started wandering again between Lesa, Morosolo, Torricella and other places. When he and Elisa were at Lesa, Signora Teresina stayed to look after the apartment in Milan. In the summer of 1862 he was at Courmayeur with Rossari, to paint and to take the waters. He had left Elisa at Lesa. He wrote to her often. He took care to write as clearly and simply as possible, as she was not exactly illiterate but unaccustomed to reading. 'Elisa, I'm writing you a line or two to tell you I arrived safely yesterday evening. . . It's a good hotel and I have good accommodation. . . The address is *Signor Stefano Stampa* (never put *Count* unless I tell you), Valle d'Aosta, Courmayeur. . . Elisa I'm writing another note to give you some instructions you must follow exactly. Take care not to wash your legs with cold water from the fountain, and *at certain times* don't even wash with lake water. Don't go washing in the sun. Always wear a straw hat when it's sunny, even to go into the garden. Never stay at the fountain in the courtyard, for washing or for anything else. Take care you don't get overtired, especially ironing, because the fire from kitchen stoves can make you quite ill at this time of year. . . Eat well and don't worry about the cost and drink some wine if you feel the need. . . Meanwhile, keep well. Best wishes. *Stefano Stampa*.'

Manzoni and Stefano remained on affectionate terms, but they did not see each other often. When he wanted to tell him something, Manzoni would write to Rossari: 'As I don't know where to find that vagabond Stefano. . .'

If he wrote to Stefano, he signed himself: 'as 'twere, your father'.

The rule his mother had taught him about the *u* was impressed on Stefano's mind for ever: you must not say *buono* or *cuore*, but *bono* and *core*. As long as they lived, Manzoni, Stefano and Teresa never forgot it. All the others, Vittoria, Bista,

320

Pietro, Enrico, Filippo – all put the *u*.

However, Enrico wrote *core* once or twice, perhaps by chance. He read of Teresa's death in the newspaper. His father had not written to him, because he was still angry with him about the story of the innkeeper at Bizzarone.

Enrico then wrote to his father:

'My dearest Father,

'Only from yesterday's paper have I been able to find out today of the misfortune which has recently stricken your heart, and our family, with the loss of poor Mama. My heart [*core*] shares your grief, and I accept as a punishment that I should have been informed only by the gazette, as if I were a stranger to the family. Yet you must believe, dear Papa, that nothing that moves you can be indifferent to me, my heart suffers with you. May the Lord mitigate the extremity of your grief with the thought that after so much suffering She now enjoys the bliss of the Blessed. My whole family respectfully begs you to accept this expression of our grief.'

In 1862 Enrico and family left Casatenovo and came to live in Milan. They encamped in a small apartment in via San Vittore, with a long gallery common to all the tenants overlooking the courtyard, on the third and top floor of a building with a cook-shop on the ground floor. The tenant on the first floor, one Santamaria, later described to some friends all he could remember of this Manzoni family who had come to live above him: a large family with children of all ages, living in considerable discomfort. The father, 'a man of fairly short stature, with a top hat, almost always with a long cigar in his mouth', had no occupation and spent his days on the bridge, 'as if he were on guard', motionless, staring at the waters of the Naviglio. The mother had distinguished manners and modest clothes. She was always busy, as she had no maid. There were two slender girls who looked alike, and on Sundays they went one at a time to mass, because they had only one overcoat and one best coat between them. Often one of the girls would knock on a neighbour's door to ask for a bit of bacon or butter, with the excuse that the shops were shut. Then one of the girls got married. It was the eldest, Enrichetta, who was then twenty-one. She married one Preti

321

from Casatenovo, an elementary schoolteacher, town clerk and organist. The tenant observed that it was a 'marriage worth having' in their conditions. Word went round among the tenants in the building and the neighbours that the famous Alessandro Manzoni, grandfather of the bride, was coming to the wedding. So they all drew up in serried ranks on the stairs, and watched 'the great, admired old man, pass by with slow step, somewhat bowed'. Then he left and there was a great dinner at the eating-house on the ground floor. The tenant went on to relate that when the meal was over, the bride was not there. They called vociferously for her; she ran downstairs shouting in dialect: 'What a hurry you're in, all of you! Now you've eaten and drunk. . . just have a pause and draw breath!' To the poor girl who never had enough to eat, that meal must have seemed the most important part of the day.

When she went back to live in Casatenovo with her husband, she wrote to her grandfather saying she was very happy. He replied that this news afforded him 'real and solid consolation'. In the past, when she was a little girl, he had sent her a copy of *I promessi sposi* with a dedication which said.:

'Enrichetta! a sweet, sacred and blessed name to all who were permitted to know the one you were named after; a name signifying faith, purity, wisdom, love of her family, benevolence to all, sacrifice, humility, all that is holy, all that is lovable. May this name, by the grace of God, be to you a perpetual counsellor and living example.'

He transcribed the same words in a letter to Cristina's daughter, Enrichetta Baroggi. The two Enrichettas had become friends. Enrichetta Baroggi, who had grown up in the Garavaglia family, relatives of the Baroggis, was very sorry for these cousins who were so poor, and tried to help them with presents and her cast-off clothes.

After the marriage of the oldest daughter, conditions did not improve for Enrico's family, but became still more disastrous. Enrico sent a succession of letters to his father with thanks and requests. 'For several days now I've been without wood and only with difficulty have I been able to keep a little fire alight. . . I owe three months to the laundress. . . if you could let me have something *tomorrow*, father dear. . . While you have been in the country I have only received the rice twice. . . and for some

322

time now we've had none at all. – I hardly know what I suffer at having to write to you all the time, and certainly for annoying you. – Also for need of a hat, at least for Alessandro, who could not appear at the Institute tomorrow with the one he has without incurring humiliating observations. For myself, I can have patience and wait for a better moment, but I exhort you not to leave Alessandro in this state. . . Just as I was taking up my pen to thank you for the beautiful basket of fruit you sent yesterday, I received some superb apples, three pullets and some potatoes. Dear Papa, my heartfelt thanks, and double thanks for the good things you provide and for the good it does my heart to know that in your great kindness you do not forget your poor Enrico and his family. Unfortunately, in spite of the vigorous measures we have taken, the tertian fever has not left us yet. . .' In 1863, Erminia, their last baby, was born. 'With great delight I can give you exellent news of our dear, good Emilia who a few moments ago gave birth to a little girl, who is a real angel. . . You can't imagine how my hand shakes after such prolonged agitation and such joy.' At last he had a small post in Customs and Excise. But he earned very little and there were so many of them: and this small salary changed nothing.

Manzoni was reconciled with Filippo in summer 1862. All year he had been receiving dramatic letters from him.

'It's a matter of life and death. . . Clemente has seen my abject poverty, so he can tell you it is no pretence. I have no shoes for my feet, if I don't pay for the room I can't sleep, I don't know where to lay down my head. I'm living on soup and potatoes. . . if you could kindly see your way to not counting the 30 francs you've already given me, I would thank you with tears in my eyes. . .'

A few months later he was asking for five hundred francs to settle his debts in Milan, and a delay in the monthly deductions from his allowance to meet advances. He went to Turin to look for a job.

From Turin:

'I would like to ask you, if it does not seem too bold, to be so kind as to help me with something to buy a little wood for the winter, which is usually a fairly harsh season in Turin, so that I can at least take refuge in my little room; I beg this favour of you, because if I had to make this provision myself it would so unbalance my little Budget of about 3 and a half lire a day, that it would be quite impossible for me to proceed without embarrassment in this town, where board and food are quite a bit dearer than in Milan. . .'

He left Turin and went to Genoa, but he found no work there either. He ran into debt. Manzoni received a letter from a creditor in Genoa. He replied in the usual way:

'With sincere regret I am obliged to state that I cannot accept responsibility for my son Filippo's commitment towards you.

'The said son left Genoa provided with sufficient money to have no need to beg. . .'

After Genoa he returned to Milan, where he had probably left his wife and children, but he made no mention of them in letters to his father. In 1862 he was thirty-eight. He had four children: Giulio, Massimiliano, Cristina, Paola. It seems that Manzoni occasionally sent the children presents through the Nanny, or the valet Clemente.

When he got back to Milan, Filippo fell ill. He wrote to his father:

'I take the liberty of writing to you, appealing with most heartfelt prayers to your good will, that you will not abandon me in the deplorable state of health to which I am reduced. The presence of gravel increases each day, and yesterday again, after the most acute spasms, I passed a piece of a quite considerable volume; vesicular erythema is appearing on my skin, and a continuous itching torment, both of which indicate a corruption in the blood. . . The wretched state of health in which I was carried away as a hostage, in spite of various treatments I have taken since which always proved imperfect, is now producing its fatal effects.' A certain Doctor Viberti had recommended sea-bathing. 'Your heart, always so kind and generous, even in far less important and serious circumstances of my life than this, will not remain closed to the imploring voice of a son who is suffering and appealing to you for aid. . .'

His father came to his help. Filippo met Pietro, with whom he had broken off relations so many years ago.

Vittoria's baby, Matildina, was growing into a sweet, healthy child; 'rosy lips' Manzoni used to call her in his letters; she was a great comfort to Vittoria. Giorgino, too, was growing up, a healthy, alert boy. But Vittoria was always ill. She contracted a deforming arthritis. She felt she had become ugly; she searched in the mirror for signs of the illness on her face and her person. Moreover, she suffered from Bista's long absences, always travelling on political commitments, summoned to a thousand and one duties.

She recalled in her memoirs:

'One morning when Bista had left for Turin, I found on my desk these verses, written by him:

O dolce amica dei miei dí che furo.
E dei prosperi casi e dei dolenti,
Perché tremando interroghi il futuro
  E ti tormenti?

Quel che ci aspetta, investigare è vano,
Ma sempre il mio cammin, qual ch'egli sia,
Mi sarà lieve infin che la tua mano
  stringa la mia.

[O sweet companion of my days that were, / In moments of prosperity and pain, / Why tremble as you search the future years, / and thus torment yourself in vain?

For vain it is to question what's in store, / I know my path, whatever may betide, / Will be an easy one for ever more, / so long as you are at my side.]

'"My dear Bista," I thought, "Yes, life is easy for you! even joyful for you, as you are fêted, applauded, in the House, in groups of friends, in ladies' drawing-rooms – but me?" and I fell into one of those moments of proud distress, by which I was often assailed in those days. But God had mercy on me – I soon found myself again – and from these brief struggles I emerged stronger and more serene, because I was clinging more tightly to the Cross. . .'

She did not write to her father. She had been told not to tire her eyes. Her father did not write to her either, but he wrote very often to Bista. They were working together on the *Vocabulario della lingua italiana*, which Manzoni had planned with Gino Capponi years before at Varramista.

In spring 1864 Manzoni went to Tuscany; he travelled with Bista, and Giovannina, Pietro's wife. He stayed at Pisa for a few weeks with Vittoria and the children; and then at Florence as the guest of Gino Capponi. He saw Tommaseo whom he had not seen for many years. He spent a month in Tuscany.

In December he and Bista went to Turin. Manzoni wished to cast his vote for the transferring of the capital to Florence, which for him meant getting one step nearer the possibility of Rome soon being the capital. The Arconatis and Massimo d'Azeglio had seen Bista in Turin where the Arconatis now lived – and had asked him to get Manzoni to stay where he was, as they were strongly opposed to the transferring of the capital, and wanted Manzoni to abstain from voting. Pietro was afraid his father would catch cold in the train, and he called Doctor Pogliaghi to dissuade him from travelling. But Manzoni was determined to go, and set off with Bista at dawn. 'It's obvious these gentlemen don't know Papa,' Bista wrote to Vittoria from Turin, 'not I, nor Donna Costanza, nor any other would be capable of making him change his mind; the *idée fixe* of Rome is rooted more firmly than ever in his head. . . I will look up Massimo, for I am sure he won't fail to come and meet Papa. Addio.'

Massimo, on the contrary, did not come to see Papa, and Manzoni and Bista went to call on him: but they did not touch on the burning topic of the capital at Florence, and Massimo spoke only of his current passion, spiritualism; he had begun to conduct experiments, and believed he was in close communication with the world of the dead.

Massimo was almost always at his villa at Cànnero, on Lake Maggiore at that time. A nephew whom he loved like a son, Emanuel, had become an ambassador. But he felt he had been left out of Italian political life, and said that, after the death of Cavour, who had sometimes asked his opinion, nobody ever asked him anything now. He was tired and disillusioned. He

326

suffered from his old war-wound in the knee, which had never healed properly. He spent long spells at Cànnero. In spring 1865 he came to Pisa and saw Bista and Vittoria; they found him changed, and very much older; he spent hours drawing and making little toys to amuse the children. He went back to Cànnero, and from there wrote to *tante* Louise:

'I don't know why people suppose I have *retired altogether*. Certainly, I can't ride, or play the assiduous minister, or even senator, because my age and health make me unfit for it. But it seems to me I have always worked, and published; and that I have been sufficiently scorned and abused to have no wish to woo the populace. Close to my seventies, with the life I've led, and not being strong, it's understandable I should find it difficult to do much more! As far as I'm concerned, I have no regrets. I wish you good bathing.'

From the priest at Casatenovo, don Saulle Miglio, Manzoni received a letter, written and sent to the priest by Emilia, Enrico's wife. It was full of bitter resentment against Pietro. She accused Pietro of living at his ease while they were in abject poverty. She accused him of running them down to his father, and dissuading him from helping them. On the one hand she said she hoped for a reconciliation between the brothers, and on the other hinted at her intention to *make it publicly known how things stood*. Manzoni wrote back sadly to the priest, sending a list in minute detail of the sums sent to Enrico and expenses sustained on his behalf in the course of the year.

Then one of Enrico's daughters, Sofia, became seriously ill. She was fourteen. Enrico wrote to his father:

'My daughter Sofia needs foods which I unfortunately cannot provide, after exhausting every possible human endeavour on her behalf these last three months; I should therefore like to beg you to send her a morsel of some of the dishes from your table, which would give her so much pleasure. Doctor Garavaglia insists I should take her to the country with the others, who are all more or less unwell all the time, and he wanted me to ask you to let me take them to Brusuglio for a few days, after which Sofia could go for a while to her sister, which is impossible at the moment. I wrote to suggest it to Pietro, so that he could tell

327

me if you were delaying much longer going there, but I had no answer. If this is not possible I should have to find some sort of small house, as it is my sacred duty to provide what is required for Sofia's health.

'If you could see the poor girl's exhausted condition, it would move you to pity. . . Sofia asked me to write all this to you, which strengthened my courage. She would like a little bar of chocolate, and, if it were possible, perhaps a pullet, such as you used to send some time ago, would be very nice. . .'

It seemed that Sofia got better. But they did not move from Milan; and Enrico gave his father a fairly desolate picture of the family and himself. It was July, and he had to go to the office in his winter clothes: 'and I assure you I am suffering because there are times when I feel I am stifling.' He had had to borrow money from friends and ask for advances on his salary. 'My children's health is suffering because for six months and more they have not been able to leave the house as they have neither clothes nor shoes, and I am blamed for this; moreover I will soon have no more indoor clothes for them. . . Your cast-off clothes and linen would do very well for Eugenio and Lodovico. Unfortunately there are eleven of us, and you know how I was without anything from the time I arrived in Milan. . . Now I have to feed Sofia on chicken. . . and I have to make her soups almost like jelly, and your cook will tell you what they cost.

'Oh Father, please take thought, allow me to trust in your goodness and mercy, as I kiss your hands, with a heart deeply moved. A son implores you at a moment of supreme need.'

His father came to his aid. The family was sent to the country, not to Brusuglio but somewhere else. Enrico remained in Milan; his father sent Filippo to speak to him; he declared to Filippo that he would accept no intermediary in his dealings with his father. Then he told his father he was thinking of moving house; his father found him a place, paid the rent, and arranged to have some of his own furniture sent there. But Enrico left that apartment and took another that he preferred; he moved in with the furniture, and wrote to tell his father the new address when it was a *fait accompli*. His father:

'You tell me you've found a new place to live, and send me the address as if it were the most natural thing in the world. . . You had asked me for wood, and, as usual, I had given orders that it should be sent to you; but I have cancelled the order, as it cannot be delivered to your home, and I do not wish, by sending it elsewhere, to seem to condone this removal.'

At the same time Sofia, who seemed to be recovering, fell ill again and died. Enrico's oldest daughter and her cousin, the two Enrichettas, came to tell Manzoni. Manzoni sent money.

Enrico:

'My excellent and sacred Father,

'God bless you for the benefit brought to a desolate family by your affectionate words and the merciful offerings you sent yesterday by our two Enrichettas.

'We are all broken by the physical fatigue of caring for the Angel we have lost. . . and I accept, dear Father, your per mission to come to Brusuglio for a few days; but as I do not wish to sadden your heart at the sight of our desolation, I shall be happy if you will allow me two rooms, where I shall remain hidden with my family, to seek the calm and strength I lack today. . .'

In the New Year of 1866 news reached Milan that Massimo d'Azeglio was very ill. He was in Turin, and Provost Ratti set out to go there. Rossari informed Stefano, who was at Morosolo; then the news appeared in the paper *La Perseveranza*. Stefano wrote to Rossari: 'I can't get used to the idea of not seeing Massimo again, after I've known him for thirty-two years and had such a special affection for him! All my castles in the air that one year I could show him I was a worthy pupil, have vanished! . . . And he is hardly sixty-seven! . . . I should like to go and see him, as so many others are doing. . . but what then? would Massimo have confidence in me as a nurse? . . . would I be in the way or welcome at such a time? I really don't know what to think. . .' Rossari sent him the text of a telegram which had come to Provost Ratti's house: 'The Marchese's condition is still grave though better than yesterday. – His wife arrived in Turin yesterday. – The patient received last communion. – They are expecting Ambassador d'Azeglio tomorrow' [Emanuel, his nephew].

When he saw his wife before him, Massimo said to her: 'As usual, as you are coming, I am going.'

He died on 15 January.

Manzoni to Bista:

'You can imagine how heartfelt are the thanks I send you on my own behalf and on behalf of everyone here for the rather better news you give of our poor dear Vittoria. Let us hope soon to have *much better*, and before long really good news. Your own feelings will tell you what a blow the death of poor Massimo has been to us. It is some consolation, especially for those who had strong loving bonds with him, to see how he is universally lamented; and rightly so because the fact that one did not agree in every point with a man who did so much of great value and distinction does not mean that his passing is not regarded as a public tragedy. . .'

Vittoria had become 'our poor dear Vittoria', this was how her father referred to her in his letters; he was in the habit of writing not to her but to Bista, with whom he had a cheerful relationship that grew closer with the years. He was one of the people he most enjoyed talking and writing to. He had Pietro; but Pietro was essentially a prop, the shoulder he lent on, or his faithful shadow as he walked. But Bista moved in a different world: he was close to him, yet different from him. He sent Bista little notes almost every day with persistent questions on points of language:

'Which is the common or prevalent term in Florence, *Orologiere, Orologiaro* or *Oriolaio?*'

At the bottom of every letter he wrote greetings for 'poor dear Vittoria' and the hope that she was a bit better. But he had detached himself from her by now; perhaps he was too old and too tired to take another illness to his heart.

Vittoria and Bista came to Brusuglio with the children in that summer of 1866. Bista had given up his teaching post.

In the autumn they took a house in Florence. 'Babbo' Gaetano came to live with them. Matildina was sent to the Conservatorio di Sant' Anna in Pisa, because her mother could not take charge of her. Giorgino was sent to the Military Academy in Milan.

In the summer of 1867 Manzoni made a will, annulling a pre-

330

vious one. He would have liked to disinherit Enrico and Filippo in favour of their children, but the law no longer allowed this.

In his will he favoured Pietro, and absolved him of any obligation to account to the other heirs. 'My son Pier Luigi shall be protected against any loss or damage he may incur in the realization and effective obtaining of credits as a result of advances already made to his brothers which were in no way imputable to him. . . . Whereas the management of my affairs by my son Pier Luigi was never authorized by power of attorney, but was founded entirely on mutual trust and good faith. . . it is my intention that the said Pier Luigi shall not be molested by my heirs, nor required to account for any actions whatsoever taken in the course of his aforesaid management.' Furniture and furnishings and linen at Brusuglio and via del Morone were left to Pietro, since Enrico and Filippo had already been given furniture, furnishings and linen.

In a letter to his father Filippo spoke of his children. Giulio was a soldier. Massimiliano and Cristina were away at school. He said nothing about the youngest or about his wife.

Filippo died in February 1868 of the kidney trouble he had contracted years before. Enrico wrote asking his father for money to buy a black coat to attend the funeral.

Tommaseo wrote of Filippo: 'They say he married a lady of low life.' Because of this reputation, poor Erminia Catena had never been received in the family.

After Filippo's death, Erminia Catena wrote to Manzoni every New Year; she sent her best wishes, and thanked him 'for all the kindness and help which, in your exquisite goodness, you continue to show towards the children of the lamented Filippo.'

Enrico lost his job. It was not his fault, he wrote to his father, others had been dismissed, too, for economic reasons. He had the idea of sending an appeal to Prince Umberto. Prince Umberto replied, 'expressing his regret', but it was impossible for him to do anything. His wife than asked for an audience with the prince, which was granted. She obtained nothing.

They asked Manzoni to write to the director of the Savings Bank. Manzoni refused. Now Enrico's wife, Emilia Redaelli, was also writing to him. She would ask for clothes for Eugenio or Lodovico. 'My revered father-in-law. . .'

At last Enrico got a small job as an assistant at the Braidense library. But other misfortunes befell him. He had a bad hand. It was 'a carcinoma on the middle finger'. He wrote to his father:

'From my earliest years I was taught it is our duty to preserve our life until it pleases God to take it from us. . . It is my sacred duty to continue to appeal to you. To whom could I appeal for help to cure an ill I bear from birth, if not to you, Father? Besides, you never refused anything to Filippo or to Pietro, and I too am your son, and child of my poor mother, like the others.'

He asked for money to go to Salsomaggiore to take the waters. He got the money. He sent his son Alessandro asking for more money and swearing it would be his very last request. Shortly after, he asked again.

In the summer of 1870 his father wrote to him:

'Enrico!

'After so many years of sacrifice and pain on my part, and of promises not kept and repeated with the same persistence on yours; and after a recent more considerable sacrifice and a new, more solemn assurance given to me on that occasion, I should not have had to expect another request from you.

'What I give you annually, arising from your receipts, would, in the opinion of any honest, practical person, suffice for the decent upkeep of a family, even a bigger family than yours, if properly managed. . .

'I am eighty-five; and you should be content to compensate, by allowing me die in peace, for not allowing me to live in peace for so many years, not only by the distresses which came from you directly, but also by the many, many people you have brought down upon me, who have been one of the most painful experiences of my life.

'Any speech with you can only serve to recall and repeat for me so many painful things; your letters have already hurt me so much that I have had to declare, over and over again, that I would not receive any more, unless you had something new to say: a proposition I mean at last to carry out.

332

'I do what I can and more; you should do what any honourable feelings dictate. And I pray God, from the bottom of my heart, to grant you all the blessings I could desire for myself.'

> Non è ver che sia Pierino
> Il peggior die miei ragazzi,
> Tutti e sette sono pazzi,
> Dalla Giulia al Filippino.

[It is not true that Pierino / Is the worst of my brood, / All seven of them are mad, / From Giulia to Filippino.]

This was a jingle Manzoni had written years and year ago, when Matilde was not yet born. How far away the jingle must have seemed, if he still remembered it, if it still danced in his memory! That was a time when he was still under the illusion that parenthood was a cheerful, easy affair. Only a few years later he knew this was not so; on the contrary, for him it was a very difficult area to cope with. Now it was a deserted landscape where his gaze no longer ventured. It was true he had Pietro and his family: but all the other tempests and losses made that family group seem less solid and secure: and in this winter landscape he was like a solitary tree buffetted by the north winds.

There is a studio photograph of Manzoni, sitting, with Pietro's family around him. He is there, small, bent, shrunken, solitary. Behind him stands Pietro, in profile, serious. Women and girls fill the space, parading their satisfied expressions, pleased to find themselves assembled to pose for a portrait. He is shrinking there, shut away in his thoughts as in a shell, exiled in a world with which he no longer had anything in common.

He must have asked himself endlessly in his old age for reasons and explanations. He must have wondered why, when Matilde was calling him and dying, he did not move. And why those two, Enrico and Filippo, limpid and gentle in childhood, had became two such strange, querulous, unfortunate men, full of subterfuge and lies, and if the cause was in their natures, or some fault of his, or a hostile fate. Perhaps he would have thought he had been somehow to blame, at some remote point in his life: but what and where was too difficult now to estab-

333

lish, and futile.

His friends came to via del Morone every evening, and he conversed with them. There were Rossari, don Ghianda, don Ceroli, Francesco Rossi, librarian at the Brera, the Marchese Litti, Giulio Carcono, Ruggero Bonghi. Usually, Pietro was there too, They were happy hours: for Manzoni, perhaps the best of the day. The friends who survived him remembered those hours with pleasure. He would talk with obvious enjoyment; he was quick-witted; he told a thousand and one tales; he had a prodigious memory. Among these friends, whom he had known for so many years, he never stammered. 'His voice was naturally weak and habitually humble,' Cristoforo Fabris, who often attended these evenings, wrote of him. He would stand, snuff-box in hand; he would poke the fire; this is how they remembered him.

In the summer of 1868 Vittoria came to Brusuglio with Matildina. It was the last time she and her father saw each other. Her father did not go to Tuscany, and she did not come back to Brusuglio.

However, Bista came there alone, the following summer; he read aloud to Manzoni, to their mutual delight, the letter A in the *Novo vocabolario della lingua italiana*.

In 1870 Rossari died. Manzoni was asked to write an epitaph for his small tomb-stone. He wrote one, but it was too long, and was not used. It was published in the paper *La Perseveranza*.

To Stefano, Rossari's death was a tremendous grief. He had been a brother and father to him. He left an aged sister, Peppina; Stefano took her to Morosolo with him for a while.

Stefano took another, bigger house in Milan, in via Monte di Pietà.

His uncle don Giacomo, the priest, died, and his other uncle, Giuseppe, became ill. Stefano cared for him. It was a long illness.

On 20 September 1870 the Italian artillery entered Porta Pia; on 2 October Rome was united with the Kingdom. The next year, the capital was transferred there.

Bista was made a senator. He invented a 'calculator' for the application of grist-taxes; he was trading in agricultural implements, and thoroughly enjoying himself.

In January 1873 Vittoria received a photograph from her father. On the back was written: 'Eyes, ears, legs, alas! and mind, / not one I have that tells the truth, I find.'

Still in January, Bista wrote to Manzoni, asking him to write an epitaph for a monument to Napoleon III. Manzoni said no. He did not feel he could. Napoleon III had opposed the unification of Italy; he did not want Rome to be the capital. How could he express distinctions and reservations in an epitaph? or leave them unspoken? '. . . I don't see how new terms can be found to touch only upon facts. . .'

This was Manzoni's last letter to Bista.

They told Vittoria her father had lost his memory, but she did not believe it. The letter he had written to Bista was so lucid and clear!

She found out he had fallen, on the steps of the Church of San Fedele, after hearing mass, and had struck his forehead.

In a portrait of the Manzoni family painted in 1826, grandmother, parents and children – Filippo and Matilde were not yet born – Pietro is in profile. He is a thick-set, strong boy, with a pronounced nose and serious expression. In one of his last portraits, now an old man, he seems equally sedate, weighty, serious. He preserved something of his boyhood appearance, having had, as a boy, an adult appearance.

When he was twelve, he was translating Aesop's fables, with Fauriel's help.

Giulietta admired him because he swam well, and dived from the boat; and because he was a good rider; and because he picked up languages easily; and because everything he did, he did well. Teresa said he was 'an excessive drinker', but perhaps this was an invention. There does not seem to have been any sort of intemperance in his character.

Pietro was completely devoured by his father. He was simply his father's prop, and nothing else: his faithful shadow. He bent his mind patiently to resolve all his anxieties; he took upon himself all his problems, the most insignificant, the simplest, or the

335

most inextricable; book-proofs and lands; Filippo's affairs and Enrico's affairs. Only once did he choose to act upon his own initiative, without consulting his father, when he got married. It was a happy marriage.

Pietro died on 28 April 1873. He was sixty. Manzoni did not realize he was dead. They told him he had gone to Bergamo.

At times he was surprised not to see him, and went through the rooms looking for him. He got very upset. Years ago he had told Vittoria he could not survive a month without Pietro.

Since that fall in San Fedele, he was not clear in his mind. Strange, lacerating thoughts must have passed through his darkened mind. He used to ask: 'Will the forgiving Father have forgiven me everything?'

He died on 22 May, at six in the evening.

Stefano III

The funeral took place on 25 May. He was buried in the Famedio.

Stefano had a letter from Abbé Paoli, who had been secretary and friend of Rosmini, and was now living at Rovereto. He asked him to represent the Academy of Rovereto at the funeral. At his side would be a cousin of Rosmini, Count Fedrigotti.

Either Stefano or Abbé Paoli found that, in the many articles that appeared in the various papers, nobody spoke of the friendship between Manzoni and Rosmini. Only Ruggero Bonghi mentioned it, in *La Perseveranza*.

There was a lengthy exchange of letters between Stefano and Abbé Paoli. The abbé wanted to know if, at the funeral, Count Fedrigotti had been pleasant to him, 'or otherwise'. Then he asked him various things about Manzoni. He wanted to know if he had really been an atheist. He wanted to know if his wife, the Genevan Blondel, had really converted him to Catholicism. Stefano wrote what he could remember. *It was the grace of God, my son*: this is what Manzoni has answered when he questioned him. As for Count Fedrigotti, he had been pleasant.

Stefano seldom went to Lesa now because he, too, felt a profound melancholy there. He only went there for practical reasons. On the other hand, he often went to Morosolo, and to Torricella d'Arcellasco.

His uncle, Giuseppe Borri, was ill for three years; he had to accompany him when he wanted to go to Torricella, and take him back again to Milan. Giuseppe Borri died two months before Manzoni. Stefano was his sole heir. So he had more farms, more possessions, more lands.

He was living with Elisa Cermelli. He took her with him wherever he went. It was many years later that he married her.

337

The house in via del Morone had been stripped of its contents; Pietro's widow and her children had moved elsewhere.

In 1875 when the estate was wound up, Stefano received his mother's dowry.

Enrico wrote asking him for money. 'If you, my dear Stefano, can do me the truly charitable office of lending me something, I shall be grateful to you all my life, and I promise you an exact repayment.' So far he had received nothing from the winding up of the estate. At last he had obtained a small steady job at the Brera National Library, but it paid very little. He had separated from his wife and was living alone. But he had to provide for the children. Twice he asked Stefano for money, and twice Stefano sent it. The third time he apologized, saying it was difficult for him at that moment. He suggested Enrico make economies. Enrico wrote again. 'I economise as much as I can, and I live in a wretched little fourth floor room where I thought I would die of cold this winter. Those of my relations who have been able to go on living in L2500 apartments are more fortunate than I. . . In the inventory they drew up, a great deal of stuff was omitted, which constitutes a crime, and they even refused me a blanket I asked for to protect me from the cold.' He still hated the dead Pietro and hated all Pietro's family. He tried to win over Stefano. According to him, Pietro and his wife had brought suffering upon the unfortunate Teresa, whom he represented as a poor suffering creature obliged to swallow insults. Neither Pietro nor Teresa was mentioned by name; he expressed himself in an obscure, tortuous manner. He depicted himself as the only person with whom their 'revered father' had enjoyed a little peace. The fact is that his 'revered father' had known no peace in his relationship with him. Then he fantasized about the winding up of the estate; he would use the money for a certain small business affair. And finally he confided that his father had imagined he was extremely poor and had been consumed with anxiety. People had encouraged this belief. Only, he, Enrico, had tried to tell him the truth, and for this reason they had waged war against him, 'a treacherous war'. 'I must tell you that my revered father, about six months before his infirmity oppressed him, had a conversation with me, which ended with him kissing me on the brow and forgiving everything, with words of comfort and

338

consolation.' Then he returned to the question of the loan. He enclosed a receipt. 'By this means I could provide myself with items of clothing I need, and make some other indispensable little purchases, and would thus be saved from the damage I would unfortunately incur if I had to resort to other means that are so ruinous, because those who lend money, that is, the so-called 'bru brú', always demand disastrous interest. . .'

It seems Enrico was an excellent employee, hard-working, scrupulous, conscientious. Which leads one to think that, if it had not been for the silk-worms, the legacy from Giulia, the villa of Renate, the desire to cut a dash in the eyes of his father and brothers, Enrico might have led a normal life.

In 1876 Matildina came out of the Conservatorio di Sant' Anna, where she had been for nine years. She had copper-coloured hair and a pale complexion, and when she went to her first ball, with a taffeta dress with fine blue and white stripes, she looked so much like Matilde that Vittoria was disturbed.

'Babbo' Gaetano had died in Florence in 1874. His wife, Signora Carolina, the one who was mad and moved from house to house, had also died two years later.

Bista and Vittoria decided to settle in Rome. Bista took a house and arranged the removal. They set off in December 1877. Vittoria and Matildina had never seen Rome. They arrived in the evening and saw a great expanse of light. 'Rome,' said Bista.

The house was in via Cavour. Enrico came to call on them. He had arranged to be transferred, and was now an assistant at the National Library of Rome. He was living with his son Alessandro, who had a wife and small children. It was a great pleasure for Vittoria to be with Enrico again. They had not met for such a long time. And now they were the only two remaining of the nine children. They had so many things to talk about! Enrico got in the habit of coming to see her often with Alessandro, his wife, the wife's sisters, and the children. But Bista was not so pleased with these visits. He did not like Enrico. He said he had caused his father so much suffering and he could not forget this. Whether Enrico asked them for money, whether he talked to them of Pietro in the obscure, tortuous way he did to

Stefano, Vittoria does not say in her memoirs.

Enrico died in Rome in 1881, attended by his son Alessandro and family. He had lost his reason. He said il Caleotto was his again, and the property at Lecco, and all the places named in *I promessi sposi*.

In 1878 Stefano painted two pictures: *Emanuele Filiberto, lost on a hunt, asks the way of a mountaineer*, and *Beech Wood*. They were enormous paintings. He maintained he was more successful with large than small paintings. He wanted to show them at the Brera, but first he wanted an opinion of the *Beech Wood* from Couture, a French painter he had once met on his visit to Paris ten years before. He wrote to Couture, asking his permission to send him for his comment a painting, with which he would include some bottles of wine. Couture replied coldly that he did not give opinions of other people's works, he only judged his own. He should keep the picture and just send the wine. However, he could if he liked wrap the bottle in one of his studies, 'which would be sufficient for me to judge your talent and tell you all the truths I found in the bottom of my glass. Yours, Couture.' Stefano sent him the wine, 'the bottles of *Lacrimacristi* you wished to sample,' and in the crate he put a tiny *Beech Wood*, done during his stay in Paris. 'I beg you to tell me if it has *verdure, light, truth*. . . On the other hand, if you think it is an abominable crust, tell me frankly all the same, I shall still be grateful for I love truth above all things. . . Believe me your most humble and obedient servant.'

Matildina got married in 1880. She went to live at Modena with her husband, Roberto Schiff, a professor of chemistry.

Bista and Vittoria wanted their son Giorgino to take up a military career. He did not want to. At twenty-seven, he left the army. Bista had a marble quarry at Massa Carrara; Giorgino decided to take charge of it.

In 1881 Bista and Vittoria left Rome and settled at Montignoso. Vittoria did not like it, especially in the winter, but resigned herself to it. She began to write, with great difficulty because her sight was so bad; she wrote poetry, and her

340

memoirs. As for Bista, he was never bored; like his father and grandfather, he had a weakness for *mortar*: he had dams, walls, houses built; the walls he had built along the mountain streams were always collapsing and having to be rebuilt; she thought all those wretched little houses spoiled the view.

In 1882 Stefano brought out a book of philosophical and religious writings, called *Il numero infinito*. It did not bear his name, only his initials, S. S.

He sent one of the first copies to Antonio Stoppani, the great scientist and geologist, priest of liberal ideas, a student of Rosmini. Stefano knew him only by sight. Stoppani replied: 'I have dipped into your book, and in general it seems to me an excellent work, worthy of a Rosminian. But why did you not put your name to it? When I read a book by an anonymous author, I feel as if I am listening to someone speaking through a keyhole. I am always keen to look people who talk to me in the face. . . I believe you are a priest, like me, and perhaps not unknown to me.'

Stefano wrote to him:

'I confess I had the temerity to try to present my scribblings to you before they were printed. . . But this scheme failed. . . and I printed them *à la grace de Dieu!* . . . It is not because I lack the courage of my convictions that I appended only my initials to the volume, but for two reasons. The first is this. . . Accustomed since childhood to hearing home-truths not only without compliments, but also without regard, even harshly, accustomed to being taken seriously by nobody. . . in the course of time I grew accustomed to live completely unknown. . . so I calculated that, if the book were worthless, no one would speak of it. . . but if the book were considered to have any value, I could not bear the idea that I would not hear the same home truths as in the past, or of being treated with any greater regard than that accorded to any middle-class citizen: this is the reason for the initials, and I think you cannot altogether disapprove the second reason. If it should ever be true. . . that my book could do a little good to anyone, I tried by remaining anonymous to avoid the application of the fatal saying: you have already received your reward. . .I had to smile at your error in imagining me to be a Priest! I am an artist; that is to say, a mediocre landscape painter who had some bent for music, some love of science, but no bent for philosophy, and still less for metaphysics, and none at all for poetry. Indeed, I devoted to the book only the winter hours of the evening, and of the morning by lamp-light. And if I had not feared falling into humbug, I would have put an inscription on the frontispiece *Loisirs d'un artiste*. . .'

That summer Stefano wrote to Vittoria. He knew she was putting her father's letters in order. He had not written to her for a long time and had thought of her with affection. He told her a little of himself, but only a little. He said he spent a lot of time at Torricella, and that he had with him someone she perhaps remembered, as this person had cared for Teresa in her last years.

Vittoria replied:

'My dearest Stefano,

'Perhaps you won't believe this, but the other day. . . when I was in my room, with poor Papa's letters in my hand, I was just thinking of you, dear Stefano! and saying: if this is ever published, I will send it to Stefano myself, with these words: To dearest Stefano, her last surviving Brother, his poor affectionate sister Vittoria sends this sad and tender memory of times past. And I was so absorbed in these thoughts and this fond plan, that I heard my name called repeatedly without even thinking of answering. Then my Matildina (who will be a mother in a few days) came in saying they were calling me to give me a letter (which she had in her hand). I told her to read it, that it must be from such-and-such etc. "No," she replied, "guess who?" And I went on to suggest such another etc. etc. "No, no," she went on, "do you want to know? It's from your brother Stefano!" And she began to laugh at my air of bewilderment, and asked me why ever this news should affect me like that! "Don't you know," I answered, "that I was just thinking of Stefano? . . . thinking back to so many things from the past, I was saying to myself that I now had only him to turn to and say: do you remember? It's true that this thought has come to me many times (like so very many others from those happy days!) but today I couldn't get it out of my mind. And just at that moment I receive a letter from him and have the comforting proof that

342

he too has not altogether forgotten me!" Then reading this dear, good, affectionate letter, I saw, poor Stefano, not only that you had not forgotten me, but that you even remember the name you gave me! . . . Unfortunately *le petit écureuil* has changed into an old monkey! . . . Yes, dear Stefano, these memories of happy times appear to us now like a sweet dream, and make the sad reality of life appear more bitter. . . and perhaps you, poor Stefano, are the only survivor from that vast and terrible ship-wreck! the only friend remaining from so many who had a little affection for me! I assure you that this thought, in the midst of so much grief, so many tremendous losses, has always been a comfort to me, and now I feel it still more strongly. . . Dear Stefano, in your first letter (if you will write me another) I should like you to tell me a bit more about yourself: if you are *painting*, if you are *playing the piano*, what sort of life you lead. I think so often of the furniture that surrounds you, and I see it so clearly!. . . Please tell me if the lady you speak of is Laura. If so, give her my affectionate regards. And you, my dearest Stefano, do think again some time of poor Vittoria. . .'

However, she did not want to see him again, and they never met. She said the taverns in their valley were uncomfortable, and they could not put him up in their house, which they were sharing with a brother of Bista's.

That summer, at Montignoso, Matildina had a baby boy, who was called Ruggero. Two years later, at Modena, she had another boy, Alessandro. This second child died of typhus. Matildina spent another winter at Modena, but it was a sad winter for her, and she was ill all the time; the cold climate at Modena did not suit her. She came back to her mother. They spent a few months at Massarosa and a few at Montegnoso. Matildina's husband came to live at Massa Carrara; he had asked for leave of absence from the university, and busied himself with a tram-line going from the quarries to the sea.

In 1883, when the monument to Manzoni was inaugurated, very many articles appeared about him, and some said things that Stefano thought false and senseless; he wrote letters to *La Perseveranza* denying them. Vittoria laughed with him about them. Someone had written that Manzoni had tried to kill him-self when Enrichetta died. That his mother put two lire in his hand every week and Manzoni put them in the little pocket of

343

his waistcoat. That his son Pietro threw a bucket of water over his door every evening so that Manzoni, who hated walking on a wet floor, would not come out of his room and wake him up. 'And isn't that one about the scales stupid?' Vittoria wrote to Stefano. They had said Manzoni had a barometer and a scales in his room, and every morning he would look at the barometer and weigh out on the scales according to the weather the clothes he would put on. Vittoria: 'As if a garment of coarse cloth were not heavier than a warmer one of cashmere! In any case, who ever saw him do such things? *certainly* not I!'

In 1885 Stefano published a book of memories and testimonies of the years he had spent close to Manzoni. He still put his initials, not his name. The book was in the third person, and he spoke of himself as 'the stepson'. He was especially concerned to combat what Cantú had written of Manzoni in his *Reminiscenze*. He kept quoting Cantú's statements, and opposing his own reflections or memories. But the reader often feels Cantú is right and Stefano wrong; there is a forced ring about Stefano's statements that is not at all convincing.

Vittoria read the book with irritation. There was an extract from a letter she had written to Stefano the year before; just a few sentences, affectionate about Teresa, but alluding to malicious rumours; and a footnote said 'there follow intimate thoughts'; Vittoria thought it indelicate of Stefano to publish an extract from her letter without asking her, and found the footnote indelicate too. And he spoke of her sister Cristina in a way that seemed to her brusque and rough. And what of Pietro? he was hardly mentioned. However, Vittoria was pleased that Cantú should be opposed, for she detested him; and all in all, with many reservations, she liked this book of Stefano's.

In 1887 Stefano got married. He had been living with Elisa for many years. She had a lot of relatives at Campolungo; they were all Stefano's peasants, as he had inherited the land from his Uncle Giuseppe. They were flabbergasted.

The same year he brought out another book, *Il simbolo rosminiano*.

In 1888 the Holy Office condemned the *Forty Propositions of Antonio Rosmini*. Violent disputes broke out. A periodical appeared, *Il Rosmini*, edited by Stoppani. It included an article by Abbé Paoli, 'Le opinione di Antonio Rosmini'. Stefano was writing to him continually. Abbé Paoli was eighty The condemnation had disturbed him profoundly. It was clear that the Jesuits were determined to attack the Istituto della Carità.

Cristina, one of Filippo's daughters, wrote to Stefano asking him either for money, or for a picture, a portrait she knew Stefano had done of her father long ago. Stefano sent her both money and painting. Cristina had married a cousin, a son of Enrico's called Eugenio. They had both started off poor, and in marrying they became even poorer. Stefano helped them. Eugenio was an assistant at the Brera National Library, as Enrico once had been. He lost his job. His wife wrote to Stefano again. 'Would you, Count, be so generous and courteous and kind as to supply me with 50 lire?' She undertook to return it to him in five months, at ten lire a month. This time Stefano refused. 'I am not rich enough to be able frequently to provide sums that are asked of me.' He also replied in the negative to Enrico's widow, Emilia Radaelli, who was asking him for money. He had been told she was getting help from relatives on her mother's side.

He began to fear that he was no longer rich at all. He wrote to Vittoria complaining of the anxious, laborious life he led, visiting his estates, and of all the new claims advanced by the peasants. Vittoria: 'Poor dear Stefano! What tribulations you too are experiencing! . . . What trials and tribulations, poor Stefano! Once at least there were not all these strikes! Alas. . . they may well say the world is not what it was in our day! It is true, there has always been evil! But now evil is good; and men are no longer responsible beings! but let's leave it there, because one could say so much!' She was writing from Massarosa. 'You won't remember that Papa was here at Massarosa in the autumn of '52 with poor Pietro. I was expecting my Giorgio who is now 37 going on 38. He is always involved in business, which means involved in vexations. At the moment he is at Massa where he has his office for the marble trade. Of course, it's called trade, though it's selling marble from our estate. He also has a tram-line at Massa, going from the sea to the quarries. . . Please give my affectionate regards to your excellent wife, and

345

thank her from me for the real and respectful love she bears you which makes me feel more at ease about you, poor Stefano, in the midst of all the woes that surround you! Oh! if only one day we could be together in the Kingdom which is not of this world! I do not deserve it, but. . . the Lord will help me'

Vittoria and Stefano exchanged opinions about medicines. Stefano had always been obsessed with medicines, like his mother, and now Vittoria had the same obsession. 'I take the lithia in wafer-powder. . . I've had to take it in water because it was upsetting my stomach. . . as soon as I can, I shall start taking it again between February and March, because in the spring, and even between February and March, I am worse. But it's not the arthritis that's worse, it's my general condition. . . the lithia usually slowly dissolves the deposits that form in my joints; It facilitates and clarifies the water; and in every way it's the king of remedies for arthritis.' She was writing again from Massarosa. They had spent the summer at Montignoso. 'Bista and I have been here since the fourth of this month [it was November], and our life is solitary and monotonous. But as far as I'm concerned it is my good habit never to be bored when I'm alone! my daughter Matilde is not far away.' She was at Massa Carrara with her husband and little boy. '. . . I come here in a closed carriage, a couple of hours drive, and I'm at home. What about you? are you in Milan? what are you doing? how do you feel in health and spirits? do you really not play the piano any more? You paint, or not even that any more? . . . And now goodbye, dear Stefano. My eyes are getting appreciably worse! My best regards to your wife. . . What is your wife's name? Which year did she come to us? You did say I knew her. But you also said it wasn't Laura. I've wondered this so often, so do tell me.'

That was Vittoria's last letter to Stefano.

He heard, from a letter from Matildina, that Vittoria had died of pneumonia two months later, on 15 January 1892.

That year Stefano published another book: *Let us combat atheism – Reflections by S. S.*

He settled at Torricella. He subscribed to the *Nuovo Risorgimento*, a periodical that came out in Turin, and maintained a lengthy correspondence with its director, Lorenzo Michelangelo Billia, whom he had known for many years. Abbé Paoli was dead, as was Antonio Stoppani, and there were few Rosminians now. But the *Istituto della Carità* and the *Pio Istituto della Providenza* still existed at Milan.

He used to go for long walks in the fields and woods, looking for places he would like to paint. Elisa would follow him, carrying his easel and brushes.

If he met the Torricella doctor, Cesare Sala, he would stop to talk to him. His wife would pull at his jacket, 'Steven! Steven!' to get him to go home.

Enrichetta Garavaglia Baroggi wrote to him. She was one of the 'two Enrichettas' and daughter of Cristina and Cristoforo Baroggi. She had grown up in the Garavaglia family and married a relative of theirs. She had lost a little boy of five, Tognino, in 1869, and Manzoni had written an epitaph for him. All those years later she still wept for this little boy, who was gifted with extraordinary, precocious intelligence, according to the epitaph. She had come to call on Stefano at Milan and failed to find him. She wanted to see him, simply because she 'jealously preserved the affections of her childhood' and knew how 'close to my poor Mama' Stefano had been. In fact, Stefano had not been particularly close to Cristina but now that whole vanishing world seemed to him radiant and precious.

Poor Emilia Radaelli, Enrico's widow, was living in a garret in piazza Beccaria. In 1896 she was put in a nursing home. She had quarrelled with some of her sons, Eugenio and Alessandro. It was Alessandro who declared her mentally ill, and had her shut up in the asylum at Mombello. One of her daughters, Bianca, had married one cavaliere Pietro Fregonara, a clerk in Rome. Her mother wrote to her: 'I thank you from the bottom of my heart for the good news you send me. . . I hope you will never doubt my sincere affection for you and your husband, and that if I lack words to express my rapture, it will nevertheless be understood by you. Please believe, me, my darling. . . I do not wish to darken your just and sacred joy! But my heart and mind are full of anguish which I feel an overwhelming need to express to you! Shed a tear for your unhappy mother! On the 10th of last month, by the most disgusting trick, they removed me from the nursing home (while the distinguished Director was absent) and I was brought without a word of warning to the Mombello asylum! I could never tell you what I have suffered! and you could never imagine! . . . The Superiors are quite good to me: but Bianca, it's horrible to live in the infirmary among these unfortunate wretches and their cruel spasms; how can I ever forgive it? If you and your husband can save me, in God's name, do so!' She died at Mombello a month later.

This was the Emilia to whom Sofia, Enrico's sister, wrote loving advice, the Emilia who from Renate sent Sofia strawberries, flowers, cakes and live lambs.

On the occasion of a wedding, Matildina sorted a small group of Manzoni's letters to Bista and had them printed, and she sent the opuscule to Stefano. He thanked her. He told her that the first time he met Vittoria they had all been sitting at luncheon, and she had got up and walked round the table to shake hands with him. He was twenty at the time, and she sixteen. Teresa had given him a sharp tug, because he should have been the one to get up; so, embarrassed and mortified, he had walked round the table in his turn and shaken Vittoria's hand. Everyone had started to laugh; and Manzoni observed that they were behaving like princes, who always exchange visits without delay.

Matildina had another little boy, Giorgio, who was born in 1898, four years after her mother's death.

Bista lived until 1906.

Stefano became ill with diabetes and cataract. Then Elisa became ill, and died in February 1904.

He commissioned a portrait of her by the painter Tallone. He sent him her photograph and her clothes.

The portrait was done. It shows a tall, sad, gentle woman, dressed in black, two large hands in her lap holding her missal.

He made a will, leaving everything to the *Istituto dei Figli della Provvidenza*, apart from some legacies to all the Cermelli relations. He left his art-books and lithographs to the Brera Academy, his music books to the Conservatorio, his theology books to Ambrosiana. 'I do not want flowers at my funeral. I wish to be borne like a poor man to my grave.'

He quarrelled with the local council at Lesa. He had become touchy and quarrelsome. They excluded him from the council. Then he heard they wanted to knock down the cemetery. So he

348

arranged for the remains of his mother, and his father, Decio Stampa, to be taken first to Morosolo, then to Torricella, where he had a family tomb built.

He became completely blind. He never moved from Torricella. He used to sit under a chestnut tree, near the house, which they called 'Stefano Stampa's chestnut'.

He died in February 1907.

List of Characters

ALFIERI, VITTORIO an aristocrat, author of tragedies and of an essay on tyranny, written in Italian; through his plays many Italians became acquainted with contemporary political ideas. Manzoni's early uncritical admiration for him changed when he realized how much Alfieri hated France.

ARCONATI, MARCHESA COSTANZA and **MARCHESE GIUSEPPE** exiled by the Austrian regime to Belgium, where their home was a centre for Italian liberals; later settled in Cassolo in Piedmont; the Marquis became a member of the Chamber of Deputies in Turin. Costanza's brother Lodovico married Manzoni's daughter, Sofia.

ARESE, LUIGI son of a conservative, patrician family; a freethinker and with Manzoni a passionate bibliophile; died young.

BECCARIA, DONNA GIULIA Manzoni's mother.

BECCARIA, DONNA TERESA DE BLASCO mother of Donna Giulia, after a runaway marriage with Cesare Beccaria; died when her daughter was twelve.

BECCARIA, MARCHESE CESARE when twenty-six published his book *Dei Delitti e delle Pene*, hailed by Voltaire, Diderot and Hume; it caused Leopold of Tuscany to abolish capital punishment. By his first marriage he was father to Donna Giulia, Manzoni's mother.

BECCARIA, GIACOMO a cousin of Manzoni's, for whom his daughter Giulietta developed a sentimental attachment, and to whom she wrote many letters.

BECCARIA, MARCHESE GIULIO son of Cesare and his second wife; he took over the administration of Manzoni's property at the latter's request.

350

BERCHET, GIOVANNI poet and patriot, a member of Manzoni's circle; fled to Paris in 1821 when the Austrian police discovered his activities; remained in exile for twenty-seven years.

BLONDEL, ENRICHETTA Manzoni's first wife; daughter of Swiss Calvinist immigrants who objected to her marriage (at sixteen) in a civil ceremony and even more to her later conversion to Catholicism.

BLONDEL, ENRICO Enrichetta's brother, who married his own niece, Louise.

BORRI, GIUSEPPE brother of Donna Teresa, Manzoni's second wife.

CABANIS, PIERRE-GEORGES brilliant physician and philosopher, one of the leading members of the French 'Idéologues' who were devoted to an analytical search for truth in the traditions of the Enlightenment; friend of Fauriel and of Sophie de Condorcet, to whose sister he was married.

CANTÙ, CESARE long-standing friend of Manzoni's, author of lively *Reminiscenze* (1885).

CARLO ALBERTO became King of Sardinia in 1831; declared war on Austria in 1848, after Radetzky abandoned Milan; defeated at the battle of Novara and abdicated in favour of his son, Victor Emmanuel II.

CATTANEO, GAETANO member of the reforming Lombard group; tried to introduce scientific method into antiquarian research; provided many of the source references for *I promessi sposi*.

CAVOUR, COUNT CAMILLO DI aristocrat of liberal opinions; with Count Cesare Balbo founded the newspaper *Il Risorgimento* (1847) advocating a system of representative government; led the petition for a constitution which was granted by the King of Sardinia in 1848. He advised Sardinia to take part in the Crimean War; the question of Italy was thus brought into the settlement discussions (the Congress of Paris, 1856). With Napoleon he planned to drive the Austrians out of Italy; the peace of Villafranca left Venetia in Austrian hands. In 1860 popular feeling brought central and northern Italy together; Cavour bought French agreement by ceding Nice and Savoy to them. He secretly encouraged Garibaldi's expedition to Sicily and southern Italy. In 1861 Victor Emmanuel was declared king of a united Italy, though Rome and Venetia were still outside it, and

Cavour died the same year. He and Manzoni admired each other, Cavour offering the writer a seat in the Senate of the united Italy.

CIONI, GAETANO helped Manzoni with the language of *I promessi sposi*; the use of Italian as spoken language was current only in Tuscany; dialects were spoken in every region, e.g. the Milanese dialect in Manzoni's own home. The official language in Milan after the Napoleonic period was German.

CLARKE, MARY devoted to Fauriel, active in Paris intellectual life for many years; later the wife of the distinguished German orientalist, Julius von Mohl.

CONDORCET, SOPHIE DE *la belle révolutionnaire*, whose husband was the most prominent intellectual to support the Revolution, in which he died; she survived and had some power under the Directorate, when the 'Idéologues' were generating ideas for the reform of the education system. Manzoni's mother, Donna Giulia, became a close friend of Mme de Condorcet and her lover, Claude Fauriel, on whom she relied when Imbonati died. Manzoni and his family spent some time at their house, *La Maisonnette*, in 1819.

CONFALIONIERI, FEDERIGO schoolfriend of Manzoni and later a member of the Italici party, when he helped to introduce industrial machinery such as the spinning-jenny into Northern Italy; helped found the radical journal *Il Conciliatore* (1817). In 1819 he was among those who planned to drive the Austrians out of Italy by concerted action with the Piedmontese constitutionalists, but the uprising broke out in 1821 just after the Austrians had entered Naples and suppressed the Carbonari government; Confalionieri's irresolution and the defection of Carlo Alberto (heir to the throne) collapsed the revolt.

D'AZEGLIO, MARCHESE MASSIMO landscape painter, writer of romances, statesman; married Manzoni's eldest daughter Giulietta. He eventually became Prime Minister of Piedmont, and helped forge the unification policy. His second marriage, to Louise Blondel, widow of Manzoni's brother-in-law, was unhappy.

DEGOLA, ABBÉ EUSTACHIO the Italian delegate to the Constitutional Church in France, led by the Abbé Grégoire. The two became the leaders of a small group of French Jansenists (a doctrine similar to Calvinism in its stress on divine grace as opposed to salvation by works); Degola in particular converted Calvinists to his section of the Catholic Church. He was adviser to Mme Geymüller and through her to Enrichetta Manzoni, then to her husband. His spiritual guidance was extremely rigorous, and continued in correspondence with them both, after he had handed them on to Tosi.

DE MAISTRE, COUNT JOSEPH French diplomat and philosopher, believed in an ordered theocracy as the only protection against anarchy.

FAURIEL, CLAUDE critic and historian; wrote studies of Provençal and Italian literature; the first to hold a chair of foreign languages at the Sorbonne; translated Manzoni's tragedies and was his close friend for twenty years. He was briefly private secretary to Fouché, Minister of Police, in 1799; withdrew from political life in 1802 to settle with Sophie de Condorcet at Meulan. Although they lost touch in the 1830s, Fauriel was a profound influence on Manzoni.

FOSCOLO, UGO briefly a close friend of Manzoni. Published his most famous poem *I Sepolchri* in 1807; when the Austrians entered Milan, Foscolo left for London, and died in poverty and neglect there in 1827.

GEYMÜLLER, Mme ANNE-MARIE Swiss friend of Enrichetta, leading Calvinist convert to Catholicism through Abbé Degola.

GIORGINI, GIOVAN BATTISTA lawyer, married to Vittoria Manzoni, and wrote the State-sponsored Italian dictionary, along principles Manzoni had laid down. Had the Chair of the History of Law at Pisa, played an important part in political life.

GIUSTI, GIUSEPPE poet and political satirist; elected to the Tuscan Chamber of Deputies in 1848.

GREGOIRE, ABBÉ a noted cleric of radical convictions; leader of the Constitutional Church in France; prominent in the Revolutionary Convention; pioneer in the abolition of slavery; his funeral in 1831 was attended by twenty thousand people. Manzoni revered his example.

GROSSI, TOMMASSO close friend of Manzoni, composing an epic poem on the Lombards at the First Crusade as Manzoni worked on his novel, had a study in the Casa Manzoni in Milan.

IMBONATI, COUNT CARLO lover of donna Giulia, with whom he lived in Paris after her legal separation (1796) until his early death in 1805.

JOSEPH II, EMPEROR son of Maria Theresa and Francis I, whom he succeeded in 1765. Developed a centralized administration whose bureaucrats were mostly Viennese or Tuscan, without any Milanese representation in its hierarchy. The government of the duchy was quite enlightened by contemporary standards – Manzoni remembered his mother speaking of it with approval – but it was by foreigners in a foreign language.

LEOPOLD II, EMPEROR in 1765 succeeded his father as Grand Duke of Tuscany where he attempted unsuccessfully to reform the Church along more Jansenist lines. Succeeded his brother Joseph II as emperor in 1790, began to form a coalition of states against the new France (he was brother to Marie Antoinette) but died before the war broke out.

LEOPOLD II, GRAND DUKE OF TUSCANY Tuscany was the most liberal of the Italian states, though it too was ruled from Vienna and the Duke declared his allegiance when he suppressed the last liberal journal in Italy, *L'Antologia* (1821-33). In 1848 republicans captured the government in Tuscany; they forced the Duke to agree to a Constituent Assembly at Rome, which would settle on the form of government for central Italy; he fled the province in 1849. His eventual return with Austrian troops – he kept ten thousand in Tuscany – and his abolition of the constitution in 1852 inclined the Tuscans to look north to Turin for leadership. He was expelled finally in the revolution of 1859.

LUTI, EMILIA read *I promissi sposi* aloud to Manzoni, substituting Tuscan words for Milanese expressions; decisive influence on the revised edition of 1840.

MANZONI, DON PIETRO from a solid provincial landowning family; his main interest was the management of his estates, and his marriage to Giulia Beccaria when she was twenty and he forty-seven was unhappy from the start. Although always aloof from his son, he made Alessandro his sole heir on his death in 1807.

354

MAZZINI, GIUSEPPE ardent liberal advocate born in Genoa (1805); his mother was converted by the Abbé Degola. He founded the enormously influential Young Italy Association in exile in France (1831), whence he was expelled. Took refuge in England in the 1840s. Participated in the Lombard revolt of 1848, with Garibaldi tried to keep the revolt alive after the capitulation of Milan. Planned various abortive uprisings in the 1850s; elected as parliamentary deputy by Messina as a protest in the 1860s. He died in Pisa in 1872 and was given a public funeral by the government. He and Cavour distrusted each other; both were essential to Italy's unification. Mazzini was too extreme for Manzoni's liking; he thought that Manzoni should have seized the chance to be 'the Luther of Italian literature', though his general remarks about the writer were warm.

MONTI, VINCENZO the most celebrated poet of Manzoni's youth, their relationship was chequered, but Manzoni visited him often in his last illness, and after his death wrote famously in his praise.

MUSTOXIDI, ANDREA Greek writer and historian, in exile until 1824, publishing works on archaeology and classical history. Became Minister of Education after Independence.

NAPOLEON I ended the first Austrian occupation in Northern Italy in 1796; crowned himself King of Italy in 1805. Seen by Manzoni and his friends as a last hope against reaction when he promised constitutions to every state during the Hundred Days. Manzoni was shattered by his defeat at Waterloo, and on his death wrote an ode, 'Il Cinque Maggio', which was translated all over Europe (Goethe was among the first translators).

NAPOLEON III in 1859 supported Victor Emmanuel (then King of Sardinia and Piedmont) and Cavour in the war to expel the Austrians from Lombardy; the French victory at Magenta made possible the occupation of Parma, Modena and Milan, where the French were greeted with great enthusiasm, but without the active support that had characterized the civic uprising of 1848. After the difficult French victory at Solferino, the war came to an abrupt end; in the treaty of Villafranca the French and Austrian emperors agreed that there should be an Italian confederation; the Austrians surrendered most of Lombardy to the French, who undertook to cede it subsequently to Piedmont. In

1860 Napoleon took over Nice and Savoy as a condition for Piedmont's annexation of central Italy. In 1861 he suggested to Cavour that the French garrison in Rome would be gradually withdrawn if Italy would allow the papacy to keep a reduced state around the city of Rome. He recognized the unified Italy, and among European statesmen had been the most helpful to its progress, if only to further his own schemes.

NICCOLINI, GIOVANNI BATTISTA with Cioni, advised on the language of *I promessi sposi*.

PAGANI, GIANBATTISTA schoolfriend of Manzoni, and responsible for his losing his faith at that time, Manzoni wrote him the *Sermoni*, verse letters, in 1803; because of their attacks on Napoleon and the French occupation, his mother destroyed all but four.

PARINI, GIUSEPPE tutor to Imbonati, author of *Il Giorno*, a satire on fashionable life in Milan; combined the theories of Rousseau with a broad form of Christianity. Much admired by Manzoni.

PIUS IX, Pope began as a reformer but became a stern conservative; after 1860 papal territory was to a great extent incorporated into the Italian state, which the Pope refused to recognize. Once his power was no longer secured by the French garrison, he lived as a voluntary 'prisoner' in the Vatican.

RADETZKY, COUNT JOHANN JOSEPH Commander-in-Chief in Lombardy from 1831. In March 1848, after the news from Vienna of the students' revolt, the republicans of Milan took to the streets in the revolution known as the 'Cinque Giornate'. With a population of 156,000, few trained soldiers and about 650 firearms, they opposed Radetzky's garrison of about 12,000 men and thirty field guns, and succeeded in driving them from Milan. Radetzky held Verona and Mantua for the Hapsburgs; a few months later, after a decisive victory at Custozza, he reentered Milan. In 1849 he nearly destroyed the Sardinian army at Novara, forced Venice to surrender, and resumed his iron rule over Lombardy and the Veneto.

ROSMINI, ANTONIO a philosopher priest, his most important work was his *New Essay on the Origin of Ideas* (1830); his political ideal was a confederacy of Italian states under the presidency of the Pope. When two of his books were put on the Index in 1848, he retired from public activity to Stresa, and spent the rest of his life in devotion and developing his philosophy. His friendship with Manzoni became very close in these years of mutually stimulating interchange.

SOMIS DE CHAVRIE, COUNT a Catholic and a liberal, friend to Enrichetta during her conversion.

TOMMASEO, NICCOLO author of *Colloqui con Manzoni*, compiled a Tuscan Dictionary of Synonyms; confidant of Rosmini.

TOSI, MONSIGNOR LUIGI the Manzonis' confessor in Milan for many years; less of a radical than Abbé Degola who had recommended him; Bishop of Pavia for the last twenty years of his life. Perhaps a model for Cardinal Federigo in *I promessi sposi*.

TRECHI, SIGISMONDO known to the Manzonis as 'the legendary baron'; member of the Lombard reform group, well known in the salons of London and Paris.

VERRI, COUNT ALESSANDRO Pietro's younger brother, early Italian novelist.

VERRI, COUNT PIETRO friend of Beccaria; arranged the marriage of his dowerless daughter to Don Pietro Manzoni. Founder of *Il Caffè*, short-lived but strongly influential journal for reform.

VERRI, DON GIOVANNI the youngest of the Verris, Donna Giulia's lover, and rumoured to be the actual father of Manzoni.

VICTOR EMMANUEL II King of Italy. Became King of Sardinia and Piedmont in 1849; appointed Cavour as his chief minister. In 1859 the Austrians demanded the disarmament of Sardinia and were refused. The French aided the Sardinians when the Austrians attacked and they defeated the Austrians in the battles of Montebello, Magenta, and Solferino. Lombardy was ceded to Sardinia via the French; in 1860 Modena, Parma, the Romagna and Tuscany were peacefully annexed. Savoy and Nice were ceded to France when Sicily and Naples were added to Sardinia by Garibaldi. In 1861 Victor Emmanuel was proclaimed King of Italy in Turin, and the capital was transferred to Florence. In 1866 the end of the Austro-Prussian war (in which Italy was allied to Prussia) gave Venetia to Italy. After the fall of the Empire in 1870, the French ended their occupation of Rome, and the province was added to the kingdom of Italy.

VISCONTI DI SAN VITO, MARCHESE ERMES one of Manzoni's greatest friends; wrote in *Il Conciliatore* and works on the philosophy of aesthetics; in the small group who came to talk with Manzoni in the evenings in later life.

SWITZERLAND

AUSTRIA

OTTOMAN EMPIRE

Savoy

Lombardy
Milan

Venetia
Venice

ISTRIA

Turin

FRANCE

Piedmont

Parma

*Mo-
dena*

Romagna

DALMATIA

Genoa

Nice

La Spezia

Pisa

*ADRIATIC
SEA*

Monaco

Livorno

Florence

Tuscany

*Papal
States*

COR-
SICA

Rome

Naples

Naples

Sardinia

TYRRHENIAN SEA

Palermo

Sicily

ITALY
IN THE
RISORGIMENTO